# SOLD SHORT

## *in America*

A true David vs. Goliath story
**exposing the corruptions now
fleecing America.**

# Richard A. Altomare

SOLD SHORT   IN AMERICA
AUTHOR:   Richard A. Altomare
EDITOR:     Richard Begelfer
COPYRIGHT © 2010 Barbara Altomare - Encore Holdings, Inc.
PUBLISHER:   The Encore Press, Pompano Beach, FL
FIRST EDITION:   September 2010
COVER: Concept – Richard Begelfer; Artistry & Mastering - SFD Studio, NYC

PRINTED IN THE UNITED STATES OF AMERICA

$24.95
ISBN 978-0-615-40620-6
52495>

9 780615 406206

Mr. Richard A. Altomare
CEO Universal Express, Inc.
2006

To all our children and grandchildren:

May you live in a future America that understands why this book should NEVER have had to be written.

May you NEVER live in an America inhabited by robotic citizens who have fearfully suppressed or, God forbid, forgotten those freedom loving qualities that stir the courageous actions necessary to bring about honorable changes within our government.    Our faith in those freedoms once defined the fabric of this great country. NEVER forget it.

To my memories of an America, when leaders were filled with Integrity, Constitutional accountability, and a sense of equitable Justice.

With special gratitude to the United States Marine Corps, which instilled in me the importance of fighting for the truth - no matter the pain, effort, or sacrifice.

To the memory of Universal Express (USXP), its employees, shareholders, ideas, and investors that built our exemplary business model.    The positive dream continues to exist, and the truth of their efforts live on.

To all of those government officials currently "above the law ", who made this work painfully necessary ... can you now hear the footsteps of our impending justice?

To My Dear Wife Barbara,

When you agreed to marry me, neither you nor I could have fully grasped the depth or extent of "for better or for worse" as it would eventually apply to our life together. You have stood by me during what has surely been the "worse".

You have been publicly humiliated by those who sought to get to me, through harming you. They did their best to frighten and intimidate you with threats and financial attacks. Yet, during it all you never wavered — (maybe "swayed" a bit at times - justifiably).

Thank you for gently teaching me more about love and loyalty than I was forced to learn about the vindictiveness of wounded bureaucrats. I'll never forget the pain I felt being separated from you for so long.

I love you

To my Attorney and friend, Chris Gunderson,

As General Counsel to USXP, some blame you for this entire event.  I do not.

In fact, I admire your loyalty, steadfastness, honesty and tenacity amidst this tumultuous adventure.

I'll never forget you visiting me daily, and subjecting yourself to the visitation process at MCC.

Thank you for calling me regularly and ever encouraging me on those dark days that justice will eventually be served.

Like some of these prison characters, you have been unforgettable.

You were a great General Counsel!

To Rich Begelfer,

During this four year travesty, I made many new friends, and couldn't find some of my old ones. Fear of authority has taken on a new life under today's Patriot Act mindset.

However, as my closest friend, and like the "Illustrated Man" in this book, you have courageously believed in me and my cause, embracing it as your own, and taking action.

Rich, because of your enthusiasm, technical assistance, editing and listening skills — this book has become a reality.

Thank you Richard, for your friendship, your support, and your numerous skills, as well as your fearless attitude towards fighting for justice. You were certainly sent to help from somewhere special.

I look forward to the next few decades of our friendship, laughter and success together.

# Contents

Forward – A National Scandal .................................................. i

Prologue – Case Profile ............................................................ a

Introduction – Questionable Destination .................................... 1

Chapter   1 – Orientation ........................................................ 5

Chapter   2 – Settling In.......................................................... 13

Chapter   3 – My Dysfunctional Neighborhood ........................ 19

Chapter   4 – In Contempt?   Or Contemptuous? .................... 27

Chapter   5 – My Counselor meets "Al".................................. 35

Chapter   6 – Today I became a Prisoner................................ 41

Chapter   7 – Could this be the "Twilight Zone"?.................... 49

Chapter   8 – Waiting "Listlessly".......................................... 57

Chapter   9 – Read Between the Lines .................................... 63

Chapter 10 – Shaking Out Memorial Day ................................ 69

Chapter 11 – "For Lack of a Nail" .......................................... 75

Chapter 12 – The Escape ........................................................ 81

Chapter 13 – A Heart to Heart with You................................ 85

Chapter 14 – The Mickey Mouse Club .................................... 89

Chapter 15 – Please! Don't Make My Eyes Roll .................... 95

Chapter 16 – The Salute .......................................................... 101

Chapter 17 – Brother Lovers .................................................. 107

Chapter 18 – Next on the List! ................................................ 111

Chapter 19 – My First Fashion Class ...................................... 117

Chapter 20 – Condiment Class ................................................ 121

Chapter 21 – Finally, I'm Authorized ...................................... 125

Chapter 22 – Move Over Mummy – The Family's Here! .......... 129

Chapter 23 – "Celling" Out .................................................... 137

Chapter 24 – Close to the Edge .............................................. 141

Chapter 25 – Movin' on Up...................................................... 147

Chapter 26 – Changing a Broken System................................ 151

Chapter 27 – Head Slave "Perks".......................................... 153

Chapter 28 – 3,000,000 Seconds … and Counting.................. 155

Chapter 29 – Arab Spitters .................................................... 159

Chapter 30 – Respect.............................................................. 165

Contents

Chapter 31 – Showers Without Towels...................................169
Chapter 32 – "Sockopoly"...................................................171
Chapter 33 – Thirty More Days … and a Paint Brush?.......................173
Chapter 34 – Sanitary Tears .................................................179
Chapter 35 – "A Fine Mess You've Gotten Us Into, Ollie".................183
Chapter 36 – My Coming Out Party.......................................185
Chapter 37 – Expanding the Team .......................................193
Chapter 38 – I'm Seeing Changes in Here ...............................197
Chapter 39 – Playing Ball in the Day Room ............................201
Chapter 40 – "Shift"ing Priorities ........................................205
Chapter 41 – "Dogman" Appears........................................209
Chapter 42 – I Smell Smoke! ..............................................213
Chapter 43 – Toilet Thoughts..............................................215
Chapter 44 – All Washed Up and Out....................................217
Chapter 45 – Burn Baby Burn!.............................................219
Chapter 46 – Conjugal Shower Visitation?..............................221
Chapter 47 – Tattoos for Everyone! ......................................223
Chapter 48 – My Snickers Bar Melted!...................................225
Chapter 49 – Come and Get Me!...........................................227
Chapter 50 – Mount Underwear ..........................................229
Chapter 51 – My Supply List Gets Posted ...............................231
Chapter 52 – Killing My Plumber .........................................233
Chapter 53 – Good-bye "Bloody Evil" ...................................235
Chapter 54 – Becoming Management ....................................237
Chapter 55 – A "Solitary" Father's Day...................................239
Chapter 56 – My First Prison "Power Lunch" ...........................241
Chapter 57 – The Vending Machine Caper..............................243
Chapter 58 – My First Suicide .............................................247
Chapter 59 – Soulless in New York .......................................249
Chapter 60 – Sammy the "Bull" and Me .................................251
Chapter 61 – Felix and Oscars (I want to thank the Academy)...........255
Chapter 62 – Illegally Cutting My Nails .................................259
Chapter 63 – The Tail Wagging the Dog ................................261
Chapter 64 – Book Brigade ................................................263
Chapter 65 – My Fans Speak ..............................................265
Chapter 66 – Choke on those Pretzels....................................267

Chapter 67 – Napoleon meets his Waterloo ........................................ 269

Chapter 68 – Fireside Thoughts............................................................ 271

Chapter 69 – How do Urine and Feces Feel? ..................................... 273

Chapter 70 – One-legged Suicide Solved............................................ 275

Chapter 71 – Happy Birthday First Timer!.......................................... 277

Chapter 72 – Mr. Clean ....................................................................... 279

Chapter 73 – I'm Not Here? ................................................................ 281

Chapter 74 – Cookiegate ..................................................................... 283

Chapter 75 – Trust Our Military.......................................................... 285

Chapter 76 – The BOP's Statue of Liberty.......................................... 287

Chapter 77 – I'm not eating Garbage … Yet....................................... 289

Chapter 78 – Turning Grey Without Sunshine .................................... 291

Chapter 79 – A Rose by any other Name … ....................................... 293

Chapter 80 – Sign-In, Sign-Out – Who Loses? .................................. 297

Chapter 81 – Missing Picture .............................................................. 299

Chapter 82 – Being a "Lifer" – On the BOP Installment Plan ............ 301

Chapter 83 – It's your desk, Deliverance ............................................ 303

Chapter 84 – Strip Searched by Little Richard.................................... 307

Chapter 85 – Papa John Delivery ........................................................ 311

Chapter 86 – Booty Bandit & the Broken Washing Machine ............. 315

Chapter 87 – One Minute of Freedom................................................. 319

Chapter 88 – More or Less … I'm Chillin .......................................... 323

Chapter 89 – Roaming Around My Ponderosa..................................... 327

Chapter 90 – What Came First?   The Chicken or the Bone? ............. 329

Chapter 91 – How does a "Patriot Act"?.............................................. 333

Chapter 92 – Did you read my letter?.................................................. 337

Chapter 93 – Incoming!........................................................................ 339

Chapter 94 – My Exercise Class.......................................................... 343

Chapter 95 – Two-Ply Forever!........................................................... 347

Chapter 96 – Yes, Blind ...................................................................... 351

Chapter 97 – Rent … Not the Play ...................................................... 359

Chapter 98 – Chillin' in the BOP ........................................................ 365

Chapter 99 – Spanky and His Gang..................................................... 369

Chapter 100 – Into the Secret Prison .................................................. 375

Chapter 101 – It's Déjà vu, all Over Again ......................................... 381

Contents

Chapter 102 – Bottom of the 9th – Two Out.........................................385
Chapter 103 – Black Plague in New York ............................................387
Chapter 104 – Heat on the Plantation...................................................391
Chapter 105 – Rat, I mean Rat .............................................................395
Chapter 106 – I'm Resigned to It ..........................................................399
Chapter 107 – Sent Me Off, Like it Never Happened...........................401


Court of Claims Case Profile..................................................................405
Bull & Bear Financial Report.................................................................413
An Overview for Offenders....................................................................419
Inmate Rights and Responsibilities ......................................................421
BOP Rules & Policies ...........................................................................425
Prohibited Acts and Sanctions..............................................................431
Special Housing Unit Rules and Procedures – Inmate Copy ................443

# FORWARD

<u>A National Scandal</u>

Much has been said and written during the past year regarding who is to blame and exactly what caused this complex economic meltdown and loss of confidence in our trading and capital systems.

The public needs an understandable explanation of the truth, as well as, the confidence that those in charge will correct the past mistakes.

Following is a straightforward presentation of past and recent events that any individual can follow, understand and derive a logical conclusion from.

The past SEC administration was incompetent or conflicted. They permitted and covered up the gross abuse of established securities trading rules.

One small American company identified the problem of "naked short selling" and even went to Court to prove it existed. They won substantial jury-decided lawsuits against several investment brokerages. They then were compelled to sue the SEC administration for its failure to protect the company and its shareholders from these activities.

What was their reward for being the Whistleblowers who took on the SEC in an attempt to prevent the continuation of these violations and possibly prevent the economic meltdown of late?

Read the following pages and meet real Americans who experienced, first hand, what happens when you have the righteous indignation, the courage and the true cause to "take on City Hall" (in this case – The SEC). What you will find are the root sources and causes of this seemingly complex "naked short selling" calamity. It has taken its toll on these valiant individuals, their thriving business, and will ultimately affect the confidence that this great Nation and its Patriots have relied upon as a result of the actions of heroic whistleblowers.

The story will anger you.

It's time that those regulators who were entrusted with our financial safety in the markets and, therefore our financial futures, are exposed as the true cause of the confusion, distrust, illegalities, fraud, and outright thefts that have been perpetrated upon the American public.

When the public sees that the SEC is neither a formal nor a transparent agency of our government, their reaction will be predictable.   They will demand to open the SEC's books.   Then, the cause of the current economic problem and its solution will be in the hands of the public.

Naked shorting is a significant cause of the present financial crisis, which the SEC failed to regulate for years in the interests of Wall Street firms, as well as itself.   (just as it also failed to prevent the Madoff scandal)

A number of Senators have recently called for a ban on naked short selling, which, in the past, the SEC vehemently and repeatedly denied the existence of.

This failure by the SEC to regulate our trading markets for years has led to the destruction of thousands of small public companies, substantial devaluation of investments, the loss of 401Ks by millions of Americans, and the tragic loss of hundreds of thousands of jobs.

The SEC has permitted, and actively covered up this national scandal of naked shorting for more than 15 years and, as you will painfully witness in the pages of this book, it actively harassed and persecuted prominent whistleblowers to silence them in the interest of the naked short sellers, and the SEC itself.

Trillions of counterfeit and unregistered shares in the names of small public companies have been permitted by the SEC to be traded - destroying their market values and thereby contributing to many of their eventual bankruptcies.

Naked short sellers do not have to purchase the stocks they originally sold short, when the subject company fails due to the downward stock price pressure of the naked short selling of its stock, as well as the internet posting of negative propaganda on the company.

Proper taxes are not paid on the revenues the naked shorters collected through the illegal selling of these phantom non-existing shares. These unpaid taxes, it is estimated by the Wall Street Journal, would be enough to pay off the National Debt.

Naked Short Selling, selling shares you do not own and never deliver, is Grand Larceny under the laws of every State. It is also a violation of the counterfeiting Statutes of the United States.

Those who commit these crimes and those who, by their denial fail to prevent and thus perpetuate them, deserve to be imprisoned … not their victims or the whistleblowers exposing them.

PROLOGUE

CASE PROFILE

Universal Express (USXP) operated as a pristine and exemplary small public company for 17 years. It was ignominiously silenced by rogue government officials in days. For the good of our future economic trading system and other vulnerable United States public companies the following facts need to be exposed and understood. We ask the interested public to simply allow these chronological facts in this profile to speak for themselves.

The present Securities and Exchange Commission and the United States Court of Claims need to address the facts that this book will present.

This case involves the failure of previous SEC administrations to stop naked short sellers and to expose SEC employees who destroyed Universal Express and permitted the destruction of thousands of other small publicly-traded companies.

Despite the ongoing efforts of Universal Express and its officers previous SEC administrations had failed for more than a decade to take any effective regulatory or enforcement action against illegal naked shorting or naked shorters themselves.

The failure to regulate and enforce naked shorting rules by previous SEC administrations bordered on criminality, cover-up and, gross fraud.

Naked short selling is selling shares one does not own, and has no intention of ever purchasing or delivering. These are unregistered and non-existent shares not issued by the companies in whose names they are sold. Each such sale is an illegal violation of the securities laws and the anti-counterfeiting statutes of the United States. It is also grand larceny under the laws of every State. This illegal trading process was long covered-up and until just recently, its existence denied by previous SEC administrations that profited along with culpable Wall Street interests. Naked Short Selling has been a significant cause of the present financial global crisis, and resulted in all the events that made the writing of this book an historical necessity.

Previous SEC administrations denied and ignored frequently requested assistance by Universal Express and its officers to combat the naked shorting of its shares on behalf of over 65,000 of its (USXP) shareholders.

Failure to enforce existing securities laws as well as congressionally ordered regulations adds to the active cover-up of the naked shorting scandal. This has been an ongoing gross breach of the SEC's fiduciary duty to small public companies, their investors, officers and employees.

The previous SEC administration's willful and paranoid destruction of Universal Express and its continued vindictive efforts to silence and defame its officers as whistleblowers constitute gross fraudulent misconduct.

The naked short sellers operated like gangs or economic terrorist cells usually from within Wall Street houses such as Bear Stearns and Lehman Brothers. They attack, by selling large quantities of the stock of small developing companies for the purpose of driving the stock price downward, destroying investor confidence in the stock as well as the company's ability to maintain cash flow to the point where the targeted companies were often forced into heavy dilution or bankruptcy. They simply were allowed to sell vast quantities of stock that they did not own.

The naked shorters who attacked Universal Express combined their raid with false and negative internet postings of more than 700,000 messages on the Company's chat board, thus attempting to destroy the Company's stable image. Universal Express heroically fought long and hard since 1998 and continues to do so even now, although Bear Stearns and Lehman Brothers collapsed in only one weekend under the same type of internet postings and naked short selling attacks.

The sole purpose of pushing these public companies into bankruptcy was that the naked shorters would be able to keep the entire proceeds of their illegal naked short sales because they were never forced to "cover" by purchasing and delivering the shares when the targeted company failed. It remains a common practice that these "SEC" protected naked shorters do not have to report these ill-gotten revenues on their taxes.

After the naked short sellers drove down the target company's stock price, it destroyed the ability of the company to obtain credit lines and maintain existing credit relationships. This further resulted in shareholders' lack of confidence and often predictable panic selling forcing the corporate failures.

On numerous occasions since 1998 Universal Express and its officers complained to the previous SEC administrations about these illegal practices. Surprisingly, the SEC always helped the naked short sellers through its denials, first by fraudulently doing nothing, and then by actually attacking Universal Express and its officers.

Failing to get any help from the SEC, Universal Express was forced to sue some of the naked short sellers directly. The Company obtained two Florida jury verdicts totaling $700,000,000 against the naked short sellers. These were the same judgments which the previous SEC administrations seized by fraudulently forcing Universal Express out of business. The SEC has been attempting to permanently silence those naked short selling facts which two juries determined appropriate for victim compensation.

The Company filed 68 annual and quarterly reports with the SEC over a 17 year period to accurately disclose the additional shares of stock authorized and released for sale to generate needed capital so USXP could attempt to outlast the naked short sellers and continue building the company. These reports prepared and certified by CPA's and Tax Attorneys, were timely filed, received and approved by the SEC without any questions or criticisms, again – for 17 consecutive years.

Despite the SEC's fraudulent statements of denial and even mistruths to the courts, Universal Express had the absolute right to issue stock to counteract the SEC protected naked shorting of its shares. Under SEC fraudulent statements, it orchestrated a questionable summary judgment against Universal Express. Its six subsidiaries were immediately and improperly seized, closed, liquidated and corporate documents shredded despite the ongoing trial request and appeal against the ill-founded summary judgment.

While Universal Express was being dismantled and silenced by the SEC, Bernie Madoff was writing, with the SEC's cooperation, the short selling rules for the financial industry. He was, as we sadly note today, operating one of the biggest unregulated naked short selling scams in history.

Finally on July 15, 2008 and again on September 15, 2008 the previous SEC administration admitted, under intense media scrutiny, that naked shorting not only existed, but was a huge national problem underlying the failure of major financial institutions and was a major cause of the Nation-wide financial meltdown. It was during this period of public disclosure and admittance that the SEC shockingly incarcerated and sought with deceitful efforts to fraudulently maintain in <u>chained solitary confinement for 83 days</u>, Universal Express' CEO, Richard A. Altomare, the most prominent speech giving whistleblower on naked short selling. No crime. No justification. Just flagrant abuse of power, to silence the most damaging potential witness to the SEC's failures and corrupt behaviors.

Universal Express was one of those estimated six thousand small public companies to be destroyed by the naked short sellers in league with the previous SEC administrations, that had been  paid (yes, paid) for every counterfeit naked short share traded.

These SEC actions to fraudulently harass, destroy and silence Mr. Altomare on behalf of the naked shorters culminated on May 2, 2008 when, at the behest of an SEC sympathetic Federal Judge, Mr. Altomare was brutally incarcerated into chained solitary and illegal confinement for eighty three (83) days under a now purged civil contempt charge. Mr. Altomare, after a 40 pound weight loss, due to being imprisoned, then defiantly proved the civil contempt charge to be improper. This former 12 year U.S. Marine & U.S. Army veteran, Political Candidate, college Educator, and internationally recognized business leader refused to allow this violation and abuse of governmental power to end there.

It is time for the guilty to be exposed and punished, and the innocent to be vindicated and rewarded.

Questionable Destination

As I walk hazily through this quiet and impersonal Florida airport, I wonder if today's Americans will ever again protest any governmental injustice. Has the Patriot Act erased our innate ability and Constitutional right to question authority? Just observe the obedient, lemming-like passengers mindlessly undressing on those "security" check-in lines. Have we lost our love of freedom and the American independent personae? Have the non-uniformed Americans (us) been effectively neutralized by the uniformed TSA "security providers" under the imposed fears of terror from the Patriot Act, which paralyze us from even thinking about challenging this daily cattle herding?

I reluctantly find myself sitting on this commercial airplane rushing me to New York. I know today that I possess the courage and integrity to stand up to misguided governmental forces. I have definitely proven that I would not watch silently as I or my neighbor was abused or even confined for speaking the truth. Lost in the mist of the clouds outside my window, I consider injustices to others, like my shareholders, no differently than an abuse of the rights of my own children. My cries for help on this matter fell on deaf ears … tragically, as high as those in the White House.

Would most Americans place themselves on this plane with me, or would they avoid engagement with anything that did not directly affect their lives and could endanger their own personal freedoms? Would they stand up for a stranger, let alone as I have, hundreds of thousands of them? How long would they protest an injustice, and would they jeopardize their own safety zone for it? Today, knowing what may await me at the end of this flight … I'm not sure I'd blame them if they wouldn't.

Most of us have convinced ourselves that our American society is beyond despotic behavior. There are rules to prevent seizure of our property. Planted and false stories and propagandized accusations against innocents are no longer possible. For decades, I have rested comfortably knowing we possess a fair judiciary and responsive media that will eventually expose any unchecked governmental abuses. Or do we? Did I need this flight to make me question these assumptions?

I have been experiencing a legal situation which not only exposes a series of injustices, but has the potential to also prevent future regulatory abuses. As my eyes tear up, I must admit that I am questioning if it is all worth the battle. Why didn't anyone in our government do as they promised and act in the best interests of its citizens?

My unwanted flight today seems to be uneventful and not life defining to others. Or is it? Will this particular flight be remembered and studied in universities and history books? Do others on the plane realize the significance of this flight? Should they save their boarding passes?

During the past fourteen years my developing public company demonstrated good old American know-how and created a well-respected and insightful business model. Our six new subsidiaries were growing in much needed security related businesses and tens of thousands of shareholders believed passionately in our future success. My company employees, partners and consultants grew in number to thousands from only my Wife and me at its inception. All was progressing as planned and then the initial reason I ended up boarding this flight occurred. I may never know by whom, but the company and I were targeted to be destroyed. Was it after I exposed a larger than Watergate cover-up by an agency of our government or did it occur as a result of our $700,000,000 victory party?

After I arrive at my unique destination, will I be told to return home? I expect the media will be there. Maybe simply getting onto this plane will be enough for my misguided nemesis, and I will then be told to return. As a rule, altar boys, Marines, college professors and business leaders like me are not sent on journeys like this. Does everyone on the plane know why I am here, or are they unaware of the historical significance of this airplane's "wheels up" event?

I remember as a young boy the clean and pure smell of the religious drapings worn by a nun or a priest. Why do I flash back to that now? Do the drapings of our Judges and government agency employees still smell that pure to me today?

Have you ever wished for time to stop while a part of you paradoxically wanted that same time to speed up? I've nurtured my diet coke and exhausted small talk with my neighboring passengers. I bet they don't know why I am here. I wonder how many messages will be on my cell phone after this flight.

The Marine Corps offers basic, advanced, and survival training to those of us willing to participate. Today I am embarking on an unusual life journey and find myself unsure if that training will make today's events result in a life victory lap, or end up as a premature eulogy. My company was like working in Camelot. But was I King Arthur or Merlin? Only these soon to be shared travails may crystallize and answer that question.

When Camelot ended, did it self-destruct or was it overtaken by villains? Did their marauders also seize, liquidate, plunder, burn, and shred those positive memories and were the victims, like me, simply ordered onto a transport like my symbolic plane?

I wonder if I should have flown yesterday or if today's flight decision was the better one. In either event, it won't be until later tonight that I can relate the events, actions and stories that may unfold after this plane lands in New York City.

As the plane now taxies to the gate, despite my desire to stick my leg out the window, like a child on a fast moving sled to slow it down; my hands, normally dry, moisten. My occasionally intense eyes, now steel to watch the opening of the cabin door. Who might be charging on? I keep re-reading my full page New York Times response ad to this situation in the event there are any media questions.

I see that there were fifty-nine phone messages left during my two and a half hour flight. Listening to these messages will not be possible as my legal team greets me at the gate, not outside security. Can one man actually do this to me? How will my parents, children, grandchildren and wife process what may very soon happen? Will the following days be an adventure, a nightmare, a non-event or a life altering tragedy?

In less than an hour in the now awkwardly silent ride from the airport to lower Manhattan, a 60 year old, respected former political candidate, businessman and law abiding American citizen, without a parking ticket, will actually change his name from Richard Altomare (that's me) to 60981-054. I will report to the Metropolitan Correction Center to be placed in a high security solitary jail cell with no permitted trial, no crime committed and no knowledge of the events he and you, the reader, are about to share. Over the following unbelievable days we will better understand together one of America's best kept dark secrets, never before so clearly exposed by an innocent whistleblower.

During this soon to be life defining wrongful incarceration you, the reader, will see and experience a prison world yours and my defensive psyches refuse to admit could be allowed to exist.

Chapter 1 - Orientation

I must confess I often have looked past the barbed wire of prisons thinking that our government ran a "tight ship" with our prisoners. Prisoners were bad. They obviously were guilty of something. These prisons kept law abiding citizens like me and you safe from them. Yet, tonight, Friday May 2, 2008 as stated, I have erroneously been accused of civil contempt by one Federal Judge, and I have been ordered to report to the Metropolitan Correctional Center located in downtown Manhattan, NYC.

Anger, embarrassment, shock and disbelief were only some of the emotions I felt as I boarded a plane in Florida to arrive the same day that the Judge refused to allow a forensic accountant to explain what he obviously refused to believe. I simply did not have the money to pay his outrageous fine, which was already on appeal. I am sure this "stay" will be a one or two day occurrence, so the judge can show his power and "make a point", and I will be placed in some non-criminal minimum security facility. Maybe, I will be assigned to a prison like the one in which I was a warden, when activated to serve when I was in the military reserves many years ago. Now I, someone without a moving traffic violation, was actually going to prison! Life is filled with many unusual experiences, so having had a pretty full life, I figured I could at least have some new interesting dinner stories and be home by Monday.

I will discuss the aspects of this case throughout my diary which resulted in this incarceration, but to every American reading this diary, hold on to your hats and read about the "world within our world" called the Bureau Of Prisons (BOP) which spends over 60 billion dollars of our money annually.

Closely follow my story, as I visit but one "Club Fed", for what I thought might be a short weekend junket, and I report (in far greater detail than I had originally anticipated) on what is happening inside the barbed wire at thousands of U.S. prisons nationwide.

Everything you will read is true. I will endeavor, through my observations to expose the reality that you or someone you know, innocent of any crime, and without a trial or conviction for anything, could suddenly and unwillingly be checking into any one of the "Club Feds".

This diary can be a primer for "What you always wanted to know about prison life but were afraid or not previously interested enough to ask." The purpose of this personally psychologically revealing diary is to give a pro and con of a broken system through one non-criminal's eyes. I am not a criminal but have been sent here by a lifetime appointee to be "put in my place" or to be silenced. After reading this book, you can decide for yourself.

For "my protection", (non-felons) are often placed in solitary confinement for 24 hours a day. That's a 10 foot x 6 foot cell to be described in grizzly detail later on in this diary.

This diary is presented without prejudice or elaboration. It is devoid of any slanted facts due to my obvious negative feelings towards my Judge and his tactics or his attempts to endear his governmental employer. It simply reports on a place most of us, including me, never thought I would live in for a minute - certainly not 83 long but insightful and educational days! And that means 24 hour consecutive days and nights.

On the day I was to report, the Federal Marshals removed my shoelaces and belt (suicide tools). The initial check-in process took about 3 hours with 8 other inmates. All of us were handcuffed, frightened or angry. This is where I began my initial observations of our penal system.

We were placed in filthy rooms with no windows as we filled out prison forms with rubber pencils or only wiggly refills to prevent us from attacking another inmate or hurting ourselves. Suicide occurs far too often in here. This is where I first met a 27 year old, William F. from Manhattan, accused of selling a gun. Based on my initial dialogue, the Marshals abruptly removed him from a drug clinic boot camp which he was attending. This young frightened father of three babies was my first roommate along with at least six mice and rats in our cell. I watched him and the mice during my first sleepless night.

Our first "food" delivery was served in small brown plastic trays about 6"x8" in size. It appears that some of the guards try to treat the inmates with courtesy; I will elaborate throughout this diary on the behavior of those who mishandle their unlimited power over many of the inmates.

That reminds me of my initial undressing from my civilian clothing in front of a prison trustee. I guess depending on his sexual preference, this may be a dream job for him. The undressing is done in front of only one inmate and prison clothes are issued while your civilian clothing is put in a numbered hanging bag.

I was given "rules and regulations for MCC-NY (attached) and "sexual abuse guidelines", which aids in one's first night of one-eye closed sleeping in that 10x6 foot cell. The toilet bowl and sink is one unit and located directly in front of the door which has a small window. When going to the bathroom an inmate either covers himself with his own blanket in order to not be seen by his bunkmate or to avoid the plain view of anyone looking through the window on the door. An inmate's cot is similar to a hard poolside lounge. The surrounding noises initially are frightening or later on humorous if you can detach yourself from the sounds of mice (or rats) in the walls. There are screamers, some yelling at each other, some yelling at imaginary people, and most yelling at guards. Unfortunately, the guards are forced to become as noisy and crazy as the inmates under their charge. The initial sounds alert you to the painful fact that this is not like any other place you or I have ever experienced.

During my check-in interview I answered yes to two questions, which resulted in me being moved into a solitary cell the next day. Frankly, it should have happened immediately upon my entry, but I was soon to learn that prisons are not operated like our outside world expects them to be. The questions were: Was I ever a political candidate or political official, and was I ever in law or prison enforcement? Since both answers were yes, I was hastily removed from William F. and moved into a solitary cell for my "own protection" 24 hours a day. At least, I didn't have to put a blanket over myself when I went to the bathroom (some initial relief). What to do? ... What to do? My "counselor" would arrive by Monday - phone calls, visits, supplies, all were only possible through the counselor. They injected me with a TB test and I was told that seventeen cases of chicken pox were circulating through the population estimated at one thousand prisoners. The previous inmate had left an old envelope and a four inch rubber pencil. I made a deck of cards and sat like Papillon or Rainman for the next nineteen hours playing cards. I began exercising but without any change of clothing for the next three days, I tried not to add to my anti-social appearance and scent by exercising. Showers were Monday, Wednesday and Friday. I had no soap or toiletry items.

Fortunately, I experienced something that most inmates do not receive, making these diary pages possible to sneak out. I had legal visits. Those legal hours gave me contact with the outside world and a constant reminder that my incarceration was not for any crime. As a former Marine, I fought for the right to exercise my freedoms of disagreeing with a "life time" appointed Judge and his own arrogantly self-appointed one man jury. He needed no second opinion. My second day was spent alone except for my legal visit.

I am writing this initial diary entry on my sixth day and still no counselor has arrived. I realize that William F. has sat without contacts for those entire days. William F. and I started speaking a little through the walls, but that doesn't use up too much of the twenty-four hours. Maybe I can read a Bible? That is the best I can hope for now, since it is the only book I was given. Perhaps a future anthropologist, studying the demise of our great Nation, will explain why the Bible was banned from our classrooms, yet appears to be standard issue in our prisons.

On day three, I received clean bedding (a sheet, a pillow case, no pillow and a towel). This Monday will be my first handcuffed prison shower and my first change of clothing. I will receive one pair of socks, one tee shirt; one used underwear and one orange jumpsuit. No shampoo, no razor, no shaving cream, no toothpaste or toothbrush is issued. However, I will get a shower overlooking the center of the "Day Room". After I go into the shower, they will lock me in and take off my handcuffs. At least I can see what is going on around here from there. The Day Room is like a 70x70 foot central command with one old desk and five unmatched chairs in the décor of an old subway station with a black and white vinyl tile floor.

After each departure from my solitary cell, I am strip-searched upon my return.   No writing materials are permitted, but I was able with a piece of snuck-in legal paper, to make a rudimentary set of Scrabble letters to play on my twelve inch steel desk that is bolted on the wall of my cell.   My Scrabble set joined along with my self-made deck of cards as my own form of self-created entertainment.   Sometimes I get unusual meals; today it was a piece of cauliflower, one whole pepper, two packets of jelly and three packets of mayonnaise.   That is really all there was!

On my fourth day of isolation, for society's own good, I received some generic medicines which my earlier physical check–in required.   Most inmates get drugs in prison.

Breakfast has been the same every day.   It consists of 1 half-pint of milk, 1 cereal packet and 1 tangerine.   The cardboard milk carton must become my glass for the day.   Tepid sink water is all that we get every day.   One white plastic teaspoon/fork will be with me for my entire time.   The nights are very cold, so one must sleep in the standard prison issue orange inmate outfit, but fortunately, I am told that, in a few days; I will meet my counselor and be able to get toiletries and commissary privileges. Unfortunately, the toilets began to overrun in neighboring cells so the complaining noises and odors add to my initial civil incarceration punishment.   I did today leave my light on all night to hopefully keep away my night visitors of mice and rats.

I received a mystery book which had the last six chapters ripped out, but I read it anyway.   Twenty-four hours in total isolation is a very long time. The book had a note from a previous reader.   It said, "I ripped out the ending - fuck you.   In here, none of us have an ending."   How prophetic that statement was to become.

On day six, one of the inmates gave me some opened toothpaste and a small finger sized used toothbrush.   No counselor.   No Lieutenant.   No Warden.   Forget about me, I listened to inmates pounding on the doors because some have been waiting three weeks and have received no phone calls, no visitor forms, and no contact with the outside world and, unlike me, no legal visits.

As I write this initial report on this sixth day, still catching up because I just snuck in refills and paper, I remain in isolation.    I look out my narrow door and see 8 other rooms or cells and hear these inmates at night. This diary is not only about the mice, rats or ranting of the inmates; it is about the minimizing the underbelly of our society and creating an expose' about this prison system and the invalid causes of my incarceration.

Guards have a very difficult job dealing with gang members, rapists, murderers, hardened criminals and now one sixty year old grandfather who dared to not have the ability to pay an appealed and ridiculous fine imposed by a Judge.   How dare one question the wisdom of a man who is part of this unsympathetic, unresponsive and unprofessional system of supposed justice?   This facility is right in the center of New York City. Always remember that as you read the stories and descriptions that follow.

If a society is measured by the way it handles its prisoners.   Boy, did I see a lot this first week.   It is not a recommended spa but if one wants to lose weight, find religion or learn to enjoy handcuffs - reservations can be arranged by incurring the unchecked wrath of a politically appointed lifetime Judge, whose poor decisions will ultimately be exposed in an objective Courtroom and the more important court of public opinion.

It is now May 10<sup>th</sup> and my eighth day of incarceration and in addition to my still being here, it amazes me more that a counselor has not appeared. More than that, NOTHING can be done, no calls, no supplies, no visitation forms UNLESS this counselor gives them to you.   Men are begging to call home at night and the Corrections Officers simply say, "Talk to your counselor".   It is a continued emotionally abusive game, or a sadly stated organizational ploy.

When an inmate psychologically snaps, and snap they do; they scream gutturally, pound and kick the door and make the longest and most unnerving sounds.   Then the guards let them make a telephone call even without a form.   What then is the expected behavior of an unbalanced inmate to call or get their requests?   You guessed it!   Act irrationally and get attention.   On the outside of each steel door is a muted mouthpiece speaker, which forces an inmate to scream to be heard.   Normal voice volume levels elicit no responses.   Polite questions posed to guards are ignored unless the inmate irrationally performs like the zoo animal the guards are accustomed to conditioning. The guards tell me that some inmates throw feces and urine at them. Today I do not wonder why. In the days to follow, I will wonder why that is *all* they do.

Chapter 2 – Settling In

All I have requested during my first eight days is for a book to read. Neither any counselor nor any education employee has aided me in receiving one. Today from another inmate, I received the "History of Salt". That book is not a page turner or best seller, believe me!

At night the guards play and party. I can hear them. My only fear is in a fire or evacuation or medical emergency I would be trapped due to their inability to put down their pizzas, donuts and Chinese food. They could not possibly hear us during their loud and uproarious clubhouse shenanigans when no one is watching them. They appear to be more closely supervised during the daytime.

I would be remiss if I did not try to describe the daily food distribution in the Special Housing Unit [SHU], which may or may not be different from the food received by the general population inmates.

Breakfast: Contains one packet of cereal, one half-pint of milk, and six or seven chunks of a sugary fruit or a tangerine.

Lunch: Consists of boiled potatoes, oatmeal and a slice or two of some sort of inedible and foul smelling bologna. It is not the texture or taste of any bologna that I have ever known. It could be hardened to become shoe leather if I wasn't so afraid of the mice or rats getting to it during the night. Sometimes there are two slices of bread and a boiled egg.

Dinner: Pretty much the same as lunch but rice is often the replacement for the potato, oatmeal and bread. Cold oatmeal is often the side dish.

Obviously, prison food should not be reviewed by Zagat, but we could do very much better. Pride and self-respect improves anyone's self-image. By destroying an inmate's self-image what long term rehabilitated help then is within this penal system, which costs taxpayers sixty billion dollars annually?

It has now been almost ten days that I have been in the "hole" and the men who came in with me are still waiting to make a phone call, see a counselor or get a toothbrush or toothpaste. However without the proper form or Counselor's visit, we sit and wait. Nothing can be purchased if you cannot communicate with the outside world to wire funds, speak with family members or have the peace of mind that is essential in isolation to get through the long and dark twenty-four hour days and nights.

Many hardened correction officers, who unfortunately have to deal with this bureaucratic bullying, cease to see the inmates as fellow citizens. That same thought process that enables soldiers to kill when humanity is stripped from your thought process exists within this corporate mind set.

Today I had a one hour and thirty-five minute prison shower, which deserves some clarification. I wish to help you visualize this three times per week shower ritual. After cuffing an individual and moving him to a shower cell, he is then "caged in" a small grey metal shower and locked in. Cuffs are then removed through a similar slot like the one we have in our cell door. One then undresses and normally lays his clothes on the floor of the shower due to the filthy condition of the floor and growing bacteria. Since this day I was the eighth or ninth to shower, I "stepped up" on the wet orange suits, underwear, socks and towels to shower and shave. If you are issued a razor, they attach a metal magnet which reminds the guard who is releasing you to get back the disposable razor. Today, they forgot to attach the reminder for me. I told them. "Boy, do I belong here."

After my shower with one very small cold water spray, I dried and stepped out into the 1' X 2' outside caged area with only a towel on. The thin orange prison towel is a large washcloth with minimal absorption capability.

Unfortunately the changing of the guards occurred when I stepped out of the shower and despite my fearfully polite reminder, I watched four or five of the officers rush to go home and the night guards began sitting about to discuss sports, what food to order, women or union rights - thus leaving me standing there waiting for clothes. There are no shower shoes without commissary purchasing so, therefore no shower shoes.

Over forty-five minutes later, I was still waiting to be handed my exchange of clothes and to be escorted back to my solitary cell. There were some female guards during this guard change over and I must confess I was a bit embarrassed at either being ignored or not noticed at all or noticed more than I thought appropriate.

As I am approaching eleven days into my incarceration my elusive counselor has yet to submit my phone list or get me books to read or find out why I still do not have shampoo, toothpaste or mouse traps. I still await those basic requests. Yes, mousetraps are the basics in here.

Today, I was honestly told by a guard if I wanted more palatable food I should convert to one of the Middle Eastern religions. "Jews and Muslims get a diet of vegetables and fish", he said. Some of the inmates then "sell" their vegetables for other supplies in this institution. I am not yet ready to sell this food. What I have been eating is far from my perception of currency. I was to learn later about currency exchanges in prisons.

My book "On the History of Salt", which makes me feel like Bubba and his Shrimp discussions in the Forrest Grump movie, is really my only book (except for the Bible which I read until I fall asleep.) The time in solitary would pass more productively for me and others if there were positive books for the young inmates to turn their lives around or to improve their emotional thought processes. I have observed that prison life seems to not be so difficult for most repeat offenders. They and the guards seem to actually enjoy the banter which appears to be gang slang more than acceptable English. There will be more to follow on that slang gang talk later on in this diary.

After thirteen days the room and the accommodations have not grown on me. I trust that my hardened "sin" of not having the money for the appealed fine of this Judge will one day end my solitary confinement, although I have been told that, under the Patriot Act, I can stay in prison for no crime for up to three years at his discretion. I do have some difficulty with the unchecked power of a politically appointed Federal Judge, but I have to save that for another time, and only after we win our Appeal.

I started reading another book given to me by an inmate, "All God's Children" and on page fifty-five the following quote did give me reason to think at how the term "lynching" came about. The passage states that the word "lynching" probably took its name from Captain William Lynch, a backcountry settler of Scottish-Irish descent who lived first in Virginia and later in South Carolina. In the 1760's, he and his neighbors developed the custom of handing out swift and violent justice to "lawless men" or any unwanted stranger by flogging or killing them. Due process and evidence were not always necessary.

Since I believe my Judge also didn't consider due process and evidence, I guess the genetic "Lynching" problem goes back farther than I realized.

I was informed today that my telephone form was filled out incorrectly because I left a space between the area code and phone number. I must wait another four or five days. Who doesn't leave a space between the area code and the number? Why does it matter?

In addition, I have been told that the "books" are not being delivered because there is chicken pox in my ward and all child bearing library women will not visit. So yet we find another excuse to not work. If I wasn't crazy before entering prison, I would become such as a result of this system. My counselor told me that my commissary form, not honored last week, also had to be redone in ink. Then she said "I've been here 18 years and I'm today as crazy as this system". "The system will do that to everyone", she concluded. My compassion goes out for those foreign speaking prisoners trying to get a pencil, get a form, and meet a counselor, Chaplain or Warden. Everyone says, "Fill out this" or "fill out that" but the results of continual inactivity are the same. I asked why I was exposed to chicken pox and was told that, "You are not exposed because you are behind the door." As one of the other inmates asked again for the basic form which the counselor does not have, she told him to shut up and stop bothering her.

I did receive today, in exchange for my coveted History of Salt a copy of the "Perks of being a Wallflower" - another quality education selection. Without "child bearing visits", I guess I should just silently enjoy the isolation breathing in of chicken pox germs. At least I am not child bearing, but I am starting to "bear" a grudge for a broken penal system that prevents rehabilitation and creates childlike inmate dependency on the idiots who run these institutions. How tragic that Mrs. Andrews, my counselor, will retire one day and be paid for spreading such incompetent insanity. There will be more on this woman in the pages to follow. By the way, my question of why men can't deliver the books was ignored.

I use my plastic spoon/fork for breakfast, lunch and dinner. I have the same white spoon/fork with three small perforated edges to serve as a quasi-fork and will have it until my final day. It leaks as a spoon and is not sharp enough as a fork, but it will become a cherished friend, like "Wilson" the volleyball was in Tom Hank's shipwrecked adventure movie, "Castaway".

Today I also got an extra blanket from our orderly, which I could roll into a pillow. My first pillow in almost fifteen days enabled me to celebrate this humble yet often taken for granted sleep item. I slept through the night with my self- made hard wool pillow.

I obtained last night a Torah which was printed so small it was unreadable without a magnifying glass. I am not permitted reading glasses due to the fact that I have not been sentenced and I have not committed a crime. "The Perks of Being a Wallflower" was another classic I must have missed during my twenty years of teaching English. Unfortunately, it is a "Catcher in the Rye" type of work about committing suicide, feeling alone and going crazy. I kid you not! One can't make up the attention to rehabilitative detail of this finely run institution. Give this type of suicide thought process book to an inmate whose mattress has written on it, as in my isolation cell, "suicide watch". What a system of support!

It is a good thing I can still detach myself. I still say good morning when they wake me at about 6:00AM instead of "What's up?" Remember, I have no clocks, mirrors or time references.

As this travesty of injustice continues, in a place with no area for individuals who have not committed a crime, I must be held in solitary confinement within the walls to satisfy the temper tantrum of an all-powerful Judge. Soon I will be able to report to you on those neighbors actually convicted of a crime.

I now have a pillow. I sleep more than I am normally permitted at home and I now have a book on how to justify suicide. The New American Dream compliments of a Judge wrongly appointed for life. Maybe our weathermen should also be appointed for life whether they are correct about the weather or not. It is time we as a society hold our Judges to a level of proficiency and sanity without having to repeat that Holocaust poem:

"They came for my neighbor and I hid behind the door".

"They came for my other neighbor, and I hid under the bed".

"When they came for me, there was no one there to help me".

## Chapter 3 – My Dysfunctional Neighborhood

I eat about six hundred calories daily with my white fork/spoon, yet I am happy because after fifteen days I was told I may get to call home for the first time and that my toothpaste and toothbrush order may come soon. All this has happened because one Judge can't figure out my wife's check book, and he has denied our offer to have a forensic accountant present our finances. What has happened to America's judicial system? Is there a quota within the prison system? Is *that* why I'm here?

I am the victim of a judiciary that made an initial mistake of closing our fine young company and now it is trying to justify that mistake by flexing its muscles and to continue its character assassination of one innocent leader and whistleblower.

We empower our fellow citizens to rule over us in conformance with our laws without a speedy mechanism to correct them when their rulings might be politically motivated or simply wrong.

Today the absurd took on yet another degree beyond my comprehension. I heard an announcement "Psychologist on Floor". I ran to the door to watch a dark suited white-haired frightened man actually running past each of the doors saying "Are you O.K.?" As he came to my window, I said, "May I" ... and he continued running past the doors and out of the area with the cell doors locking behind him. He spoke to no one. His time on our ward was less than one minute!

As I was writing to you, over eight suited officials now visited. One of them, I'm told, is Warden Star - the others have badges and name tags but they are unreadable as they walk through. I did stop one and asked him if I could be moved from solitary confinement after fifteen days for civil contempt - His answer was "It doesn't matter what you are here for murder - arson - or no cause at all" you are here and when they get to your name on the "list" - they will move you. What list? Move where? By the way, the "suits" were deep in discussion on improving the Special Housing Unit [SHU] wing by moving the bunk beds one way instead of another. Eight salaried professionals and that is the only innovative thought they were discussing today or any day I observed them.

I then demanded to speak to the Warden.   They said he had left the area. I said "May I speak with him".   They said "Maybe, next Thursday".

Let me go back to reading about suicide.   This bureaucratic, politically placed bunch of hacks, really don't care about the rehabilitation of those inmates within these walls.   They are only focused on their small job within their fiefdom called the Metropolitan Correctional Center (MCC).

Today after the psychiatrist's Mad Hatter "Alice in Wonderland" experience I thought that the only thing missing may have been the psychiatrist's wearing of a big watch and a top hat.

I would like to explain how one actually reads in solitary.   One may lie on the hard bed and slant the book towards the wall lights, which are on the opposite wall.   Or one can sit on the sixteen inch hard circular metal desk chair until your back or your posterior hurts.   Finally you can sit on the small desk bolted to the wall, place your feet on the chair and keep your back against the wall until your back or backside hurts from the cold steel or the damp wall.

Today I await some toiletries from the commissary!   My only toothbrush is a borrowed two inch brush, which I have had since day five, but today I may actually receive toothpaste.   To think I would send back a drink, in our society, if I didn't like the mix of vodka and juice or the size of the glass in which it was served.   My situation certainly has changed.

My two hour shower last night caused an event to occur which may have captured the entire prison institutionalized mind-set for me.

I have explained the process of shower shaving before, and the magnetic "razor" sign, which is attached to the fence engulfing the shower.   It reminds the guards that the inmate has a razor.   As I touched the magnetic sign, it fell down and became hidden between the floor and the stair edge. When the guards came to get me (one hour waiting with only a towel wrapped around me) I told them that there may be a security flaw in the system because an inmate not wishing them "well" could knock down the magnetic sign and the guard might forget to check for a razor with no visible sign to remind them.   They thanked me, and I handed them the razor.   Then they told me to turn around in my 1'x2' fenced in area because I may poke them in the eye as they retrieve the fallen razor sign. My response was one of disbelief. "Would the one who pointed out the problem, returned a razor you didn't know I had, then poke someone with my finger"? "We have policies sir", was my officer's response. Could this mind set have won World War II?

There are many issues that still amaze me. Pens are forbidden in the cell. All of my forms, documents, requests and even letters of complaint have been in ink. No one has ever asked how I got a pen. Another astonishing occurrence was that I did receive a handful of books today. Unfortunately, they were in Spanish and Chinese! The predominant language spoken amongst the guards is Spanish. Many are bi-lingual, but when given their choice they often choose Spanish. All night and early morning many speak quite loudly in their Spanish language. Add that to dealing with the gang slang and you may wonder how one ever sleeps in prison.

The legal visits for over a thousand prisoners contain four 10x10 conference rooms. The wait for attorneys when the room is occupied can be hours before they are allowed to come in to actually meet with their clients. Add that to the length of time to get the inmate or the attorney to the legal section and it is difficult to get representation. On paper, legal assistance is always available. In reality, the inmates have very little opportunity to defend themselves.

I submitted a request today for toilet paper and socks. I was told maybe Monday on the socks, but they'll see what they can do with the toilet paper request. A few hours passed and one of the more violent and hardened inmates called for toilet paper this way "Hey, toilet paper, mother fuckers, - not next year - now!" The paper came within minutes for him and me! I hope he's also without socks, because I could use them as well. Insanity begets insanity in this institution.

The Mad Hatter psychiatrist came to the cells again today.        I stood naked as he repeatedly asked, "Are you alright?" "Are you alright?" to the cells not really waiting for a response and not really loud enough to be heard. He stopped at my window - he stared - I said "I'm glad you" ... and he was gone! The Mad Hatter in Alice in Wonderland - A true caring professional. I feel psychologically better already. What is he paid? What does he do for these needy men?

The weekend prison meal requires further analyzing. I simply do not understand it. One portion of oatmeal, one portion of boiled potatoes, one egg and one piece of inedible mystery meat (it may be tongue or baloney or something else because after 60 years of eating foods from various cultures, I have not been able to figure out what it is!) The same meal repeats like clockwork every weekend. I just wish I could grasp the reason for this uneaten combination and the origin of the meat.

Today I asked if I could go to the clinic to cut my nails and be weighed, since I am losing weight (total weight loss 40 pounds). You would have thought I had asked for a sex change operation. Good news I am "on the list" for a visit. I am reminded of the Seinfeld Chinese Restaurant episode and can imagine months after I depart from here that my name will come up on the "list" and some other poor soul will be waiting because he was still on "the same list".

Yesterday when I came off the elevator at the same time as the Chaplain, who is now on jury duty, I was hustled away from an ongoing extermination process - water bugs the size of mice or birds! That night, unfortunately, I was served some sort of water bug looking black bean sauce, which I just couldn't try. I still await my mouse traps for my room. I'm on the "list" for them so I shouldn't have to wait that long. The mice are lucky there's a "list" system here. They are safe for a while. Today's breakfast and lunch dirty meal trays are still here at almost dinner time. I guess the weekend crew doesn't have the same time schedule as the weekday crews. I am only concerned with insect and rat attractions and our general cleanliness.

Tonight the word on the ward is that the old man (that's me) had some extra writing paper so one of the new inmates sent a line across the floor for me to pass him envelopes and paper. I may remind you this is the counselor's job. The young inmate was creative as he ripped a thread from his blanket - that was his rope. He tied it around a small salad dressing packet that was the weight on the end of the line. He threw it until it came to the front of my door. I attached it to an envelope with paper and a pencil. He pulled it back to his cell. A 60 billion dollar budget and an innovative creative young man has to do *this* to reach out to his family from prison. Tonight after fifteen days my phone call home was still not recorded by the phone system. It astounds me that Mrs. Andrews (my counselor) can be permitted to negatively influence prisoners' lives due to a broken system or her own incompetence. She also has three different names and enjoys confusing the inmates by pretending to be different people.

Tonight the guards have their own partying lives going on the Day Room. They are not any quieter at night than they are during the day. Their radio playing, TV sounds and laughter are annoying throughout the entire night.

In addition, we do have one prisoner who must have a variation of or actual Tourette's syndrome. He gutturally screams at constant intervals throughout the evening hours. The guards simply laugh and argue with him to cause more turmoil to this lost soul. This personal guard "fun time" saddens me and speaks volumes of their professionalism and undeserved and unchecked power.

The Chaplain visited me today and we spent 30 minutes speaking. He also apologized for my incarceration shocked at the "debtors' prison" situation in which he has found me. He agreed that the guards, the counselors and the system are broken and quite damaged. I received Communion! I was hungry! I couldn't tell him about my conversion to Judaism last year! It would have been too much for a man who thought he found an intelligent Catholic adult. He was going to try to see if there was anything he could do to help me with a call or to find some books for me. I still await my daily legal visit; it seems much later than usual today. I'm sure the attorneys must have some stories or explanations as to their difficulty of visiting me.

I was just informed that the elevator was broken and they have cancelled all attorney and other visits until they get the elevator working.

I don't have the words to express my disappointment. I had so much I wanted to give, get and hear, and I felt so painfully isolated today.

Using the stairs, it goes without saying, is simply not permitted. Why not?

I'm sure my attorney is as frustrated wanting to get in, as I am waiting to receive a visitor.

I will wait, I don't think there is a "list" for this - so I do have some hope that it will not be too long.

This feels like childlike disappointment - almost a total let down. When you have been focused on a time goal, prepared for it, go to sleep thinking about it, an unexpected cancellation like this with no alternative plans for visiting is devastating.

Then your mind starts to wonder. When will they fix it? What about future visits? How long before I can communicate with anyone other than writing diary entries to myself? I do get them out daily. For the sake of my other inmates, I will not divulge the method. It is not fair to those who remain behind.

A broken elevator in this rigid system may require much more flexible solutions than the prison system is designed to handle. A broken elevator means no one has to work and no one has to move prisoners. I'm not suspicious at all of lazy guard ill-intent. But today I have unfortunately allowed that thought to slip in.

I will wait, and I will report in future writings when I find out what really happened.

A few hours have gone by and unfortunately it appears that I will not get to meet with anyone, exchange e-mails and give my writings to my attorney. I shouldn't let this bother me, yet I would be less than honest if I said it didn't hit me hard. I can take the cheap hits of stupidity - but I felt this one. It's a funny thing about disappointment sometimes you can accept it, but it doesn't assuage the initial wound.

Listening to these guards laughing, eating and being unconcerned about all of the disappointed visitors and attorneys shouldn't get to me. But they really don't care about these inmates and attorneys. They are not intellectually or spiritually capable of anything other than collecting their pay check, assuring their own job security, and they do not want to make the world better even by one or two acts of kindness. These rehabilitative thoughts are beyond their pay grade and emotional levels.

Here is further "elevator-gate" dialogue. It will require further investigation to get to the truth. As dinner was being delivered by one of the laziest and most angry guards CO Deliverance, I said, "Thank-you, have they fixed the elevator?" He yelled, "How the hell do you know about that elevator story?" I replied, "One of the guards told me because I was expecting a legal visit". He then said, "Take your fucking food, and don't talk about what isn't your business. You fucking mole."

I paused ... I hesitated to stare or scoff. I simply stared as a child in the presence of an alcoholic or abusive parent.

He concluded, "You want your fucking food, or I'll take it away?"

I only got rice and carrots for dinner. I wonder if the Captain or Warden knew the elevator was allegedly "broken" today. Remember a broken elevator means no work for the guards to do.

After almost eighty continuous hours of solitary since my last legal visit, I decided that today I would speak to you on two issues, which further symbolizes the silence of my days. One is the surround symphony of sounds and the other is my estimated caloric intake over the past twenty days. I continue to lose more weight. I can feel it. I shiver much too much.

The sounds I must confess are unique to my jail world and my sensibilities, try to imagine the following sounds continuing throughout your hours of solitude. There are no melodic rhythms just intermittently the following sounds. Some days one is dominant, often they seem to take turns. First, there is the Tourette syndrome guy yelling bizarre sounds and horror movie laughter at a sound decibel level off of the chart. Then there are two Jamaican characters who are housed very far from each other and yelling some sort of Hatfield-McCoy feud hours and hours at a time. I have no idea what they are saying. It definitely is anger, and when it begins and when it ends is a surprise to the silence of the ward in which I am housed.

Now appears my newest sound, which just arrived. This inmate has obviously beaten the telephone list problem. He spoke loudly and coherently for over 3 hours last night on the phone to a fellow gang member. This language was not as foreign as my Jamaican fighters, and it was at times translatable, "You know what I mean, bro"? The problem with his very loud telephone call was - there was no telephone! He is a pure psychotic imagining and carrying on to no one at all. I know this to be true because, as I said, the guards stand outside his cell laughing like children trying to understand a problem beyond their intellect.

Amidst these symphonic sounds, there is the hysterical "banger". He is the one trying to break down the door throwing whatever is in his room and pounding his fists for actually minutes at a time followed by eerie silence only to begin again. He's not as scary as "the crier" who actually cries at the highest and most piercing pitch moaning like in a horror movie. The surround sound effects are enhanced by the guards trying to ignore all of the above sounds by laughing and playing. These are some of the regular sounds I am exposed to during the evening hours as I try to go to sleep.

Only because my lonely cell is bolted and locked, can I sleep.

<u>Chapter 4 – In Contempt?   Or Contemptuous?</u>

So many of these individuals are psychologically damaged and so very ill. It is tragic that this is the rehabilitation solution which best serves our society and them.   Fortunately, they have the non-contacting mad-hatter psychologist or my inattentive counselor to guide them through their various issues and to return them to society, improved.

My caloric intake seems like an afterthought to these surround melodies, but during this questionable incarceration, I try to find some other things to report to you.

Although I believe "on paper", (like the legal visiting room availability) they serve an adequate caloric intake for prisoners to maintain their weight, I only eat about 700 to 900 calories per day.   Let's once again *try* to go through a typical day, (estimated of course).

My breakfast has been exactly the same each day - one packet of cereal (90 calories), half-pint of milk (80 calories) and either a tangerine or a slice of some canned fruit (60 calories), Total calories = 230.

My lunch may include potato salad or macaroni salad (inedible because mayonnaise and unsanitary conditions plus heat heighten my fear of getting sick), salad (1/8 cup normally hot - I also pass).   That leaves the rice and the vegetable and sometimes mystery meat.   Estimated Total Calories = 300.

Dinner is pretty much the same except sometimes I do get a tangerine. My breakfast milk container is my cup for water at lunch and dinner. Estimated Total Calories = 300.

Some of the positive effects of my "visit" to observe the prison system is no snacking, a little more forced reading, more Bridge Solitaire than I'd like to say and more push-ups and sit-ups while I drown out the sounds and the loss of some weight.   How much have I lost?   I'm on the clinic "list" to be weighed.

As I wait to see if the elevator is "working" today, I know now that it is selectively working "depending" if the guards want to "work" themselves.

I hope we can have an investigation just to help those who may never have the opportunity to question this type of power abuse.

Abuse of power by the SEC and one Judge is what placed me in this institution in the first place. I guess it is shortsighted of me to think that the same ethical guidelines in the same Department of Justice wouldn't remain consistent.

My company was attacked ten years before we all read, just recently, about Bear Stearns and our stock financial meltdown caused by what is today called naked short selling. Naked short selling is the counterfeiting of a public security with no intention of ever buying or delivering that stock certificate. Naked short selling results in more shares trading than actually exist or that have been issued by the company. The stock normally devalues and more often than not the company goes out of business. Over six thousand developing companies have failed during the past few years.

Those traders who have sold what they did not own pocket the profit. They do not even have to cover their sale (or produce the certificate) because the company is then out of business. No taxes are paid on the pure profit made by the counterfeiters. Such companies are normally "attacked" as well by vicious lies on the uncensored internet during the process.

We took our case to the Florida courts. Although highly unusual, we were the only American company able to identify some of the crooked counterfeit sellers. We were able to prove the existence of naked short selling to two Florida juries and were awarded approximately $700,000,000 USD for our shareholders. We were finally able to explain why our stock price was decreasing while the company was continuing to grow and improve. More on this to be discussed later, but for now let me continue my prison expose' while I am being wrongly incarcerated.

As I was watching the steel cell doors close today, I had to think of claustrophobia. How horrible that problem would be for an inmate confined as I and others have been.

Take away my legal visits, my writings, my books, my self-created games and it's easy to understand some of the literary stereotypes of prisoners from Papillion to Shawshank Redemption and to "Escape from Alcatraz". We really haven't improved the process of rehabilitation and healing. It appears that these are buildings of societal confinement and other forms of socialistic welfare. We justify inconsistent law enforcement, unconstitutional legal court processes and we keep the prisoners in the same type of place as we did in the Eighteenth century.

The constant yelling and bantering during the daytime is more annoying than my evening symphony of psychopaths. Trying to read, pray, concentrate, even exercise is constantly interrupted by the immature "playing", "teasing", "yelling" and childlike bantering which replaces actually working as the guards daily activities. I wonder how long a sensitive, intelligent, caring officer remains that way before they either acquiesce or shut down. It seems to me that the better doctors should be where they are needed most. The better psychiatrists are really not here. I look in the inmates' and guards' eyes. The guards are part of that welfare and political patronage cycle of intellectual poverty that we have permitted to exist in our society.

It's been many days and my nails and hair are beginning to make me look like Howard Hughes!

These two grooming services are not permitted without the counselors or a CO presenting a request. You get on the "list". This "list" seems like a "permanent record" in high school. I believed in that high school list - I am having some difficulty believing in these prison "lists".

Some of the guards do nothing and they don't hear, or choose not to hear you screaming at the cell door because that is the only way you may dialogue with them.

Still no first phone call. Today I met, during my post legal visit strip search, a young man who couldn't call anyone to even tell them where he was. He wanted to speak to someone but the same counselor told him he can make one call every thirty days. So much for being able to inform family and legal defense. The system is designed to house criminals and it shouldn't be a hotel, but with Sixty Billion Dollars budgeted annually, an effective prison system should prevent more criminals. Do they want that? There are many questions to be asked like eight salaried "suits" discussing the moving of a bunk bed and not enough Counselors (or at least caring ones). Believe me, I would tell both sides of this story if there was another side. It's broken.

Everything that you have read, from the night screaming to the lost and overwhelmed guards to inmates appearing even brighter than the guards, are my heartfelt observations. I may be here longer - so I will report positive or professional actions when they occur. There just hasn't been that many to report. Therefore, I decided to write a letter to myself.

Dear Me - On the eve of your second week anniversary in solitary what are your thoughts?

Dear You - What have I learned? Well I'm stronger and more resolved than even I thought I was. I haven't found religion or taken an oath to say what I don't believe. I guess if others can do it - so can I. Whether it was growing up in 1950's Brooklyn, Marine Corps training, multiple businesses, politics, sports ownership or simply being almost sixty - that combination, coupled with complete confidence that the forces of God must have a reason for giving this opportunity to me, convince me that this is an opportunity . When I win the Appeal, my life will shift into tenth gear.

I say tenth gear because, to date, I have lived what others would explain to be a very full life. This legal victory can activate me to a new level permitting me to act as a positive enabler for so many regulatory issues and so many worthwhile causes.

In two weeks I've learned I can absorb what others could not. I believe that God is present in every religion and that they are all connected and not different. I know that someone really loves me in this dimension and the next. Upon reflection, I am happy with my journey to date, and have no painful regrets from these SEC events, that have not crept into the silence of solitary. I have been given time. I am not doing time.

I have learned that previously I, like most of us, ate too much and I can get by with less. I have learned that I can survive easily on basics and adjust as quickly as anyone else, despite my privileged life style.

I have flourished in solitude due to my belief in the righteousness of my actions prior to that solitude.

I feel sorry for those who have made prison their world - that now includes staff, inmates and Judges. Guards actually report to prison every day for twenty or more years.

I have found I can live without things I didn't think I could live without.

I have realized the depth of the love and attachment I have to my family and friends.

I do not fear the unknown of this experience and I find this solitude to be similar to a religious retreat. I appreciate the "time" life has given me. It certainly stopped my familiar world and introduced me to an unknown one. That unknown world has required a resetting of who I am and what I will do.

I didn't lose my optimism, my sense of humor and my expectation of my personal performance. Hence my disputes with prison employees and the Judge who wrongly put me here continue to be presented in this diary.

I am hopeful if the Judge continues his persecution based on his loyalty to the SEC and not to the law, his personal goals and dreams will be stopped, not by his judicial limitations, but by the will and actions of this writer and his supporters.

Today my stay in MCC (which I am told by the guards means more charges coming) took an unfortunate but expected turn of events. My frustration with my three (3) named counselor, Mrs. Andrews or Mrs. Compton or Mrs. Johnson, who has accomplished nothing except to frustrate or confuse this already broken system, heard that I had told another CO that "anything she was paid over a dollar for her services was a waste of taxpayer's money". She told me today, "Remember your $1 dollar statement and see how much help you get now."

This level of bullying behavior is reprehensible. I guess for telling the truth, I was put in here by a Judge thinking the Constitution was his alone to interpret and I now have a psychotic three named counselor teaching me a lesson for expressing my frustration at her inefficiency, inactivity and her professional burnout. It's just like the organization I sued. Remember I was the plaintiff in this silencing effort of the SEC regarding my naked short selling expose'.

Whatever the consequences of this truth, I will deal with it, just as I am forced to deal with the ignorance of this punishment. Over a thousand financial pages have been presented to the Judge. Civil Contempt is not an inability to understand the documents but a person's unwillingness to cooperate with the system. I cooperated fully.

When I win the reversal - who gives back our company, who gives me back the prison time and who finds jobs for my hundreds of loyal employees and who will recapture the stock valuation for our tens of thousands of shareholders?

The Judge and his broken system have tried to destroy, rob and then crucify those of us unwilling to acquiesce. Similar to Naked Short Selling isn't it?

The Securities and Exchange Commission (SEC) is in charge of protecting the sanctity of our trading system. <u>By the way, the SEC is paid for every stock transaction, real or counterfeit.</u> They denied the existence of naked short selling and immediately began to harass this whistleblower with subpoenas and actual business interference. The SEC and friends planted stories on the internet and in some newspapers; indicating their "suspicions"; although for 17 years they accepted and approved all filings of quarterly and annual reports from my model company without question or comment.

Following the advice of my General Counsel and outside legal team, my company sued the SEC and they "suddenly" decided, within hours, that our company had been reporting "improperly" for the past fourteen years. My company knew it had functioned properly and provided the proof. We filed an Appeal to question the government's attacks and their vindictive questionable claims.   All appeals were rejected by the same judge.

The judge assigned to our case was a former Justice Department prosecutor.   He is appointed for life with a reputation of never biting the hand that feeds him.

The Judge ruled no trial was necessary.
The Judge ruled no appeal could be heard in his Court.
He, without a trial fined my company $30,000,000 and fined me $3,000,000.
He refused a "stay" while the company appealed to a higher Court, and he ordered every officer to step down immediately.
He even banned me from working in a similar capacity for life in America.
Did you ever hear of such a verdict?

Sounds pretty draconian?     Then the SEC seized control (yes, seized) and shut down our fine company in days by a questionable receiver who constituted yet another layer of corruption, ignorance, and sub-standard credentials.   Despite her inaccurate reports on our company, she never told the Court she represented naked shorters and was herself the target of lawsuits on those matters.     Comparing this woman's looks and intelligence (respectively) to Phyllis Diller and a monkey would be unkind to Ms. Diller and the primate.   She dismantled our fine company in days like a monkey throwing a complicated computer around in its cage.   The monkey then threw the computer in the water and subsequently claimed that it didn't or never worked.   What were we doing for the past 17 years?   What did reports like the one at the back of this story say about our "too complex for her to grasp" unique company?

Countless eye witnesses have come forth to report on her vindictive actions.   But, nobody listens when three or four writers, working in unison with the SEC, post inaccurate articles supporting the sanctimonious stand of those dismantling power-abusing bureaucrats? The SEC receiver liquidated (yes, liquidated) the company for pennies (to her friends?).   They shredded (yes, shredded) the company's documents (before the appeal!).    The SEC itself then seized the $700,000,000 judgment.   It cancelled the original case by the company against the SEC. Let's go back to the diary, before I get too angry to think clearly.

By the way, I promised positive stories when they occurred. I was promised by the education director, my counselor and one of the "suits" today that books would be sent to my isolation cell.

No books from any of the three employees have arrived today. I continue reading the Bible and unfortunately I keep re-reading "We're All Doing Time". Of course, multiple pages are ripped out so I guess I'm reading "We're All Doing Some Time" with hundreds of pages removed through old age, usage or vandalism.

It is important to note that although I had been mechanically lucky in my cell until today my prison water is now inoperable and my toiletries are still not here - but I'm not worried because I'm on the "list" for toiletries.

One Chicken Pox infected cell neighbor is now getting medical attention for dehydration - I guess being unconscious can move you up on the medical "list". What a cracker-jack run organization.

Chapter 5 – My Counselor meets "Al"

No one comes on our little tier or ward without wearing Hong Kong air filters on their faces. I'm not worried because my counselor told me I'm behind the door most of the time and I'm probably not on the list to get Chicken Pox or whatever the masks are being worn for this week.

Today I await the Appellate Court's ruling on emergency relief, or do I have to stay one more week to have the new ordered deposition in here instead of answering questions in a more humane setting. What a vindictive action, hopefully someday impeachable.

I was told that regarding my water and broken toilet the plumber would handle it immediately. That was about 2 hours and 45 minutes ago. Immediately, only works one way in an institution like this. We perform immediately when the slot opens for food; they don't have to respect us - so inmates gain respect in other ways. It's so clear to see the double standard of respect in prison.

Today I was awakened to my first concert while in captivity (if that is an acceptable term because even wild animals have larger cages). They are installing a new shower on our Ward. The old one has been out of service for years. The construction crew is top-notch. They began singing doo-wop "I got to get out of this place if it's the last thing I ever do". Hey, that's my song! Maybe they are inmates too? From what I can see - they look like they have as many tattoos as the inmates have. There are so many tattoos on guards; it seems to support my premise that we become like those with whom we work. The workers are guards! It's a reflective and pensive thought that something is wrong with an institution where both the guards and the inmates have the same school song.

Good News - they fixed my water. With contempt, (can I use that word?) the corrections officer (CO) shook his head when he arrived after six hours of my calling. "It's only a switch outside your door" was his comment …as if I could get out the door, or if I could touch the switch. "It was simple to fix - no problem" were his comments, as he walked away in disgust. Why should I feel inadequate? Speaking of inadequate, this shower project by the doo-wop crew of four has been going on now for the better part of five days. It's difficult trying not to listen to the dialogue. "Fuck this"," fuck him", "I told him to fuck off!" I started meditating (self-taught) on my bunk today - can anyone blame me? I must try anything to block out the sounds and negative energies of this place.

By the way, my counselor who is no longer speaking with me tickled me yesterday (not really). She answers to three names and often does not respond if you call her one of the names she is not pretending to be that day. She wanted to know why I call her Ms. Andrews, et.al. "Who is this Al guy? I don't know no Al," she said. What a laugh she gave me. Instead of my self-taught UMMMMMM meditating mantra, I decided to use ALLLLLLLL. It made me smile, and I probably accomplished the same internal joy as if I had been surrounded by incense, llamas and a mountain peak. This inept counselor operates under three different identities. When you address one of her names, if she doesn't want to engage, she becomes one of the other characters. Nothing gets done. She gets away with this mentally painful treatment of needy inmates. Mrs. Andrews, et.al, causes more anguish to these young men and no one even addresses her manipulative or psychotic behavior.

I still have not received books, so I keep re-reading these letters from inmates to this prison guy, who is the Ann Landers of prison life, in "We're All Doing Time". He's a sensitive guy but some of these letters remind me of why I am in solitary. For example:

"I stabbed this guy 38 times in prison until he was dead. This is my eleventh murder, but I now feel the presence of the Spirit in my cell. What mantra should I hum?" I've also gotta get out of this place. Hey, maybe I can help them fix the shower!

From what I can gather from the terms "unbelievable", "fucking ridiculous", and "I can't take this much longer", the work on the shower has halted because a toilet instead of shower handles was delivered for the shower repair order! All I know is that the yelling indicates someone did something the crew didn't expect. I guess we'll continue our across the hall walk for our shower. Institutional brain dead thought occurs when the negative energies outweigh the positive ones. Someone defecated in the shower. That's what the yelling is about. They do not know which guard (yes, guard) did it! What a system.

As I await today's legal visit, I savor the silence, but wish I could know exactly why the shower construction appears to have more challenges than the Verrazano Bridge, the Great Wall of China or me finding an honest and fair-minded Judge to view all of the facts before destroying a company, attempting to destroy a personal reputation and giving me a two-week, or longer, hiatus which I hope will soon end.

Material for this diary comes faster at me than I could ever imagine. As you remember the elevator was "broken", (I am told today the builder of this building was arrested because of how poorly it was built). So after my legal visit on floor three I have to climb with a guard up to floor nine. No big problem, just another creative exercise in my Club-Fed diet program. Climb six stories with your hands cuffed behind your back. Upon arrival at the ninth floor I was put in a holding pen until one of the five eating and resting guards decides to move me to my cell.

Today was very eventful because Ms. Andrews et.al, my counselor, who to this date has not accomplished one of my requests, was walking about the Day Room, which is flanked by numerous holding cells. She saw me, and I silently stared at her. I stared because I knew she had decided to put me in "my place". She started down the stairs to lower cells (about 5-7 concrete steps). Either it was only justice or maybe it was Al who tripped her, but good old Ms. Andrews took quite a tumble.

That humorous tumble has consumed the entire staff for more than an hour. Their panicked reactions were comical and their ability to stand one very overweight 4'8" counselor up again could have been a comedy skit on late night British Television. I didn't say anything, but Ms. Andrews knows that my stare was the last thing she saw before she did a seven stair high-dive into the holding cells. Like Harry Potter, I'm feeling wizardly empowered. All I need now is a Potter escape from my cell beneath the stairs.

When I returned to my cell, my lunch was there (for hours) so I was very selective as to my eating choices. Of note, today is something new.

Instead of milk for breakfast and nothing for lunch and dinner they gave me two small packets of granulated fruit punch. It is a very blood-like color when mixed with water. My mind is not a criminal mind, but the last thing I would give these prisoners is a substance that would resemble blood. I can think of too many reasons and ideas of how it could be used to keep a guard off-center. By the way, it's not very tasty anyway. No surprise there.

It sounds like they are finally taking Ms. Andrews away now. I don't know where they store 4' long x 12' wide stretchers to move her. Just my luck she'll be getting her disability checks long before my phone form gets processed. With no counselors there is another set-back on my "list" hopes. My only real hope is that they take her to one of the prison hospitals to correct her leg. From what I can observe, legs obviously can only handle a certain amount of "dead weight" for just so long. This hospital is probably run without patient rights and competent staff.

During that climb up to the ninth floor today, I had a discussion with one of the guards. This guard happens to be a sensitive and non-BOP loyal one. He is not a regular on my floor. He said something which got me thinking. He said when discussing the Justice Department system that it's all business. The FBI has to justify their budget. The Courts have to pretend they are dispensing justice. Even the prisons have to rationalize their respective budgets. No criminals would be like no war for the Pentagon budget. This can be a very interesting topic for one of my post publication debates, which should follow AFTER I win my Appeal because only then will anyone believe our side of this insanity. Another tier shower just finished, one more meal, sleep and I'm one day closer to being able to publish these stories.

Today I received an orange jumpsuit truly four sizes too large. Anyone looking at me would think I had lost 100+ pounds. I still have no clean socks. Was it King Richard who said "My Kingdom for a sock" or something like that? Maybe it was a horse.

Today I once again asked for a nail clipper. "We bite our nails here, bro" was the guard's response. I'm not surprised because a few more weeks here and nail biting may be the least dysfunctional behavior I can develop.

There's still no word on Ms. Andrews and her leg injury. When and if I ever find out, I'll share it with you directly.

After my shower, I did sneak my old socks in with my new underwear. Yeah I thought about leaving the old socks in the shower, but then I would have no socks at all and no pocket to carry anything in. This oversized suit doesn't have a pocket so the only way I can carry some of these diary papers to my attorney is in my socks. If clean socks ever come, I will give my old pair of socks to another inmate. No one has socks.

Four o'clock in the afternoon is the changing of the guards. I've previously described the changing of the officers' precision, but today I listened to two guards talking about how last night they had to "mess one of the inmates up". That's all I could gather as I stood waiting to be returned to my cell. Some may wonder why I don't comment more. I have learned the rules and regulations here and additional time or penalties are like my incarceration …without due process. Each offense has a designated official number. For example, insolence may be a 312. The rules inside are too ominous to risk extra time after this Judge is finally finished with his teaching of one of "us" a lesson. I would be forced to extend my stay for alleged acts of insolence as defined by prison employees who need their customers to stay.

Chapter 6 – Today, I became a Prisoner


Yesterday, I tried to describe my evening symphony of noises.   When I re-read it, I choked up with some degree of personal discomfort.   As I sit in my cell tonight and dinner is a bit late (almost -2 hours by now), I listen to my solitary confinement neighborly orchestra gently reminding the guards of the lateness of the dinner.   From "Where's my fucking food" to "you cock-suckers, did you fat fucks eat our fucking food?"   All of the voices came to life.   The two Jamaicans started arguing over whose fault the food lateness was.   My newest friend called his imaginary alter-ego to start ranting about these white mother-fuckers who have taken his freedom and now have taken his food.   The banger has been trying violently to break down the door - doesn't he realize that if an inmate breaks down the door, there are at least five additional locked doors which are worked by keys and others only by electronic central command.   Hey maybe, that's the job they'll give Mrs. Andrews now that she is immobile.   No doors will ever open.   My Tourette syndrome neighbor seems to be quiet now - I guess he's waiting until the moon comes out.   What I didn't remember (I think psychologically I blocked it out) were the other "sounds" which contribute to my Club-Fed nocturnal experience.   The creatures that live in the walls are so very loud.   I hope they are prison cats chasing the mice.

If this was your apartment house, you wouldn't sleep here.   The running and scratching noises are continual and I can only imagine that the population of rodents is being handled as efficiently as they handle the prisoners.   When someone knocks this building down, anyone in the area should go out to the Hamptons for a few weeks.   These non-stop rodent noises must be added to my evening symphony.   Lights remain on twenty-four hours a day in this writer's cell.

Normally after a two week vacation, I am anxious to go back home.   The same is true of this incarceration vacation and forced diet program that the good Judge thought was important for my character and his ego.   The fact remains that I have more character than both the agency and the Judge on this matter and other issues.   Maybe someday they'll get a similar vacation, although now they think it is impossible.   Life is funny and God certainly has proved He or She has a twisted sense of humor by what I have observed through only my little prison window and my abused inmate neighbors.

I am told that although the food is 2 hours late it has finally arrived due to the "elevator problem". Thank goodness I don't have to keep the broken elevator secret to myself any longer. I wonder today like Holden Caulfield would - how did they get Ms. Andrews down the stairs? That is a sight I would have paid to see. They probably have a freight elevator and that would have been an appropriately ignominious departure for the woman who has prevented telephone contact for me and everyone except my friend with the imaginary phone. He simply may have been trying to get on the "list" longer than me. Food tonight was only a cup of rice and two cold hot dogs. I wonder how many calories that was.

Tonight I spoke across the hall with the 25 year old young man who has been contained in the system for six years. As I spoke with him, watched his smile, thought about the last six years of a boy who could have been my son, I cried. He was in solitary confinement because he yelled at his counselor. She put him here in solitary. I am a reasonably good judge of character. The boy was incarcerated six years ago for a non-violent offense. What are we doing to young men like him? Give me a young man like this and I could make our society proud of him. What a waste of humanity. When they are done with him, this young man will be a repeat offender.

I selfishly talk about the injustice of my civil contempt and my loss of weeks of a maturely fully lived life. What does a nineteen to twenty-five year old lose? Our prosecutors and Judges have been giving long sentences for non-violent crimes. We need to re-visit and restructure our sentencing guidelines. That BOP budget could be reduced to less than twenty-five billion and fewer lives would be ruined - and that includes citizens, inmates and guards. I am sad tonight - not for me, but for the countless lost lives that have fallen through our governmental cracks. How I hope I can persevere in this legal case of mine and will use the knowledge to financially adopt some prisoners and show the BOP an alternative way of looking at their antiquated system of rehabilitation. From prosecutors to Judges to prisons to parole officers, we have the highest incarceration rate in the entire civilized world based on population percentages. Dare I say it? I feel like Ebenezer Scrooge after the spirits have visited in the Christmas Carol. How can I ever again look at these institutions as I have? My heart is selfishly irritated but tonight broken when I see the young men so abused. Our society deserves a much better human repair shop. If cars kept breaking down, we would inspect or close the faulty repair shop. Our repeat prison percentages are abysmal and from what I have observed - we owe it to our society to take a much closer look. This is a political campaign issue! The BOP is the cost of the Iraq War every year!

This morning I was taken to the clinic for a physical exam and they scheduled my blood and EKG tests. Fortunately I was put on a medical "list" so these tests may never occur prior to my departure. The doctor and guard had never before met a non-criminal civil contempt inmate held in isolation for almost twenty days. How fortunate for me.

Although it is early morning a few of my fellow inmates have begun banging and screaming. God knows why? They claim it was two rats fighting from cell to cell.

Well, the shower project appears back on the front burner. Today, they sent up the five guys to work on the shower and our related water issues. They have been on the project for over three hours as I listen to them complaining. At the rate of this 4'X3' shower repair, the Great Wall of China would have taken the BOP over 35,000,000 years to finish.

Well Mr. Mansion and Ms. Black are to be our new replacement counselors. Today a suited woman came to "make rounds". I asked what she was doing. She said I'm here to make "rounds". "Rounds for what, may I ask? Medical? Counseling? Telephone? Psychological?" She quipped, "I am here to make rounds". I can't make this stuff up. I said this was a most productive round. What did we do? She said, "Mr. Mansion will be told he needs to come up here". You tell me what happened? Wasn't Mr. Mansion here with her? The other inmates who had been quiet during the "round" now started laughing and yelling about "rounds". The two Jamaicans started fighting about which of them understood "rounds" better.

Good news. I was given one white sock (one sock only) and two double extra-large pair of underwear. Don't ask me to explain, I only sign on the "lists" – I don't issue any of those things. (Yet)

I'm sure by now Ms. Andrews' legacy will be passed effortlessly to my new Mr. Mansion. I'll keep you posted. As of now, I've still not made a phone call home after almost twenty days in isolation. Unlike the others here I am able to visit with my attorneys and sneak out my messages. What about those unable to do so? Something just doesn't smell right, and that is a figurative odor comment because the odors here on this ward and in my cell are what I would never even try to describe. Some rats have started to complain about the filth.

I am reminded of when the missionary, Tom Dooley, went to work with lepers and he himself caught leprosy. His sermon that Sunday started with "We lepers" and everyone knew he had become one of them.

Well, this afternoon I became one of them. A black inmate's cell had water problems so they planned to move him into the young twenty-five year old white inmate's cell across from me. The one who made a fish line ... you remember? So the black guy doesn't want to bunk with the white guy. He says to the guards because I am watching from my window. "Why can't the two white guys room together?" The guard says, "He (me) has to be alone." "Why" yelled the black guy. Without waiting for the guard's answer "I said because I kill my bunkmates at night" - and stared at him with my best Charles Manson evil face. It was more of a lost and twitchy stare. He said, "Shit, get me in here - that dude's crazy". The guard smiled and I had entered slightly into their world of insanity. Hopefully, it will pass before someone gets me a telephone call, the new counselor makes "rounds", I find the other sock, or I get to the clinic for my blood tests.

If I were creating fiction, I couldn't make up these characters as they now have started flowing in front of my door. A new psychologist (female) came by this afternoon. She stopped and engaged me. "Hey, are you my new counselor?" She calmly said, "No, I am a psychologist. Can I help you with anything?" I replied "Yes, I have been here for almost twenty days in isolation, can you help me to call my home? I have not made one phone call since I arrived." Her answer was, "On Thursday the Warden comes by tell him. Have a good night." She walked away. If there is a phrase beyond speechless, that is where I am tonight.

I laugh whenever I now look out the window of my cell door and the black inmate looks and runs inside quickly so I can't see him. I must confess a sense of Hannibal Lector persona starting to take hold as I attempt to survive in this emotionally un-survivable governmentally created bizarre world.

I was told again that I am on the phone "list" tonight. Whether it comes to me, or even if my call actually goes through, I will publish a book exposing this sixty billion dollar poorly run machine called the Bureau of Prisons.

Tonight's dinner was as bad as lunch. Lunch was that mystery meat and two pieces of bread; which meant only the two pieces of bread could be eaten. Dinner was also disappointing. It contained one wing size piece of bony chicken, a little potato and some indescribable beans. Damn those inoperable vending machines in the legal room. I could have gotten through the week with only a few candies and a soda. Well, discipline builds even more character. The vending machines in the legal meeting room continue to be non-functioning. Seeing the food and not being able to get some of it is often more difficult than not seeing it at all.

It doesn't seem like the phone is coming tonight, but there is some bad news in the cell. The guy who talks to himself just had a fight on the phone with his alter-ego. I hope they make up before I leave. They seem to be planning some sort of a "job" or a "hit". No psychologist ever visits him.

When my caloric intake is less than normal I get tired earlier. That doesn't mean I sleep through the night until breakfast. It just means that I get sleepy or depressed before the inmates begin their evening serenades.

Many tonight are screaming about "rashes". So far Ms. Andrews was right because apparently I'm on this side of the door for chicken-pox or new rashes. I'm starting to hum like the shower builders. "I got to get out of this place". Oh, by the way, the shower project is on hold as they have been put on a new "list" for parts. I wish this wasn't happening. It's like being in some crazy man's dream with nothing making sense. I've never taken drugs, so maybe this is what they experience during a flashback. Could this be a hallucination?

The phone call never happened! The inmates tonight seem to sense my disappointment. They are howling like dogs. I kid you not. They are screaming for a guard to come. No one has visited since dinner. If they don't come, they don't have to "do rounds"; they don't have to, like the psychiatrist, ask if "anything is alright"; they can just stay in their clubhouse and do nothing. I am disappointed because I thought that when my counselor went down the stairs, I stood the chance of a phone call.

How does an inmate contact his outside world? I have experienced twenty days and no contact. Despite what they say in their literature, their purpose is to isolate and deprive those prisoners. If the result of that deprivation is these repeat inmates as we have been describing, then the system needs an overhaul quickly. As a former Marine, I seem to adjust quickly due to my life experiences. What about the young impressionable ones? What about their families? A phone call alone will not solve this problem; it just simplifies to this layman the arrogance, incompetence, lack of concern, and total disregard for their fellow citizens. And these inmates are citizens! We either can fix them or make them worse.

Tonight CO Deliverance who I believe has the most anger and does the least at night took and ripped up my request for a telephone call and said "yeah-right". He walked away from me despite my calls for him to speak and to explain to me why I have not been able to make a phone call.

It's a dilemma. Do I formally complain about someone in here and then have an inside the prison enemy when today I just have a non-combative lazy governmental worker. Or do I just wait and wait until the system finally catches up and does what it should do?

In addition, tonight I sadly received thirty more of aspirin and thirty more of a cholesterol medication substitute. Do they know something I don't?

My continued incarceration has to be addressed before Friday. Am I staying more than thirty days? How could this be allowed?

Chapter 7 – Could this be the "Twilight Zone"?

The SEC actually demanded that their Judge send me to a Manhattan jail for "civil contempt" for not being able to pay the $3,000,000 fine, which exceeds my total salary earned over the past fourteen years. My attorneys told me it is highly unlikely to be incarcerated for civil contempt. Nevertheless, I am still writing from inside a prison cell with no crime committed.

I think the loss of a developing company without any hearing or trial is a crime. Confinement without a crime is a crime.

This morning, I began to wonder at what price one finally acquiesces. At what stage of pain, loneliness, fear or loss does one drink the Kool-Aid? Is authority always the victor? Is integrity worth your freedom, your family, your life, and your dignity? Do we genuflect, and at what price? Each individual must make that choice. There are some willing to martyr for their belief, and yet others say "OK, if you don't want me to believe that way - no big deal"?

Is my Judge someone who has been told to believe (and believes) that the SEC is right, no matter what they say? Has he simply "parroted" the SEC's opinion and disregarded my position and me personally as an individual and respected member of society? In this society do most agree with him? Are most afraid of authority? Does my pain this morning need to be further expanded or simply accepted? Will I lose forever the world I built? Does the pain ever subside, or will pain get more difficult each morning? A true patriot, Patrick Henry said, "I regret that I have but one life to give for my country". This is how I still feel today.

What are my limits? What are my loved ones limits? Why do others in political re-education camps acquiesce? Can one "pretend" to believe or does a "pretend sell-out" still mean a sell-out? To whom, am I selling out? How long must I suffer for a cause which may or may not ever be admitted? Who pays for my financial destruction? What if the system is broken all the way to the top? If my destruction is so easy, why will they relent? When and if I return home; will I ever recover financially? Will others look differently towards me? Not heroically, but with contempt or fear? Do members of a society see when that society has begun to die?

I have sold all of my remaining personal assets to fund the appeal of this unconstitutional decision for my shareholders and myself.

How many mornings away before loved ones forget about you?

Waking up in here has become "normal". Time has been taken away as well. I have committed no crime, but have the perceptions of the propagandized lies of my fabricated wrong-doing made me appear toxic and dismissible from other's lives?

Who will trust to work with me? Will this diseased SEC-created leper (me) now be distrusted by those in the financial establishment? Will the wrongs created by one Judge and the fearful mistruths of the SEC, as well as their conflicted receiver ever be reversed? Have they successfully painted this victim as the criminal and improperly punished him - despite his honesty and integrity?

I persist, and I suffer. I suffer for my country. Has my America forgotten? Have my fellow Americans chosen to not fight for what has always made us different from other civilizations? In these deep dark morning moments, like a shaggy dog, shaking water off after a bath; I shake, but I must not forget it isn't water I'm trying to shake off, but injustice. When such injustices as these occur, City hall can and should be defeated, because Americans are given the opportunity to define themselves, their character and their reputations. No matter how vulnerable, pained, angry, disgusted or righteously indignant one has been made to feel - one must persevere and fight for truth. Take everything from me - but you can't take away the TRUTH!

I am listening to a dialogue between an inmate and a prison representative. Apparently, the inmate didn't listen to a guard. The representative basically sentenced him to sixty days of no visitation and thirty days of no commissary privileges. What then about my phone rights? When will someone recognize that no crime has been committed? Hearing my attorney tell me I am innocent and this is an outrage, does not rescue me from a world foreign to any well-balanced society member. I left a note hanging outside my cell demanding a phone call. After listening to that "counseling" session on disrespect, I decided to wait until they let me call. I ripped up the request. This is like playing cards with the guy who made the cards and who changes the rules of the game as it is being played.

As this gum chewing cow-like woman CO counseled two other inmates about not disrupting the system and following the rules, I waited until she finished. Maybe she could help me make a phone call. As she finished, I requested to speak to her. She walked away ignoring me as her gum chewing continued, unabated. The young man in solitary was put here because his counselor didn't fill out his requested visitor's pass and his mother was not allowed to visit him after coming from Kansas. He expressed his frustration and questioned his counselor's professionalism. That's a crime? There is no professionalism in this macabre world of disorder and inconsistent laws. It is the exact opposite of what on paper they pretend it to be. That is the truth. Save these young people and damaged individuals from more damaging behavior. Completely reform this prison system. Privatizing it only assures more unnecessary arrests to insure private corporate profitability.

It's frustrating not knowing the results of today's call with the Judge, which was to discuss my release. Not hearing anything however makes me think that the answer was no release again today. I'll wait until tomorrow morning, and still hope for a degree of civility and my eventual release.

Tonight there is not much to report, but the phone situation remained the same. I did receive the phone tonight, but the prison computer said "no way". I plan to hand the warden another letter tomorrow on his Thursday morning walk through. I hope my letter is also met with some degree of professionalism and responsiveness.

Showers occurred again tonight. This was my first mouse in the shower experience. At first, it seemed the guards were trying to treat me with the same courtesy which I extend to them. – Then the mouse. I just miss my family. I worry at the financial challenges that this incarceration, as well as these appealed fines will do without my legal victory occurring. Yet still, I didn't step on the mouse.

I may be trading a book tonight with a cell neighbor. I hope I get one in English that I can actually read.

It's quiet tonight and I hear it is only 8 PM. That's not a long time until I try to sleep without thinking about going home tomorrow. Remember we have no clocks, and time management becomes a mind exercise in here.

Today after my legal visit, it took over an hour and forty-five minutes to get me back upstairs. They had only one elevator and I am a low priority, I guess. Lunch was three hours cold waiting for me. It contained a pretty hard piece of meat, which I put on a sandwich. Dinner was spaghetti and two ounces of an inedible spicy sauce. I'm certainly not overeating.

Tonight's book trade was typical of this institution, and worth trying to explain. The inmate next door yelled to me "did I want to trade books"? "Yes, tonight", I said, "I'm just about finished." I had over 200 pages to read, but he seemed anxious and I didn't want to keep him waiting. I read from the end of my legal visit to just after my shower. "I'm ready", I said. A guard came by and both the other inmate and I explained the trade. The guard gave me his book, I handed my book to him to give to my neighbor. There was silence. I began reading. Then the sad voice from my neighbor was heard. "Did you give him the book"? "I didn't get it," he said. I started yelling for the guard and one of the orderlies found the book I was yelling about. The disappointment in the voice of my neighbor made me somehow feel I had let him down. I could see the book that the orderly was holding. He said, "I'll bring it in when they unlock the doors." I felt relieved. I hadn't let this poor reader down. One hour, two hours. The book was still missing. No book could be found, and my neighbor had nothing to read. It's so revealing of a system without professional consequences.

This morning I awoke early (before breakfast) to prepare for the warden's walk-through, to update my diary, and to organize if I am leaving. I won't be disappointed because appropriate actions just don't always occur in a world permeated by malaise and lack of attention to detail surrounded by men and women "doing their time". That's the employees of the Justice Department as well of the inmates of whom I am speaking.

With the help of the orderly, I had another book delivered to my neighbor. At least he will have something to read now.

As I await the Warden's visit, I was visited by one of the CO's (Rutgers) who has been trying to "figure out" the phone problem. He truly seems perplexed. He asked me if I had paid for my PAC (identification numbers). "No, and no one asked me to do so", I said. In fact, I have my PAC number on my commissary form I didn't pay for my inmate number or my PAC number. This CO has been here in this system for over 15 years from what I can assess. Why is my phone snafu unique? No one pays for the number given to you when you enter prison. Certainly if this were true, how are my commissary products being delivered? Why wouldn't the counselor have done it? Why wasn't it in my documents? Frankly, after twenty days shouldn't I have been told! Others have never heard of it - but in the air tight system of double-talk anything is possible. Confuse, confuse, confuse. Therein lies their power and control.

At moments like this I am reminded of the James Baldwin quote from "Another Country".

"The aim of the dreamer is to go on dreaming and not to be molested by the world. His dreams are his protection against the world. But the aims of like are antithetical to those of the dreamer and the teeth of the world are sharp." (James Baldwin)

"Their teeth may he sharp, but so is the skin on my neck. The neck of a "leatherneck" (U.S. Marine) is impenetrable." (Richard Altomare)

Well, I gave a note to the Warden. He appeared surprised but appreciative. The rest of the "suits" rushed to find out "what my problem was?" I told my problem to the one who was in charge of phone calls. He was going to "get right on it". We'll see! In my letter I simply explained the facts, gave a brief background on why I was in solitary and I offered to discuss "my observations of this prison" if anyone was interested. Let's see if I get to the top of any list. The book lady wasn't there, but all the "suits" copied something down on their clipboards. It's so pathetic that one has to go through this method to get the basic printed and promised human rights.

Today my legal visit is late. They served me lunch before I went downstairs. This could be a very good or very bad sign. Maybe they went to the Judge's chambers for an order to release me. Or maybe they couldn't get into the legal conference room because they were waiting for others to finish. I really can't speculate. Maybe they just served lunch early. With no clocks or frame of time reference beyond the meals, I could be simply over reacting to an early lunch. We shall see!

This afternoon a "case manager" appeared at my door. "Hello," I said. "Are you a Counselor or an education person, medical personnel, or a psychologist?" "No", she quietly said, "I am a case manager".

Anticipating the obvious answer I said, "Other than managing a case, what does a case manager do, which might be different than a counselor or any other professional?"

"Nothing really", was her response. "I just manage cases". (Damn, she still got to say it). For example, the masochist in me continued," if I hadn't made a call in twenty-two days, could you help me?" "Only twenty-two days? we have until thirty days, and then you can complain," she responded. "Is there anything else I can help you with today?" she concluded with a smile. "Oh no, what else could I possibly want, except do you need a partner to do this job?" was my flippant response.

Whenever I lull myself into a sense of understanding, they seem to move the administrative bar of disbelief yet another degree lower.

With the most sincere of intentions, I do not know with whom to speak. The CO passes the ball to the administrator, the administrators pass it amongst themselves, then the "form" or "list" people never appear, so the administrator and the CO's can continue to blame this secretary, who supposedly works 24/7. In the Bureau of Prisons that probably is 24 days (or hours) a month for 7 months a year.

On paper, our family is told that we can call whenever we want. In reality, silence and non-communication assists the prosecution in disorienting and performing verbal and intellectual lobotomies until they either acquiesce or apply for one of these jobs to work here.

An examination of their managerial qualifications reminds me of two tongue-in-cheek 1960 military draft stories. In the military, I always believed they were too lazy to make up new exams year after year. Yet, some soldiers would cheat. So to avoid cheating, the administration would not change the test - only the answers.

Yesterday, one of the guards (almost 350 pounds) told me that FBI agents and prison guards took the exact same test. Fortunately one of the more realistic guards said, "Yeah, but we don't have to get as many questions correct as they do."

If these suited professionals take a test to get this job, do they toss and turn at night pretending they work, or are they incapable of describing their actual duties on a future resume because they really did nothing? Filling time is more difficult than actually working or doing time.

There is one guard whose eyes and demeanor tell me he knows what is wrong here and makes me want to apply for the job of Director of Prisons Nationwide. Who better qualified than a former inmate without a criminal record? I have listed twenty-five suggestions for improvement with the warden to discuss. Care to make a bet on if anyone talks to me?

Chapter 8 – Waiting "Listlessly"

As an experienced business professional or hunter plans for an important project or hunt, I have decided, as I await the wheels of justice to release me and while I remain in solitary shackled or cuffed whenever I go to Court or to a legal visit, to embark on the following projects. The first would be some toilet paper acquisition. Second would be an appointment to cut my hair and trim my nails before I can use my nails as keys to leave the cell. Lastly, I want to ascertain the progress of my letter to the Warden.

I am on a list to spend one hour every day out of solitary. So far, it hasn't gotten to me in twenty-two days. I must remind you that at the present time I am on a great many lists.

To review:

I am on the telephone list.
I am on the book list.
I am on the blood test list.
I am on the visitor form list.
I am on the PAC list to see if I have to pay for the identification number to make calls.
I am on the sock list.
I am on the towel list.

I'm sure that I've missed a few, but I am now going to simply fill out a form in my cell and request the toilet paper and the hair appointment.

I'll keep you posted, but I would be remiss if I didn't discuss toilet paper usage by the inmates. It's also used as paper Mache'. They wet it and actually fill in all of the rodent holes, air vents, and any open crack including the bed posts which are long gray jagged uncapped steel posts. Excuse me; we have a stand-up count being screamed for by a female guard. In case you are a voyeur being able to have half-naked prisoners of the opposite sex stand up for your personal inspection seems to be a job some might enjoy.

Let's go back to the paper Mache' Olympics. I have only been in two solitary confinement rooms to date, so my frame of reference is honestly limited. If these two cells are typical, it might be cheaper and certainly safer (when heat comes in the winter months) to exterminate instead of empowering the inmates to individualize and to protect their cells from nocturnal rodents with hardened toilet paper.

I'm going to submit my request form now that the stand-up head count is over. By the way, counts in prisons for obvious reasons, are conducted three, four and sometimes up to six times a day. I think the count is for the prisoners, but it could be mental stimulation for the professionals who work here. After dark, although secured by at least six electronically locked doors, they frequently turn on the cell lights to make sure you haven't decided to check-out in the middle of the night. Unless they have counted the rolls of toilet paper and believe that they can be weaved into an escape rope from nine stories up, where could an inmate go?

Yet, who am I to question the procedures of a tip-top organization devoid of any administrative lapses or complaints? I am going to submit the forms. I'll report as the events unfold. Why do I think there is a future story coming?

To ensure a story or a response of appropriate merit, I requested a non-gay straight barber nail appointment and toilet paper preferably white to go with my decor. Let's see the response. My form has been sticking out of the door for a few hours. As soon as someone takes it and responds, I'll share it with you. They intently watch over us here.

By the way, during these painfully long challenges that I am enduring, I wanted to thank you for being there. Without you, I would have been in solitary with no one to speak to.

Eating is an unusual experience in solitary. Much time and thought are consumed wondering, imagining, and even planning about meals. Yet, when it arrives, first you have an approximate time of day reference and coupled with the conciseness of the meal (dare I say, small) ... it's over in minutes. Ten or fifteen white spoonsful and a drink of water from the milk container and the meal is over.

Prior to returning to my newest vampire mystery book, I was asked today by my attorneys about the law library availability to prisoners in order to prepare themselves against the governmental prosecuting attorneys.

The law library is a 10' x 12' cage with about fifty old legal books with a sign that reads: please stop ripping out pages. If you need Xerox copies contact Ms. Andrews to get on her "list". Fortunately, I missed that "list". The only two times I've been in there, I was handcuffed. One of the times was the seven step swan dive by my favorite counselor and her imaginary friend Al (you remember Mrs. Andrews, et.al.). I imagine that when the Warden contacts me (no phone list yet) to discuss the observations of a former Warden he will probably assign Ms. Andrews to effectuate change. Yesterday a very bright, serious and worried stock broker went into the law library to research from the one old computer that is also in the library. I was finishing my shower and waiting my normal hour to be removed and I observed the following dialogue:

"CO, how do I get on the computer?" "Oh, you have to have a password to get on it". "How do I get a password?" "I don't know but I'll put you on the "list". An inmate has a limit of only one hour in the library, unless the guards like the inmate.

As I walked by, his eyes met mine, and I told him to try Disney character passwords or Three Stooges names. They would be the most 'appropriate' ones. He laughed, and I hope I returned reality to him, if only for a moment.

I'm sure that I mentioned it previously, but one of the reasons I have been placed in solitary confinement is because of another Federal rule. I am therefore placed in solitary for my own protection, because I had previously been a warden in a State penitentiary. As long as I stay in this institution, solitary confinement is my only placement. I can also never go to the general population due to my non-criminal status. Only convicted criminals can be housed in the general population. Does anyone else see the flaws in this bogus incarceration for purported civil contempt? No electronic bracelet for someone telling us the SEC is broken – just throw him into solitary.

After receiving the booklet on "how to handle sexual-prison attacks", I must confess, solitary at least meant I sleep without fear.

Six CO's have walked by my note sticking out of the door and I guess it will be picked up before bedtime. I still wait for a phone call. I'm sure the Warden won't let me down. I know my wife is told every day by the prison telephone operator that inmates can call home every day. The operator said, "I guess your husband just doesn't want to call". How helpful that dialogue is to assuage concerns for those family members awaiting contact!

It's bedtime and my request for white toilet paper (obviously it's all they have) and a hair appointment have not yet been picked up to get me on the "list". In addition, I guess the Warden will be visiting me with a phone shortly before bedtime (Why shouldn't I believe that?). Well, so much for Warden professional courtesy.

The inmates seem especially aggressive tonight. There is a great deal of yelling, complaining, banging and arguing. The energy is a sad energy, so tonight I'll read and play some Bridge solitaire and my made-up Scrabble type game with pieces of paper. I'll play until the Warden comes. I'm sure he will respond to such a polite, professional and pragmatic note given after I exhausted his entire chain of command. I am sure that since no crime has been committed, his response would be the same as he would expect if the circumstances were reversed.

But, one of the inmates has been banging against the door for hours screaming for a phone. I think it's being delivered to him as I write. Move over, Alice; is there room in that Wonderland hole for me? Do I have to become a fully irrational prisoner first before a phone is given to me?

Good news, I have learned of another sixty billion dollar high-technological solution to the toilet paper delivery problem. I was told, and I kid you not, "when you want toilet paper just put the inside cardboard center on your outside door knob". An intelligent retort to that is, "how do I get outside to do that"? I realize I have to be taken out of the cell in handcuffs with the cardboard center in my mouth to then try to put it on the door handle.   Oh, yes, that's much better than asking.   I'm sure this solution came about in a management meeting after the Warden discussed my phone deprivation.   As long as I can put toilet paper centers in my mouth, I can avoid the toilet paper "list".   Don't worry, the next time I'm going to do it their way and I'll report to you.   In case you are wondering about my request, to have a sense of humor, intelligence must precede it. The toilet paper delivery CO said "White is the only fucking color we have".   (He missed my attempt at humor)   With a heavy heart and my eyes awaiting the Warden, I enter my third week in MMC.

## Chapter 9 – Read Between the Lines

I guess the Warden or one of the staff members that diligently wrote down my phone issue is probably planning some sort of celebration or surprise for me. I must admit I have been "eyeing" the center cardboard of the toilet paper. How anxious I am to be able to work within the system the next time I need that roll. I keep reading and re-reading the orientation manual, and I find nothing about how to get out of your cell to put the cardboard center on the door handle. This could begin to better explain "making rounds". Those cardboard centers are "round". Maybe there is a higher level of intelligence and professionalism than I have been able to understand. If we could connect them with the strands of clothing that the other inmates use, could we possibly make kindergarten-type telephones with the string? I may have broken the communication code in this place. Maybe by walking around with toilet paper centers in my mouth while I am unnecessarily handcuffed, I can yell loud and demand more. Maybe that's what the others have been using? Had I had one in my mouth, would the Warden have respected my request? Does it have other uses that I foolishly may have ignored? What about this system for socks? If I put one sock on the handle, will I get the other? If I put the ripped pages of a borrowed book, will another arrive? My free-floating creative mind feels I may have broken the prison code here.

If I put the "center" of the toilet paper roll on the front of my jump suit, will I become "one of the guys"? I must be careful not to mistakenly put it in the rear of my jumpsuit that would probably be frowned upon. All in all, I'll be working on my newest breakthrough. Friday, as I remember, is the mad hatter psychologist visitation who hastily runs through rounds. Today, maybe I'll paper Mache' my room and even paper Mache' myself to get to the "secret center." I'll put that in my mouth covered with toilet paper; let's see if that stops him on his rounds? "Solitary confinement I am told makes one re-evaluate their crimes, their lives, and possibly their future. I never heard of the toilet paper center breakthrough. Hopefully, I will not have flashbacks every time I return to society and get to the end of a roll. Will I discard it, will I instinctively put it in my mouth, and will I put it on the front door? What will the mailman think? Does he know the sign? Will my neighbors begin doing the same? Will it affect property values? Oh, I must return to the here and now. Could I begin seeing other uses for the center? There is so much more for me to learn, and to think I thought all of those "suited" visitors were doing nothing. They were counting toilet paper "rounds". I feel so ignorant, so misinformed. Thank goodness I have not ventured into the next week without this information. Do all solitary confinement people know this signal? And I thought a few of them just had large noses. With all the creative signals going on here, no wonder the Warden disregarded my paper written note. Now, if it had been written on a toilet paper center (TPC), he would have known I was worthy of a response.

Friday seems to be an administrative moving day in and out of solitary. I go from newcomer to old timer every week. You can tell the seasoned "solitaries" because they have "list-marks" like "hash-marks" on their sleeves or a few tattoos for effect. Some have the toilet paper center "round" in their mouths as they jubilantly leave solitary. Alas, my sin is so great my societal offense so heinous; I must stay to be rehabilitated so I may one day exhibit the compassion of a Warden, the wisdom of a draconian Judge, and never again question the professionalism and integrity of an agency that itself is under investigation and is the only agency influenced if not paid by the brokers it monitors. In essence, the SEC is on commission. Sorry, for my venting slip-up. I'm going to do what any self-respecting inmate confined to solitary for no crime should do to show some respect; I will put a toilet roll center on my mouth with the bolted door closed and I will not say another word of complaint.

I finished another mystery novel. Now begins the struggle to get another reading book if I am to be here yet another weekend. I'll leave a written request. Who knows what wisdom or dialogue will follow. I have ceased requesting a phone call. I can't go higher than the Warden. After all, I did have seven more days before indignation is officially permitted despite prison regulations to the contrary.

Honestly, there are many lost historical figures in life who sacrificed more, their freedom and even their lives. But as far as I can research (and that's not in the law library) none of them had a Jewish wife in Boca Raton, Florida waiting for him. This will not be a supportive, "Donna Reed" type dialogue that I am anticipating. She wants this battle over. She has to live in a community of retirees who relish in gossiping about this type of unusual intrigue. That poor woman has to deal with that, while I am getting on "lists", consuming 700 calories daily, now walking around with a cardboard round in my mouth and living in a modern gray and white cell, accentuated by orange contemporary understated decor.

Today I must confess some optimism as well as fear. Am I to be released? Will there be a deposition? Can I see my grandchildren soon? Will my wife ever forgive me for being stubborn, and fighting for what's right for us and other Americans in the future? Will I remember how to swing a golf club? Hey, maybe if I save my roll centers and paper Mache' and put them together, I could at least make a putter.

Soon I will go downstairs to meet the attorneys. Will the Warden spring (wrong word) his telephone surprise then? Yet, he seemed so understanding when he took my note. We'll see...

What an amazing dialogue is going on as the inmates are packing and many of them are shipping out to other prisons. I am amazed to hear these prisoners proudly speaking of friends, family and neighbors in multiple prisons. They are talking about a prison riot last year where some men were killed. It was a Super Bowl event with some Mexican dudes having been killed. I don't remember reading about it. Yet their descriptions seem vividly similar. They are telling each other prison names like you or I would have our children speak of Ivy League colleges. This system has become self-serving. Who would say "selectively open the prison gates?" Today, I am saying that. Not for me, but for future generations in America. Remember that doing the same thing over and over again and expecting a different result is the true definition of insanity. This system defines insanity.

Insanity is truly what is happening here. Forget about my sarcastic, tongue in check, observations of a broken system. For people like us it's wasteful and broken. What happens when it breaks a person? What happens to that person's family and children? We in the Marine Corps used to say that we as a squad or platoon or company were only as safe and successful as the one member who broke silence or gave away our position. Our society is the same principle only larger. We should never forget that these forgotten children weigh on the future of our children's safety, tax base and sense of long term societal well-being.

My legal visit has just been announced. I don't mean to continue our laughing at the ridiculous, but sometimes when reality sneaks in, I must share it with you. But first, a little more of the bizarre. When an Attorney first arrives for a legal visit, the announcement is made – in my case, "ALTOMARE ... LEGAL VISIT!!!" After that, it could be 10 minutes or two hours until the guards decide to get up and escort me, in cuffs, to the legal conference room. If you are paying your Attorney by the hour ... I don't think this insanity requires any further elaboration.

I swore to myself because I was feeling "blue" about not being released as expected today, that I wouldn't write in my diary tonight. But then showers came, and I couldn't contain myself.

Believe it or not, the new shower being repaired was the one I was sent into! I was initially impressed that it had been finished. As they put me in, I immediately noticed that there was no door, and therefore, visibly exposed to the stairs directly in front of it. I undressed and found it surprising that there was no place for soap, shampoo, or shaving gear; but without lights it didn't seem to matter. What did matter were three female guards that kept coming up and down the stairs while I showered. We did exchange glances. What I was most interested in was the water was actively flowing to the two foot square area one dresses in after they shower. The shower was slanted away from the drain! The dressing area was covered with at least three inches of water. Getting dressed in a totally wet area makes it impossible without soaking the bottom 10 or 12 inches of the legs to put on a jump suit, which you must lay down to step into. I had joked that I might never get to use that shower - I wish I hadn't. It astounds me that the number of wasted man hours could have created a slanted peep-show without a door, or lights to add to the eventual mold, water damage and complete re-do of the same shower in months - if the female guards allow it!

In the movie "Castaway", Tom Hanks created a character to speak to named "Wilson" out of a volleyball. I don't have a ball in this solitary cell, but I've been thinking about drawing a face on one of the toilet paper center rolls.   It's an interesting idea if this unlawful incarceration extends, thus causing me to begin creating characters in the cell.

The four day Memorial Day weekend begins tonight and I tried to call to comfort my distraught wife due to the fact we thought this capricious abuse of power would be over by now.   You guessed it - no phone access and none until next Tuesday.   My disappointment is aggravated by the constant indifferent laughter and daily ineptitude of the guards.   How disappointed I am now all the way to the top of the chain of command. This behavior is reprehensible, and the responsibility of these caretakers has been completely lost in the MMC.   Tonight a phone call was all I needed to comfort and inform my family.   Shame on them!   Shame on this system!   This diary speaks of only my challenges.   Can you multiply this ineptitude and disregard throughout the country tonight?   Tonight as a former Marine, I am disgusted with my country's poor handling of justice and decency.

Tonight I finished another mystery novel about a family that was distraught with the legal system.   They had kidnapped all the characters that had beaten the legal system and conducted a trial, on worldwide TV mind you, convicted them and then the Federal Judge thanked them for correcting justices' errors.   Wow, is that something for me to look forward to, or should I just be happy with a toilet paper center in my mouth, to get out of here without losing my sanity, family, reputation or financial future?

I have been reading books to mentally escape from the walls which seem to be getting smaller and smaller with every layer of paint.   Since these cells haven't been painted in years, it is an illusion.   But as time goes on, the stark reality of the situation begins at times to remind me of time passing, opportunities lost and memories un-had.   I know "un-had" is not a word, but it certainly defines time in solitary.   What may have been is un-had.   The reason I discussed reading earlier, was a subtle and psychologically revealing bit of advice I received this morning from one of my resident correction officers.   I returned two 500 page paperback mystery novels.   As I asked him if there might be any more novels around, he calmly and as a representative father figure of this institution or maybe our present society, told me, "to read slower!"

Read slower and we may let you go.   Read slower and your family's pain will be over.   Read slower and stop telling others what's wrong with our governmental trading system.   Read slower and you can kiss your grandchildren and children again.   Read slower and we will embrace you. "May I please have 5 more books?"   Unfortunately, reading slower is not an option.   It's like telling a fish not to swim or a bird not to fly. "Read slower", no, you people start reading faster.   God damn it!   These young men and women need you to read faster!

Chapter 10 – Shaking Out Memorial Day

It's quite interesting to observe the ups and downs of solitary. Depending on multiple factors, some days you can rise above the negativity and laugh at it, and some days it hits you directly and you can feel all of the emotions that this destructive human creation can do to you. My visits with attorneys do nothing more than remind me of the cause, the price one has to pay for it and my responsibilities to all of those counting on my perseverance.

The correction officers (they hate being called guards) have all started to appreciate my low maintenance requirements. They are amazed at how fast I read books. They may start monitoring my toilet paper ordering to ensure that the books are actually being used to read and not "other uses" for that paper.

I have decided after shaving a few times to now grow a beard in prison. This is not because I have decided to burn the flag, although at times I must confess a disappointment in the judicial system. Not shaving is because the last razor given to me had been used before. I know they are supposed to dispose of used blades because of HIV possibilities, but in a system "not that exact", I have decided not to take any more chances. We had sixty-eight prisoners in solitary and over forty have been transferred today. There are no familiar faces staring out the door windows yet. No conversations. No late night serenades. One new inmate across the hall is unfortunately a drug addict. He is regularly administered methadone. The thought of us exchanging razors has caused me to go for the Don Johnson look of Miami Vice or the white full beard look, if necessary.

I don't like weekends because of the mystery meat meals in general, but also because of the one CO Grant. She's a very sweet lady, but has the loudest piercing voice I have experienced here or elsewhere. Her voice is explosive, happy, mad, argumentative but relentless. As I read or do anything, her voice just penetrates. No complaints - just an observation to continue to try to capture the sounds, moods, up and downs in case you ever are invited to visit. If you really want to visit, disagree with a Federal Judge, take out a full page New York Times ad on his actions, be unable to pay his ludicrous fines and you too can experience this vacation paradise. After all, many have gone to France, the Hamptons, Florida, and Italy etc. Have any of your friends ever raved about the mind altering experience of solitary confinement in a Federal prison for weeks upon weeks? That will help you gain control of the conversation. "Oh, so you saw the Leaning Tower of Pisa but have you ever had a toilet paper center roll in your mouth?" Have any of them lost as many pounds at any other spa? Or have they ever met such memorable characters and group showered as often?

I certainly have too much time on my hands. Well, I guess that's to be expected. I just wanted to touch on two simple topics tonight, as I dig in for a long weekend. Tomorrow I will be doing the twenty-four hour in the cell marathon added to the time after today's legal visit. I'm looking at as much as sixty hours before I speak with anyone. I am remindful of the monk who entered an order of silence, but every nine years he was permitted to speak. After nine years, he was called in to the head monks' cell (it probably was a room, oh my God, have I been here that long?) And the head monk said, "Is there anything you would like to say?" The monk said, "Could I get a new mattress, mine has had the springs sticking out for the past five years." After the next nine years, and the same dialogue, the monk said, "Could I possibly get a pair of sandals as I have not had any sandals for seven years?" After another nine years, he announces that he had decided to quit the order. The head monk said "I am not surprised, you have been complaining ever since you got here."

So I guess today I'm complaining. My toilet bowl sometimes flushes for five minutes after flushing. I hate to waste the water, but to get on the plumbing "list" and to have that "crackerjack" repair crew that did the shower repair could possibly destroy any sense of humor or objectivity I may still have left. So with apologies to my fellow earth conscious "Green" friends, I can't risk it. I am so close to the end of my stay, I hope.

I will leave a note for the next guest when I fill out the "comment card", or when I visit the prison gift shop to purchase some of those orange suits or orange sheets as I leave. I'm sure they wouldn't miss these gift shop branding opportunities. Do you think they steal the sheets? Maybe that's why there are no pillows. The bathrobes probably went in the first few years. Now the towels are without absorption but the size of three washcloths and despite my weight loss I cannot tie it around my thigh, let alone my waist.  My waist I may add is not a 30" but it's not that much more than that - so these towels are quite small.  Because I have the time today (do I sound bored?), I'm going to measure it "by eye" right now.  The measurements are 12" x 32" (approximate), but they are orange and that appears to be most important factor.

I experimented tonight.  I decided to ask another CO how do I put my toilet paper center on the outside door knob.  This has really been a keen issue with me over the past forty hours.  The guard came by to ask me why the hell I would want to put a toilet paper center on my door knob.  Obviously, this CO did not read the manual the other guard read.  Rather than get the first guard in trouble and then, in turn, me; I decided to answer that I thought one had to do that so a case worker would know to stop when making "rounds".  He walked away saying, "We don't have case workers, you mean counselors".  It's going to be a long weekend for me, and I'll try to not take it out on you.

I've written long letters to every family member to avoid this diary becoming even longer than "War and Peace".

The early sounds of morning are the initial noises coming from the Day Room.  Like robins on a quiet summer morning, you might hear "you get the fucking food" or just the noisy pre-delivery sounds of that same breakfast of milk, cereal and ½ an orange.  The sounds of toilets flushing can be best described as engines at a NASCAR race.  Each toilet is truly an eight or nine on the decibel scale similar to a motorcycle starting up next to a baby carriage and revving for a few minutes.  Each flush has its own life span.  Noise discretion in the middle of the night is simply not possible unless you fear flushing because of the noise and in my case the length of flush.

After arising in a damp chilly room, I awoke again before breakfast service.  Remember breakfast service is a 4" x 12" slot that opens with a key and a conditioning bang.  The food is coming through that slat or slot or slit.  That noise is my morning alarm clock, or my robin singing in the forest.  But today I wondered do I flush before the food service arrives?  What if it continues "flushing" like last night's five minutes?  What if they find out it is broken? Will they send the repairmen? Will I be moved to another cell? I just got this one paper Mache'd and cleaned! My decision was to wait and then monitor the button (yes, a button because a "toilet flush arm handle", I guess, could be used as a weapon) or maybe too many inmates would get confused over whether to hang the toilet paper center on the toilet arm or the outside door knob.

One can only hypothesize on the high level executive decision which went into the button selection. Or more simply, some politically connected brother-in-law had the specifications written so that he was the only one to have a "button-flusher" (does that sound like mother-fucker?) The term could be used so that some of the inmates felt at home, "button-flusher" is indeed a unique technical term.

Before I eat today's surprising breakfast (it's the same), and while we are on politically connected friends who may benefit from the prison system not being changed; one of the inmates said in dialogue, which even this skeptical pen has difficulty absorbing, that Ms. Bush's family are directly connected to prison food delivery or food manufacturing. I just hope it's not the mystery meat! That would be a National scandal! Once Americans tasted, smelled, looked at, or even just walked by it; it would become mystery "meatgate" or "baloneygate" or "tonguegate". I mention what the inmate said because if buttoned toilets and orange bedspreads make sense to these people - there may be a bigger political scandal. If it's not Ms. Bush (she seems so nice) let's at least get the last administration looked at. I'm sure its fingerprints or continued political financial rewards will be found out by an effective journalist examining who other than the salaried "suits" do not want to change this status-quo system. By the way, my button flusher shut off in reasonable time.

In case I may have lost you during today's early morning thought process... Well I've played a word game, exercised, ate breakfast, straightened up my room, walked about the fence limits of my Ponderosa cell, checked the other door knobs for toilet paper centers (I can't help it) and only 23 ½ hours left to read and write to you.

Some days not much happens in solitary confinement. I started reading "Sole Survivor" a mystery novel about a mysterious plane crash. A funny thing happened today. Although it doesn't seem to be a damp or cold day, I have become a freezing monk. For the first time, I am draped with my blanket because I am so cold. I don't feel sick, I'm sure I am not. But the sight of me writing to you covered with a blanket, or reading with a blanket has even resulted in some comments from the guards as they pick up lunch trays. I don't think this could be a result of weight loss, but one never knows. My window is blackened so no sunlight passes through. One of the guards sympathetically asked, "Are you going fucking crazy?" I simply responded that I was cold. Unfortunately, I have to wait to push the button for hot water tomorrow at breakfast. The interesting observation of the button used to get cold and hot water from my unique button-kitchen-bathroom unit is that it is instant and it shuts off immediately. We all have experienced those institutional faucets that you press and you almost make it to the water before it shuts off. Not this one, the second your finger is off the button, the water stops. To utilize it, one finger pushes while the other hand washes or fills up a milk container. Forget about mixing hot and cold unless you have a bunk mate who hasn't read that sexual attack brochure. It's either very hot (1 Hour) or all cold (23 hours). Today, I hope it gets warmer. Maybe the heat in the rest of the building was shut off for the long weekend. I feel like a family cat left at home when the family goes away for the weekend without the ability to adjust the thermostat.

At least they left an automatic feeder (egg, oatmeal, mystery meat and today uncooked frozen French fries). See, I told you it was cold today.

Chapter 11 – "For Lack of a Nail"

While I am doing a poor impression of "Orange Sitting Bull" I am reading this Sole Survivor book. Once again that cracker-jack education department probably is unaware that there are about 6 suicides in the opening 100 pages. Another subliminal message brought to you by the Bureau of Prisons - "The Bureau that doesn't give a damn what you think because we can do whatever we want to whomever we want because no one gives a damn about those whom we control. "That public service announcement should be on its advertisements. Hey, what an idea, privatizing prisons and letting prisoners and their families, like college, choose the one which has the lowest rate of return. Believe me, think outside of this box (no pun intended); a prison monopoly is still a monopoly, and it's not working as it is.

Memorial Day has always been a tender day in my life. Since the Marine Corps, and having lost some close friends and Marine brothers in Vietnam, I normally golf alone pretending they are with me and laughing to myself about things they would do or say during the round. Well, the traditional tournament has been cancelled this year, and I invited them to spend the time with me, here in my cell. Because of our lifetime friendship, they told me no way will they come; they'll wait until I get out. Those are my friends and I can't blame them. On a more serious note today, I honor those who gave their lives so that I can hope to defeat governmental "employees" who have chosen to conveniently forget the difference between right and wrong. Without these fallen heroes I could be living in a totalitarian system with no hope of restitution and vindication.

It seems that a few Spanish inmates have arrived because of some disciplinary problem in population. Their "property" has been an issue for the past few days. The system can't locate their "property" and the inmates are hysterical. That's all they are talking about, and the solution is, of course, wait until Tuesday when a counselor can help straighten it out. I do not have an opinion or comment on how long it will take to find the "property". When you are reduced to so little, your "property" becomes all that defines you in here. From headset music (which I would eliminate) to personal effects, one would think the property would travel with the prisoner instead of disappearing into a system run almost entirely by the criminals who are put inside here. You figure this logic out. I am going back to reading. Dinner must be only three hours away.

Well, much is happening. First, the Chaplain came by and said he was in a hurry because it was a very beautiful day outside. So much for his consolation. He did also tell me that he looked up my case, and the government's position seemed to be correct from what he had read. He also had jury duty again next week. Hopefully, this will be his final moment of tenderness. Also, he can't help me with a phone call. Total visit time was one minute. I feel better again. Where can I purchase one of those Muslim prayer rugs?

Speaking of Muslims, on the commissary form, from which inmates can purchase items weekly, is pork-free Dove soap. This list and prices are pretty interesting for any reporter who might like to follow the money on this monopoly. Isn't there some sort of law about price gauging when a hurricane or tragedy occurs thus forcing people to pay more than others normally would?

Call me a masochist, but I'm trying the phone attempt again tonight. If I don't keep trying they can say it was available and I didn't use it. I'll not let them slither under a rock on this issue. Over 24 days without contact due to incompetence, disregard or arrogance. This call was not permitted once again!

Today we did have two visitors to the area. "Good morning" the first woman said, "What are you here for?" As I hurriedly attempted to respond, she was gone. Following behind her was a doctor or at least someone in a white lab jacket. He looked at me, and he was gone. At least in a zoo they throw you some peanuts or make faces. I guess I should be pleased that unlike the insensitive Chaplain, they didn't try to tell me what they thought of the government's case. Is it not the task of any leader to try to uplift rather than to devastate?

During the past three weeks I was able to clean and disinfect my little cell to where I felt it was not overrun by transmittable diseases and rodents. Well policy is policy. Today I had to be moved to another cell. My cell was for one inmate, this one is for two. Nevertheless, I just saw this room for the first time. My God, I have just literally removed one 45 gallon trash bag of oranges, paper, old food and old clothes. The walls are covered with filth and mold. I will be cleaning for the next few hours.

For the sake of your personal enjoyment, I have been moved directly across from the fully tattooed Illustrated Man. This is the methadone user. I'm sure after I clean my cell and after I settle in, I'll get to meet the "neighbors".

No time to do anything other than try to clean-up my little section of the world. This cell has not been cleaned or (even paper-Mache'd) for months based on the amount of garbage left on the floor. I'm afraid I have a place which may have very spoiled mice or rats.

When a cell is vacated, shouldn't it be standard operating procedure to clean it up somewhat? No kidding, I really removed a full 45 gallon garbage bag and there are excessive amounts of mold on the walls. The button-flusher works so I guess I should be happy for that.

Psychologically, this cell movement doesn't do much for one's centering. If they had wanted me to clean all of the cells, they didn't have to keep moving me. I would have been happy to do it and stay put in my disinfected and clean cell.

The CO's said they would bring me disinfectants and a mop in five minutes. Two hours later I have finished cleaning with only the hot water and my bar of soap (with pork) and I am totally wet with perspiration. Yes, we can get soap with or without pork. Who's winning this war on terror? Unlike my other room this one is very hot with minimal air circulation. Maybe that's why the mold exists. I have cleaned as best one can with only a bar of pork soap and a wash cloth.

How could the previous inmates have been able to leave it that way? A simple glance and lifting up of the two mattresses would have exposed the mess. Looking under the bed would have clearly shown oranges uneaten and partially eaten food (I'm hoping it was the inmates). What exactly are we teaching inmates in prison? This is not about my indignation at the filth. It is my indignation over the fact that the CO's never came with the promised supplies. Like the Warden, promises but no follow-up. This goes beyond my phone call and incarceration ... this is a clear set of eyes telling you what you (and I) never wanted to know. Hold on because I'm now taking a societal leap - It's worse than the Iraq War because it will never end and there isn't even a debate about how much this broken welfare system costs. Look at the BOP Budget. Examine where monies spent actually go. Examine what relationships between friends determine contracts. No one cares because these are society's invisible people. Until after they fester in here and then they rob, rape, frighten, or kill someone you know. This place makes them much worse, not better. Even in solitary confinement we don't have them clean under their bed! As they listen to head phones in the jail, the CO's have no problem with them. What garbage rap music do they listen to? Continue the stereotype that only music soothes the savage beast. Consider hard work, pride, discipline and respect of officers that say what they mean and do what they say. These inmates already have enough broken role models.

Sure I remain indignant at the Judge who wrongly put me here. But this is just another part of the broken justice system that Judges simply don't understand, and don't care to understand. Every coin has two sides. The court room and the jail should complement each other.

Trust me; this is a poorly run and weakly administered facility from top to bottom.

As a former Marine and real executive, I am appalled at what I see on a minute to minute basis in here and we continue to pay without comment.

My sons know the following poem by heart:

> For lack of a nail, a shoe was lost.
> For lack of a shoe, a horse was lost.
> For lack of a horse, a rider was lost.
> For lack of a rider a message was lost.
> For lack of a message, a battle was lost.
> For lack of a battle, a war was lost.
> For lack of a war, a country was lost.
> The country was lost for lack of a nail.

I'll pick up the nails and I'll clean under the bed. You and I have been doing such for all public employees, Judges to guards, who are simply contributing to the country's economic decline. The Wall Street Journal recently said that counterfeiting of securities (Naked Short Selling) costs Americans 3 billion dollars a day! Some governmental agencies and Congress are questioning the SEC's police tactics. My reward, while they ponder my criticism, is prison. Could naked short selling be funding terrorists? Are these prisons weakening America's future?

Chapter 12 – The Escape

Well my new best friend across the hall has taken me under his wing. He has been yelling at the guards for me. He also told me to shave because we can't let those guards get to us. His entire body, fingers, face, and scalp are tattooed. I'm glad my 3 day beard growth was so noticed by him and considered unattractive.

Well, just when I thought I would be boring you with meaningless complaining about my new dirty room, I was given my finest prison story to date.

My new tattooed friend told the guards that they had forgotten to give me a shower. He keeps track, I guess. They took me to one of the lower showers. Our shower is out of order (no comment). I took a pretty long shower because of my cleaning efforts and they also gave me a new razor so I shaved. Everyone, including my Illustration Man Friend, would be happy. So, I finish, dry down and step out with my small wrap around towel. As I am standing in my most provocative position (I wish) female inmates working on the floor with a female guard handle me standing there semi-naked like a Brad Pitt sighting. They are clapping and whistling. I am still there waiting for my clothes, and the guards are simply mulling around discussing some basketball game. The female guard says "Honey, you better get in the shower you "upsettin' my girls. Go in the shower, boy". With embarrassment, I did.

As I stood in the shower, the "count" began. The "count", as a review, is the quality control, like a prisoner of war camp, of this fine-tuned BOP machine. I couldn't help myself. I decided to see if they would miss me in the count.

The female guard and her harem left. The CO's began the "count" while I stayed now out of sight and in the darkened shower. The dialogue was priceless. It must mean I'm going home soon. Please let this be my final story.

"What you mean Altomare's gone?" "I brought him back from legal 2 hours ago"; (Apparently no one remembered they had brought me to the shower.) Despite the fact that both of those guards, who were part of the search, were the ones who placed this nude, chilled and toweled hider in the shower; they were like the Keystone Cops in their search approach. They all started yelling at each other, as I quietly stepped out of the shower and now stood waiting to be noticed and taken back to my cell. The search and recount continued until one of the guards finally saw me quietly standing where I had been placed over 1 hour and 30 minutes ago. They were so happy to see that I hadn't made a break for it. Can you imagine that paperwork? Everyone started blaming everyone else, and only I knew that for at least 20 minutes I enjoyed some retaliatory "sunshine" against a system that *tries its best*, but it is broken. My escape was short-lived, and the head guard couldn't have apologized more that I had been left over an hour during the count and had been so missed. I'm really going to have to send pizzas to him when and if I finally leave.

When I was in the military in the 1960's there was a joke that asked the difference between a drafted Army and the Boy Scouts. The answer was that the Boy Scouts had adult leadership. It simply flashed back to me tonight as I disappeared for the count. Where is that adult leadership?

The pile of garbage I left outside my cell, during its initial cleaning, remains piled in front of my window as I return to my cell. The pile of garbage, which has been there for hours, represents the disdain those inmates and prison employees have for our society and our system of justice. How different a prison could be run if those in charge really cared.

I'm really not going to forget that on Memorial Day weekend the Warden went on a 4 day vacation while disregarding my polite and professional request for phone call assistance.

Initially, I was going to let Warden Star hide behind the "suits". If a fish stinks - it stinks from the head down. I intend to try to assist in whatever investigation this Sing-Sing, Shawshank Redemption story may one day find itself. Normally the truth does come out. It's similar to the reason I was invited to visit prison by a Judge, who like the Warden, thinks he is above reproach. The cleanliness transformation of this cell, if I may say so, is remarkable. I have disinfected, mopped and changed the linens as well as protected the perimeter with toilet paper that may inhibit evening visitors. I am quite proud of my efforts.

But that's not all I wanted to speak about. The real issue is that along the perimeter of this new cell are ripped out baseboard heaters. Connecting them are 5" or 6" long metal spikes (knife like) that are quite easy to break off and use now or whenever appropriate. I, of course, still care for the safety of these CO's. I may hide during a count, but these young untrained and unmotivated men and women are dealing with hardened criminals or hardened civil "contemptors" like myself. The point of interest is the CO stated, "We know, we told management." We are on a "list" to have the cell made safer and closed off from the walls. Yes, the holes in this cell are massive. I would have to use the center of the toilet paper instead of the paper itself to prevent rodents from entering.

My wife is more superstitious than I am, so I will not talk about leaving. As I wake up this morning, a little earlier than normal, I would like to reminisce about my stay here. Maybe today I will leave.

First, I will miss the personalities of some of the guards. A few of them are definitely likeable. Maybe like a dog, you wag your tail for whoever feeds you and takes you "out" for a walk to my legal visits. I remember that my dogs used to go crazy when I picked up the chain, and they knew they were going out for a walk. Honestly, it is the same each time I hear the keys or handcuffs rescuing me. After initially "tabling" my ego and pride, even strip searches after visits became worth the departure from the cell for an hour or two. Some of the guards touched me (not that way) because they care. Some are simply more evolved and competent than the others who are overwhelmed by the task and the responsibilities at hand.

Without my diary notes in front of me, since I sneak them out through my daily visits, I hope my stories and comments are not too redundant. For you see, my mail is opened, read, and stapled together and I am pretty sure my letters and stories would have been censored by someone with the same qualifications as the more inept characters who have already been presented .

Before I go down prison memory lane and all is well again with the world because I, a non-criminal, am finally leaving to return to the "non-toilet paper center world".   Let us pray for those for whom today is just another day in this non-productive system of make believe.

Chapter 13 – A Heart to Heart with You

Often "patriots" resent any criticism of good old America. My country "Love it or leave it". "My country, sure we have problems but we're a hell of a lot better than any other country in the world". As a lower to middle class former Marine, I've said and believed what these "patriots" today believe.

I have poked fun and was even sacrilegious towards many of the procedures, policies or inept actions of the unchecked authority during my stay at MCC. I have discussed and described a criminally negligent counselor, a Chaplain devoid of compassion, the sounds of the night, the relationships between prisoners and guards, the internal shower construction, my escape during the count, "button-flushers", toilet paper centers, clothes, and the parade of psychologists, "rounders", and countless other uncaring middle managers. I gave the top management only one test (my requested phone call) and they failed with impunity. I've shared with you the loss of personal freedoms and the thoughts and, in some cases, the practices, games, books and activities one does when his world has been taken away.

But remember, whether today is my final diary entry, or yet another disappointment on the road to release; there are hundreds of thousands of souls, many like you and me, living within this broken system today and tomorrow. There are countless families trying to hear the truth from those with whom they speak. There will be countless dialogues today of promises not kept, innumerable thoughts of despair, hatred, unacknowledged depression, humanity ignored, filthy cells, supplies not given, words not heard and America getting weaker - not stronger. It has been said that a society's character can be judged by the manner in which it cares for its indigent, which includes its prison population. From Guantanamo, which all patriots have given carte blanche for my fellow Marines to waterboard and detain without the semblance of due process, to even MCC and my brief stay with no hearing and an incarceration without my civil liberties respected; our prison and judicial system needs an examination and full overhaul.

To the alarmists who believe that my remarks constitute an opening of the "Willie Horton" doors of justice, their indiscriminate and parochial conclusions are ill advised. Let us consider that our prison system is now a very large business that is not scrutinized. It needs prisoners to grow. Frankly think of it as a fire that needs wood. We pay for the salaries, construction, upkeep and repeat returnees because that's their built-in obsolescence. Many still discuss that the Packard automobile company went out of business because the car was too well constructed and consumers didn't have to repurchase them every few years. Are our prisons designed for rehabilitation or a lifetime of generational dependency? Are we packing them in for generations to follow?

So today, this morning, my walk down memory lane may be short lived and the Judge may forget, or feel my punishment still does not make him feel good about his absolute power. Nevertheless as I imagine my counselor with 3 names, the mad-hatter psychologist seemingly afraid of the inmates, to my tattooed neighbor, my neighbor who beat the telephone system by creating an imaginary phone and countless other memories; I wish to thank-you for giving me some reason to write. Whether this diary results in cocktail party dialogue or a reporter deciding to examine the financial books, or a lawyer having the courage to file a lawsuit on behalf of the system's responsibilities to his or her clients continual incarceration, to maybe a TV talking head beginning an investigation; I contend that all sides of this issue need to be heard! Prisoners may not all be eloquent.

But during my brief visit to their world, their eyes spoke volumes. Please hear their silence.

If you could have read these eyes and mannerisms with the same intensity that I was blessed to see; then you would never compliment this diary but you would know how far short of the expose' my simple words came to the intensity of the challenge before us. The solution is not within the Bureau of Prisons. The solutions must come from the hearts and minds of our American collective intelligence and our desire to be the bearer of freedom which symbolizes our nation.

This, my captive diary reader, is one man who has been punished from misguided authority. The media tells us that some of our financial problems are caused by our involvement in the Iraqi War, or it's the next election, or it's the revolution of our social divide. No, it's how we handle this bleeding ulcer in our economy and our collective soul. Let's focus on this problem. It affects multiple societal issues.

We laughed and maybe cried together in my unwanted twenty-five day stay in a Federal prison. There haven't been too many diaries that get out. There were many "Anne Franks" who probably had their diaries destroyed. We need only read and see the truth in one story, and that should be enough for us to believe in the many ongoing tragedies which thousands have experienced and yet have gone unwritten, disbelieved or unread.

Like the reason I am here, sometimes life calls upon us to be touched by a mistake or an injustice and to act in support of others who may never know what you did for them. This work is a dedication to those inmates who cannot or are prevented from speaking for themselves.

I would tell you at the very least to call your elected officials, but unfortunately, their approval ratings are lower than the President today. But we must accept that we live in a "selective" democracy and these elected men and women only work on what the polls and their constituents' letters tell them to address.

This is an issue that deserves more attention than steroid use in baseball. There are some BOP officials who should be taken in and out of hearings in cuffs or with bags over their heads. We have questioned the tobacco industry for attracting and then killing their customers, but do our prison officials ever get questioned for the psychological deaths of millions of these less than hardened criminal inmates?

My Illustrated Man dialogues or inmate serenades of nocturnal sounds ask you to look into where and how they will be treated, and how much we will be forced to pay for the next few generations. These inmates will only be replaced by maybe one of your offspring. Once you slip in; it is close to impossible to get away. They need customers. They require more customers. How do we change this? It's your move. (And I hope mine out of here today).

If it's worth the effort, I'll relate my actual move out of this prison. Who knows what indignities or laughs the system of BOP still has to show us. (How prophetic when you finally read of my final day)

You see, I think the BOP is subconsciously crying out for help as evidenced by their actions, can't you hear them?

Although I had hoped this entry would be my last, I must still relate an incident while I wait to go to the legal room for a visit this morning, hoping to hear of my release.

The shower crew has returned and all hell has broken out in the hallway. I only wish this were fiction because, at least, you would credit me with a degree of imagination unequaled in American literature.

The hullabaloo is that someone defecated again in the shower. The dialogue is that they are not sure if it was an inmate or a guard. That has me sitting here telling you with a childlike uncontrollable giggle as I write with my wiggly pen (refill not the pen) which I also sneak in daily. I have always been amazed that during my strip searches for contraband, they inspect bodily orifices but don't look inside the bottom of my shoe or inside the pocket in the front of my jumpsuit or even in my long messy hair.

Chapter 14 – The Mickey Mouse Club

Nevertheless I am still torn between leaving today or reporting on today's "shower defecation gate" update.

I know that one should leave after saying goodbye, but can anyone blame me for telling you about the defecation incident, let alone who they think did it. I have a theory, it's the Warden - No it can't be him - he doesn't give a shit about anything. (Apologies for the painfully inappropriate language)

Well, as I wait to hear the results on whether I will be released today; I returned to my cell from my legal visit. I have received three lunches! It appears the standard, a Jewish kosher lunch and it seems also a Muslim Vegetarian. If this is true, Jewish people eat the best in prison, followed by the Muslims. The Muslim meal was only a raw onion with skin and stem, some leafy salad and 1 and1/2 green peppers with seeds still attached. This was much better than the standard Christian lunch of an inedible chicken meal with spices never before experienced by me, other than as the recognized smells of cleaning supplies.

I have started storing little packets of shower supplies, soaps and salt packets (you can never be without salt after what I read) in an unreturned clean breakfast tray. But, today when I returned to my cell, it had been dumped out and the tray returned to the system. It is important to note that in the initial cleaning of this cell yesterday, I returned seven such "trays" with green molded food still in them! I'm glad that I could assist in returning this clean one back to the system. I mention this tray incident simply to let you know about the multiple freedoms that take a holiday when you "take a holiday" in a penal institution.

This cell invasion and tray return - I don't understand. "Storing" property is difficult in solitary confinement but doing it in a container which impedes insects and rodents seems to far outweigh leaving "things" on the floor or near the toilet bowl. It is important also to note that my illegal refill pens were left intact and not confiscated. Inconsistent actions add to the confusion of prison thought.

I was told by one of the guards after my repeated alerts of the danger of seven or eight potential knives sticking out of the wall in my cell, that if I remove them and give them to him - I will be put on a "list" for a commendation.

All of the "lists" I am on have not yet worked out for me in this system. I did however meet with a Lieutenant today. This is one of those guys who I have observed to be a paper-moving do nothing guy. The guards are non-responsive verbally when I ask what this political officer crony does. Their eyes only tell me they fear him.

So I requested to meet him today and to tell him my telephone plight. Well, low and behold, he's going to give it to my case worker. A new layer of efficiency! Could a case worker be that woman who made rounds? I asked what my case worker's name was. I wish I was lying because he told me it's Mr. Mansion. "Isn't Mr. Mansion my new counselor, who I have never met since the swan dive of Ms. Andrews et.al?" He didn't respond and like an elementary school teacher whose student couldn't understand something - so the teacher simply repeated the exact same words slower to exert his authority, he simply repeated, "Mr. Mansion is your case worker ... dismissed!"

Dismissed? I haven't been dismissed in decades. It reminded me of a Marine Corps world long forgotten.

Normally, "dismissed" is not done by someone brighter or more evolved than yourself. It is normally like the feeling we got when a parent said "because I said so", and we were unable to answer back, or too young to know better.

If I am to be dismissed today, should I verbally lock the heels of that under-worked liver damaged red nosed, dead in the eyes Lieutenant? Not today anyway. Dismissed? Maybe he was the shower defecator? There are so many potential suspects.

I must confess as I re-read the last few days of entries, I wonder how funny a Woody Allen or Larry David movie or book on this could be. I often see very menacing prison films, which make most of us, turn the channel and let the BOP handle the nightmare. Granted there are some prison institutions where the mood is intense, but the majority of these prisons should have the Mickey Mouse Club Song playing for the guests. The final scene in Platoon indicates the feelings of the soldiers about the war in Vietnam. They whistled the Mickey Mouse Club song as they marched into the rice patty. There really is no difference in here.

Politicians will react if they covertly investigate and see how these prisons are really run. Those in power will react only when public opinion about inmates gets hot, but make no mistake about it, they have the same blood on their hands or gavel as their BOP executives do. When we send our children to camp or school, we visit, don't we? When we kennel our dog, we visit, don't we? When was the last time one of those Judges visited and observed a prison? They're not too busy. They are appointed for life. They have the time, but not the stomach or courage to see the real results of their actions.

Judges owe it to those they sentence. They owe it to the Senators who confirm them. I only wonder why the Pope, a dictator, and an American Federal Judge are appointed to serve until death. Other than some government employees who seem appointed for life, who else can get away with such ineptitude?

That being said, I have decided after this is over to bring administrative charges against my "three named counselor". I know the system will protect her for multiple reasons. Nevertheless, I plan to do whatever I can to remind her someday of one of the faceless inmates that her laziness and disorder hurt. Since there are three of her sharing her 18 and 1/2 years of tenure; I should at least be able to get *one* of them fired for incompetence. Like it says in the Bible, "Let ye who is without sin cast the first stone". This is a system where no arms are left to throw stones. How do they use the "button-flusher" sink and toilet bowl?

It's a quiet night and the Illustrated Man, my legal expert, has told me that I may go home or I could stay here for a year. He told me if he had to stay in isolation for any more than a week, he would freak out. I didn't want to tell him that his tattoos freak me out while I am talking to him. I have never spoken to a fully tattooed person before. Have you? I now understand how Ray Bradbury, in the book "The Illustrated Man", had them start moving and acting out several stories. I find myself looking at the tattoos when I yell across the hall to him.

The "Loneliness of the Long Distance Runner" was nothing compared to the loneliness of solitary. No one who knows me would have ever pegged me to be engaged in political and societal discussions with a man covered with body art even on his shaved head and ears.

Despite the fact that I hope to be leaving, I am rushing to finish reading every one of my novels and historical books tonight. Should I be rejected again by our one man system of justice, I may be without books tomorrow. Then, for lack of intellectual stimulation - I'll be hoping that the BOP sends in its employees, spouting their commands and observations, which only they can do to create the visual absurdity that I will then get to further share with you. It's not that I haven't grown close to you. I really miss my family, and I repeat I still don't know why I am here. I feel like a foreigner who may have been in Guantanamo with no phone contact and no knowledge of when the nightmare ends.

Tonight a doctor visited the ward, and boy did the Illustrated Man let him have it. He's not getting the medications the Judge put on his confinement order, and he is suffering from withdrawal and having a painful night. The discomfort is unsettling. His noises alone would prevent my drug use. I guess my painful nights wondering if I'm going home, and my tattooed neighbor's concerns that his condition is life threatening, are proportionately quite different.

Sometimes I feel so petty when I observe the pain of the others. Aside from that raw onion as the major ingredient of my Muslim lunch, their nighttime music and chanted prayers in the background are quite peaceful. Their onion lunch prevents me from a prison conversion even if they have special soap without pork fat. Only in America would we declare war against a religion based ideological culture, but when they get into our prisons, we afford them all of their religious privileges such as special meals and the freedom to practice that religion. *I am proud of that fact?*

As I was waiting for my legal visit, and I did hear them announce my lawyer's arrival two hours ago; I was told I had to take a shower now or, possibly miss the legal appointment. Knowing that my lawyer is already here, I chose to hope my shower would still be available upon my return. It was another leap of faith. Only time will be the recorder of the accuracy of my decision.

Today, the "Judge's departure conference" was postponed again until tomorrow. So I wait again. Good news, however, all signs are the prison phone professionals are now working on my phone request in a manner that any top notch organization would be proud of.

This morning I was visited by three new "suits". I don't even ask anymore because neither you nor I would believe their titles. I once again told my plight. They asked me to fill out a third copy of the blue phone request. I did. They left.

After I came back from my legal conference, I was visited by another "suit" because Lieutenant Dismissed asked her to talk to me. I told her the same story. Her solution was sincere but not too comforting. "Tomorrow, I'm going to visit you and we'll fill out a fourth copy of the phone request form, then I am going to deliver it directly to the phone room", she told me. I think they must know that I'm going home. I hope I am, but the fact is that through super-human complaining we keep going back to the same blue-form. This fact probably highlights the clearest governmental repetitive and inaccurate management "style" for all to see.

Let's forget about this over-educated, over-verbal, overly persistent inmate, who is visited by attorneys almost daily (to sneak out the diary). What does a frightened 20 year old do in a broken communication system? It's easy to criticize complex organizations. It is not easy to accept a system that just doesn't get it. Thirty days and nights, four weekends and over 50 formal and verbal requests and we are still working on a blue form for a phone call! Forget every one of my other requests. How does this not add to one's anger and frustration?

Case in point, today, I was going to legal and I had to sacrifice my shower until Friday. At that time, I felt it a wise choice. One of the newer inmates apparently did not wake up during today's early morning shower. As the guard and I walked by his cell, the dialogue went as follows:

Inmate: Hey CO when can I get a shower?

CO: You missed it. Wait till Friday.

Inmate: I didn't hear anything.   Come-on I need a shower and shave.

CO: Too bad.

Inmate: Fuck-you, Mother Fucker.

CO: Fuck me? Fuck you!

Aside from the maturity and eloquence of the dialogue, another guard came over to the guard just discussed and said "He gets nothing for 5 days".   "Let's see how that prick likes being ignored".

"Tit for Tat" may work on a playground, but let's not add this troubled inmate's challenges to the ones I have shared with you.   Let's imagine him out into our world and tell me why he wouldn't become explosive and release all the pent-up frustration and anger caused by "respect" issues within the BOP system – if a regular citizen should casually disregard him.

"M - I - C,   See ya real soon!"   (60% return rate!)
"K - E - Y,   Why?, Because we *need* you!"
"M - O - U - S – E"

Chapter 15 – Please! Don't Make My Eyes Roll

During my two hour wait today before I returned to my cell, I had a brief respite in the law library holding cell. I was able, as an inmate and as a functioning adult, to observe the play by play in this Day Room. My troubling concern was the sounds emanating from the various cells. Rap music was playing in headphones loud enough for me to hear. With the inmates mouthing and repeating aloud either from the cell and two of the sweepers, painters, and "moppers" also singing a song containing gang dialogue that I could not understand. I could however, make out "Fuck Whitey", "Fuckin Pigs", "Policeman Junkie" etc. I'm troubled about the emotional climate of inmates and guards. The "suits" have no stress. They walk about complicating basic needs which should require no forms. By the way, when they do get forms; the inmates have no writing implements. Once in a while, they get a pencil that wiggles, but the phone list must be filled out in pen! You and I can clearly see the conflict. That's because we never worked for the BOP. Forms in pen! No pens allowed!

Books, logs and sheets of paper are all moving about and are all disregarded and obsolete by morning. Forms, lists, titles, procedures, rules, regulations, and brochures all contribute to a system that is clearly understood only in the "eyes" of the "suits".

Today the Illustrated Man, who is still begging for the medication which was promised yesterday, told me in prison-talk how to accept the way things are. "It is what it is, Brother."

Am I so wrong in wanting "it" to be more? Maybe, that's why I'm in here?

Today I finished my books and that's why I went to the law library. The Education Department is supposed to visit on Thursday with the Warden. We only have Chinese, Russian, Spanish and Muslim books and all are tattered, ripped and incomplete.

Tomorrow is my next encounter with the Warden. As you may remember, he walks the prison on Thursday and the "suits" copy notes so they can "re-copy" them the following week. It's an inspection of sorts.

One can only judge the effectiveness by the results of your requests. To date, not one call in twenty-nine days! That's the real truth! I have struggled with writing another letter, ignoring him, writing a nasty letter or to stand at the door and pretend I am disoriented. Frankly, I can't take any chances disrespecting an authority figure, or they could extend my time here, even though I couldn't have been disrespected more by any of them. By the way, I have been very quiet about the food. It remains inedible and were it not for the bread and water, I might not eat anything. I am not a picky eater. It truly is inedible. I cannot tell you how the brown suits (general population) eat. I am an orange suit (solitary confinement) and I can only pass judgment on the food I receive here. Does anyone taste it? As a former mess officer in the military I did eat what the men got served. Like Frank Costanza in the Seinfeld show, who had flashbacks to when he was a military cook - I may for years be unable to even look at some of the food groups served in this prison. Granted, prison food is not a reward, isolation and time away is our punishment - but destroying taste buds when that simply does not have to happen is just another visible example of the ineptitude at all levels of this place. Dare I mention food to the Warden? Believe me, it's just a walk through. It wastes everyone's time, but it looks great in the time log and it fills empty hours for do nothing administrators.

My attorney said that I have a very long diary. I think that's because I live very long nights. I never thought about how long twenty-four hours were before. Those who are free fill it with multiple activities like travel, work, fun, family, TV, and love. But sitting at this cold white desk in this room of loneliness, I just wonder how men with ten years to life sentences miss their families and their lost opportunities. That reminds me of another illogical thought that this civil contempt is creating. How long could anyone not work before their economic world collapsed? I raise that question due to the fact that this is also an economic issue. Which is better; me earning money and being able to address this fine, or being here and making no money? Which do you think an intelligent Judge should prefer? Well, you are living it with me. He would prefer to be sure I was unable to pay his appealed fine than for me to chip away at it while I work. Or is this a governmental puppet punishing someone who dared to question the autonomy of an agency that has obviously not been doing its job? Let's examine what the SEC's job seems to be. Litigate, litigate, and litigate. Ignore the real issues so that the SEC can beat the "bad" non-governmental citizens into submission. The more spectators, the more they have to frighten others, using my beating as an example of the consequences for questioning their autonomy.

Unfortunately for everyone involved, they picked the wrong issue, wrong CEO and simply the wrong individual to genuflect before their golden calf. I worship only the truth on the top of that mountain, and all of their standard slander procedures will fail this time. This time they will have to pay my shareholders and myself and return what they have stolen from honest Americans who built this in a way that the Judge and those governmental agency bureaucrats could never understand - through creativity, hard work, integrity and tenacity. These are four qualities necessary for absolute success.

As also a respectful former political candidate, I believe that I will eventually hear what twelve Americans on a jury would say to this governmental cover-up and attempted persecution and silencing of this well-intended and very much correct American whistleblower.

Looking out the cell window, (for a short period of time one of my cells had a street window – even though it was painted 95% black) and seeing workers in some of the neighboring offices kills me more than the institutional ineptitude that defines the BOP and SEC governmental minds. Make no mistake; forty percent of these employees deserve to receive appreciation and gratitude. However, the majority should be removed.

Today one of the guards who childishly acts like he comes to a clubhouse each day, told me he makes $80,000. Wow! Had I known institutional pay for doing nothing paid so well, I may have given my sons different career advice.

Who works here? Come on investigative reporters. Check the family lines. Check-out the patronage. There can't be that many incompetents throughout this system without some thread of dishonesty or some sort of political interference. Look at the "appointments" of the BOP in

Washington. Try to fathom the forms, titles, games, kickbacks and patronage. You almost can accept the costs, if anyone is really doing what they say they are paid to do - but believe me, they are not.

My prison friends come and go here The Illustrated Man was moved today either to the hospital, Syracuse or Riker's Island without a goodbye. He has been replaced with two Jamaicans who unfortunately have a few other friends either down the hall or in New Jersey because they are loudly yelling and speaking in their native Jamaican dialects. They have certainly turned up the "tempo" of the ward. I don't know much about them yet, but the noises have become louder and the dialogue sounds like I'm on a Caribbean Island.

I don't know if it is today's luncheon meal or the emotional "ups" and "downs" of the past few days, but I definitely am having my first prison food and stomach disagreement. I hope it doesn't continue for long, but this discomfort coupled with my new Jamaican neighbors is keeping me up tonight. Sometimes when the people you love are in pain, it can upset your body more than today's funny tasting tuna fish. At least it will keep the mice away tonight, because I will be getting up throughout the evening. I don't think the CO's get involved or ever silence these yelling inmates at night. The sleeping of others doesn't really fall into the night crew's assignment. "So, 'Mon,' I have a craving for a drink with an umbrella in it, after a few more hours of this noisy Jamaican reunion".

Tonight, I can hear the crawly creatures actually breathing in the walls. I swear to God … BREATHING! I certainly hope they are cats doing "rounds" in the walls. But I don't think so. I guess the city doesn't inspect the Federal Prisons for rodents. If they could, this would be a front page newspaper story. It seems as if the new inmates have settled in. Some have been moved closer to each other, so the loud yelling has stopped. Yelling that you hear in your native tongue is very different than when it's in a foreign language. You sort of know what they are saying though because every once in a while I hear "Counselor", "rat", "toilet paper", "list", and other expletives preceding "phones", "visits", "Chaplain", and the list goes on. There is a time of mental fatigue when you simply accept the noises. I'm almost there, so good night. I wish I wasn't surrounded by such aggressive noises and breathing. They really are within the walls. That wouldn't normally upset me except the baseboards are exposed in this cell. Once again I wanted to thank the BOP for its attention to detail and the public's money well spent.

My patience, begging and asking for even partially ripped books or anything that gets me from day to day has finally run out. During the past few weeks I have read six mystery novels. I even tried to translate a Spanish one. I found the Fight Club (another socially redeeming work of art for these inmates from the BOP's Education Wing). I found it stuffed against the wall to block a gaping hole so it's a little crumbled. Recently, I read Inverness Island by the writer of Mystic River. Of course, this was also a book about a prison of psychological deviants. Yet aside from the Bible, most books I have "found" have had a prison motif. I also found a 1962 printing of "Religions in America", which is another real "page turner". My Jefferson book on his relationship and discussions on slavery enables me to at least go to sleep at night. Plato's work on the Symposium of Love based on homosexual Greek love is yet another work that makes me search for another pair of adult eyes to meet so I may experience the thrill of "rolling my eyes in disbelief again". I finished a book on a Muslim man killing his wife because she didn't show him "respect". (In case you can't see my eyes rolling - please imagine it).

Chapter 16 – The Salute

Today the dentist came by to inspect me through the door with a light. "Open your mouth". I did. Now date of birth, and have you been in a hospital in the last two years?" "No", I responded. "Thank you, have a nice day". "Wait" I said. "Can I get my teeth examined or my gums inspected?" One cannot really clean teeth with the 2" toothbrush and no other whitening products. "Have you been sentenced for longer than a month to this institution?" "Well, I haven't been sentenced to anything - I am here until the Judge decides to release me on a civil contempt claim." (I use that instead of CHARGE). "Then you're out of luck. - Even if you are here for years, unless you're charged with a crime, we can't do anything other than emergencies. I will put you on a "list" to visit". At least you can admire the list consistency in this place.

I have decided that today before my legal visit and when the "brain trust" walks by, to not ignore them as originally planned. I must engage these imbeciles.

Self-respect aside, what will they do if I sit on the toilet bowl as they all come by and try to talk to them? Maybe that will get me the notoriety and attention to get one thing done. I could hand them the toilet paper roll. If I knew that today was my final Thursday of being part of this morality play of actors walking about pretending to be competent and caring, I might have more resolve and courage.

I returned my Spanish book to a CO begging for him to possibly find me an English one. His heartfelt response, well-intended as it may have been, can give you a feeling of the amount of reading material here. It was "I may be able to find a Spanish dictionary if you want to translate the book. It will take longer to read it. "

While I'm sitting on the toilet speaking to the Warden, I can 'for effect' be translating a 500 page Spanish paperback. How's that for drama? Comedy?

Some of my "anti-prison" problems could be my fault. I may have to readjust to the environment into which I have been placed. Take the Education Department for example; I wish you could take it, I just don't know where to send it. I have a belief that if this education department went to work for the Taliban, who only permit the reading of the Koran, they could effectively slow down or eliminate the one book to distribute. Within a year they would be reading it in a foreign language trying to translate and eventually maybe just go to work and build their society for their children. Enough said about solving the education problem in the Middle East. Today I will change the typical book requests which have been: "May I have any fiction, any non-fiction or any Bridge Playing Books, any biographies or any current or past classics or current best sellers". This has resulted in "nada". You can see the benefit of my cross-cultural language training that I have received from the BOP.

Today, I am going to ask for books on mass murders, dysfunctional societies or anything they may have on revolutions, rapes or prison uprisings. I may further ask for manuals on bomb or weapon production. *That* they will have.

As I prepare to see if I have the courage to sit on the toilet bowl in front of the window as the Knights of the Roundtable saunter by to ask, "How's everything today", and copy down inmate requests with absolutely no desire or ability to correct those requests, knowing they will only say "Have a nice day": I ready myself for their arrival. I am only a few minutes away from my Thursday fix of authority in MCC. I could lie in my bed (bunk) with a note facing the window saying, "Same old - Same old", or "How can you improve upon perfection?" or "will work for edible food or "where's my phone" or "A book, a book my Kingdom for a book," or "sorry, mice took him away" or "gone to the prison in Guantanamo" or "went looking to find a Counselor".

How about a ZAGAT book on prisons? I guarantee they could sell it in their Commissary.

One more day and I find out if this silliness has an ending, or if I have more to observe so I can actually publish this story for others to read. As of now it's been only you, but more readers have to laugh, question, be shocked, investigate or simply say, "I'm not surprised", if any real change is ever to occur.

Sometimes at night I shudder to think of my rescue during a fire or an emergency. Aside from the lack of professionalism, they could never cuff and escort this many prisoners, and by following the rules during a fire, they would still be more concerned with "policy" rather than the saving of our lives.

I just couldn't believe today that there were 15 "count them" 15 "suits" and executives actually bumping into each other. The Warden saw me reading and said "I see you got a book". I said "No books have been given to me; I found this 1962 book on religion in the law library". He didn't hear me. He smiled and wished me a good day. Now comes a communication breakdown which revealed a truth of which I hadn't thought. First, a man came by and said "Psychology" - I said Boo!, and he left. The next woman asked me "How's it going?" I said, "How can one improve upon paradise"? She misheard and said, "it isn't possible to improve upon a paradox." In fact, I'm going to have to look up the word. What's a paradox"?

Realizing that she couldn't understand my voice through the door, I said, "paradise like heaven". She said "we don't sell dice and there's no gambling allowed here". "That's the paradox". I said. She shook her head, and I only wish I knew what she wrote down. She called over a guard because she claimed that I had a pair of dice. Paradise!

While I await going to legal, there's another commotion outside. An inmate claims he has a broken arm and he can't "cuff-up". Cuffing-up is putting your arms through the door before you are permitted to leave your cell. There are a few "suits" talking with the inmate. They have compromised, it seems, he's cuffed one arm, and they are checking his medical records to verify his broken arm. The dialogue is tense, the guards are upset and they are taking him to the medical office. I'm such a low-maintenance inmate.

Oh happy days. While the broken armed belligerent inmate is at medical, the guards have moved him directly across from me. I hope I'm going home, but dialogue with him I feel has some writing potential coming to us all. Maybe he's the one with the dice.

I must compliment the BOP when appropriate. The commissary operators do a good job. Privately operated or not, the three times I have filled out the Wednesday sheet, requesting specific products, each time, many of the products have been delivered when available. I must relate all of the facts, positive or negative, as I observe them.

Oh boy! The broken armed inmate is being dragged back. He's spitting and kicking. They just threw him in and slammed the door. He's spitting at them. I'm a little reticent to meet my new neighbor yet. I'll wait until the anger moods settle down. I won't look out the window now. I will have to look tough and "bad" to bond with him. He can't see me washing my spoon. Oh my God, he's pounding on the door threatening to kill the guards. The guards are calling him a punk and they're going to "fuck him up." Oh boy, has my neighborhood changed. Where's my Illustrated Man to settle things down? Oh, he's really smashing the door now. Should I hide under the bed? I wonder if he's "in" for civil contempt too. My prison instincts tell me to stay low for a while. Tensions are hot, as I await a legal visit or my actual departure.

I learned from the Illustrated Man that an arm across your chest (like Sammy Sosa, remember?) is hello. Although this inmate's pounding is intense and he is hysterical, I think I'll stay low until tempers subside. I'm going to however use the salute. What if the Illustrated Man was cursing at me? I hope this arm across the chest is a friendly sign. Here's the problem. The bathroom in that cell is broken. It's been broken for the past 3 inmates. I guess they think if they change the inmate, the water problem will subside.

While this is going on, one of the guards brought me a roll of toilet paper. Did someone put an empty cardboard center on my door knob? No they did not. Like Sally Fields would say "They like me, they must really like me".

Well, the consistency of the system has revealed itself yet once again. A doctor or psychologist is talking to the inmate. Solution? They're moving him to where his friend was. He was rewarded again for dysfunctional behavior.

What have I been doing to get my toilet paper? I must have become a "bad" dude. Yo, know what I mean?

I'll never get to use my hello arm signal now, since no one is in that cell. I'll have to wait. I'm going to watch the move. I'll get back to you. I gave him "my signal". He gave me the finger and said something like "go fuck yourself". Well he's definitely off my prison reunion party list, which is being planned.

Chapter 17 – Brother Lovers

Six guards the size of Pluto, plus a doctor and the Lieutenant have just arrived. I wanted to ask if this was a good time to get a Book, but I kept quiet. I exchanged "the signal" with another inmate while we all watched intensely …like a car race, anticipating an accident. They escorted this new inmate into one of the cells where I think you stay chained even while you are inside the cell. I can't see him anymore. I'll get the whole scoop on my next trip to legal. By the way, that Lieutenant Dismissed did a good job; he handled this situation quite impressively. Perhaps this guy is in here for *double* civil contempt. My prison instincts tell me to be quiet for a while. Tensions are hot, as I await my long anticipated departure.

I just returned from my legal visit. Once again we must now wait until a conference call scheduled for Monday or Tuesday. What a system! What hubris from this self-appointed demagogue. Lunch was inedible. I can't do justice to the mystery meat. It resembles baloney in shape and its color is like an old man's tongue. Its texture is rubbery and the smell is repulsive. Other than that, someone in BOP knows someone who sells it. Everyone laughs about it. There were two pieces of bread, corn flakes (yes, a bag of cornflakes and ketchup) (you never know - hamburgers may be coming soon). Obviously I can only eat the bread and butter. Maybe dinner will be better.

Across the hall, another inmate "Love Brother" arrived and is now waiting for an investigation. He and his "brother" were caught in the same bunk. He is pacing, and behaving in a tearful manner, unlike a hardened criminal such as I would spend the day. As soon as the facts of this high level drama unfold, you will be the first to know. For the record, I was told today by the elevator operator, the CO's think I'm "doing time" like a real guy, and I have more legal visits than John Gotti when he was here. It's always encouraging to be acknowledged by your contemporaries. This kid across the hall is a real crier. If he appears at the window, I'll be able to settle him down. Only a few more hours and I get a second chance of eating dinner. I am astonished that despite my weight loss, solitary confinement has re-activated my Marine Corps survival training; I am just so repulsed by the look, smell, feel and taste of this food. I amaze myself at how nauseous I am. It amazes me over and over again. In the future, if I am served a meal I used to enjoy to excess, I may recall this BOP food repulsion perk, given to me erroneously by a judicial system that simply is out of touch with the reality of where they are sending our citizens – and that will help to keep my waistline in check. Positive reconditioning run by caring professionals has to be better than a pre-Revolutionary War philosophy of lock 'em up, throw away the key and they'll never do it again. Quite the opposite, you revitalize your opponents by mistreatment. You endear and engage with proper judicial handling. In other words, love is a greater motivator than controlling hate. It doesn't make sense when a civil contempt guy is housed down the hall from someone carried in with six fully dressed riot control guards. When that inmate is sedated for days on end; and the civil contempt detainee is looking for a nail clipper and socks - the system needs massive overhaul. But we'll save that for another day. I'm going to salute and engage Brother Lover. I'll be back to you if I am successful.

Well, the Priest came by to speak to my neighbors. It does mystify me that the Priest doesn't visit me anymore. He visited me once, and he now seems to ignore me. Well to be honest, that Chaplain seemed more interested with the brother love story. It seems, putting together what information I can, the two inmates didn't have sheets for two beds and only enough blankets for one bed. Since, like clockwork, everyone gets a pillow case (no pillow of course), it's a 50-50 possibility that there was a slip-up, and now I have been listening to another inmate screaming for a blanket for over 2 hours from my old freezing cell.

His blanket requests have been polite, continual and of course, without response. Remember the day I was freezing in that same cell? The CO's responded 'five minutes' the first four or five times, now they are yelling back for the inmate to wait. With the party going on in the Day Room no one wants to be disturbed. From the CO's ignoring this simple request to the brother/lover claiming they only had one set of sheets, to the Chaplain turning his back (is that the right term, Father?) on me; it's all about a general climate of being overworked, under motivated and underperforming.

It is not possible to put this many incompetents into one location.   It is not possible, so there must be other answers. Recruitment and proper compensation for those who actually want to work should be considered.

Today, for example, after my legal visit the elevator operator sat and "shot the breeze" with the female guard about children and life.   Because I was waiting to be returned to the 9th floor, I waited over one hour while they spoke.  I sat.  I paced.  I tried to convince myself someone upstairs was coming down because this operator couldn't have such a task completion deficiency (TCD).  I was wrong again.  They keep lowering the bar of expectation.  Communication is crippled by their procedures.  Add the "Rank" structure to a governmental mind set and this group sinks below the National Guard during the 1960's and the draft.  No one wants to be there.  No one wants to do anything.  Everyone wants to get paid.  Pride is dead here.   Not in my cell, but it is dead throughout this slowly moving enigma called a prison.

As of now the brother/lover has had no investigation and he keeps crying.  The other inmate has no blanket and I remember how cold that room was.  The other two inmates are sedated, and the Jamaicans are having Family Sunday Dinners.  Yeah, this is a system that's really an example of excellence.  Do Judges understand the results of their decisions?  Do Congressman, Senators, Governors ever spot visit?  Has there been one presidential Candidate to have a town meeting in a prison or with prison families?  The questions go on, and so do these tragic stories.  When should we give felons back the right to vote?

I have to admit Sunday night's dinner was one of their best.   It contained rice, vegetables and four ounces of stew.  I could survive in here on rice alone.  They can't do anything to ruin the taste of plain rice.  The Deliverance brothers are on duty tonight.  That may explain the delay in the blanket request.  Here's how it went tonight when they delivered dinner.  The blanket requester asked again face to face, as they served the food.  Unfortunately, he now also needed a spoon.  He either never got one, or he broke it, or he threw it out, because he didn't understand that this is the only "spork" they want to issue, no matter how long you are here.  Their response took me back.  It was, "Blankets, you want blankets OR you want a spoon?  Which one"?  As the inmate tried to process this, they walked away. I do not know which he got, or if he got either. I only worry about getting cleaning supplies and new linens with Deliverance working tonight.

Since I started reading these books in here, I was not as knowledgeable on salt, religion, Jefferson or black owners of black and white slaves. The list goes on, however, because dental hygiene here is a few steps beneath phone call efficiency and sensitivity training for some of the employees, "I have had to do what an inmates' gotta do". I just read that salt rinsing was the earliest form of mouthwash and used for other dental improvements. With no mouthwash and nothing except toothpaste I have religiously (sorry, Father) rinsed with my little packets of salt while I am here. I hope I find out when I get home that this was a good idea. Jefferson and Washington even referred to using it. Wait a minute! Didn't they both have wooden teeth?

Well, all is copasetic on the ward after dinner, except the crier is still crying. This is not a place to test that technique for attention. Or maybe it is? I'll keep you posted. In here, things don't happen as I think they should.

The first thing I did when I found out that I wasn't going home today was I asked for some new books when I got upstairs to my ninth floor home. I was told that the education department had been here and they were making a "list" of books we might get. Making a list? Why not just send the books? Do they have to make a list? They should be back in a few days. How about that Spanish dictionary? It's starting to sound better already.

Chapter 18 – Next on the List!

I guess I shouldn't complain about the books. If the books were better, I wouldn't today be watching the guards fill out in triplicate the "incident report" with which they are now preoccupied.

Remember my broken-armed neighbor, who's not being invited to the reunion party? Well, apparently one of the guards was spit on, hit or hurt in some way. Everyone is quiet. The Jamaicans are sleeping or resting up for tonight, the mice are sleeping, and the guards are very busy with the forms. I am going to keep reading the beliefs of each religion in America. I could easily replace the Chaplain when I am finished.

Not much has been said about my phone calls. I am still waiting to speak with the outside world. Today I read the "Appellate Brief" on my case. Not to be redundant, but I find it so hard to believe that the Court hasn't read or reacted to it. It's not like a prison blue phone call form or anything that difficult. I have heard that my wife is having a very difficult time waiting for the wheels of justice to let me go home. Her suffering on this, I am told, has been intense. She has treated the lawyers pretty strongly because she believes the situation, the loss of the business, the fines, and the incarceration are all a direct result of poor legal representation. Sometimes, so do I. So, my sweet Jewish wife, has made me stop feeling sorry for myself, helping me forget where I am, eating as I am, living as I am and on more "lists" than I can possibly remember; she has taught me a little more about Christianity than I had ever thought or read in my religious training.

With tongue in check, knowing that I will for the rest of my life pay for only this one entry in the diary, I now know another reason why Christ didn't marry a Jewish woman. It could be.... (Only kidding Barbara, remember I am in solitary and not emotionally well, as well as malnourished) (I hope that covers it) ... because He didn't want to have anyone upstaging his crucifixion with her own pain and suffering. Although I try to convince my wife of the resurrection to follow, she's pretty focused on the past twenty-nine days that have temporarily ruined our lives.

Can you imagine if Ms. Andrews returns to the "hole'? How many reunion invitations should I send to the woman with three names, three possible identities and three possible paychecks? It is not important. No matter how many I send, she'll lose them or forget to show up! I hope the Warden comes. I hope the "'Illustrated man" has gotten his medicine by the date of the party.

The incident forms of the broken armed inmate have been completed. A CO has come to read him "his rights". The CO asked if he wanted it read to him. The inmate said, "Give it to me, I can read". The guard said he'd be returning in about thirty minutes. Now that can mean that he will be returning today or any time before next Friday based on time integrity in here. I'm on "pins and needles" to hear, if I can, what his punishment will be.

Additionally, I now see that Deliverance, the guard who looks like he could have been in the movie "Deliverance" is on duty tonight. Under his leadership anything is possible over the next few hours. I'll keep you updated. Hopefully, I will be released soon, but someone should expose the daily behaviors of many mediocre employees in uniform.

Two hours have passed, (not thirty minutes)! Now that makes sense to me. While I am thinking about time commitments, remember the counselor who was coming up today for me to fill out form number four? She didn't come. She didn't leave the form. She didn't even leave a message" - "And the beat goes on."

I'll find out what happened to the broken armed inmate to whom they are now "reading rights". I'll try to tell you within a real thirty minutes from when I find out. And find out I will. A place like this is a gossip mill. Would you expect anything different? Meaningless information is proportionately more valuable to the lowest degree of intelligence and maturity. Let me now go back to my book about the death of the woman whose Muslim husband killed her for disrespecting his wishes. "And the beat goes on".

Well, the education department showed up to tell me I have to fill out a new form to request a book and I'll get on another "list" for the book. I asked, "Why for the past four weeks wasn't I ever told about the "form" and the "list"? Tomorrow they will come with a "list" for me. Please may I be away from here before the weekend is over.

The unofficial gossip about the incident is that the inmate spit at a guard. The inmate claims that he was reacting because he was hit first. Nevertheless, the unofficial punishment prior to an internal hearing is loss of commissary for thirty days, solitary incarceration for thirty days and he is to be chained this weekend to his bed for three days (details on that are not firmed up as yet). If he wasn't crazy before being chained, I am sure being chained in one position will do wonders for his psyche. Apparently in today's world, spitting with or without HIV is a pretty serious jail offense. I don't know what additional jail time is added on. I only know that they have the power to do it.

Things are quiet now, but the creation of a new book "list" appearing now, and only after the numerous times I have spoken to them, (and already received some books) makes me crazy.

Tonight I asked again, "what do I do to trim my nails?" I was hoping that there would be a nail clipper I could use. The CO is checking if there is a "list" for this. When I leave here, the first person to say list may get a piece of my mind. I, of course, thanked him, still hoping that I would get out of here before another day is lost.

I am laughing so hard that I am crying. Just a few minutes ago, a CO came to tell me that I have come up to the top of a "list" and I am first to go tomorrow. Excitedly I asked, "Which list?" "The law library", he said. I swear to you, with all of my law visits and no desire to sit there, I am still giggling. This is a list you have never heard me speak about, request or even anticipate. I will go because when you are on the top of any "list" you go. Let's see if by tomorrow this is still true. Reality changes here quite quickly.

As a matter of fact, when I tried to get on the "nail clipper list", I wrote the following note: After almost thirty days, my nails have begun to resemble Mr. Howard Hughes. Could I please use a nail clipper or if this is not possible - what color nail polish do we have? I have made a "list" of my "lists" here in the cell. It's quite impressive, yet the first list I get to the top of in here, I never signed up for. Is there a coded message being given to me here?

Before I give up again waiting for the phone tonight, I wanted to take this opportunity to thank my Marine Corps drill instructors who in 1969 taught me how to tuck in a blanket on a bunk this size. My bunk probably is the only prison bunk that you can bounce a coin on. I tell you that because when I slip into this tightly made bunk, no rodent has a loose blanket or a dangling sheet to climb up and invade my sleep. I just thought I might give you a visual of my sleeping like a buried mummy. Sleep tight. I guess "tight" is my new way of sleeping.

As I slip out of my cocoon this Friday morning, I hear some disturbing dialogue even before the breakfast is served. A doctor is examining a new inmate next door. I think the inmate came in late last night. I hear, "Open your eyes. Today, I am going to recommend a rectal exam". I wait for the words, not sure if I'm asleep or having a nightmare, but the tight covers and my inability to move remind me, it is my reality. He now says these words to the inmate, "I will put you on the list and we'll get to you as soon as your name comes up". And to think, I wasn't pleased with my law library "list". There are potentially more lists that I am not on, and I don't even know about them. How do I get on "this rectal exam list" to ensure I am never called? With all of my daily strip searches maybe I have been exempted. So, instead of birds singing this morning and me slipping out of my cocoon to not disturb the covers, I hear about a new fear and a new "list".

In the movie, "Field of Dreams", after Kevin Costner's character finished building the baseball field, a ballplayer comes out of the cornfield and asks the question "Is this heaven?" It is a moving and quite cerebral moment in the film, as one debates "after life" or spirituality.

I preface that with a thought I had before breakfast this morning. Why am I not hungry when they serve the food and why am I not eating as much as I know I have in the past? I'm afraid to ask if this is paradise (pair of dice) for fear of another questioning session, but is this heaven?

In another movie, "Defending Your Life", the actors can eat whatever they want and not gain weight.  How great a visual is that?  However, in here, whether it be depression, weight loss, desire to cease existing under these circumstances, or just plain old fashioned bad food conditioning - they have succeeded in accomplishing what I couldn't do for almost sixty years; I have misplaced (dare I say lost) my appetite.  I am not seeing any massive weight loss and other than an occasional candy bar I eat at my legal visit, my caloric intake is minimal, yet I'm looking at breakfast as if I'm full before I begin.  Could it be boredom?  Could it be that I'm on the "list" for hunger and I don't know about it yet?  But as I force myself to consume the exact same breakfast as I have had for the past thirty days, I'm really ambivalent about eating it.  There's a business here the BOP has missed.  Package these meals exactly as they are served.  That means you may not even have to heat them up.  After thirty days, you'll be so disgusted, so miserable, so depressed; you'll lose weight on the BOP's thirty day diet.  Never will you crave food again.  Move over diet companies.  This obvious new income stream has been missed.  We have been trying to associate food with joy or pleasure.  The answer is that "no love" and "no human caring" can succeed in this diet business like none have before.  Everyone should want our diet program.  The demand will be overwhelming.  So there will have to be a "list".  When your name comes up, you will begin the diet.  That will ensure unfortunately that it may never begin.  Oh well, time to roll-up my sleeves (I don't have sleeves) use a little toilet paper as a napkin (we only have toilet paper) and begin my 90th BOP meal, with no desires or thoughts, hopes or dreams about meal number 91.  It will taste exactly like the other ones and I'll not eat much of it, but miraculously I really am not hungry so ... this must be heaven (or at least its alternative location).

Chapter 19 – My First Fashion Class

There are many other things going on here on an hourly basis that I have not mentioned because I didn't realize it may have been part of the "loathing food process". I've thought that BOP may mean "Better Off Passing" on this food. As I was cleaning and opening very carefully my milk container knowing it would be with me for days of drinking because my "milk container rotation" (MCR for those of us in the hole) takes about three days before it begins leaking. Sometimes we get some warm drinks and that really weakens the plastic/paper container. Before this religious experience (remember I told you I found Jesus in prison because 35% of the inmates seem to have that name) of eating less, I suggest while you wait to get on the BOP diet "list", that you pour your next glass of wine into one of these milk containers. Drinking from it is just not sexy, cool or satisfying. You may flash back to elementary school before you had ice in a glass. Ice, I remember that. Maybe that's the ingredient that causes overeating? Enough about my milk container or if I will ever have hot water again …this diet is also quite futuristic.        It may be what astronauts will use in space after we realize that 60 days on the Better Off Passing Diet may result in never wanting to eat again and still remaining nauseous for months. It's a subtle reconditioning process. Maybe that's what the "suits" have been doing. Maybe that's why there are no phone calls. Does the mice and rodent ambiance supplement the nausea? That's why there are no mouse traps. Could it be the orange and gray motif? Of course, its visage is that of unpleasant food groups. Are there appetite suppressants added to the food... as if the food was not suppressant enough on its own? Why then are the guards and staff so hefty? Maybe they are not eating the food! The toilet paper roll system may require a door knob electronic monitoring system. It's all beginning to make sense. Oh God, please don't say that I'm actually grasping the prison culture.

As early Greek students listened to the wisdom of those honored philosophers such as Socrates, Plato and Aristotle, we here at MCC SHU listen for the tidbits of wisdom from our COs as they carry on discussions with various inmates and you try to piece these bits together. Phrases like, "Then go kill yourself, see if I care"; "Who cares, she's probably with your best friend anyway", or "I'm your mother, I'm your father - get used to it". But, today there was a fashion discussion with which I have also avoided boring you. You see, this orange jumpsuit has various styles depending on the user's method of dressing.

You have to imagine this one piece of clothing that you change every three days and have no choice on what the next one will be, let alone the size. Some have pockets, some have buttons, and some have snaps. Some are cut up the sides. Some have been cut at the bottom (don't ask me how; I am in solitary, thank god!). Some have elastic on the waist. Some have had the elastic cut. Putting it on is a change in our human thought process. Initially, when handed one, you put your arms in first. No Way. You must lay it down, step into it, then pull it up and in most cases struggle to force it over your shoulders and then put your arms inside the arm holes (unless they have been altered). It appears there are numerous styles the inmates create. Some cuff up the bottoms like one is searching for sea shells at the beach. Some do not cuff and let at least 8" to 12" drag wherever they go. Some slice or rip the bottoms and tie it like a buccaneer. Sometimes they have cut the bottoms off short. But whatever fashion choice each inmate makes - that is what they will wear for at least 3 days. I hope this basic fashion overview of our orange jumpsuit gives you a more complete understanding of prison haute couture.

Now, let's add the guard discussion. Some inmates when in solitary, walk around naked in all their glory. Most either wear the jumpsuit or get by with only a tee shirt and underwear. The "look" that was under discussion was the look I have also adopted. You button a few of the buttons and do not pull the suit over your shoulders. You have pants on but have a hanging ½ suit flapping behind you like you are a center for a football team. This way when you have to get dressed you can pull it up, button and go. Bathroom use requires removal of the suit anyway. I am told that gangs have specific rules on how the jumpsuit should be worn.

This "gang look", I might add, causes the lower pant to slip down resulting in that "ghetto" clothing look of underwear exposed that surely, you have observed on our society's youth. The guards wanted to understand the various "looks" and were discussing them with the old timers.

Apparently, even in a classless society, man is still driven to create fashion differences.

I don't think much about illness because I have multiple theories on how not to get sick here, to do this time, and return psychologically unmarred. Of course, I may never eat with metal utensils, use glasses to drink or ask for seconds again. I wash my hands about 10 times a day especially when the water is hot. I figure it has to help "germ wise". Even if it doesn't, I've become like Dustin Hoffman in Rainman. I exercise regularly, read, play a scrabble type game I made, and play bridge with my hand made cards. (I could now buy cards, but I don't want to believe this wrongful incarceration will go on beyond how long my little handmade cards will last.) I am also very busy cleaning regularly with soap and a wash cloth. I do have an extra pair of socks and underwear which I wash by hand every night. This is a secret way of washing my hands again, but it is really done to maintain my personal step and dignity. In this place, clean underwear or socks even if you only wear half a jumpsuit drooping down is dignity.

There are a few personal items available through the commissary. So to quote my former neighbor, "It is what it is, brother", and then you take your right arm and tap your chest with it. It seems to work with all of the other faces in here, when our eyes meet, except for the broken armed inmate who was so angry yesterday.

I'm not sure if I am going to require jumpsuits for my reunion party. I may grow accustomed to this baggy and droopy feel as my waistline seems to have (due to the jumpsuit buttons) moved down about 12 to 20 inches between the knee and the center of my thigh. I try to imagine my civilian suits and Florida golf clothes being altered to maintain the droopy/ghetto "look". I may pass on it.

As I live in SHU, I am escorted about the prison as a very vicious inmate. The general population, (brown jumpsuits) are normally afraid of the (orange jumpsuit) guys. In my case, I'm more afraid of everyone else, but I can't blink as I walk into elevators. I am forced to face a corner. I hope when I go back to business I remember to face the elevator door. Yesterday, while I was waiting in our legal room to be taken back upstairs after my attorney left, a brown suited inmate and some other lawyers were trying to avoid looking at me. They don't make eye contact, if they do, they don't smile and quickly look away. They very often sneak looks because you look like Hannibal Lector and they are interested or fascinated at how "bad" you must be. So yesterday this brown suited inmate defied the rules, smiled, made eye contact and said, "Mon, you look like Hannibal Lector, mon". Instead of the proper response, I simply licked my lips and stared. He moved away immediately. I must for the sake of my neighboring psychopaths and murderers keep up the image of the lost souls in orange (LSO for those of us in the hole).

Being "bad" in this society is "good". Being "good" is "bad". This may have some subliminal message about the food, but this is only a working theory. By the way, my law library visit has not happened even though I was first on the "list" in case you are wondering.

This anagram usage of letters may be the initial breaking of the code to understand the real prison messages given. The inmates like to use anagrams and insider codes. So the possibilities are endless. I'm going to wash my hands now. I may be called to the law library or to fill out a book list. In here, you always have to be ready because things happen second by second without warning.

Chapter 20 – Condiment Class

Today, as I face possibly another weekend in prison and a heartbroken family, I decided to put down my flippant and caustic defense mechanism pen and evaluate as best I can, my true feelings and the depth of depression and pain I am really experiencing. In other words what does a confident narcissist have to have happen before his emotional walls collapse and he acquiesces to his captors? Well, I mused over that this morning and then a simple action gave me the answer. As I was dressing (you know that means lifting up my downward facing cape), I went to my one pair of blue $2 sneakers. Before I put them on I found myself cleaning them with soap and a wash cloth. Believe me; I clean everything with only a wash cloth. I realized how many pairs of shoes I own at home and the pride I have always taken in personal grooming. I proudly cleaned my sneakers, put them on, opened a book, washed my hands and prepared for my legal visit. So I guess I'm still holding on to that "step" and my righteousness despite the best shot attempts of society's landfill - its' prison system. By cleaning my sneakers, I realized that I am still holding on to my dignity.

I have written with a pen refill more than ever before in my life. You don't think this is hard work? My middle finger is red and stiff from pre-arthritic pain. I only mention it because I have snuck in, once I adjusted to this system, over fifteen pen refills which are forbidden. Not once did a guard find it and say, "don't worry about it". No, they strip search me daily and I simply have decided that as long as the pen is not inserted into the rectum they don't seem interested. I'm far from a danger and far from someone who would bring in an object of danger. But these pens obviously in the wrong hands are able to ruin a guard's day. I don't think anyone can break out of prison holding a wiggly pen refill, but they are forbidden. I am searched daily. I would love to tell them how easy refills are to get in. But because of "orange loyalty" (OL for those of us in the hole), I won't tell. I continually make up these asinine anagrams because that is how these lost souls talk. They so desperately desire acceptance and being special. I have such pain realizing how easy it would be to fill those needs with positive ingredients instead of the various tragedies I have tongue-in-cheek been discussing with you. All these inmates need are one caring CO, one caring counselor or one professional who went out of their way to demonstrate reliability and tenderness. Sure many prisoners are damaged, but are they unable to be repaired? That, this mild observer, refuses to accept.

There is one other food observation that mystifies me, but remember, I am not hungry. Every meal they drop in our cell has condiments or special spices to utilize with the meal. Or at least one would think so.

With my cereal I often get mayonnaise or salt and pepper. A hamburger comes with jelly. A hot dog is joined by mayonnaise. Yet a few days later mustard did come with the oatmeal over the weekend. Jelly came without bread. But bread came with salad dressing. I'm not complaining, I am only observing the "attention to detail" that collapses when people in charge have lost their way. Sure inmates save these mustards because they know they must be on a "list" for a hotdog or a hamburger soon. With the morning meal, which does have sugar most of the time, comes ketchup. I just hope that when my former counselor, Ms. Andrews gets promoted to, "condiment understanding now and tomorrow" (you do the anagram) then the quality control within here will improve. I thought of this because yesterday with pasta and meat sauce I got two packets of jelly. I have been waiting for the bread which I hope will follow. As an experiment, since I am in total food intake shutdown (TFIS), I may only eat the condiments given to me. The wisdom and secret food policies of these incompetents may still be eluding me.

This is a very, very good sign. Lunch has come and I have not had a legal visit. Could this mean they are working on rescuing me before the weekend? My mind is racing a hundred miles a second. I'm not even going to mention the new vanilla pudding over my salad in the tray topped with a tomato. I would never complain if this lateness means the BOP and I are going our separate ways. Could I be departing? Just before I was to go to the law library? No other "list" has happened. Could it be I am finally leaving? Could it be?

You realize if that happens this will be the end of the diary. If my diary is well received, we'll push for reforms for these forgotten souls. But before I turn into Mother Theresa, let's see if I really can ignore the pudding and salad with thousand island dressing on the side. Good news, I did get some bread to make that jelly sandwich. I am having a problem with my one and only milk carton. It's leaking and another one won't be available until tomorrow. Let's hope there is no tomorrow in here for me. I wait ...... I wait .... ! It is just my luck that an entirely new event occurred while I am waiting to find out my departure fate. Six fully Darth Vader like guards just carried another inmate in and placed him in full restraints. There is a movie camera (for legal reasons) and a debriefing was just given on tape. He has been administered some sort of tranquilizer and it looks like the neighborhood just got one terribly unpopular neighbor. I tried to do my "hello" salute, but no one paid attention.

This was a serious entrance. This was my first time seeing the riot controlled guards fully masked and carrying the inmate. When and if I leave here, I'll still try to report on this unusual sighting.

It will be just my luck that I'll leave today just when the neighborhood mood is in yet another state of intense change. I have no idea what the inmate did, but I'm hoping the prison or guard gossip mill is alive and well.

Now I'm thinking that I am not going home because they probably detained all visitors. I don't know why I get my hopes up so. I want to go home (clean sneakers or not). I still wait.

That legal debriefing is still going on. The mood is quite intense. You can feel it in the air. Even I know this is not the time to ask about my nail clippers. I'm on the nail clipper "list" and that should be good enough.

Imagine if I do go home today and the reason my lawyers are late is because they're getting the release forms done. Imagine if I leave tomorrow or at the latest next Monday. All of my lists will happen after I leave, I just know it.

What do I take with me? My two handmade games should come with me to show my family. Some legal papers, one toilet paper center also should come. I will give everything else to those left here. You know I don't have much, but whatever I do have should stay here.

Wait a minute! New developments. They have actually put an armed guard outside the cell of the guy they just handcuffed and totally shackled to his cell. What would cause this? Could it be something worth reporting on? Is it only a suicide watch?

The guards are actually sweating and talking about the stress of this job. Who is this guy? What did he do? Is he ahead of me on any "list"? If the guy wanted to use the law library ahead of me, I would have let him. Could it have been book related? I just spoke to a guard and he was visibly upset. Maybe this guy beat-up my attorney.

My attorney has never been this late. I'm sure something very unusual has happened.

Someone has definitely gotten hurt.

What comes first the chicken or the egg? I have over the past 30 days shared my frustrations and my observations with you. Does the BOP protect society from these outbursts or does our present system of incarceration, governmental rules and "lists" turn inmate warm water into hot. I only suggest that cold water or new ideas may be an alternative.

That poor guard is also a victim. There are too many victims in this system as it is being exposed to me and presented to you.

The inability for some of these adult guards and "suits" to multitask has now even caused me over one hour of waiting for one of them to take me for my legal visit. They are all involved in this one incident. I yell "legal visit!" and they say "one minute". I can't say anything because I don't know when I am leaving. The frustration of waiting is excruciating. Not one of them really wants to work so this excuse becomes like a "count". All movement stops.

Chapter 21 – Finally, I'm Authorized

All is quiet tonight; it's like a still ocean after the storm. I'm not going home. I got a book from one of the COs titled "Into The Wild". I know it's not about my life here. No "lists" came through for me today. I have a shower planned and yet another weekend is wasted as I sit as a perfect example of a broken judicial system attempting to flex its muscles, but not its brain. In time, this abuse of power or judicial incompetence will be ruled on by higher courts. Until then, rest easy because the BOP is taking care of the inmates sent here by Judges like mine, who inconsistently genuflect to their governmental patrons, rather than the Constitution.

I'm told by a new counselor, that she put the blue phone form in and she hopes they have processed it. I asked, "Since a prisoner can't go to the processing room, why can't you finish the job started? It has been 30 days and 3 phone forms". The answer was, "You'll just have to try the phone. If it doesn't work, we can try again on Monday." Is it possible I am not the only one who finds this inefficiency inexcusable? Over the past 2 days I have seen four inmates "lose it". Is it only the inmates? I wasn't ready to "lose it" 30 days ago. Some of these inmates have been sentenced here for years and years and years. Some are sentenced for life.

I have been told I am on today's shower "list". Since I didn't shower last Wednesday because of my legal visit, I have to shower in the sink tonight because you and I know they will probably not remember the shower. On top of it all, one of the Deliverance brothers is angry at me because I filled out a phone request and wrote that during his night shifts, the phone has not physically ever gotten to me. It was true, but that did not prevent him from chastising me because now "it is in writing". He called me a "fuck" and I, of course, allowed him to do such. Again I am forced to quote a Seinfeld episode "Serenity Now, Serenity Now."

If I self-shower, shampoo and wash my clothes in the 12" sink tonight, it will be yet another example of a system that has no ability to effectively or consistently perform.

Since the officer is angry, I can probably forget about the phone, as well. Exactly what moral lessons does this criminal justice system teach the imprisoned? Hopefully I will be able to have some prison changes made after governmental investigations and the media does their job exposing this prison system.

Despite no showers, phones, books, mouse traps, etc., I still look forward to my law library visit. By the way, nothing happened - absolutely no further dialogue after the CO told me I was "first" on the law library. If so many mistakes weren't hurting everyone involved, it wouldn't be as criminally neglectful, and I would not be revealing them.

Deliverance electronically "scanned" me today when I returned from my legal visit. Were my pens going to be finally caught? The scanner beeped but he continued on. He then asked about the yellow paper I had in my front pocket. "Is that authorized?" he asked. "Of course, I said without blinking, I am an author". He said, "OK". I guess that's what makes paper authorized. Serenity Now!

With all of the waiting time available for showers, I hear many of the inmates actually screaming for them. When, if at all, will the guards stop laughing and "partying" while the reason they are here "screams" for the basic promises made in the BOP manuals? I can "field shower" in my 12" sink. I can wash my clothes and not wear what is still wet tomorrow. But will the Warden wear wet clothes tomorrow? Where is his responsibility? If you tell the truth, you are ignored and chastised. I now realize the intellectual and moral limitations of the government I am fighting against in Court. I remain encouraged.

My new counselor stays late into the evening to flirt and talk to the COs. Instead of going to processing or helping those inmates who she told tonight that she had no pencils or writing paper, forms for phones or forms for requests… she hangs out in the Day Room. She follows in the pattern of excellence initiated by her predecessor - probably the real reason I and others still have no phone access. Exactly what is she required to do?

I will continue this weekend with my "authorized" paper to report to you, and I hope you never will have to see or feel first hand this debauchery of wasted tax dollars.

## Chapter 22 – Move Over Mummy – The Family's Here!

Both Deliverance officers are not speaking to me. That's the silent treatment at night we get when they are in charge. Their eyes tell me how much they hate what they do, as well as, the inmates with whom they work. There will be nothing, no shower and no phone call. All I can hear is the constant laughter of Ms. Black, the new counselor, who shouldn't be here during the evening hours (hopefully not logging overtime).

A new guard came by three times to tell me he's going to get me that shower. Want to bet?

If I could just get a change of clothes, I would forget the shower. Ms. Black has now actually started singing in this professionally run operation of the BOP and its' evening staff. This graveyard shift attracts individuals like these characters. I have to remain non-confrontational. But hopefully there will be a time in the future when I must, for the sake of these young and troubled men, publicly expose this because a more mature team should be in charge. It's moments like this that I concern myself again with an emergency evacuation. Think about how that feels? They won't look or speak with you, so how about opening the steel door in a fire? I guess I shouldn't become too maudlin; I'll probably not make it out of my covers; they are so tightly tucked in and squared.

I should start cleaning my clothes because the party seems to be going on down in the Day Room and no one has walked or come to complete their promises in the past hour.

J.D. Salinger in "Catcher in the Rye" had Holden Caulfield wondering, before his nervous breakdown, where fish went when the water froze. As I ponder equally cerebral thoughts, I wish to know what prisoners do to cut their nails. After thirty days, I don't have a clear answer where and when they use these instruments. I realize the problems here are many, and to wit; there are plenty of doors being pounded on by inmates tonight. I guess the only way to get a shower is to begin washing myself and my clothes in the sink. That should probably do it. The surveillance cameras, I am told, are in every cell. If there are cameras, they probably don't work anyway. It is a comforting thought, when I use the toilet.

The last time I heard of the Uniform Code of Military Justice (UCMJ) was in 1969. I remember finding out that the UCMJ replaced the Constitution and these military rules and laws actually remove personal American born freedoms. The punishments are draconian and the terms are severe. Today, I found out that, as an inmate (even though I have not committed a crime), I am now governed by the UCMJ. That, my friend, is frightening. A guard could accuse me of anything and I could be sentenced to years of additional jail time. Prisons are in reality, and by their very nature, a necessary dictatorship isolated within our democracy. If the initial judicial sentencing doesn't put someone away long enough to keep the BOP financial machine fueled with new customers, then the dictatorship's internal disciplinary rules add extra time to that cash flow. Thus, they can hire more family, friends and political party members to continue this dual welfare and patronage system called the Bureau of Prisons.

Well, I learned how to beat this system tonight. I started washing myself and even though it is past 10 PM they came to tell me I was next on the shower list. I went, but I lost my socks. They have no socks. Maybe I'll get some tomorrow. I am on the "sock list" again now. I couldn't shave because it was so late (like it was my fault, I've been sitting here all day). So the next time I can shave will be Monday. My beard will be pretty long by then; at least the Illustrated Man won't be around to yell at me. It was uncomfortable showering and undressing in front of that young female counselor, but I'm sure under UCMJ, I should keep my comments to myself. One of the guards holds a grudge a little longer than the others. Do you know how you can tell? You know when they put the handcuffs on you. If they only click them gently, it doesn't hurt. If they hold a grudge, they apply the handcuffs a lot tighter. It's only prison and "it is the way it is".

It's close to 11:00PM from what I can gather and although my poor family believes I have forsaken them and chosen not to call, I once again fall asleep feeling like I failed. What makes a Friday failure so horrific is that on Saturdays and Sundays no phone calls are allowed. So officially the BOP has not permitted me after 30 days, without having been convicted of a crime, any phone contact with my Wife and family. It's deplorable and now it's documented. Their policy is quite clear and their counselors and computer staff have prevented this basic human expectation. What is my recourse? When will Americans realize that we empower ignorance and incompetence by our silence? I am an example of someone who refuses to accept stock trading ineptitude. Where then do they put me, but in the motherland of incompetence?

Showers and clean clothes mean a great deal in our lives. When you only possess a plastic spoon/fork and toilet paper, a shower followed by clean clothes creates a feeling beyond the written word. Not having socks doesn't sound that disconcerting until one hears the nocturnal noises of the prison walls. My socks were another line of defense in case my squared corner mummy bed procedure (SCMBP) ever had a malfunction. The concrete floor remains cold and damp.

I have become quite the surviving eccentric as I objectively analyze my current actions. As I wake up and carefully crawl out of my tight square cornered bed to greet breakfast, I now find myself repeating the following activities: Two milks delivered today means a carefree weekend of drinking water; now if only I can get those containers to open without a rip. As I plan my container opening attack, I re-tighten the bunk. It goes without saying, I then wash my hands. On those mornings when the water is hot, I then rewash my 2 inch toothbrush and spoon/fork to disinfect them. I then begin cleaning the floor with my cleaning washcloth (remember no socks). That sock issue will be with us this weekend. I now have to dispose of my empty wiggly pen refill. I can't throw it out on my food tray for fear it may be a violation of the UCMJ. Failure to follow instructions or use of a wiggly pen may be punishable by making me become an assistant counselor or even worse, in charge of organizing the institution's "lists". With my beard now six days old, I realize it's no longer a "'cool" look for me because it is white (Moses style). Without a comb or brush, my dry scalp and hair, look like I've reached mad man status. I have become a veteran of this solitary thing and knowing that today my attorney will not be visiting, I must pace myself. That poor lawyer arrived yesterday at 11:00AM and had to wait for me to come downstairs until 3:45PM. What normal person would still be there when you came down almost five hours later? So much for easy access to your defense.

The milk carton opening operation, with my long nails, has been a success! Maybe that's why they don't issue nail clippers! Prison wisdom comes with practical experience. During the night, I gather, we were a busy Motel Six. Many new inmates arrived to spend the weekend and beyond. The cell across from me has that continual broken "water issue". The inmates feel the "'weekend spirit" because some of the guests seem to be either old friends or family members. This is one way to beat the telephone and visiting "'list" issues. In an attempt to improve occupancy issues the BOP may, once again, have developed the answer. It is so much easier to get into prison through the Federal Guidelines for sentencing than it is to get a phone call or visiting form. Innocent future criminals on the outside can come in faster and easier than inmates can call out. Once again, I may have overlooked the creative marketing ideas of the BOP. They probably won't need that gift shop selling orange jump suits and linens if they continue at their present rate of growth, they'll be able to eliminate the phone and visiting programs altogether. If they had their way, we'd all be inside the prison so we could all communicate directly. My morning exercises are soon to begin, followed by reading a few pages from multiple books, none of which I would choose to read, then some yelling for socks, wash my hands a few times, and before you know it, it will be 7:30 AM.

I have been placed in jail because after mugging my company and myself, the Judge was angry that I didn't have the resources to pay his ridiculous and unfounded fine. Let's forget about all that for a minute. How do I pay basic bills while I am in here? How do I find a job while I am in here? What does my family do to survive? What would you do? My wife cries due to worries, and I am not there now for us to "start over" even though we have appealed his ill-founded rulings. By the way, if a higher Court (what could be lower?) rules that we should have had a jury trial (6th Amendment of our Constitution) every fine, every action, every ruling goes away! So, let's sum up. When I win, why was I here? When I win, where is my company? When I win, who pays the damages? The Court of Claims and the Securities and Exchange Commission (SEC) will pay. These are some of the "'pangs of guilt" I feel while I sit, without having committed a crime, in an unconstitutional debtor's prison. When all is corrected that Judge may say, "Oops" but does he still remain appointed for life? You go figure. From my observations, I would let him get a job here with the BOP - he would fit right in.

I remain proud that I continued to operate my company and planned for exciting acquisitions, strategic partnerships and continued loyal shareholder growth and involvement after the Judge refused us a trial. I still remember planning our Appeal when I took out a full page ad in the New York Times telling our side of the story.

The SEC lied. They claim that I have hidden money with which to pay their summarily imposed fine. The Judge claims he didn't "like" the thousands of pages of financial evidence given him, to prove that I couldn't pay - and he simply refused to hear mine or any expert accounting testimony. He, in my opinion, was told to silence the one voice that clearly showed what naked short selling was doing to our economy because someone in the SEC didn't want naked short selling known to the American public. What were they up to? Were they just trying to hide the fact that they were not protecting the American investor, as is their charge … or is there a much larger truth being buried here?

Unless the Appellate or U.S. Court of Claims reverses the destruction of my company and the investments of my shareholders which were done without any hearing or trial, I must await the collective justice and indignation of my fellow Americans.

I have submitted a request to the guards on duty today. I have modified my needs to only three requested items which would complete my simple life. One; is a phone call. Two, would be a pair of socks and a towel. Three, is a book. I didn't ask for nail clippers because I've been thinking about sending flyers to the neighboring cells; so I could open inmates' milk cartons flawlessly with my claws. I have to work while I am in here. After all, I have been working since I was 14 years of age. Only because I questioned governmental malfeasance have I been banned from working in America! That company, my company, was over twenty-four million dollars in debt when I took it over and from that, I created five new

American industries growing at over 200% a quarter. So I guess this Judge's knowledge on the economy and American work habits are like the BOP's knowledge of effective prison operations.

I have received a major job offer, which I am considering. I knew it would only take a little time before BOP employees would see my worth. I have been asked if I want to be the orderly who sweeps, mops and does the laundry for the unit. The "perks" are no handcuffs when they let me out and I could get closer to central command (the Day Room) and gather more prison stories and characters yet to be discovered. The drawbacks are that I may be so good making their jobs easier or obsolete that they could try to keep me here longer, and I might lose my writing and hand washing time. Well, it won't be officially offered until Monday and maybe I'll know if I am leaving or staying by then. There have been over six attorney requests to have a phone conference with my Judge. This wizard decided the issues of my case were too complicated for a jury to understand. Believe me, that is why he also decided there were no issues, motives or facts for us to present. Remember, we were the original plaintiff and we are out of business, and now I'm out of toilet paper and socks.

My new job offer is on my mind. Does this writer want at 60 years of age to be ordered around like a plantation slave by grade school or high school minds whose idea of efficiency is making a new list and destroying the old list? Yet, this creative opportunity entices me.

If you'd like to see the June 28th, 2007 Full Page New York Times National ad ... turn the page – it's reprinted here for your information.

A full page New York Times National ad ... and not one single elected official even called Universal Express to inquire.

# The New York Times – June 28<sup>th</sup>, 2007

The hundreds of employees and tens of thousands of shareholders of our fine company have requested our CEO, Mr. Richard Altomare write an equal response to the undeveloped articles recently published in your newspaper and to help focus the public on our National naked short selling scandal.

Our Chairman is a creative leader, and a proud former Marine, and we invite all to visit www.USXP.com to read further on this company and his recent press release response to these SEC attempts of questioning the character of our company.

**Now his formal statement:**

After the Company received Florida jury verdicts in excess of $700,000,000 against "naked shorters", an embarrassed and conflicted SEC commenced a pattern of harassment against our Company, as it has against many other "whistleblowers". The Company then sued the SEC on these issues and the SEC retaliated shortly thereafter with a New York case to silence the Company, not to protect our shareholders. Universal Express will vigorously defend all aspects of the SEC's nine year abuse of power attack on our Company.

**Ours is a landmark naked short selling case!**

The Company and its officers specifically have absolute and complete immunity from the allegations of the SEC on these discussed matters under the United States Bankruptcy Code which supersedes the SEC's authority. The Company is entitled under its reorganization charter and the Bankruptcy Code to issue additional shares to match the recapitalization of the Company on a daily basis caused by the issuance by market makers, broker-dealers and hedge funds of "naked shorted", counterfeit and unregistered shares, not issued by the Company and for which the Company has received no consideration.

The Company filed a timely notice of appeal of the expected lower Court's decision on May 31<sup>st</sup>, 2007.
The Company has moved for a stay of all proceedings pending such appeal and a jury trial.

Our Company has now requested a jury trial on all matters, including the "naked shorting" scandal, which has put over 6,000 small public companies out of business over the last 15 years and which the SEC has ignored and condoned.

Universal Express and its 9 vibrant subsidiaries refused to be victims of "Naked Shorting" and will vigorously resist any unwarranted and criminal control over this company by those at the SEC seeking to silence the Company on the "Naked Shorting" scandal and prevent a trial that the American people deserve.

The "Naked Shorting" scandal, long ignored by the SEC is at the forefront of our Company's campaign against this massive damage to thousands of public companies, their stockholders, investors, and employees. **No one at Universal Express expected this landmark issue to be a one decision ruling and welcome, if not embrace, the exposure necessary to bring an end to the SEC's flagrant and illegal acceptance of a practice that must be halted to ensure confidence in our trading system.** Our Company's good name will not be damaged by an agency that has acted as if it is above the Constitution of The United States and our elected officials.

To read the full content of this full page ad, go to www.richardaltomare.com.

Chapter 23 – "Celling" Out

What happens if the "brain-dead" disease is contagious? What if I start viewing the inmates as a bother? What happens if prison "lists" begin to make sense? What if they invite me to one of their parties or meetings? What if they like some of my jokes? Where will you and I be if I become their slave? We've grown so close. What if I can't take you with me? What if my privileges cause me to take too much toilet paper? I'm sure there will be a nail clipper in this for me as well. Can I be bought for those perks?

Extra food is all about the Day Room. Can you imagine? Will they take me on their nocturnal rat hunts? Will I have extra socks? Will I use their phone? My head is spinning with the possibilities. I'll know the gossip. I'll be one of the guys. I won't be one of the inmates. Hey, wait a minute! Didn't the Nazis do that? Didn't they take some prisoners to be in charge of the others? Didn't those prisoners have perks? What a model of efficiency the BOP system has copied. The "count" is also a German prison camp procedure. On paper, the count is designed to make sure one cuts down on escape time. In reality, it is similar to multiple prayers throughout the day of a religious fanatic. Like God really cares if you say the same prayers multiple times daily. The count, as stated before, is either a test for the guards to see if they can count to one thousand or it is another meaningless activity to pretend efficiency. Remember my shower count experience? - Exactly how detailed is the count? It reeks of the phoniness of lists. Well, enough rambling about selling out to the establishment or keeping my VW and surfboard. Decisions, decisions. I remain ambivalent, and who knows, like the law library "list"; it may never actually happen. I'll discuss this prison job opportunity with my attorney on Sunday. It's almost 10:00AM and the Saturday of my life now requires some bridge solitaire, scrabble solitaire, reading about Jefferson's possible affair with a slave and a dysfunctional young man who ran away from his family and killed himself (another topnotch BOP motivational novel).

Saturday's lunch was exactly the same weekend lunch and often dinner meal every weekend. Today I simply couldn't do it. I examined and studied the "thing" on top of the potato. I am not kidding; I do not for the life of me know what it is. It initially looked like a mushroom. When I cut it open it resembled a hollow biscuit which smelled like a seasoned meat. It sort of reminded me of two elderly refined women who were examining defecation on the street. "It smells like it, it feels like it, it even tastes like it. I am certainly glad we didn't step in it." I didn't taste it! I decided, today, to eat the two pieces of bread, ignore the egg since my history in here has indicated a feeling of malaise after I eat the eggs. They seem to be moving out some extra milk today. They gave a THIRD container to me. I am considering making it into a "planter" with some of the seeds from one of the oranges I may get in the next few days. Dirt will not be a problem. A few more weeks' of this and I'll be washing my hands, talking to myself, humming while I watch my planted orange tree growing in my milk carton. A few more months, and I could have a plantation here in my room and possibly if I take the "head slave" job; I could make some "contacts" and sell my oranges to the BOP. Self-sufficiency. It is only a matter of time and ideas. Maybe I can pay that fine.

Although at times I may be a bit flippantly caustic, I want to thank the BOP for teaching me that I really can subsist on minimal daily calories. Looking at their food, my appetite is gone. I am constantly repulsed by that which is served. Am I the only one? If I become part of management, I can study the garbage and see if anyone really eats this food.

In fairness, the positive stories should be told along with what some may say is complaining. I'm really not complaining. I am truly reporting, and I will rave about something done right. I had one of my requests delivered. Well, it was partially one of my requests. No, not the phone. No, not the socks, as I re-clean the floor in my room. No, not a book yet. I got a washcloth! I made it to the top of the washcloth "list"! I already have four washcloths that I now use to clean my cell. I embrace my new orange washcloth. It will have a very special place hanging on my bunk bed away from those washcloths responsible for finding the dirt necessary to fill my planters.

To spruce up this room, I can draw pictures on my cartons with my pen and pencil to add character to my little piece of the universe. I do have one snickers bar that I purchased from the commissary because I thought I was going home last week. It took all of my self-discipline not to make a snickers sandwich. I really thought about it. But if dinner is the same as lunch, I decided I would have that to look forward to.

Keeping busy and mentally active helps the time go by at a rapid pace. It is almost 11:00AM. I am now going to read about the history of Christian Science. Oh, please make it stop!

It's a good thing you are here, because like Tom Hanks, I have been considering making that "Wilson" not out of a volleyball, but either my milk carton or a toilet paper center. And to think the BOP is accused of not effectively rehabilitating those that commit crimes against society. We have those inmates creating their own world and blocking out ours. Yes, that may do wonders for the "repeat customer needs" of the BOP, but what about our society needs and these young men's futures?

Chapter 24 – Close to the Edge

Remember weeks ago I told you about that carefully selected powdered fruit punch which when mixed with water resembles blood?  I saved two of the packets and with my extra washcloth and milk container; I have decided that next week just before the psychiatrist comes by to smear it on my white beard and face.  I will say nothing.  Let's see if anyone notices. This will be my final exam to see if the psychiatrist actually stops at a window.  Just a thought, as I go back to dissecting the various religions in America in 1962.  By the way, as a relevant historical comment in 1962 this country did not include Islam or Muslim in the Religions of the World book.  Yet we wonder, with the worldwide population of that religion, why 40 years later we have these problems?  One of the brighter inmates said that the guy who was carried in yesterday by the Darth Vader Uniforms might have been Bill Clinton when Hillary said she wouldn't take Obama's VP job.  It might only be rumor, but I share it as this diary has gone to the length of a small book.  I am so sorry.  When I began it, I didn't know the oil reserves beneath the surface of this place were so plentiful.

I don't want any of you to begin worrying that my pre-stated eccentricities might get worse in this solitary world.  Keep in mind there are only three of us solitaries here.  Two are shackled and then there's me.  No one but me is here for 30 days or more.  None are as hardened a criminal as I, I suppose.  Being alone increases loneliness but you can go to the bathroom without a blanket over your head.  The reason I mention my aloneness and eccentricities are they allow one to experiment with washcloths replacing his socks. Don't laugh! I may be on to something. We have washcloths - we don't have socks.  The reverse would be ok for you, right?  If we had extra socks I'd be cleaning with little puppet like mittens ....hey, maybe that's why there's a shortage of socks - the inmates are having puppet shows in their cells.  If you take the washcloths and lay them in the bottom of these expandable sneakers and then gently put your feet in, when you pull up the excess you have "socks substitutes" (SS). The only initial drawback with this prototype is you can't really walk without it getting lumpy.  But in solitary we don't walk much.  This may be some advanced experimental sock program I have been selected to work on for the BOP. The cameras may be studying me right now.

Tomorrow if I showed up holding my orange seed container and washcloths for socks, I'm sure my attorney would have serious reservations about giving me more pens and paper. I'm saving that red dye for the Mad Hatter psychologist or God forbid next Thursday's (I can't still be here) Warden walk through. The attention to detail here would force me to study their reactions. Because of the UCMJ punishment criteria, I will always make sure they don't put me on any "lists" to see if "these people" can help "me" better understand the "real world" and "reality".

Dinner should be coming in about four hours, so let me go wash my hands, practice my secret "hello" in case someone moves across the hall. The day is young. My books are real page turners and I remain confident that there will be something more important on the horizon than the ramblings of one victim of judicial power abuse.

Let's touch on reality just for an instant. It is important for me in prison to remain in touch with reality even if the BOP has tried to alter or remove it. Remember the same CO who came by this morning, to whom I gave the three requests? Well, he just came by and said, "I am glad I was able to get you everything you asked for." I almost put down my planter. Did I get socks? "No, he said, we are out of socks." (I didn't dare bring up my washcloth substitute program). Did I get a book? "No, Monday when the education department comes in. "Did I get the phone? "You're on the list". I found myself thanking him and then I needed to get back to our reality. It was nice for him to visit. It was nice for him to remember I had given him a three issue list. Unfortunately, we have a disconnect (dare I say that phone word) with "I got you everything you asked for." Could someone who looks like me, have gotten the socks, be speaking on the phone and reading that new mystery book? That must be it! Because the BOP would never train and fine tune an adult whose concept of task completion ends with the receiving of the request. That's what the counselors and the education department have done. Mice live and multiply because of this philosophy. I'm returning to my projects of time denial and projects galore until bedtime (PGUB). There may be an anagram matching column A and column B exam at the end of this diatribe. Quickly, which one was (CUNT)? Oh, you remembered.

Time is tough to fill up in the hole. Consider my problem of no socks. Let's for a moment believe putting your feet in these "living" moldy sneakers due to previous unclean shower stories is your problem. Your feet are cold on this concrete floor when you are forced to go barefoot. What do you do? Plan one could be just using the sneakers and I might have done that with social graces still intact in the first week of solitary. I'm in my fourth week here! Try this advanced "hole" solution, upon which I am still marveling at the thought process but not the final appearance. Let's start with the washcloths (we have those). Let's put them on the bottom of the feet and wrap them on the sides. What do we have that could hold them to feet generating warmth and not causing undo germ phobias from the sneakers? Well, remember the multipurpose use of my issued toilet paper? I'll admit with or without me holding orange tree planters that it looks a bit unusual, but my feet are warm. Who would know in here? And, it could serve as that additional layer of defense tonight as I attempt to prevent sheets and covers from touching where the mice and rats might be crawling.

Yeah, I am really "doing fine" in this rehabilitation center and contempt lesson instruction center (CLIC). As long as I have my COs and counselors to return me to reality when this unconscionable ordeal is over, why should I worry? I used to be a contender. Where's the boxing ring because I am still ready to go in?

Deliverance brought the meals tonight. One of the new inmates asked the same questions you and I have beaten to death. The answer for visits, phones, books, etc. was "you have to see your counselor". "Who would be my counselor?", the inmate asked. I watched from the door hanging on this answer. "Ms. Andrews, A-N-D-R-E-W-S, write it down", said the guard. I wanted to remind him that last night until after 11:00PM the new counselor partied with him. I dared not upstage an idiot. Ms. Andrews left weeks ago! She's not coming back for months based on her dramatic departure, but the "beat goes on" and this inmate will begin his trek Monday looking for someone who doesn't come here anymore! The guard has to know that! He's in the command post! This is like Captain Kirk not knowing where the Earth is located.

Good news, bad news with dinner. There was an orange but not one pit. The plantation project is on hold. Dirt however has been rolling in. Good news, dinner wasn't the egg and oatmeal and mystery meat. Bad news it was cold pasta with indigestible (not inedible) sauce. I know this from previous eating efforts. So the final tally today was bread plus a slice of cheese, equals today's food. Oh, also don't forget my Snickers bar. Ah, the day is only six hours from an end, and then maybe I am almost out of here.

I am sure the "authorized" question about my paper means that when this diary is published others will probably not be permitted to sneak their observations out through legal visits. It never could have been mailed out. It would have been censured. I'm on the phone list again tonight. Jimmy the Greek would probably place the odds at 35/1. But hope springs eternal. I laugh as I try to picture what 4 weeks have done to my physical appearance. I marvel that one American without the consensus of a jury of Americans can be permitted to have that much control (unchecked) on a law abiding American. Nevertheless, my hair, beard, toilet paper supported washcloth for socks, empty planter and my wiggle pen writing on "authorized" paper, make me smile. My meaningless mental activities assure my leaving here more balanced, more focused, and more committed (is that the right word?) than before.

Unless others acknowledge what courage it takes to stand up to injustice, no matter what the personal cost when you see or hear about it, I will sit alone in my cell for some time.

Some say I am a hero for standing up for a belief greater than myself and having the courage to sacrifice everything so that others may one day benefit.

To see that counselor's name continuing to be passed on to hurt others (even when she's no longer here) and the guard just last night spent over ten hours with her replacement counselor still didn't crack into the cranium of an empty brain matter individual, is infuriating. If I tried to correct or embarrass him, my phone odds would have dropped to 85/1.

As the night approaches our two other troublemaker "solitaries" are either medicated or chained while the third one (me) is probably causing them more political fallout without kicking or requiring those riot control Darth Vader outfits - by just writing the truth for Americans using my societal microscope to observe. I hope my ears are clear, my vision is focused and my heart purely honest in what I have been sharing. If I had stayed home and pretended to be here and made up stories on the way things are run here, I would have fallen short of the mark. The bizarre reality here requires this to be a political issue.

I got the phone! I called. It was rejected by their internal computer system. There are no words of disgust that I can muster at the feelings of desolation caused by a telephone system that, in thirty-one days, can't even connect a simple call to my family! This issue is shared by 100% of all the inmates in this ward. No one could make contact with anyone they called tonight. This emotion generates wanting to stand outside the prison after I am released to verbally tell off some of these responsible "suits". They'll do it when they get around to doing it. Shame on us for allowing this type of ineptitude to exist in a technological society. One phone call and I wouldn't have had this many diary entries. The smaller the hill in war; the more significant the battle becomes. Can you imagine what's not being done that you can't easily measure? Despite my day of experimentation, growing of an orchard, and countless observations, I go to sleep with a heavy heart because the definition of this BOP staff is the uneducated telling the unwilling to do the unnecessary. When it is necessary, there is no one capable of knowing and more importantly caring what to do. We fought wars over "taxation without representation being tyranny". Why are we not responsive to a 1940 prison system operating on two cylinders in the year 2008? With apologies to my family for letting them down again by not calling, I am (during my stay) an unwanted extension of a bunch of undeserving governmental workers. Warden, how do you answer this? Stop aimlessly walking around on Thursdays and get your counselor inmate debacle repaired. If you can't, watch what good Americans do when we finally publish this story.

Chapter 25 – Movin' on Up

It's been an interesting night. I seemed to have beaten the rodent problem. I decided, because the noises were out of control last night, to leave my light on and let the guards shut it off from the outside. I also banged the walls intermittently and just screamed whatever came to mind. This may just be why the other inmates have been screaming: to send the rodents to my quiet cell! No one shut off the lights, and I slept through the night. I've decided, due to the wall noises last night and my effective solution, to forsake using any neighbors as future references. Although I may, to the untrained prison survivor, appear to have developed Tourette's syndrome, I slept like a baby because the ominous wall noises abated. After this extended period of arbitrary and improper persecution, I guess yelling at these walls is perfectly sane and understandable. As long as I previously removed the sock washcloths, one dysfunctional activity at a time may qualify as true survival technique. More than one dysfunctional activity at any time constitutes cause for concern.

I remain this morning more resolved than I ever thought I could be. Any government capable of creating, within its staff, the world I have observed, also has the capability to do that to its other institutions. My adversaries will eventually fall, not only because they are broken and defensive, but because they are on the wrong side of truth and justice.

Whether or not I have socks, phone calls, mouse traps, books, or contact with my loved ones; they cannot hide the truth of the facts here forever. It has been said that "the wheels of justice grind slowly, but they grind very fine." I do believe that before my "orange grove" is fully developed, these injustices will have been corrected.

I have really been trying to observe whether my existence (I can't say life) here would be better if, like George Jefferson, I "moved on up to the Eastside" and took that orderly/slave job. I saw today that the present orderly inmate, who's retiring on Monday, has put up curtains (newspaper) on his window. Privacy, now, that's power!

While I am considering my options, the broken toilet cell has just been occupied again. A young man who is crying doesn't want to be separated from his brother. Do you remember my previous comments on the "getting all family members together" program? (AFMTP). From what I can gather, this young man is hysterical at being put in a cage alone. I try to not think about that fact because that is where I am. There is going to be an investigation conducted into his case "soon". (That could be next Thursday or three weeks from today) I think I heard they were also in the same bunk. I can't swear to that. Yet I will have to listen to the debriefing on this one. Still, that bathroom won't work for long and I hope they are reunited (if that is the right term).

Just as I waited for a legal visit and thought it would be a quiet cleaning and reading day, my little window to the world got yet another view.

In case you are wondering about the orange seed program, I must marvel at the consistency of governmental know-how and the method of reverse psychology that must be implemented to maintain this karma. Consider these facts: For weeks I have been served tangerines with so many pits they were almost inedible. Finally, I got a planter and shared with you my plans for the orchard and sales program (OSP). The tangerines stopped and have been replaced by seedless oranges. This is a very interesting and comical development.

That young man across the hall said this was his first time in prison. The way I look I couldn't tell him "me too". I look like a "lifer" with this beard, hair, washcloth socks and singing to my planter. But, here's the rub (HTR), I did my prison roman salute to settle him down. He did it back! It must mean hello, so I guess that the kicker and spitter just didn't speak prison lingo (PL) when he ignored me.

As I look out the cell window, I am going to bond with him. Don't worry they won't let anyone in here. Let me give him some reading material. How do you think he'll like Plato's Symposium on Love? Yeah, that's like giving a diabetic a box of chocolates.

Let's wait until the investigation. I hope there's not a "list" for investigations. This kid will be here long after that retired counselor returns. I don't want to say her name. Let's just say et. al. (EA). It could mean elephant's ass (with apologies to the elephant).

This is just an afterthought as I was trying to read, "Fight Club" today. Remember that was the book stuffed in the wall to prevent easy access for my rats at night. I'm not saying they are big, I'm saying the rats should be registered. But, now back to my "afterthought". They censure our mail. They read everything, but in the first six pages of "Fight Club" the author tells one how to make explosives by using basic household and commissary items!

Only twenty-four hours more and I may get my "head slave" opportunity. My lawyer said as long as I don't get myself in any trouble, and I can enhance my exposure to report on what is occurring that I had his blessing. I'm sure it is only another false alarm from my legal team, but I'm told I'll only be here a few more days.

But in defense of those believing that the Judge doesn't give a damn about right or wrong or of my family's future, he's already decided what should be done, but he's too stubborn to admit he made a 180 degree mistake in all aspects of this case. But if he hadn't, would you and I have met? I hope this book activates an investigation on all fronts of corruption and ineptitude.

I have, to date studied the laws and customs of Baptists, Catholics, Jews, Christian Scientists, Congregationalists, Disciples of Christ, Episcopalians, Greek Orthodox and Jehovah Witnesses. There are many more to study and escape from the very slow moving 24 hour clock in solitary. With the intellectual exercises of writing, card games, physical exercises, reading multiple books and the Bible itself, I have avoided becoming brain dead since it's quite possible for that to occur in here. Caloric decrease adds to depression, guilt, and frustration coupled with the loss of human contact. Humor, positivity, righteousness and resolve, along with personal mental discipline, can enhance those inmates subjected to this never ending negativity. Solitary deprivation may be cruel and inhuman treatment no matter how we as a society blindly empower our heavily budgeted sixty billion dollar Bureau of Prisons to do it. I hope that I will have left prison by the time this book is digested, debated, praised or vilified. The hard facts remain that, in tiny cells with questionable nourishment devoid of adequate stimulation, we need to ask the question - does man improve or deteriorate? I simply report what I am seeing close up. Often we ignore war time correspondent's opinions and choose to believe political spin from those in power. Tonight, so far, has been quiet, so I wanted to balance some of my at times, tongue-in-cheek silliness with pensive hard hitting reality.

Chapter 26 – Changing a Broken System

I never thought I'd be in a jail, let alone, cuffed and in solitary confinement.  You probably still think prison is a far cry from a possibility in your life.  That belief doesn't minimize what a gift has been given to us both.  Are we to turn the page?  Are we to turn our direction?  There are many issues this democracy has to address.  I am strongly suggesting this one issue because I have walked through the coals of hell, and report to you herein, so that you may make the effort to question it.  Economically we can lower our taxes, psychologically we could prosecute fewer, and spiritually we can look into the depths of our social consciousness, although that will necessitate a change to this system.  Believe me, the BOP is like the Tennessee Valley Authority, a governmental organization that is no longer capable of doing the job Congress originally empowered it to do.  This is not about containing the "bad" Americans; this is about reducing their numbers and aiding, like an emergency room, the families, the victims, the perpetuators and the emotional needs of all those involved in the crime.  Before some of you want to throw out my ideas like the "baby with the bath water", I am initially speaking of non-violent crime reform.  We can work on the violent; only after we properly utilize the wasted resources presently being spent on the *business* of prisons, rather than to effectuate the real *purpose* of prisons.

As a quick aside to the heartfelt statements just written in solitary, a new CO came by to see if everyone is alive.   Really they just kick the door if you're sleeping, or even if you are up and about.  There is no count.  They just make sure no one committed suicide by cutting themselves with milk carton planters or whatever pen refill one can easily sneak by them.

He kicked the door because its 7:00 PM and the "crier" was sleeping.   The crier asked, "What time is it"?   He is a bit overwhelmed with his situation.  He also is without paper, pen, book, or snacks.   I asked if I could give this young man some paper, pencil or a book (I'd be glad to give these away).  His response (the guard, that is) "Fuck him", and he walked away.   This is not a hardened young man's heart in that cell.   Must our system, to insure its own perpetuation, make his heart harder?   I am not a card carrying bleeding heart.   I know by now that you know that.

I also want to correct a previous error in my diary. I said hot water was delivered only one hour a day. In my new cell, I now have hot water for the entire day. I guess each of the cells has, as the one across from me, its own personality. I just don't want any positive aspect of this prison to not be credited to the BOP. Heaven knows, the rest of the facts should not be discounted because of that legal term "falsus in uno, falsus in omnibus". That means if you can prove one falsehood, the rest of the claims come into question. I only wish my Judge had learned that term in law school instead of spending time looking for political friends to advance his career. I wish he had studied harder because falsus in uno, falsus in omnibus should be on his courtroom door ... because if he could be so wrong on this unnecessary and unconstitutional incarceration - he must also be wrong on his questionable and ridiculous summary judgment as well as his refusal to let a citizen jury hear our reasons for initiating this lawsuit against the SEC in the first place. Remember, the plaintiff is sitting in solitary while the defendant has seized and shredded his judgment, company and reputations. How can this be permitted?

I experienced an act of kindness tonight from Deliverance. The "head slave" brought me a pair of socks. He put it on my door knob (because I guess I didn't have my toilet paper center on it). Deliverance saw me standing at the window. I didn't ask. I figured my socks would be gone by morning. I wouldn't ask. We stared at each other. I walked away. He then opened the cuffing shoot (CS) and threw in the socks. No words were spoken but he may have secured an invitation to the reunion party, and one of the first oranges from my plantation. I am still a little concerned about the crier. He's been sleeping all day. His room is dark. It will be a long night for him. I hope he's OK. No one else considers it unusual because everyone really finds their "own style in solitary" (OSS). I hope tonight, the testing of my new theory of light and intermittent screams to keep rodents away doesn't scare them in his direction.

Chapter 27 – Head Slave "Perks"

Just a brief postscript on the socks recently received, they are tattered and different colors but much better than my old wash cloths. I often think how my legal adversaries would handle these challenges, and that's what empowers me. They couldn't handle this, and when the actual case springs back in our direction; I will crush their lies like Kafka's character in "Metamorphosis". He crushed a spider with his hands until all that was left was liquid paste. But other than that, I guess I am ambivalent about how they have acted.

I spend the night filling up wall holes with toilet paper. For some unexplained reason the tissue paper keeps "falling out" (or being pushed out) by morning. And you wonder about my tight cover tuck in! I've completed about 1/2 roll of paper to simply add to my defense line against the noises in the walls. With the lights on and the paper inserted coupled with some infrequent banging and yelling by me, I should be okay tonight. This is my new theory on rodent control: light and intermittent screams – (LIS).

Aside from my flippant pen and anger towards those who perpetuated this low level behavior of human development, I am returning to our world in my mind tonight. This darkened room with a crying young man, alone and afraid, breaks my heart. I am powerless to aid his grief. I am unable to give him even my socks, if that would make him feel even a touch of human kindness.

The crier is really afraid. I am so physically close, and yet because of locks, so far away. I am nothing more than a detached stranger watching a turtle cross a busy highway. Praying for him sounds like the politically right thing to do, and I will. But the pragmatist, father, son, and grandfather feel more for the stranger than I ever thought I could. If I was "head slave" tonight, I could slip some food or a note of support under his door. This is my first time in here seeing a darkened room for more than ten consecutive hours with the long dark evening still ahead of us. I find myself standing at the door hoping that he'll put on his light. I'm sure I am overreacting to his mood and my own concerns that I have about his well-being; nevertheless I pray all is well with my newest neighbor across the hall.

The head slave gets to shower every day and he may even get to eat the leftovers of the various meals brought in and served to staff members. Those meals look a little bit different than the slop-buckets we get. The head slave just came in and the officers were escorting him back without cuffs. Now, in this world, that's power. I only wish I could have spoken to him to ask him to do something for the dark door across the hall. I feel that agony all the way over here. It's gnawing at me and I hope that by morning all is well.

The young man got up! His light went on. I spoke to him. He said, "Thank you", and the neighbors on both sides are talking to him through the wall. Human kindness, it works every time.

Chapter 28 – 3,000,000 Seconds … and Counting

How could a morning be bad when you have two socks?  Even if they don't match, the bounce in your step off of the cold gray, pealed painted concrete is an indescribable sensation.

My defense light system worked again (no rodents), but these bright lights burning all night do affect my sleep.  Despite knowing that socks awaited my wake up, my sleep was repeatedly broken in my anticipation of possibly putting an end to solitary, or as I have grown accustomed to calling it (a twenty-four hour exercise in self-discipline, positive thought, mental control and time management (SPMT).

The crier was cuffed and brought to an R&D hearing.  I don't know what R&D means in here.  It can't be our worldly definition because prison research and development could only exist here in theory not in practice.  Should he disappear like the Illustrated Man never to return and never to say goodbye, I still intend to invite him to the prison reunion party and even his brother.  I'll keep them in separate rooms until I get the whole story about those linens.

I have much to do today.  Whenever I imagine my moving from here or even possibly taking my first step towards prison orderly management, I get excited.  Since I am without many expensive "toys" here, if I am released I only intend to bring my two handmade games.  The books belong to the BOP, so they'll stay.  I'm sure I can reproduce the orange wash cloths and one orange and one teal sock set, so they will also stay.  My bars of soap should be left for the next inmate because I remember when I first came into this prison and there wasn't any soap for me.  Agricultural laws probably prevent me from moving my soon to be orange tree and planter, so they will have to remain for the next tenant.  I'm considering trying to take the spoon/fork as a memento.  Any unwritten paper, pens, pencils will stay as an act of charity.  A few partially written pages would come with me.  So after careful analysis, I would take a small envelope, a plastic spoon and a few pieces of written paper.  I think I can make this move without the help of friends.  I could call for an "estimate", but by the time I get on the moving "list" and then get to the top of it, I could be here another sixty to ninety days.  So I'll risk the bodily strain of self-moving. All of my hidden toilet paper rolls and wash clothes used to "stuff" the perimeter defense of nocturnal protection (PDNP) will also stay for the next hardened offender. My feelings towards my Judge are based on his dysfunctional prejudice against men like me, who dwarf him in integrity and intelligence. His actions have indicated that his faulty decisions are based only on his judicial sense of self-importance and absolute hubris.

With the Deliverance brothers working last night we didn't do weekly cell cleaning. Hopefully as I plan my pack-up and departure I won't be here for it. But if the wheels of justice arc still trying to find the connecting axle, I'll be here until Tuesday. It's tough mentally packing and unpacking for the move, but I have showers and maybe a shave tonight if I am still one of the chosen ones for a shower. Hence the BOP continues like an overeating house guest to strain the host and society without a need for them to still be here. My revised penal system idea where families pay for the incarceration, will remove this badge of courage that has been created within the underbelly of our gang and ghetto indigent society. Boys and young men of these gang societies are actually expected to do time in prison as a rite of passage to be respected in their crime ridden neighborhoods. Having the family pay also contains more personal responsibility for all involved parties coupled with a drastic revision in our judicial sentencing guidelines. Unfortunately the Warden never responded to my initial list of issues and ideas that I handed to him. Sometimes I'm a bit hard on the upper management of MCC. It's possible that the Warden's personal library burned down while I was here and both books may have been destroyed. It's also worth mentioning that one of those books probably hadn't been colored in yet! Maybe he didn't choose not to read my phone and improvement requests; he simply may have been unable to do so. The Warden looks good, has a nice smile, is an obvious status seeker, and he must have the right friends in the BOP. A true professional needs much more to put together a top-notch organization like the one described here. I invite dialogue, visits, open forums and a one on one debate against the Warden at any time. This will occur only after the UCMJ no longer gives the other side an unfair advantage, and I once again become a free American and not a mole or afterthought.

If I am to leave, I have to finish all my books today. I have tried to not be without an activity because the twenty-four hours of silence seems to fly by like pushing the Statue of Liberty across Manhattan. Yeah, that pretty well describes 31 days x 24 hours = 744 hours so far or 44,640 minutes or more realistically 2 million six hundred and seventy eight thousand four hundred seconds (2,678,400). That time was not only spent here. It was that much time away from my family. Yet enough thinking about lost time at the moment of one's departure, I'm sure my dedication of this diary will cover that issue. I have decided to dedicate the book to my Judge for without his vindictive behavior and poor judgment the book and expose' would have never occurred.

I may also list the few Senators who confirmed my Judge to the bench. They too have their hand in this revealing expose' of a world we should never have visited. Their constituents must be alerted to see what these Senators' lack of attention to detail and disrespect for the imprisoned citizens has created.

My shower came early today. Through my newly developed prison savvy I traded off not changing my jumpsuit for a pair of socks and a new towel. Since during the weekend my jumpsuit hung on the bunk, it was a great trade. I was asked again if I would consider the "head slave" job, if it became available. I also received a new razor from CO Rutgers, a prince in this place (along with a few of the day CO's, who I may get to meet and tell you about). As I shower, I see some of the other tier inmates. (You remember our tier's shower/toilet combination is still out of order). Some of the other inmates are very verbal and yelling loudly today at the CO's. Without the CO's this place comes to a grinding halt. The "suits", well, that's another story.

The crier's property has been thrown out onto the floor of the hallway. He's definitely been moved. I'll try to find out the prison "gossip" about him as I go to legal today. I'm definitely ready to leave because now I have two pair of socks, two pair of underwear, three blankets (one is my pillow) and I have the "head slave" opportunity about to blossom for me. There are still no pitted oranges this morning. If I didn't know better I would think they are reading my diary before I publish it. My orange plantation tree program remains on hold.

Learning that hand salute (Roman right hand with a fist across your chest) from the Illustrated Man is like a secret handshake here. The second it is done, you make a friend. Today I had the opportunity when waiting after my shower to salute often; and the reactions were remarkable. Inmates' eyes open, and you become a brother. Now here I am at this stage of my life's journey and I have learned the first symbol of a strange culture. This underground and forgotten group of men has created a language of handshakes and signals like a third base coach in baseball. Their spoken gang words and gestures do not assimilate to the outside world, nor are there any attempts to prepare them to return to our society. Now this "civil contemptor" may soon strive to become their orderly facilitator. By the time the inmates are returned to civilian life they don't sound like us, don't dress like us, don't walk like us, and even face the wrong way in an elevator. I'm going to be studying that on my next visit to New York. When the Jamaicans and brother lovers have their loved ones in prison, can you explain their reluctance to return to the non-prison world? When you are turned into a more dependent and fearful human being, how quickly does the need to be independent occur again? Remember prison nurturing may be dysfunctional but like the child of an abusive parent, one still forgives and sadly embraces the abuser. Therein lies today's muse. Has the BOP recreated an abusive family causing those damaged souls to continue repeating crimes and returning to prison? What is the return percentage? I'm willing to wager it exceeds 60%. Family is family; and that's what we have created in this prison system as it is. It may seem overwhelming to change this broken system, but from looking into the eyes of these abused CO's and their deteriorating prisoners, what choices do we really have? Remember the cliché' that repeating activities and expecting a different result is the true definition of insanity? Do we have experimental jails? Are innovative studies available? Are they funded or resisted by the BOP? Do governmental agencies or unions ever embrace something that might eliminate jobs? Heaven forbid! That's the task of strong and independent politicians. Hopefully that has not become an oxymoron in today's elected officials' world and we will soon find a sympathetic political spokesperson or a courageous journalist to initiate and effectuate change.

Chapter 29 – Arab Spitters

Due to simple guard disinterest, returning from my legal visit took a little extra time today (about 2 hours). Anything that the crier or the previous guests owned has been left in a pile in front of my cell window. Should I say something about what this will do to my property value or resale ability? I probably won't, but it really once again gives a visual to you about cleanliness and jail attention to detail. If I worked here, I couldn't walk by the pile of garbage "once" without taking some corrective action to clean it away. Whose job is it? So Mount MCC's Trash (MMT) has been there for eight hours to date. I'm sure it's going to be addressed before the end of August. Let's just hope that there's not a "list" to take away garbage. If that's the case, I'll never get a real estate agent to look at this cell. Since I only have a front door, I can't bring anyone in any other way. This trash has preoccupied my early afternoon thoughts.

A good "orderly" sign occurred today because they took me in to "see" the laundry and storage of clothes cage. I hope they're not trying to "bait" and "switch" this job offer. I still await the alleged conference call scheduled for me today to go home.

I have many concerned thoughts as I watch prison employees eating everywhere I travel throughout the building. Food eating is a major daily activity here. There is a great deal of movement and variety of foods consumed by the employees. Why do we feed and also pay employees? I'm sure this is a business where lunch rooms are logistically awkward, although I know that they do have a lunch room for staff. Yet, everyone who works here always has food in front of them. Could it be anxiety eating? I'm only saying this because of my "evening terror sounds". If you restricted food consumption, couldn't you limit rodent activity? There are forgotten foods in desks, on elevators, in Day Rooms and now on the floor in front of my window. This is my one small preventive suggestion to eliminate the all night parties of mice, rats and I hope cats (because the breathing is getting so close) in the walls and in the hallways, closets and storage rooms. For example, recently when I was waiting (being held) in the law library, I moved a book and "bang" a bag of food and a mouse appeared! There went my love of the law library. Without the easily available food, the mouse would have been directed to where the extermination should be done. Now, if their pest control program requires a "list" then "let them eat wherever they want" because the BOP "list" program will insure generations of rodents living undeterred due to the fact the BOP doesn't see anything wrong with the ambiance of rodents to add to the "motif' of the building. We give our prisoners headsets to block out their surroundings. I suggest that we have them learn to improve their environment.

Allow me one additional example to try to give you a feeling of the institutional mood always around me. Each Ward of ten cells with potentially twenty prisoners has a Rubbermaid type cart on wheels to serve the food. They push this cart from cell to cell six to ten times daily. It is also used for delivery of linens and other items brought to the cells. It is completely covered with stains and fresh filth. I have offered that when I shower; I would bring it in with me to clean it. "It's good enough," is the typical response from the guards. Rodents eat off these carts at night.

Hundreds of different hands touch this food cart wheeler and not one employee has decided to be the one to clean it. The bacteria count must be off the charts, and my food is on the bottom of the pile because I am the last cell to be served. I mention this because that's one of the other reasons I try to hand clean my own linens in here. Why doesn't one "suit" on a Thursday see the filth? This institutional malaise translates into inmate and employee shutdown which ends up costing our society dearly.

As I write, I listen to the guards actually screaming at each other, because dysfunctional thought processes, faulty problem solving, lack of pride, and a confused sense of purpose exist here. This is not one inmate's agenda. No, I am able to easily distinguish between what is actually wrong and my wrongly being here. My BOP or MCC observations are supported in this brief encounter with countless examples representing multiple stories to prove my thesis. The system, as it is, is broken. Wait until I can get to open some of these other doors to expose even more.

What will it take to improve prisons? Riots? No, that only frightens citizens to keep "them"(the prisoners) away from "us". Expecting defensive government employees to believe what I am saying is a long shot. Government responds only to public opinion.

Whether you have a child or loved one in here, or you are paying too much out of your paycheck for this type of idiocy - call, write complain, question, get arrested like me and write about it (only kidding, trust me, it's probably worse than I have written because my self-discipline is not that of a normal person) as this diary has and will clearly continue to demonstrate.

Just when I thought we would be gliding to an end of this with little more to tell, God opened more doors for us today. Two very recalcitrant looking guests have moved across the hall. No, they didn't pick up Mt. MCC, they kicked it aside. They were put in the cell, and they are spitting on the floor. The CO's have left them until they either fill up the room with spit or decide to stop spitting. Of course, I saluted. We bonded. Understatedly, they don't seem happy with the situation. There's much more going to develop here. They seem very loud so we may have a rodent redirect (RR) occurring tonight. I'll stay low. One has to master the initial art of detachment in here.

Deliverance is in charge now. He said "hello" to me. I'm as good as in for "master slave" now he told me he was in the Army Rangers for 8 years. All is forgiven. As veterans, we are friends for life now! The two inmates across the hall appear Middle Eastern. It's only a matter of time before the inmate cell party will begin tonight. They have stopped spitting, but I'm still playing it "cool". I don't really know what to do after the salute. I should tell them I'm here for murder. It doesn't seem too "cool" to complain about a bad rap for "contempt". I'm really in the right place to be held with vicious criminals.

Now that I'm "in" with all of the CO's I should begin by drinking the prison corporate Kool-Aid. I'm glad my nails are long, because I realized today that I do not need a hair comb or brush. I now can use my nails. There's another solution to something I thought was a problem. Maybe in time, I will also try to accept why I wasn't permitted to call home for now over thirty-two days.

I've stripped down into my semi-naked summer look in the cell because I'm saving laundry usage time in my jump suit. My socks are being washed and dried on my bunk. All is well. My two new neighbors are now being taken for showers. With that pile of garbage still in front of their door it will be only a matter of time before they may want to borrow one of my washcloths, socks or soaps. I hope they like orange trees, and possibly we'll start with that dialogue a little later.

Tonight's dinner was two very low grade hot dogs. The hot dogs were unusually shaped, off-colored wiggly road repeating "S" design and they were served with tartar sauce. This combination even shocked me, so I checked twice before I wrote it down. Hunger caused me to try one hot dog, but I had to leave the other. Once again, the hot dog and overall ambiance of the food presentation has successfully caused me a relief, that's what it is, a relief that the meal is over.

Tonight's a big night. We have new guests. We may get a cleaning, and the guards now like me better than the guys spitting on their window and in their cell. It's good to be appreciated.

Tonight I'm not even going to ask for a phone. That may be the only way I'll get to the top of the phone list. Every time, the Day Room's phone rings tonight I imagine I'm on my way to go home. Today I had someone contact the Oprah Show. Another friend has started dialogue with a publicist on the diary supplemented by aspects of the entire case. I gave them ten title ideas for this work today. I am told we are at two hundred pages written with a wiggly pen refill and a wiggly pencil. That's a great deal of unauthorized ink.

I'm sure it is in my mind because of the wiggly almost human looking colored hot dogs but two things are now happening to me. One is I'm feeling sick from the one eaten hot dog, but I'm sure that will pass. The other is that I'm wondering about my old prison friends and especially the brother lovers. I hope those two got back together in the same cell. The Chaplain was going to "go to bat" for them. "Is that the right way to say it, Father"? I still wonder why a priest like the Chaplain would remind an inmate of how nice it is outside, ignore him and then tell him how good he thought the government's case against him was. He also was too busy because of Jury Duty and then he told me to look him up in Brooklyn when I get out. But, he rushed up here, when the alleged "brother lovers" had a problem. Well I guess I'll wait for the Rabbi or the Mullah before I decide which of these twenty-eight religions I embrace while I am in MCC. Most of these top notch professionals work poorly. The problems exist here from the top to the bottom of this management staff.

I have good diary feelings about the spitters next door. I think we may begin appreciating them as they seem, from what I gather, to be regular visitors here from time to time. Everyone knows them. I'll try to continue by playing it cool, and "I'll get into it with my BRO's in the later, you know what I mean - that's what I'm saying". What did I just say?

My writing instincts are right here. The spitters are kicking and screaming and trying to knock down their door! A Lieutenant and other officers are visiting now! Here are the basic issues, they have no linens and no blankets, they are Muslim and the hot dogs haven't gone over very well. They may keep the tartar sauce however. They are demanding "Respect". Now that's something I never tried in here. I just can't wait until their toilet overflows. It's only a matter of time! The spitters have not adjusted well and in the UCMJ guidelines under "plays well with others", they may not soon be getting the best grade.

Chapter 30 - Respect

Despite tonight's background inmate chatter these two spitters will get what they want because they carry on. Spitters are rewarded, while those of us still waiting for a phone call, nail clippers, or a simple seed for my garden will get nothing! Will I be rewarded for having the tightest bed, cleanest room, most books read and most wash cloths in the history of MCC?

If only I could get mad right now, curse and demand a "nail clipper". That would impress my neighbors.

Just as I expected, the toilet has begun backing up to add to the joy of our evening. I must confess tonight's fireworks show is beginning to unfold far beyond my original expectations.

The inmates are now putting on black prayer hats and shawls. The CO's haven't brought anything they need to satisfy their "respect" needs yet. And to think that some television shows fail because of lack of material. I can only imagine with a working camera what this place could show us. And on the sixth or seventh season, we could visit the inmates. The staff and "suits" would provide sufficient material for the initial years and seasons.

The rancid hot dogs could have added seven weeks to my "all food looks bad diet", after I introduce my Better Off Passing Diet Program.

I thought that tonight was truly going to be a "wind down" before leaving, but the other two chained solitaries (the kicker and the 6 DARTH VADER chained guy have moved it up a notch). It seems their medication is beginning to wear off and they are expressing some displeasure at being chained. They figure it is time their weekend chaining should be over. It's hard to try to figure how my life went so wrong. "Hey wait a minute; I didn't do anything "wrong".

The head slave is just leaving his cell to have a shower and hang out with the COs in the Day room. It's only a matter of time, because my window view of today's events with the spitters has more to unfold. I'll do the salute later, but for now I'll wait for the next explosion. I'm going to finish one book "Into the Wild" and read about a few more religions tonight, and then depending upon the spitters, think about my new job offer (which may not come).   Ah, prison life at MCC possibilities and subtle indecision as I climb those societal stairs to rehabilitation.

I'm practicing spitting in the sink in case these guys need me to look tough tonight.   Just yelling for nail clippers doesn't seem to add to my image on the ward with the other guys.

Every time I put down my pen (the illegal one) and the authorized paper (because I am an author) it starts again.   Remember they are directly across the hall. They are flushing and re-flushing their toilets.   The water is flowing out from under their door and it's not a pretty sight.   Remember the hot dogs.   Well it's now flowing towards me.   I've got my wash cloths and extra towels shoved under my door, or "it's" coming in.   They seem intent on self-flooding the ward.        I can't yell for help, it's not cool.   I have a civil contempt solitary confinement image to uphold.   I can't let down my Judge.   I want him to be proud of whom he sends here.   This is a dilemma.   Do I yell?   I just can't, so I'll just have to let the river flow until one of the CO's notice.   This could be a two hour or more wait based on the quick response time of the COs.

The head slave is now yelling at them because he has to mop it up. Maybe I should reconsider the job opportunity or place some mopping restrictions in my contract.   Nevertheless, the spitters weren't moved with respect.   They said something about his mother, and everyone is spitting at each other from both sides of the glass.   This is a real non-violent way of combat, but it doesn't improve my view with that excess mountain of trash plus the now flowing toilet water along with the appearance of the dripping spit on their glass.   All of this is coupled with the memories of the wiggly hot dogs, which adds to my lack of appetite.   Fortunately I am still capable of detachment.   I don't think I'm here.   I'm only reporting. Wait a minute!   I'm here?   My wash cloths may be lost forever.   The "head slave" has gone to a visitors meeting, and in true BOP management style has told no one about the water!   He knows he's not going to his meeting, if they know, and if they know, he's mopping.   Maybe this is my big chance?   God, tonight I hope not.   I've fully dressed now in case my cell becomes the first victim of the overflow of the Muslim spitters wrath

(MSW). I'm holding all of my possessions and I'm sitting like Woody Allen would on the top bunk. Yeah, I really belong here. I can't yell for help without the loss of my tough guy dignity.

I want to start yelling, but this place hasn't gotten to me yet. That's because of you, you know. Without this diary outlet, watching mankind implode alone and this close up view may have affected me by now.

The spitters are disappointed because there's no reaction! No one cares. They'll get to it when they get to it. I'm trying to get someone to knock over the feeding cart - any water on it is better than no water on the previously light tan now darkened and stained food tray. Let me read sitting on the top bunk hoping my washcloth dam holds, preventing the flow of water from the spitters new home into my cell.

Now the 6 Darth Vader guy is taking a shower. He's got five CO's escorting him, as I sit here worrying when I might get an orange seed. This entertainment, reported by me is, I remind you, brought to you by the BOP and made possible by my Judge. Without his wisdom, these views would have been lost for you and me to see and share. Imagine all of the stories and all of the lunacy that is occurring nationwide all over the prison system tonight.

I finished reading two more books, and if I am staying I will need assistance soon to obtain another book or two. My reading time is not always guaranteed like stories of the spitters and other inmates. I've still got one more book plus some Bible to finish, but I have to believe they will let me out soon or this diary length may rival War and Peace in a few more months (don't say that)! Well, the toilet water stopped flowing and no one has come by to assist. The guards don't multitask very well and they are all focused on the one shower of the one guy. So until that's finished, the Spitters aren't going to get the attention and respect they are demanding. It is interesting to see inmate reactions when the expected activity doesn't occur.

I've been practicing my screaming "I need another book" instead of "nail clippers" or "I have a hang nail, goddamn it!" Neither demand seems to have the impact of spitting on the window and kicking a steel door so hard that it sounds like a gunshot explosion. I don't think I'm going to be able to get into this yelling symphony tonight. The flushers water level came a good 6" from my wash cloths so they are still usable. I had considered substituting my planter and making it into a "bailing out" water bucket (BOWB). Fortunately I didn't have to do it. I have saved the dirt, and the orange grove dream is still there for me.

I have pieced together some background information on the spitters. They are from the terrorists' floor. Now here's the news I am trying to assimilate. The CO's have said that they have been moved because of the quarantine! Now I'm putting my wash cloths back on over my two pairs of socks. Quarantine! Is it Lupus? Is it Bubonic Plaque? It's good to know I'm in a germ free environment. Because I'm on the other side of the door … remember?

The terrorist status report is that no blankets or any of their other requests have been given to my neighbors. Everyone is completely preoccupied with the shower of the one other psychopath tonight.

I can't read. I'm keyed up like a reporter trying to get this information to you so you can better understand where civil contempt people go when they have upset someone who has lost touch with not only the reality here, but on the merits of my case. What an appeal reversal this will eventually be. I wish the Judge would stay here for one week. They'd carry him out in tears. He probably was the kid with the yellow raincoat in elementary school, but today he's able to work out those insecurity issues without realizing the societal consequences. Quarantine! I'll report as the information comes in to determine which disease now exists in the center of New York City.

The noise level tonight has returned to one of full symphony sounds. From the Jamaicans who don't know anything is happening to the addition of three new inmates and we have the spitters. Now add showers to be given and new check-ins and you have one busy night. I've finished my book and I'm about to start yelling for a new one.

"Do I have to play Bridge or Scrabble all night, goddamnit?" Then I spit. Then I salute. That may work. "How about some respect"?

Chapter 31 – Showers Without Towels

This wouldn't be a good time for me to pass out the circulars to open another inmate's milk cartons with my nails, or to give them pre-growing special rates on buying my oranges. That puddle of sewage in the center of the ward may not provide the quarantined terrorists with the respect they required.

My credibility is on the line, when I now tell you the two diseased terrorists or Muslim spitters have just been told they can have a shower and a bed roll which is one sheet, two blankets and always a pillow case (no pillows here). The problem which has been presented, as if these two guys were on Candid Camera, was that the officers have no clean towels or washcloths. Quickly, I picked up my wash cloths under the door and threw them under the bed. The dialogue was pathetically priceless. It went something like this. "Oh come on man, how we gonna take showers without no fuckin' towels"? The retort in true MCC style was "You want the shower? Are you refusing the shower"? If I had ever taken drugs, I would swear I was having some sort of flashback to some fantasy thoughts, threaded together by "damaged synapses". They'll all be coming back from their towel-less shower, don't go too far away because I have a feeling the "respect" they were looking for and the "respect" they will get may further fuel our little window in this world tonight.

Fortunately, I never have to stop writing to snack for two reasons. First, there aren't any snacks, and secondly I remain nauseas from the last eating experience. Even tepid water out of a tainted cardboard milk container can't make me feel better. Remember the sink and toilets are connected as one unit. It's not a Kohler or television ad material experience.

May God forgive me. The two guys who have now decided not to shower without a towel were told I have been here over 30 days. He yelled to me "man what you do to be here 30 days? " From the truth to silly responses that come to mind. I responded, "Manslaughter! I killed seven men". He saluted. This was a good answer?

Not knowing what is or is not happening in my world of legal escape from here "creeps in" between these macabre events which are unfolding at a pace beyond my belief. If I was in the command post (Day Room) there would be six such wards like this going on all at one time. One can see how these CO's become what I have observed. One ward is more than enough to deal with. Why can't the "suits" and the Warden visit on a shower night? Why do they come at 8:00AM on Thursdays when most everyone is sleeping? You do the numbers. I'm only glad I have been here to give you a glimpse through only one window.

One of the new inmates across the hall asked if he could be moved in with his two brothers who are in one of the other wards on the same floor. What can be said as you see my theories of bringing in all family members being supported over and over again?

It's not lupus or the bubonic plaque. It's chicken pox. The same disease you and I discussed a few weeks ago. It's still here. These two guys across the hall were told they are now on a towel "list" and although they are vehemently complaining about the filth within their cell they cannot have a mop, rags, or cleaning supplies because "this is their first day". After a while, these ridiculous phrases begin to make sense. I pray this is my final day here, but "It is what, it is" with thanks to the Illustrated Man. Tomorrow morning may be the psychologist's visit so, I have my red dye near the sink. I will put the dye on myself to see if the psychologist will stop. They use the same property system as Nazi concentration camps because every prisoner always has his property moved by others and it is presumed that it will get there properly. These two quarantined spitters are hysterical tonight about their property which was promised before 8:00PM tonight. It's moving in on 10:00PM, "Do you know where your property is?" With apologies to an old news flashback, which was "it is 10:00PM, do you know where your children are?" Our society certainly has changed. The "count" has been used as an excuse as to why their property isn't here tonight. They have just been told it will be here "shortly". Let's discuss that tomorrow morning. I have to slither into my cover, examine my perimeter defense, put on socks, and pray that morning comes after their property makes it down two floors within the same building.

Chapter 32 – "Sockopoly"

Well, you couldn't believe how much this Deliverance really likes me (in comparison to my neighbors I could be a psychopath, and I would still be his favorite). He stopped by tonight and brought me a third pair of socks. This was his sign of friendship. I'm not even going to say anything except hopefully my consistent mature personality can weaken even the most hardened CO. This was a very touching and memorable prison event. It doesn't say a great deal about the overall prison experience, but a touch of humanity, like a pair of socks, can bring many human elements into this process. I'm glad we bonded tonight. I have to thank all of my neighbors for making me look so good just by being themselves. You get to the top of the sock "list" by not caring about it. That's my new plan. Tonight I do not care if I ever get out and return to the outside world or as we have learned to call them, the no jumpsuit people (NJP). Turning Deliverance into a sensitive caring young man was today's gift to me. Now I have to work on that blockhead Judge.

Even if this may be my last morning here, it hurts getting up in the morning. I don't know if it's the dampness, the mattress, or my sleeping with my arms holding a blanket up to my neck in a quasi-fetal position; but the initial morning seconds of stiff pain hurts. As I try to get out of bed without disturbing the side and bottom blanket tuck-in and still get to the door in time to catch the breakfast tray before they move on without serving it or just let it drop to the floor, I feel my age.

I don't know why I eat breakfast, except I may get placed on some remedial "list" of non-eaters and they may punish me by giving me larger portions of food throughout the day.

If one goes back to sleep, the guards only wake you up for the pick-up of the tray anyway. Getting up so early with nothing to wear and no place to go only adds to the personality of prison. You know how Monday or Friday have a "feel". Well, prison life has a "feel". It's a difficult emotion to describe but I'll work on it. I'll try to verbalize that "feel" as events or emotions can more clearly express it. The constant, actually only choice, of milk may be a critical element of this food nausea diet. Again, no oranges. Someone must have talked about my orange grove.

## Chapter 33 – Thirty More Days …and a Paint Brush?

I'm packed up again to leave, but everything moves a bit slower in the morning as a result of the verbal explosions and neighborhood events described last night.

Today there was a new "deliverer" for breakfast. He looked familiar, but he was a very young man. With rapid inquisition, I asked him if he is the son of one of the other CO's. He was. Now we have generational replacement (GR) by Inmates *and* Staff. We really have our work cut out if we want to make this system go away, as it is reproducing far too quickly.

I have had a very good "run" on milk cartons. I now have 5 wash cloths (no turtle doves), 4 milk cartons, 3 socks, 2 sets of underwear and an orange seed for a pear (or orange) tree". The reason I bring it to your attention is the "look" of 4 blue and white milk cartons without matching plates or dishes might be something the son, cousin or son-in-law of some of the "suits" may decide to put in the prison gift shop. Oh, they'll have a gift shop soon. It's the next step in their branding plans.

Today could be my "comment" card day at departure. (Boy, do I wish!) There is so much to say on these little cards similar to the one that one gets after a hotel stay. Where would I begin? By the way, the Muslims are definitely coming to the re-union party because this morning they discreetly decided to sleep in and not have breakfast. They simply pushed everything when the slot opened into the hallway! You have to admire their resolve and consistency. I hope they find the "respect" they search for here.

As previously stated, thirty minutes later another CO, pushing the same filthy cart that the other one delivered the meal on, now came to pick up trays. Do you think anyone told him that the Muslims pushed breakfast away and didn't have any trays within their cells? Do you think this unsuspecting CO would now re-wake them to pick-up what wasn't there in the first place? Of course, you know the answer.

I don't know the Arabic language, but I may have picked up a few sounds that are not complementary or positive in nature. It's all part of the process of "respect" and communication that adds to the prison "mood". With now three pair of socks I'm as close to royalty or a "lifer" as I perceive one can be. That's why I know the end of my stay should be soon. I expect to leave today. Boy, if I have to continue writing after today; then you'll get a flavor of the prison "feeling" from me that will overpower your taste buds.

By the way, after you return your breakfast tray you can return to sleep until lunch. There are no other minute by minute requirements here. Just only the thirty minutes after breakfast. The more I look at the tray and the dried filthy water on the outside floor from last night, I'm moving in on a "feeling" for prison. I'm close to defining it. Just give me a little more time (Oh, my God, I didn't say that, did I?)

A great deal happened today. First, the bad news was the Judge told my attorney I am staying here until the deposition is done in solitary. He scheduled it to be done in thirty days from now because the SEC indicated that they were too busy to make it to the deposition until then. That's a little more time than what most of us thought. Sure, we will make an appeal on this apparent dilatory and vindictive legal decision, but I don't know when that will happen. Yesterday I thought that I could define the feeling of prison. Today's activities may do that better than ever before. You see, in addition to the Judge's bad news, I got the "head slave" job, and I just lumbered in here at about 10:30 PM.

Let me try with accuracy and chronology to explain my day. It may achieve my goal of being able to give you the "feel "of prison, and how I may be feeling tonight, as I nauseously drag myself into my cell.

Here's how the day started. The Lieutenant informed me that after last night's events they had to make an orderly change because the place was filthy and they also had to repaint the entire place. They felt the last "head slave" had lost his desire for excellence. I wonder why?

My first project test was that he wanted me to paint the cell doors on the wards. That's about 40 complex steel doors and each one takes at least 15 minutes to paint. He gave me the paint. One Russian guard supervising me told me to just paint the areas that were dirty or rusted, and this way, I could finish this first project in less time.   My second project was a total cleaning of all six wards and the Day Room garbage pails (not the carts - they don't think they need it yet).   Sometime I need to remind myself that I will turn 60 years of age in prison in a few weeks (just another thought which occurred to me today).

I began painting every cell door and started visiting every inmate.   I was also told that before I started to paint I had to clean out about six cells that had been vacated.   What an insight I received on how other inmates chose to live and what this prison mood creates.   Suffice it to say over twenty uneaten and unreturned meals, hundreds of pieces of garbage, empty wrappers and at least thirty-five books, and enough dirt to fill twenty of my "soon to be orange grove planter" milk containers, were only some of my initial findings.   I began, like Santa Claus, slipping books under doors, I found and gave pens, paper and anything I thought the inmates might like.   An elderly inmate was so touched by my random act of kindness that he cried while he was thanking me.

One would think that the gray paint given me would match the doors after they dried.   You know that no matter how many coats were done (four) the original gray comes through.   Some CO's thought it was OK, and some said it has to be done again tomorrow.

During my visits I met the 6 Darth Vader chained guy who had only refused to take his prison photo and refused to acknowledge the authority of the prison - hence his dramatic arrival and treatment (UCMJ).   Another shocker was that the crier was found in another ward and a different cell, and he was to go to general population today.   As I tried to speak and engage each inmate, one said I was too nice to be here and another begged me to help him to make a phone call home.

I found some creative activities and projects that some of the inmates made during their free time.   One had collected milk cartons cut them into four sides and made a set of playing cards which were quite nice.   This set was better than mine, yet still I gave them to another Inmate.

Three hours after beginning the paint job, I then began the cleanup of the 6 wards.   This is the most exhausted I have been since I came here.   I took a filthy Day Room, with a microwave that had never been cleaned, caked-up food on desks, disgusting garbage pails, the messiest public area I have ever seen, and made it all SPOTLESS. This cleaning could never have been done before by any of my "head slave" predecessors.

It's important to note there was a funny argument between two CO's about whether I should paint the locks and key holes of the cells or not. I thought it a bad idea to paint them but one of the COs in charge of watching me (there were three by this time) decided to have me paint the locks and the handles. With a smile, I knew future lock problems would follow.

I met and spoke with prison inmates who have become self-appointed "lawyers" quoting legal chapter and verse as to why I should not be here, but because of today's judicial decision, I have thrown myself into the project with fury and an unbridled anger.

I scrubbed, mopped and cleaned cells, several with vomit, and re-cleaned a place to such a degree that frankly no one spoke when I was finished. I carried that mop and pail up and down steps thirty or more times. I mopped halls until the black filthy water rinsed clear. I changed water two and three times a ward. Each ward was at least a forty-five minute mopping exercise. The Day Room is massive and it took me over an hour each time. I cleaned it twice.

I was, however, permitted to drink from a cold water fountain. I ate no lunch or dinner. They gave it to me, but my personal anger along with vomit and urine cleanup defeated my already minimal appetite.

That water fountain was really ice cold water, and I must confess it was the high point of the exercise. Wow, does my back hurt after doing work I must confess I haven't done for a decade. I am back in my cell nauseas, exhausted, angry but determined, and still defiantly able. I was working in the small slop sink room trying to clean the filthy mops. I had minimal cleaning supplies and a guard came in to urinate in the slop sink. He told me that because I was now the "head slave" I could do it too if I found the need during the day. I did not. I never did! Eventually, I stopped the guards from urinating in that sink and on the mops.

My nausea from urine smells, cell smells, bad news today, meeting all of these lost souls, the dried vomit and the guard urinating in the same floor sink where I was cleaning my tools, may have explained the feeling when I came struggling in to my cell.   Tonight, I "felt" prison.

Maybe tomorrow the cleaning won't be so intense.   Maybe tomorrow the paint will cover.   That reminds me I got to clean and set-up four cells for new inmates.   I painted inside their cells, left them soap and whatever toiletries I could find left behind from the previous inhabitant.   I gave out over twenty books today.   I received a couple of smiles, many "salutes", and then decided to clean up mountains of trash and the toilet hallway water stains of my neighbors from the numerous overflows that defective toilet has caused.

Chapter 34 – Sanitary Tears

When I stumbled into my cell, I received a letter from one of my shareholders and his wife who had lost their entire savings, and he wanted to tell me how proud he and his wife were of me.

He defined courage and hero with words that opened my eyes for the first time. Not my eyes, but my tear ducts. My back is killing me, and tonight I am being reminded of my age. Watching the CO's order and eat outside food was difficult and; today they couldn't be nicer to this "60 year old head slave". However, the emotions of the legal folly, the injustice, my wife and family crushed because of this hubris decision, extending my incarceration another 30 days, along with my hunger and fatigue resulted in my first uncontrollable sobbing event? The inmates were unusually quiet tonight. Could it have been my tenderness, my smiles, my sympathy, my turning each ward into something that reminded them and smelled like home? I don't know. The terrorists were fascinated as they watched me paint and clean for hours. Men respect men who take pride in what they do. If the guards worked, the inmates might respect them too.

I feel personal pride tonight in what I accomplished. In an attempt to right the wrongs I have observed, I responded today with my rags, mops, and heart. The jail looks so good one of the CO's said, "This place has never looked like this in the 10 years I've been working here. You took away the mess and clutter and everything smells clean".

I kept only one book for myself. As I looked into over 40 pairs of lost eyes today, my personal needs and anger weren't paramount.

By the way, today I ate only the dry cereal and nothing else served even merited a trial. Watching the guards eating heroes and drinking coke with ice, while I carried the heaviest mop buckets up and down those stairs, coupled with today's deposition delay news, gave me insight into what long term prisoners must feel.

By tomorrow, today's gray day hopefully will have lifted. My back and arms will not be pulsating as much. My keen journalistic eye will once again watch out the window and tell you what's going on out there.

I feel like that "Truman Story" tonight with Jim Carey.  I went beyond my one window boundary.  All of the guards really don't know what to say to me.  They can't even imagine what has to be done.  I asked if I could help with inmate needs such as working on lists.  Did I say "lists"?  What's happening to me?  I don't wait for them to tell me what to do.  After all, how can lost leaders lead?

I'm sure that every day a total cleaning like today's isn't going to be necessary, and they hinted that I may get to supervise the cleaning of the food carts in the steam cleaning operation downstairs. (They were only teasing me, I later found out.  There was no such steam cleaning process available.)

I am still writing here at 12:00P.M. and the CO's just came to my cell and asked if I have some paper for some of the inmates?  Of course, I gave them some of my "authorized" paper.  They don't have paper to give to the inmates.  With a $60,000,000,000 prison budget … how can that be?

The spitters saluted and thanked me for cleaning the front of their cell.  I don't know why that also made me cry tonight.  Tonight has a different kind of entry.  I am sort of glad it does.  It may show you that the essence of the man put in prison by a governmental organization that is as lost as the institution in which I am now housed, feels the devastation – even though he endeavors to overcome it.  I still remember why we do worthwhile things in our lifetime!  This case, this battle, reform of the SEC and the BOP, those faces I saw today, and the beating drum of my anger instills in me a desire to help other victims of this system and to expose this secret for those who cannot speak for themselves.

By the way, I also cleaned the law library, organized the books, removed garbage, catalogued the books others may want to read and cleaned the tops of multiple garbage cans. (rubber-flap types).  I scrubbed each with soap powder and they changed back to their original color!

I am desirous of symbolically remembering that this "cleaning" is a step towards the real justice projects ahead that need to be cleaned.  That means the agency trying to silence this whistleblower.

If a nail biting, orange plantation growing, civil contempt inmate can rise through the ranks to become "head slave", then every other dream we have on this matter can be accomplished.

By the way, the previous head slave was also caught making moonshine and selling it to the general population.  There's a story there, and when I sleep away these thoughts, I will return to being the eternal optimist with a sharp pen.  I will share that story with you.  Tonight fatigue slows my pen.  Oh, by the way, while I was mopping a counselor and a "suit" were going over records with the guards.  They dropped a pen, and only I noticed it.  After they left, I returned it to the guards because I thought it a "security breach". They've got the best "head slave" in prison country.  I'll try to utilize my entry into prison areas still unknown.  The stories will now continue for us beyond my window.

Chapter 35 – "A Fine Mess You've Gotten Us Into, Ollie!"

A great deal occurred during the night.   First two new inmates moved in next to the Muslims.   One guy looked like Tattoo from Fantasy Island (not much bigger) and the other guy was very heavy and big (sumo wrestler size).   I'll call him Ollie from that old "Stan and Ollie Show".

It's funny what sleep and two pieces of left over bread from yesterday with non-cold water can do to help your outlook.

As I looked outside my window I saw new stains on the floor.   During the night a new flood or mess must have happened.   Do you think the BOP has a night crew to just take cleanliness and defile it?   I'll find out.

When the guards delivered breakfast (I got up before them), I asked if they wanted me to begin early in the morning.   They looked at each other in disbelief.   Maybe a reverse work ethic can work here.   Well, the perks are flowing in now.   I received farina and plums for breakfast. Being "head slave" has delivered me a different breakfast!   They are going to come get me "later"; they were not yet ready for me in the early morning shift.   Asking them was satisfaction enough.   After I get out there, I'll check if everyone got the farina and if my "head slave" philosophy of feeding may have been coincidental.   (everyone got farina)

The doctor went to visit Ollie and Tattoo this morning.   I will let you know that story after I get around to their cell today.   I am not permitted to speak with prisoners so it is done like a prison camp whispering with Sgt. Schultz and Col. Klink (Hogan's Heroes) walking about.   In other words, it's easy, but we still have to sneak.

While the doctor is examining Tattoo, he was asking for something to read.   I feel like Batman or Superman must have felt (or at least Mighty Mouse), "Here I am to save the day".   I'll slide books under their door on their first day.   I'll give them hope and optimism.   I'll try to make them a test case.   We'll experiment together.   I'll put some paper and a pencil under the door as well.   I have to be careful, but imagine being able to become a double agent in here while living on the "edge".

My furor over yesterday's legal injustice will just have to be stored away. It has been said that diplomacy is knowing how to say "nice doggy" until you get a stick in your hand, or being able to tell someone to "Go to Hell" and have them then turn around and ask you for directions. Unfortunately, I'm only at the "nice doggy" stage, and it's already Hell in here.

I can't express how appreciated and timely last night's shareholder letter was. If you can, write a letter or email to someone who might appreciate it. It is powerful. It can be substituted with a phone call. I almost forgot, phone calls and computers are still permitted in most of America.

What a challenge! To mentally adopt all of these inmates and try, within my restricted capabilities, to perform acts of kindness by a smile, a word or an action. Here I go to the rescue........

After all, I already have a cape when I wear my jumpsuit unopened. Although the cape lays down, when I fly to help others maybe the cape will rise-up on my supporting winds of optimism.

Chapter 36 – My Coming Out Party

In my best imitation of Mother Theresa, I'm still conducting prison interviews and helping these strangers, soon to be friends, with hope, as the time passes by faster for all of us.

My head is spinning with all I have to tell you today. First of all, I was right about all the mopping I did yesterday. I only had limited sweeping and mopping needs today.

But the real news today is that I got into the ward which is not permitted by others to visit. I was there only for a few minutes and the CO's went crazy. They rushed me out. It's like the witness relocation wing. Why was I not put there? No one knows who these inmates are except the CO's. I assisted in the cleaning of those cells by supplying the materials through the bars to the CO who was handing it to them. You think some real big name snitches are there? I'll find out. I made big progress today. I'm starting to walk about without supervision. I now shower at night without handcuffs.

First, I farmed out my painting to a whole team of tan suited trustees. There's a color caste uniform system in prison. Light tan uniform trustees run the prison. They are friendly with the guards and they have the most important prison jobs. The general population is dressed in brown. Then there are the crazies. This is my team. We are handcuffed whenever we leave our cells. I, the head slave, work for the crazies who wear orange.

That reminds me of a rule in prison which takes some getting used to for civilians. Basically one prisoner of any color uniform cannot be in a room or on the floor when one of the crazies comes in. The reason I mention it is because when I work doing anything and a prisoner or visitor comes into the Day Room, I have to be put in a holding cell until they leave. When a "suit" comes in, back I go into the holding cell. What that means is I spend one hour in holding cells for every twenty-five minutes of working. When the cell opens, I'm running to get some work done before I get put back in a holding pen. During the "counts" I'm in for an hour at a time. That starting and stopping to a "task oriented" individual is unbearable. Now let me explain my second day as orderly/head slave.

Today was also my formal "coming out" day for the inmates. Showers went on for at least six hours. Each inmate would need one jumpsuit, one tee-shirt, one pair of underwear, socks (we don't have any) and a towel (we don't have many). Every inmate regardless of their appropriate size wants 5xxxx) (the bigger the better). We don't have what they want, so each post-shower dressing ritual is memorable. The screaming, joking, laughter and anger changes with each inmate. Today some inmates were angry because they were standing in the "post shower" cell for over an hour. The CO's tried to minimize their frustration but the "rules" don't let them move inmates unless there are at least three CO's in the Day Room. The solution to prisoner frustration by the CO was to tell them to take another shower and to stop yelling. My cleanliness has gotten a few of the CO's to start calling me Felix (I guess that's a compliment to get a nickname from idiots in my second day). Most just call me by my last name. It won't be too long before my gang name will be earned.

I cleaned that slop room I discussed last night for 2 hours (it's only 6'x8'). That's about 45 minutes of working and the rest of the time standing in cells waiting to go back to work. This shower experience is when the inmates get to meet you and to test you. For example, the loudest screamer and old timer on the ward yelled to one of the other inmates, while he was waiting to be taken back to his cell, that he could do another year in prison on his head. He then turned his verbal abuse to the new head slave and started to complain when I couldn't give him a 5xxx jumpsuit.) I responded by saying, "Maybe you're spending too much time on your head because you can fit into this 3XL". Well, prison humor and pack testing is a great deal like men hanging out on the corner. He laughed and said "you're alright, the rest of you guys stop fucking with him; he's the best orderly we've ever had here." The guards laughed, and said I was now their choice for inmate of the year.

The place is spotless. The guards are even taking some pride in it. They gave me an extra dinner tonight and they put it aside for me. But one of the more robust guards ate it anyway. Well, enough about my thoughts to level the playing field and eat more.

Ollie the new inmate we previously discussed, whispered, as I was picking up food trays, if I could find him a Jewish Bible? I said a "Torah"? He was flabbergasted! I said I would get it, because I had organized the law library books yesterday. I gave the CO's at least fifteen books and magazines to give to inmates. I gave out over twenty-five rolls of toilet paper because I actually implemented the toilet paper center rule on door knobs.

However the desire to have more than your fellow man even exists in a poor prison. While cleaning out some vacant cells today, I found a stockpile of twenty-three rolls of toilet paper stacked like I remember White Castle hamburger boxes. Why hoard toilet paper? I don't know, yet.

I got Ollie his Bible, and I organized the various inmate requests by reminding guards of promises they had made to the inmates during the day. We waxed the Day Room today after giving forty showers and then I had to clean and scrub on my knees each of the five green molded showers when showers were finished. As I approached the "Evening Boss" who was new to me (you see, every eight hours four new guards arrive); he said, "God, when did they get you? You are doing this alone? My other floor has three orderlies and this place is more spotless with just one".

All in all, their trust and confidence in me after only two days will probably bring us multiple story benefits as the days go on. The "suits" and Warden are coming tomorrow for inspection. I still have had no phone, no mouse traps, no nail clippers, no haircut, no law library - but that reminds me of a potential problem downstairs with my lawyer. He has been taking this diary and other notes to my wife and scanning and faxing them to her. My poor wife was yelling at someone in the prison and said she knew I couldn't make a phone call. They began an internal investigation, and my future writings may be prevented. I may have to go through a censor every day. That may end the truthfulness of this diary as if I had died in prison. Let's see what happens.

When I was cleaning a shower today I found, under the drain, (it was moving) a hiding place for what looked like a knife. I told Rutgers and he said "don't tell anyone, I'll spot check it tomorrow." If they think that you told me, then you'll be in danger. The realities of both sides of the orderly fence here add to my growing picture of prison life. We received six new inmates tonight. I also prepared their cells and got blankets and sheets and towels ready for them. In anticipation of new arrivals, normally these guards are accustomed to run about and complain about the tasks necessary to receive them. I asked which cells we were going to give them and would they like the items placed in their cells. This was "a fucking wonderful idea" and then two of the CO's engaged in an argument over which of them was dumber than the other. Move over Sgt. Schultz.

My forty-six inmates on six wards are tucked in tonight with showers, clean clothes, books and a few smiles and laughs. The guards even hung up their jackets today because I have been hanging them up when they used to drape them over chairs and desks. Today, I started giving the guards washcloths when they washed their hands in front of the laundry room, like a bathroom valet. They felt like royalty. I'm winning.

As personal inmate "property" was being inspected while the inmate watched the CO go through each item, the CO was sitting on a plastic carrying bucket. Seeing that, I rolled over a big chair. I said nothing and took the bucket away, and the same CO who the first night said "let's see if you can handle a real job like a blue collar orderly" came over later and thanked me.

Remember that new head CO I said was new to me? When we first met, I thought it was going to be a very long night as he was a real government type guy who did everything by the numbers. When the evening was over, he wanted me to call him when I get out. He said, I was the hardest working and most efficient orderly he had seen in 9 years on the job. I didn't do much except refuse to allow this place to make me yawn, dislike the people who are here, refuse to engage on a negative level, and to say "hello" with my eyes, my words and my secret prison hand signal.

Today when an inmate was walking by in cuffs, I gave him the Roman hello signal, his eyes were filled with fear and dread upon his arrival in our hole, I could see a positive facial reaction which may have aided him. I hope so.

As I return back to the home front of my eight cell tier while I have been about the "ponderosa", I realize that the terrorists now salute me and the two medicated ones in solitary are enjoying the books which seemed to have quieted them. Tomorrow I may be painting or it may be a maintenance day or I may be preparing for next weeks "inspection" by the "suits". Their scheduled annual inspection and related stories should be worth the price of admission. This unit has never passed that annual inspection, or

so I am told. Although I was promised a phone call tonight, the phone has still not arrived. It may not arrive, and then again it may arrive soon. Honestly, I do not know. I have given up caring.

Sadly, tonight I received next week's commissary form. I thought that when I filled out last week's form, I would be home by today. Since I have learned that prison is the opposite of reality, I will order more items tonight than I should need. That should get me out of here faster. I'll give away whatever I have left.

The Commissary prices seem a bit high, but who am I to say? I seem to be in here so long, I may have forgotten grocery costs on the outside. No, these prices are high! It also requires an investigation. Someone is stealing more than time and self-respect from these inmates.

Tomorrow is Thursday and its weekly inspection day. I will be up early so that I can do any last minute touch ups to impress those who do very little. These COs, good and bad alike, have a very difficult job, but they are without the necessary skill sets to create the environment, both physically and psychologically, necessary to effectuate a difference.

The camaraderie amongst the correction officers is quite understandable. Their job requires interaction with each other and the unnatural stress of treating the prisoners like animals. Emotional detachment is a way of handling the obvious contradictions of reality they witness daily. Remember they too must report to this prison daily and must absorb these emotions and actions for 20 or more years. This supports their need for brotherhood. But like in any governmental rank structure, the titles and red tape allow some officers to work harder than others for the same salary. Many, as expected, are rewarded for governmental mediocrity.

As I observe the officers, while I am locked in a cell waiting to begin working, their job is tedious and stressful. They are always living with the risk of one slip up or one criminal spitting, throwing defecation or just biting them to destroy their future hopes and dreams. That must be frightening. They run a boarding house for people who don't want to be there. They bond with some inmates. Some inmates return and some familiarity reinforces their feelings of attachment to these wounded puppies. All eventually leave and then the prisoners are not permitted to write. They also live with the fear of being recognized out of prison on the streets years later. They are only the symbolic authority figure, but the "suits" and Judges have the real authority and protection.

An example of what a CO goes through with most '"suits"' is a hardened military sergeant having to listen to young 2nd Lieutenant who has no knowledge of the task at hand. Add to that difficulty, counselors who do nothing but cause tension and anger for the inmates. Yet a CO has no real influence on most of the lists. The guards are inspected by the "suits", but why can't the CO's inspect and complete what they are actually responsible for?

All day I watch the 20 year old prison "suits", checking up on the experienced older guards and telling them they saw dirt on the floor of a cage, or that it wasn't locked or any other "suit" kind of justification for doing nothing. The "suits" appear petrified of the inmates which adds to the contempt the guards have for the "suits".

The worst are the women guards who want to be "one of the guys". Nevertheless, the yelling tonight by the guards has increased. The inmates are a bit upset about no phone calls. As I sit in my cell tonight, I wish I was out there to help them organize the phone "lists". But even head slaves have limitations.

Some of the guards use excuses not to work. On the other hand, some of the CO's are very professional. However, they all need constant counseling! They may have one of the worst jobs in the prison system -

except, of course, the "head slave" of the orange legion of psychopaths (OLP). Outside my door last night was another flood from the "terrorists". They must again have had a toilet issue. I will be getting this cleaned again this morning.

Chapter 37 – Expanding the Team

Today was one of those non-stop experiences. I got an early morning wake-up because the same water problem across the hall in the terrorist's cell has now completely flooded my cell and four others during the night. Since the terrorists are quarantined, my reluctant desire to pick up and disinfect started before 6:30A.M. My team was increased by two other inmates. No one is officially in charge, but they seem to listen to this old guy.

Their names and personalities define this system. Let's call one ""Evil"" (his name is like that) and the other one's name is a territory in New York but let's call him "Tex". Both should be in prison and serve out their initial terms. Their current terms however, are too long, as both have increased the length of their terms with added time as permitted by the BOP. They refuse to reduce their own sentences by "walking the plank", as I learned today. Walking the plank is lying about events or giving up names of other gang members. "Evil" and I painted fourteen steel doors today. All three of us then fully cleaned the entire ward. Tex is in charge of the laundry so we helped him, but he did most of the folding and organizing. Frankly, it was enjoyable working with them. They may not be too motivated. Prisoners pace themselves differently than we do with regard to task completion.

The best part of my day came when I was asked to go down to that witness relocation ward (WRW) again. This CO, who was asking to go to the WRW, was looking to get yesterday's guard in trouble. I was asked by another CO why I thought I couldn't go down to that ward. I answered, "I believe that's the WRW, Sir". All hell then broke loose and at least three other CO's were called over to hear my words because this was supposedly a big secret and I should not have known about the special ward. By the way, every prisoner on the floor knows about it! Prisoners have a terrific gossip and communication system, and it is called convict network news (CNN).

Here's my day's best story. It was determined by the powers that be that I could be the only one to paint doors on the WRW. No one else could be trusted. They knew I didn't know anyone, but the other two orderlies couldn't be trusted. They knew everyone in the prison. They have friends everywhere in many prisons.

It's important to note that this was my first dinner date since I came to prison. We three were locked in the laundry and we sat on boxes and ate dinner together. Listening to the ins and outs of prison life, the games the "suits" play and observing the special relationship both these young men had with the CO's was revealing and also perplexing. It's difficult to remain emotionally detached in a prison setting.

While locked in the relocation ward cleaning, no one was allowed in. I was directed to completely paint the ceiling, walls, floor, and desk in four cells. All cells have worn gray floors and graffiti on the white walls and a white ceiling with dirty white bars on the blacked out window. I was working in each hot cell for at least an hour. I was covered with paint. The guards said that, during the Warden's walk through today, the "suits" exhibited the best reaction they had in many years. And yet still, no phone call has been permitted me. By the way, all four food carts were cleaned by me with a comet type powder disinfectant and they may speak about how clean they were for years. I folded a white towel to completely cover the top of these carts so food would not touch the cart, and I have been replacing the towels every few days. One comment was, "He's turning this into the fucking Ritz". My constant vigilance has made these club house guards self-conscious about dropping food and things and then stepping on them. I walk about with a broom, mop, and spray bottle and the bosses (Lieutenants, Captains and "suits") have made it clear to everyone to just leave me alone.

Now back to the relocation wing, after I finished painting the second cell and decided that since no one was supervising me and because they really hadn't told me to stay only in the cells that I was cleaning and painting, I would cause a little confusion and laughter.

First, I threw my extra brush to the end of the ward so that in case I got caught walking about, I would have an excuse. I could say I was retrieving it, as I walked past the other occupied cells. All I did was pretend to be cutting my neck with a make believe knife. I then went back into my painting project laughing at the screaming from these frightened guys. Fortunately, prison quality control was in full bloom and the CO's were having a great time eating in the Day Room and never responded to the frightened yelling of the squealers, as they are called by the other orange inmates.

After finally painting the last cell, I must confess I was exhausted. I was as wet with perspiration as I have ever been in my entire life. One guard said, "Shit, I'd live in here". I however felt that I was making this world a little softer and professional. It touched me to think I would make this prison better than the way I found it. Only forty more cells to paint and miles to go before I sleep. (with apologies to Robert Frost)

With not much strength left in my shaking legs, I was told by the CO's I had come to the "top" of the haircut list. The barber wasn't allowed any scissors other than a very dull trimmer. It's not one of my best haircuts, but hopefully my hair will grow back. I am so hot and busy, so a shorter prison hairstyle will hopefully be fine.

I experienced a funny dialogue with one of the CO's who pointed to a cell I was painting. He asked me if I knew who had been in that cell. Since I knew that John Gotti was imprisoned here, I said, "I guess John Gotti." "Jesus, Felix, how did you know that?" was his response.

Fifteen inmates left to go to general population today. You know by now that means I clean out their cells and cart away dirty linens and take away garbage and then repaint the cells if possible. Often there isn't time to paint because we need the cell. Note I said "we". OMG!

The Warden and the "suits" were sixteen in number during this Thursday inspection. I sat in the laundry cage and no one acknowledged me, but I knew "something was up" because earlier in the day one of the CO's asked "have you been sending notes to your wife through your attorney?" We have to send letters through the mail so they can monitor them.

I've only been here a short while, but today I put this entry of the diary into my shoe and did not leave it in my cell. Sure enough, the "suits" conducted a search of my cell! I passed with flying colors. My bunk was admired by the "suits". By the way, today over six "suits" each checked the same fire extinguisher tag. They really have nothing to do. The weekly inspection is all show and without substance.

Tonight I received a trustee two piece type orange uniform, and in prison it is considered very cool. This is a more comfortable way to work instead of the one piece restricted movement jumpsuit. All the inmates want these two piece outfits. Why we don't have them instead of those impractical jumpsuits has to do with a governmental thought process or brother-in-law contract.

As inmates were leaving our ward tonight, many acknowledged my initial cleanliness changes with appreciation. Some went to Leavenworth, others to prison names I do not remember. Most went to general population here in our own jail.

Chapter 38 – I'm Seeing Changes in Here

Tonight I got the phone. I couldn't get through because this time the voice computer said I had "insufficient funds". I do not know how that is possible, but tomorrow I have to check with my attorney and wife.

My poor wife does not understand that calling to this prison for resolution of a problem is like calling Auschwitz and complaining about the treatment of your loved one. The result was an investigation. The diary will continue, but my wife's wrath at the prison has redirected the punishment and scrutiny onto me. I will have to be more careful as I continue getting this diary to my attorney and to write and send unfiltered messages to loved ones.

Today I saw a very large prisoner crying in a holding cell, when I walked by. I went to my cell which is sometimes left open now, and got books, paper and a piece of candy I had purchased at the commissary, and I gave them to him. Seeing a man that physically intimidating cry in appreciation was a memory I will hold for years after I depart. He had wanted a book for weeks. This was my first time ever meeting him. He stopped crying and his grateful eyes empowered me.

A Spanish inmate actually asked for one Spanish book. I gave him six. I hope he likes them. I had no idea what they were about. My Spanish dictionary has not arrived. I await a Chinese prisoner. I have so many Chinese books.

My two co-orderlies know everyone and are a new source of additional stories. They told me of some lifers who are in this prison and they seemed to know who everyone is and when events are going to occur before they actually do.

The CO's have begun gearing up for our next Thursday's General Annual Inspection (GAI). According to some of the correction officers, I am told that they always waited until the last second of the last weekend for the last 9 years to prepare. This time, they are letting me work on my check list and the inspection guideline forms.

Unfortunately, the fifty or so inmates now call my name repeatedly with the frequency of the CO's. They call me "Mr. A." or "Richard". Hearing it throughout the night while I locked in reminds me of my limited ability to help. I try to respond each time they call my name. Responding helps them more than whatever object they are requesting. Acknowledging them is critical. Engaging them is priceless. (with apologies to MasterCard)

I am most disturbed at why my phone call didn't go through last night. I am guaranteed that hundreds of dollars have been put into the inmate account. Once again this is an inexcusable bureaucratic embarrassment and prison incompetency.

While I was painting today, I must have disturbed one of the other sleeping two solitaries. He angrily charged the door and I almost dropped my roller and started running. However, ""Evil"", who does 500 pull-ups and 1000 pushups daily, came to my rescue. After he spoke to the inmate, I am now respected like the meanest orderly on the floor. It is good to have these two prison mentors.

I listen to stories of the inmates' lives and listen to my new "friends" while I still must tongue-in-cheek treat the CO's as if they are Sgt. Schultz of "Hogan's Heroes". Most of the time they do not disappoint me.

After I finished painting six more cells, I returned to the Day Room and announced that I had decided this time to paint the gray floors white and the white walls gray. Their shocked reaction was priceless, although one of them said at least it would cut down on graffiti. Individuality or creativity is not a governmental trait. All cells are white walls and gray floors with gray doors. They have always been. Until we get someone to help us change the system, they always will be these colors.

By the way, I found new paint and those doors are now perfect, although there still is a debate going on amongst the guards over painting the locks.

Morale on the floor is good. Tomorrow is another shower day and everything is not ready for the inmates because the guards often don't let me finish the jobs needed. Everything is only "good enough for government work".

Today I processed by far the most prison information of all my earlier entries. I spent time cleaning inside the upstairs actual command post of the Day room where all cell cameras and monitoring of cells takes place. It is rare to get inside this area. Even "Evil" and Tex were asking me about what I saw.

Additionally, I spent over two hours with my other orderlies and was allowed to really get into the minds of these two prisoners. This is not about understanding my civil contempt mind, but it's about their abused and very different life experiences.

I met with my attorney today who promised he will get me out because he was the one responsible for me being in here in the first place. What a relief! A truthful lawyer.

I was given a second two piece uniform. To the other prisoners this is a symbol of status and respect. Respect for me, is going home, but patience is required.

I learned about the Bloods, Crypts, Latin Kings and many other "gangs" whose names and customs I will share with you in a future entry. I will become an honorary member of a gang later in this diary to protect myself from a death threat.

I must have worked harder today than other day in prison. I snuck toothpaste and toothbrushes to every inmate. Most inmates did not have them.

During showers the inmates greeted me like Mother Theresa as I gave them whatever they wanted in clothes, and I actually responded to their sizing requests. All the jumpsuits were cleaned. They had never cleaned them in the past. They only dried them after they sat on the floor of the shower.

Today, two guards from another ward tried to steal me away because our (9 South SHU) has become the cleanest and best ward in the prison (according to my ""Evil"" sources).

I totally renovated, with my two helpers, over ten cells - complete with painting job. Cell painting has rarely been done since the prison was opened twenty years ago.

I had inmates laughing during showers because I have been permitted to engage them, and these guards are finding a different mood from the inmates. I can hear it and see it.

Oh, today I also found out I am surrounded by, including one of my uncuffed orderly helpers, mostly murderers with multi-life sentences. How comfortable I feel now to be locked up with them, as we eat dinner together, alone.

Inmates were actually bringing finished books to the shower so I could help them trade with each other. The dialogue and laughter were like children laughing in a home after years of silence and tension had been removed.

"Ollie" left and he asked me if I could find him a larger jumpsuit (brown). Well, we only have orange outfits but I told him our tailor didn't work on Shabbat. (Jewish Sabbath).

He was carrying the Torah and another book and laughingly thanked me for helping him and smiled about the tailor story. That makes me happy too.

A one legged inmate was brought in today. Yes, a one legged prisoner. More on that story to follow. I'm sure they'll put him on the top bunk. Sure enough, I was right.

Chapter 39 - Playing Ball in the Day Room

During the evening count, my two orderly advisors, (ever since I found out about their crimes, I call them advisors) got into an argument which turned from a simple argument to a "Disrespect Issue". This frightened me into believing a physical encounter, was imminent. Anger management is a critical need in this place, yet it is non-existent.

Another big event of this day was being requested by the guards to clean up their area on a different floor. I set the tone upon arriving with their lunch boxes. They told me to deliver these four Styrofoam trays and leave. I said, "Does that mean there will be no tip?" They marveled at my simple ability of task completion, pride, and cyclone cleaning effort. Perhaps my intense efforts are re-directed anger into my symbolic cleanup of a judicial system that dispatches sentences, not to protect us, but to justify their own existence. (Sorry Judge, but I will clean up your mess in due time)

Let's try to chronicle the day, concentrating on those more relevant stories in depth.

Going into that command post showed me the limited number of monitors actually functioning, and no one was watching them! When you can do something for these staff members and you make them look better than they really are, there is a trust that occurs. I will continue to do that. I can't help the inmates unless the guards trust me first.

Today I found out from my two "orderly advisors" (OA) that there are multiple ways to kill yourself in prison, and the system almost encourages it. How informative.

A big fight occurred today during the inmate's Friday basketball game (brown suits) conducted on the roof. It required screaming and running from most of our CO's. It was a full prison alert. I heard that stabbings were involved. Six new bloodied inmates came to stay with us this evening.

I should not be here, but I have changed this place in these past four days. Staff now, throughout the prison, treat me surprisingly different. When I was on the elevator, a stranger said "Are you the one that's making 9 South so clean?". None of these minimal accomplishments will be on my next resume'. None of these initial days of changing a broken corporate culture mean a thing to me except, I did it! The inmate attitude when I pick-up their trays has gone from sullen silence to "Hello ("Mr. A. or Richard"), thank-you for that book or that toilet paper". Oh yeah, I put another roll on everyone's door knob! The view of 40 rolls standing at attention was hilarious to only me. Speaking of that, I cleaned the work station (computer) of the guards and have almost made it to the cleaning of the untouchable desk, refrigerator, and private storage areas of the guards. I also saw my reflection today while cleaning the "big bosses" bathroom. The mirror showed me (being that I haven't seen a mirror since my initial arrival) that my prison haircut was really horrible - almost a Charles Manson type cut, but, "It is what it is".

Loyalty from my two neighboring terrorists was further bought today with eight smuggled mayonnaise packets and an old newspaper. They now salute me. The guards have started treating these happier and less aggressive inmates with a softer approach.

Even the seasoned solitaires that were initially standoffish were bought off for 5x tee shirts and extra towels. I found a hidden box of socks and distributed them. I could run today for Prison Mayor.

As the guards were watching me work, one said "Altomare, you like baseball?" I gave my baseball background and ended it with that I threw out the first ball at Shea Stadium last year. Men of this humble background could not believe it. So to prove to them I could play baseball, I had to throw a roll of toilet paper across the Day Room right handed. They were impressed when I then took it and wound up and threw a strike left handed. Rutgers then said he would never question me again on anything. To even men of this stature I today became "accepted". (Oh, woe is me.)

Today while inmates, due to the rules and regulations, were angrily waiting after their showers to go back to their cells. Their anger and frustration turned to complete joy when I snuck toothbrushes, extra soap and socks into their hands.

Morale for some inmates has improved, because when I assist in serving food, I bring "extra" for those who seem to need it.

My inability to get through the phone system last night exposed yet another pathetic procedural roadblock. Only a governmental system could create these mistakes. My commissary account had to be transferred to my phone account. How does one do it? Not one CO or any Lieutenant knew. Not one document or rulebook explained it. They actually told me to ask some inmates; maybe they will know the answer. The guards who don't know how to do this may have worked here for over a decade.

One of the inmates instructed me on how to transfer funds. My problem now is the evening CO's said, "You got the phone last night, you can't speak every night". I decided to try tomorrow when the day crew will be on duty.

I observed the unfairness of some guards who bully, lie and intimidate these inmates by taking away their privileges of phone, radio, letters or visits. These inmates, on paper, have many rights but the forms are never made accessible. Most prisoners increase the length of their jail time while "visiting" these institutions through UCMJ punishments. The UCMJ system entraps and checkmates many of these inmates who are without the proper legal sophistication.

My twenty-four year old ""Evil"" advisor has been in six prisons and has a long sentence. During one lock down, I could see his anger rising, as he took out an illegal pen, clicked it repeatedly and threatened to stab my other advisor, Tex. My two orderly advisors are thirty-five years younger than me and one of the guards told me that they asked him if I was on drugs because I am always working and no one has to tell me what to do. They think I am like Radar from "MASH". I guess that's a compliment, but unlike Klinger I won't be staying when it's time to leave.

Watching the guards fighting over who can use me for personal projects without any of them knowing, like Hogan and Sgt. Schultz, that I'm studying them, (like a business takeover) amuses me.

Watching them being unable to task complete and helping them with their inept attempts at forms and inspections is pathetically tragic.

Looking at the duplicitous confusion of forms, lists and memos from these "suits" and watching the guards shutting down with indifference further explains many of the organizational breakdowns in here.

A touching moment manifested itself when my big CO "Tiny" said, "If you are released before our inspection, will you stay to help us"? I gather their need to score well is critical to improve their past record of governmental mediocrity. My answer was, "I'll pretend to be sick so you can tell the Judge I'm in the hospital until you get through this inspection." He bought it and went back to being overwhelmed by the list of things to do, as I chip away at the projects. While I engage my fellow assistants to keep working, I would not spend a second longer than required to remain for their meaningless inspection. They correct and prioritize the physical building problems, but ignore the emotional inmate and staff problems.

By the way, the work ethic of my two orderlies is zombie like until I engage them. I work harder than them and give them clear tasks and praise them. On that note, I have by now done over twenty of these complete cell renovations and not one CO has come to inspect even one of them. They are so intimidated by the routine daily tasks at hand, it immobilizes them.

While inmates were standing today in the "shower waiting cell", I visited them and explained why they had to wait so long.        I explained the 3-guard rules. (no inmate can move unless there are 3 guards present) This, they now understand. It removed the disrespect and anger issues.

There is no supervision or protection when I am locked in the laundry with these two other criminals for hours at a time. No one could have heard anything if I were attacked or beaten. I should not be left unsupervised if they wanted to protect me - maybe they don't.

Chapter 40 – "Shift"ing Priorities

Today was a very different kind of day than the one I expected to have. Although the regular daytime CO's gave me a wish list of projects to be completed by the inspection date, not one of the other weekend guards "got around" to letting me out of my cell until after 12:30. By that time they had watched one video and were sitting around doing absolutely nothing and they were making the place look like a college dorm room. When one can see progress being made, watching others try to slow it down to their comfort speed is frustrating.

When I did get out of my cell, I threw myself into action. The place had been defiled. It was as if their contempt for themselves and their clubhouse were threatened by an inmate changing their dysfunctional status-quo. They were going to return it to a comfort level of filth. The transformation was so stark that it had to be intentional.

Two "counts" took place while I festered in that cell this morning waiting to get out. Fours and a half hours after they offered to release me, they walked the twenty steps to let me out. For five hours I was ready and dressed, but I possess no key to leave solitary.

One of my orderlies watched me paint ten more doors and clean four more tiers while he just worked out in the hallway with the large paint buckets as gym weights. Remember he's in for life so I continued working until the spirit to work moved him. I talked to him, as I painted and still my sense of decency and work ethic were being tested. He did nothing. I said nothing.

My nails are so long that they cut the plastic food handling gloves I wear when cleaning because we don't have the heavier work gloves. No nail clippers have been available since day One. On paper we have all of these items.

I shellacked many pieces of wood such as hand rails and returned the place by early evening back to my standard of hygiene. These guards never moved during my cleaning activities to aid any inmate. They simply get paid to watch T.V., which they bring in or surf computer porn. During the count they returned me to my cell even though I had all of my painting equipment still to clean.  I am writing this to you as I sit in my cell and they have not come to allow me to complete the tasks that need to be done. They seem to not want me to finish them.

One of the guards said, work slower you're making many of us who get paid, uncomfortable.  "Uncomfortable"!  What a broken work ethic exists here.

Even after the total renovation of multiple cells, it hasn't brought one guard to marvel at how much better the cells and facility now look.  The inmates however like the clean smell and the effort.

The inmates must sense I am upset with these guards because there is an unusual amount of banging and screaming for attention and food by the inmates tonight.  I must accept that despite my desires to improve everything today I can't help the guards change.  Being locked in the cell reminds me of the anger and injustice this incarceration represents. Returning to extended isolation after only five days of orderly release is quite painful.

Having to genuflect and work for non-task completing idiots and emotional children saddled also with a governmental mind set is a difficult assignment because it is more than a slave and master relationship.

Knowing that my adversaries would like to silence me for a longer period of time concerns me, but I know that my optimism will never allow the truth to be silenced.

When a new shift of CO's came to work, this day turned around!  The regulars came in and read the riot act to the other guards.  Boy, did I take this place up some notches today.  At the same time I distributed extra food, books and smiles to "my" inmates.          I must burn 2000 calories daily working.   I have never perspired like this.  Food wasn't too great today, but the guards allowed me to reach yet a new level of inmate window cleaning cleanliness.     I saw an officer throw a New York Post into the garbage pail.       I took it into my little slop room extracted it from the garbage and gave it to an old man who has been asking for a newspaper.  Imagine today's news!  I wanted to read it, but that newspaper means more to some of these men than me. Imagine inmates can't read about the world they are hoping to reenter.

We might have about sixty stairs total, up and down, to the cells that have only been mopped for twenty years – not painted. Today they were scrubbed and painted stair by stair and the reaction of one guard was, "My God, do you guys see what these fucking stairs are supposed to look like"?

My orderly advisors asked me tonight to help Tex with a response to a prison problem he has. Believe me what I am to tell you now is critical to Tex. It is critical because his penalty was 120 days loss of phone and 120 days loss of commissary privileges. Here's the story, but don't forget to remind me to tell you about my new "gang" friends now in prison.

Here's the problem, according to Tex. He has bottom bunk privilege. These upper bunks are very difficult to climb up to and to get down. If a CO doesn't like you, prison time can be very hard. His former CO moved someone into his cell and told Tex to go to the top bunk. He gave her his medical permission form for a lower bunk. To you and me that would be the end of the issue. The CO then brought in 100 inmates from his unit for an announcement. One of them had to give up their bottom bunk to Tex. How was Tex going to be greeted by his roommate or any of the other inmates who would have to go to the unpopular top bunk? Tex requested a complaint form and claimed that was all he did. The CO, according to Tex, then lied and said Tex threatened her and refused her direct order. It's Tex vs. the CO. It's like me vs. government, decided by a government appointed Judge. They get the inside track. I had to help Tex write his response. I could see his temper surfacing as I tried to rewrite his Junior High School writing style. He kept repeating the same facts to the point of sounding like Rain Man. All ""Evil"", the other orderly, did was pushups and laughed at my seemingly impossible task. I wrote it. I hope he submits my version, but Tex has some issues in confusing my suggestions with a "disrespect" of his writing style.

Chapter 41 – "Dogman" Appears

Today, I had my first class in gang history with "Evil". I was shocked at the size and scope of this epidemic, which is purposely or ignorantly fueled by the BOP - not contained by it. Gang members are exactly where they want to be. They are with all their extended family members who they care about in a controlled environment where they still have turf and respect issues to fight about all day. They are supervised by at least thirty percent unqualified and belligerent guards. Forty percent of the guards are top notch trying to add value to the inmates' lives. The remaining thirty percent are initially effective, but "burn out" quickly and join the initial thirty percent. As Winston Churchill once said, "most men die at forty, but we don't bury them until they are seventy-five". These men have a countdown calendar available at all times waiting to retire. This environment is one of containment, "suits" and forms. Some of the guards, I am told, may even be undercover and paid gang members.

In our unit now there are many Bloods, Crypts and other gang members. ("Evil" is making a list for me) It breaks my heart to see that "Evil" is more comfortable being institutionalized than going home to his family and society. He no longer belongs in our world. He belongs in spirit to the BOP.

The guards and the inmates have familiar historical references, common prisoners and shared history. Prisoner and guards names are discussed like you and I, when in high school, discussed our teacher's names. It is astounding to listen to. It makes you feel so left out. That feeling only lasts a short time for me until reality reappears.

Well, tonight the phone draught ended! I didn't speak. I called. Believe it or not, my wife didn't answer! At least I have completed an almost impossible task in this environment. This must be the end of my phone complaints! My wife didn't have her cell phone with her. Leaving a message after hearing her voice was devastating for me.

They now leave my cell door open. How's that for prison power? They lock it at night, but during the day I have been able to return back and forth without cuffs and without locks.

I also forgot to tell you, my other perks are rolling in now, because I work like a man possessed. I now get new clothes every night and extra food if I wanted it. My food intake has remained the same simply because the food is just not to my liking. I give any extra food to those who seem to need it the most.

The book problem continues despite my efforts to circulate those newly found books. The books often leave with the inmates (they are criminals, you know). Tonight I am a little sad that I have not spoken to my wife. I will begin reading the History of the Iroquois Indians, my newest book. I hope they at least had a salt business.

As in life, some of the CO's become closer to some inmates more than others. As this diary concludes, I'll tell you of my favorite guards. By the way, I am working on a secret cuffed tour by one of the guards to show me other parts of the prison. I don't know if I can pull it off. But I sure hope I can see some of the areas like Recreation, Medical and some other areas I have been told exist. By the way, I am now the only one authorized into the witness relocation wing. I guess some people here don't think I deserve to be in prison. I don't want you to think that these inmates are not still crazy and quite humorous. Over the past few entries I tried to show you the guard side, and I may not have given proper attention to the inmate evening sounds and daily stories. I'm not sure who it is because it's recent, but one of the inmates has truly developed a skill of sounding like a dog. His howling, barking and growling can go on for hours at a time. I'll have to watch to see who shakes after their shower or until this "dogman" surfaces. Always remember, despite my need to survive and get through this unusual ordeal, I have continued to try to find redeeming characteristics of humanity here. Never forget I am surrounded by individuals in need of psychological mending, too many of them return and remain anti-social.

Remembering Tex's problem letter tonight simply confirms that their emotional and educational needs are not solved by incarceration alone. Psychological and educational help does not exist and therefore, there is no hope for rehabilitation.

Halliburton and other politically connected prison contracts should be examined. This is a poorly run government sink-hole. The costs of prison are far in excess of our needs of an experimental rehabilitative prison Peace Corps type program. It's an alternative that should be considered.

Chapter 42 – I Smell Smoke!

What does one say at 11:30 PM after they started working at 6:30AM? I'll try my best to recall and record the highlights of the day, as I stumble into my cell.

Today's projects included re-painting ten more steel doors four times each. I re-cleaned the five showers with scrub brushes and newly requisitioned chemicals. I then cleaned, swept and mopped twenty-two cells, and washed over seven hundred towels, sheets, blankets and clothes of inmates. I was jokingly offered keys by the Lieutenant because "I was doing everything here anyway". My two CO-orderlies said I looked like I was forty-five and refused to believe that a sixty year old can work harder than them. I also found twelve "violations" which the COs hadn't corrected prior to inspection. Watching me in orange walk around pointing out violations with my long fingernails for the guards following behind me must be a funny sight. That they have accepted me as their advisor is an unusual mental activity because of their preconceived dislike of most orange inmates.

I tested the plumbing in all vacant cells and I found two that were not working. I brought it to the attention of a new officer. His response still sticks in my head. He said, "How did you determine that the toilets were not working?" I responded that I had simply flushed them. He responded "Outstanding!" I'm still trying to understand the dialogue.

With the big inspection tomorrow one of the CO's continued to do things to annoy my two other orderlies who were actually getting involved in the inspection. He knew that my advisors thought we should not be making any mess until tomorrow since everything was pristine. He wanted to be confrontational with them. I avoided the impending situation which was effectuated by simply moving them to the laundry area.

By the way, Tex "used" all of yesterday's suggestions, and I wrote something else for him today on another property issue. Some officer stole his property.

I circulated another fourteen books today and eighteen magazines.

Tonight the CO's didn't even bother to lock me in the shower. Progress and trust are developing and growing daily.

During this busy day, inmates have been well attended to and almost all of them had showers today. We are told to expect as many as ten new arrivals after the inspection tonight. I had to prepare for them.

Today a senior lieutenant, let's call him "Charity" told the CO's to stay put at their desk as he would prefer to work and speak with only me. "The rest of you don't know how to work". This is another big step because the defensive CO's said "He's like Superman. He makes us tired. Nobody does time like this guy".

While I am writing to you, the COs have just inspected "Evil's" cell because they smelled smoke. I may lose him if they find that he was smoking. How it could happen mystifies me (if it is true). I'll report tomorrow if anything does happen, and they replace "Evil" with another new inmate.

Chapter 43 – Toilet Thoughts

I find that one advantage of fatigue is that time passes faster. I'm reading fewer books, and I'm collapsing to sleep rather than angrily lying in a place I should never have been put in the first place.

Tomorrow my poor wife is going to see her, "humbled" husband for the first time in thirty-five days. From my horrific haircut, to the prison clothes, to my loss of weight, along with her seeing other convicts in the visiting room plus what she will go through to get inside; my heart goes out for *her* first day in prison.

In anticipation of the big inspection the guards slept, watched TV, ordered food and read. There is still one sweetheart of a CO who may be a bit slow and "laidback". He has been reading Moby Dick for the past thirty days and he seems to still be on the first twenty pages of the book. He rarely does much work anyway, so his work ethic and reading speed are the same.

Today became an insightful day when "Evil" marveled at how I spoke to people, and his keen observation saw the trust and personal freedoms that followed. So he started speaking like me, and a guard said ""Evil", I am so impressed at what you are learning from Mr. Altomare". I responded that we had a deal, either he became more like me or I had to join his gang. The guard laughed at the absurdity of my being accepted, but learning the high gang rank of my new orderly friend created even more dialogue later. He is a General in his gang. Future gang discussions will follow as I learn how to better explain it to you.

The water flooding from the terrorists' cells continues. I have had to clean this same plumbing problem eight separate times. The staff is unable to grasp that they should simply avoid putting inmates into this cell to prevent this continual flooding. Each work shift has refused to move the terrorists and this logistical stupidity not only causes germs and hours of mopping each time, but the damage to infrastructure continues to intensify. Even with the inspection today, time will be spent with organizational stupidity and employee laziness. Preventive anything is not within their thought process. They are supposed to be the guardians for the lives and safety of others. The amount of wasted time mystifies me.

Chapter 44 – All Washed Up and Out

Well, it's the day of the inspection! Last night, I asked the CO on duty to please move the terrorists because the water from their toilets will flood into at least five other cells. He ignored my warning. This morning my cell was flooded so badly I couldn't get out of my bunk. Everyone was literally screaming for assistance. No one came to get me until 11:00 AM! I laid there in disbelief and frustration until I finally arrived on that inspection scene. The CO's had to finally be doing everything themselves. They were being graded by the "suits". Watching them actually work showed me why they don't normally work. Multi-tasking was non- existent.

Fortunately for me, I went to visit with my Wife. Upon returning two hours later, the "suits" were gone and the guards had the place looking like Christmas morning after the presents were unwrapped. They apparently were exhausted and the place was filthy and devastated yet again.

New inmates were arriving, and I was given all of my other jobs but also now I have the entire laundry responsibility. Tex was fired for filing a written complaint against his corrections officer. "That's the way it is."

Prior to beginning my newly expanded duties, everyone had to go back to their cells for a count. My cell was still under water. Nothing was done to remove the water except they promoted the CO who caused the water problem by his refusal to move the inmates before the incident occurred. You figure it! It astounds me!

After I leave this insane place, I can only imagine the disconnected treatment of the inmates without my daily help. This was a worry I didn't care to think about today.

Chapter 45 – Burn Baby Burn!

As the night moved by quickly a few interesting events surfaced. First, one of the CO's was talking to me and he found out that he went to a school where I had previously taught. That caused him to open up a bit. He saw me cleaning the lint from the dryer which should be done every day and the lint removed filled one 55 gallon size garbage bag! I said to the CO that removing the lint would prevent a fire. He said, "Every day I drive up to jail I pray it has burned down". How's that for corporate pride?

Then I found a hidden make-shift large knife and gave it to the CO. There was no reaction. Pride is dead here.

I continued reminding the CO's to move the terrorists because we would have a tenth flood tonight. Finally, they reluctantly agreed. Today I removed over thirty pails of unnecessary flood water.

Oh, I almost forgot, when they couldn't return me earlier to my cell, they put me in the cell where they put the violent inmates. This is the cell with chains for arms and legs. They told me I would be there for five minutes because my flooded cell could not be used. These spaces are like handicapped parking spaces. They must be kept available for emergencies (they have only two of these cells). One hour and a half later they remembered that I was there.      I finally made it to the cell reserved for the most dangerous inmates. What an accomplishment and documentary on this organization.    And to think, I did it in only thirty-six days!

The stress of today was not the work or the interaction, but that of the CO's governmental personalities and their work habits. A CO who just can't take the pressure and prison culture anymore has decided to transfer to another branch of the government. He put his business card in my shirt pocket. He said, "After this is over, I would love to hear more about your case; I have read a little and I think you are right". I really didn't know the protocol of a guard putting their card in your pocket. Later in the evening one of the other CO's was pretending to pat-down all of us orderlies. When he found the guard's handwritten card, his thought process of having an opportunity to bust this other guard and possibly try to create even more unnecessary meetings was initiated. He took the card.

I'm sure we'll follow-up on this event in the next few days. I hope I am released before they try to hurt a very nice guard who could no longer pretend that he is rehabilitating these inmates.

Chapter 46 – Conjugal Shower Visitation?

Today my other orderly was not in a "working mood". He refused to work with the CO's who worked him hard last night and "Evil", this perfect physical specimen, had a headache.

The "dogman" continues barking, and still I don't know much about him yet. I'm still trying to ascertain who he is. He normally barks when I am locked in my cell.

Oh, something else astounded me today. One old timer inmate was waiting in the shower cage. I was controlling showers so I asked if he was ready to go back to his cell. "No man, I'm waiting to visit with my wife". Obviously, bizarre comments have to be rethought in prison. One of the CO's then told me that on Monday nights the women prisoners are marched through our Day Room to go to the visiting room. "Shouldn't he be getting dressed to visit?" I naively asked. "No" the CO responded, "his wife is also a prisoner here and they speak to each other as she walks by!" These inmates are almost sixty years old! Chew on that image for a while.

There were some stabbings today on other floors. Five more bloodied guests arrived tonight.

I was glad and also very sad today for the obvious reasons of seeing my wife for the first time in this long unnecessary stay. I save those writings and feelings for her eyes alone. It was a sad day, and I am not embarrassed to say it was a difficult day to control my anger and frustration.

Tonight it was over ninety degrees in these cells which have neither air conditioning (paper mache' blocked) no windows, and we are without any other air circulation. I report that prison is not for a claustrophobic individual. Maintaining a positive self-concept is a full time thought process in here.

The low point of my day came when I wanted to know the procedure for ordering cleaning supplies to continue cleaning this filthy old building.

I hope you are sitting down because the answer given to me has to astound you.

Yet, to those who have figured it out, this inept system - it's Ms. Andrews ET. Al. (the missing counselor) who has to be given all requests for cleaning supplies.

How are we to react to the absurdity that a counselor who visits infrequently would order cleaning supplies in this precision network called MCC? I informed them that she's hurt and replaced. Guards have estimated that she will be away for months. "We will just have to wash with water until she returns". I have to change these thoughts. They shut down at an obstacle. These prison leaders can't think beyond any roadblock.

Chapter 47 – Tattoos for Everyone!

In an attempt to pass my painful time even faster I woke up this morning already planning to clean and paint the vacated terrorist cell today.

What do you think happened? Yes, they moved another inmate into that same cell after I finally got the terrorists to be removed last night. No "bed-roll" was given to this individual. I want him to come to the window, but I get no salute or eye acknowledgement. I'll try to prepare my own little welcome wagon for him. I don't count the days anymore; I count the flushes until the next unnecessary toilet incident. There are many other available cells. They just don't remember or care to remember.

One other thought on that business card put into my pocket last night and discovered by the other guard, is that the CO investigating was the one who tormented my two orderlies and the same idiot who decided not to move the terrorists from the flood cell, but to stupidly put down a thin towel in an inane attempt to prevent forty-five gallons of water from escaping during the annual inspection. Remember he was also the one they chose to promote. They made him Officer in Charge (OIC). On the surface he appears to be normal but during the shifts I have observed mood and personality swings that are as difficult to understand as the personality disorders of the inmates. He will sing and joke with the inmates and without provocation become "Captain Bligh" of Mutiny on the Bounty. He has in my unofficial analysis a classic dual personality disorder. He definitely knows how to play this clubhouse game, but he does not belong in charge of caring for other psychotics.

There's another CO who stays on the phone with personal calls for at least three hours every shift. He is a joker and still urinates in the slop sink. He tries to be a friend to every inmate and obviously hates what the job requires of him. For future entries we'll call him CO Joker. CO Joker has more earrings than any uniformed correction officer should be allowed to wear. He, like many of the guards has a good heart, but has been completely worn down by this system.

The tattoos on the guards almost seem a prerequisite to being hired. I don't know whether they have tattoos prior to employment or it's the peer pressure which creates need for the tattoos. Without the uniform shirts on, the inmates and the CO's are almost visually interchangeable.

Now at over 100 degrees outside the building, the cells are without air flow and feel like they are over 95 degrees. Today I was painting doors and trading books from cell to cell and listening to the inmates' heat complaints. No matter how future officials respond to this complaint, believe me there is no air flow and the heat is criminal!

Imagine? The CO's said I really was the one in charge because I tell *them* what needs to be done. They seem to listen to me because "I alone have to do what I've told them to tell me to do." (go ahead and re-read that sentence … it IS correct!) At lunch today they set aside a chicken cutlet for me. It wasn't a full officer lunch, but they gave it to me. They seem to be adopting this sixty year old slave.

They asked me to write a list of what they should ask for from the supply room. They don't want to wait for the counselor. That's progress.

When I asked if I could clean out and disinfect every empty cell, they just looked at each other and said "If you want to clean up after those scum be our guest". I responded that it would make my time here feel valuable if a prisoner started with a clean cell.

Throughout the heat filled day I watched inmates actually having puppet shows with various items and pieces of vegetables in their cell. Isolation, heat and zero stimulation affects these souls. One inmate has been here fifteen days and asked me if I had ever read The History of Salt. I laughed. We discussed it while I painted his front door, five times. It only needed one coat. He needed to talk. Maybe I did too.

I was asked today by an inmate if I was the orderly who was selling head phones and cigarettes. One of my "partners" must have a part time business going on here. I will say nothing. I hope his business prospers.

Chapter 48 – My Snickers Bar Melted!

I received mail from my wife. I was told to throw out my envelope. The guard even told me to flush the envelope down the toilet. "Don't let anyone here know where you live". Even after I painted the doors to improve community spirit, the reunion party may be cancelled.

I have decided to donate hundreds of my paperback books and hard covered books to this ward. I will try to improve the deplorable treatment of solitary men and women. I am told they have a comparable female solitary ward. I will send books to both wards. They need it so very much.

To give you an idea of the central air conditioner in my holding cell, my Snickers bar has melted and my Jolly Roger hard candies have stuck to the Styrofoam tray they were in. Working about the tier is cooler than sitting in my cell. Two men in the same size cell increases the heat and the claustrophobia. I try to sleep in the laundry room because it is air conditioned.

Tonight I witnessed a graduation of "oranges" returning to general population. I was sitting in the law library while this mass of nine "oranges" were put in the same room to change into brown uniforms. Apparently, I was the only guest invited so as they marched out dragging their plastic bags filled with their humble food and belongings, I began loudly humming the graduation march. Only one CO "got it", and he may still be laughing months after the incident.

We did get another very scary looking guard today. He is one of those unkempt people in civilian life who has a "bottom feeder" demeanor. In prison, he gets to transfer some of his frustration. He commands without thought or tact. If he appears again, I'll call him CO Catfish.

The behavior of these men astounds me. Tonight I got all of the laundry and massive amount of clothes to wash from those "graduating". By the way, I have one additional thought on this graduation. We wear cuffs everywhere and then miraculously on Graduation day, with all their "stuff" in front of them for some ridiculous reason, the cuffs are removed. You figure.

At graduation there are now nine inmates circling one unarmed guard! Uncuffed. Potentially, they could still have weapons! Either they never ever needed the security, or they require a more secure departure from the orange ward.

Here's my newest perception tonight. Because they tell me we have eight new inmates coming in, I ask if I can clean eight cells, prepare eight bedrolls, and organize eight toothbrushes, soaps, toothpaste and, of course, toilet paper with a full explanation on how to use the center cardboard roll. I prepare the cells and have gathered everything for their arrival. CO Catfish is not comfortable with this smooth flow and preparation. The other COs just want to play on the computer, eat, tell jokes and not work. CO Catfish sends us unexpectedly to our cells. I got to watch from my window. Despite my efforts CO Catfish created a confused and stressful situation out of a simple and organized procedure. His ignorance and incompetence sometimes reminds me why men like him should be removed rather than quietly tolerated. It's an ongoing administrative disaster, yet a man like him will perpetuate his short comings with impunity. He is compensated in salary by you and me without ever being expected to perform effectively.

Today I got confirmation that both of my assistant orderlies were underground sellers of commissary products to those who are unable to utilize the commissary. They also have phone services available for inmates banned from calling. I don't want to know. I don't want to know.

Chapter 49 – Come and Get Me!

Every once in a while the pain of prison re-hits me with a vengeance. Unlike the professional prisoners who have made this their home and acceptable life style, there are those of us accustomed to a more creature comforting and "familiar" setting.   It hurts when the reality of my unusual and arbitrary incarceration hits my heart.   Maybe it's the heat or maybe it is just realizing the futility of more CO Catfishes and the continuing institutional malaise.   The problem is the corporate culture, the UCMJ and the ingrained attitude of entitlement rather than service to mankind. If I had a month to correct this entire prison, it would be run quite differently and with lower costs to the taxpayer.   An inmate this morning needed a book.   I had the book.   I wanted to give it to him.   I asked the CO to give it to him because the book was a little too thick to fit under the cell door.   It would require simply opening the cuff slot and putting the thick book through.   The CO ripped the book in half and slipped both halves under the door rendering it useless for future inmate book requests. This behavior is not taught.   It is only acquired by observing what others get away with over the years.

Well, I hope someone comes by tonight to get me for my BOP "legally required after working as an orderly shower".   Especially on a ninety degree still night a shower would be an appropriate act of appreciation for all the work I did for them all day.   If they don't come, I'm planning a sink shower.   I do not think they will remember to escort me to a shower. They may remember but they do not want to leave the Day Room to open my cell.   Sweating and covered with prison filth and still returning, unwashed to a ninety degree cell is an experience of prison I may not soon forget.

There was a remarkable power shift in the prison tonight.   CO Catfish and the Officer in Charge (OIC) came to my door.   They opened it and said "Never in our time here has the OIC of the day shift called to make sure you were showered.   CO Rutgers said to let the other assistant work in the laundry and let Altomare rest!   "What the fuck do you have on him"? Little do they know that I would prefer to work rather than remain alone in this cell at 9:00PM.   Their perceived reward for me is not working, while mine *is* working.   CO Catfish uncharacteristically thanked me for what I did tonight.   This was a remarkable breakthrough.   I smilingly savored the shower and still had time to write this entry before I fell asleep reading the Bible.   Again, as I wrote earlier ... how come Bibles are mandatory in prisons, but banned in our schools?

Chapter 50 – Mount Underwear

I await being let out of my cell in the morning.  However after last night, the shift of power reversal seems underway, but I still want to go home.  "Head Slave" or whatever I am called in here has had an evening shower and is going to read Cat and Mouse, a mystery novel.  Today I will meet eight new members of our dysfunctional society, but as the saying or song goes, "Something Is Happening Here".  I can feel a shift of power between the Cat and the Mouse.

Well, today we actually passed the inspection.  This was the first time I am told in nine years!  I was officially made Inmate in Charge (IIC) of Sanitation.  With all of these accolades why do I still want to leave?  Today, I even began a project never conceived by these men.  I decided that in the laundry room we will organize the inmates' underwear.  We never have adequate sizes for the inmates during their showers.  I took control of the laundry today and I did over ten commercial loads and even washed with laundry power.  Yes, they had not been using soap.  I dumped out every clean pair of underwear and decided to organize them in size bins.  This is not terribly innovative.  Remember we have forty inmates on average in this section.  How many pairs of underwear did I uncover?  One thousand four hundred and fifty three!!!  I was able to pack up over three hundred extra pairs to send to other floors.  I have more underwear to give away, but I'll wait until I am "authorized" to send more away.  Don't forget that we never had the right sizes for the inmates until I opened and organized all of the storage bags.  It is only underwear, but indicative of the entire system.  Future showers may now be less stressful.  Can any intelligent citizen or executive imagine this absurdity?  It is painfully obvious that nothing happens from those wasted Thursday inspections.

Because of my new status, I don't even go back to my cell for counts now.  I can stay in the laundry room working and organizing.  I'm sure someday it will change because sanity simply doesn't remain consistent in this inconsistent environment.

One of my former orderlies, Tex, went back to the brown suits (general population) and I helped move "Evil", the other orderly, into his own single cell. He was in a cell for the past two weeks with a very messy individual who did not speak English. During the one hundred degree days, neither of them was very comfortable.

Tomorrow I hope that one of my most innovative suggestions may be implemented. By the way, thank you for being here tonight, I am just sad tonight. I miss my loved ones as this anthropological experiment continues. Here's my suggestion. We have two unutilized cells because they are filled with sixty gray hard storage bins which fit under a bunk bed. Keep following this. The guards didn't know where to store the bins. I suggested (I know you see this coming) that each inmate get one to store their personal items, clothes and food stuff. At the present time these belongings are laying all over each cell. Inmates step on them and they are attacked by mice at night. Was this simplistic idea ever considered? No, was the initial answer, but my solution could solve a few issues. At the present time I am alone in my cell so I utilize the entire empty top bunk for my spare clothes, books, food, toiletries, paper, cards and medicines. Where would these supplies be placed if I had a bunk mate? (Where would his stuff be stored?) I have gone into multiple cells while they shower to remove graffiti, and I have seen clutter beyond your wildest imagination.

Chapter 51 – My Supply List Gets Posted

While I'm thinking about today's box storage suggestion, I began painting other cells. The CO's cannot believe how much better the newly painted cells look. A new paint job every twenty years when you have thousands of free workers seems like a good idea to me as well. "Suits" are roaming all about the ward. I'll tel1 you now - we were the "best" ward during this week's inspections. So as I finished cleaning and renovating a cell, I went to the laundry room to go to rotate the wash. Three "suits" walked into the newly wet painted cell and left their wet paint footsteps all throughout the hallway and all over the newly polished Day Room. "Serenity Now" (with apologies to Seinfeld) Nothing can be said by me. As a UCMJ non-person, I must embrace such uncultured ignorance. No one even considered apologizing. They arrogantly or ignorantly just left the unnecessary footprints for me to scrape off and re-clean.

Believe it or not, nail clippers are once again being discussed. Inmates have brazenly begun responding to my cleanliness. That's progress. Such thanks from them to me have been most touching. Most of the guards have told me the same. The CO's are now asking *me* to just talk to a few inmates who seem to need some kind words. The counselors here are just non-existent or non-effective.

The lack of phone usage, insufficient books, and countless lists remain a constant frustration for me, and tomorrow the Warden and the "suits" will perform the do-nothing ceremonial walk-through ritual again. I hope when they walk through, I'll be able to discuss these issues.

My requested tier supply list had seventeen items. The CO's actually hung it up for all to see. One said, "Can you imagine if he gets these things, what this place would look like?" The items include new serving carts, desks, cleaning supplies, brooms, spray bottles, mops with pails that have mop ringers that fit, mouse traps and multiple sanitation products for the laundry room.

Chapter 52 – Killing My Plumber

Due to my successful underwear project, "Mount Altomare", as the COs were calling it, I now have seventy-four bags of organized underwear. The underwear pile was more than six feet in height. Even one CO said, "How stupid are we that we always had all this underwear, and we never had enough to give the inmates?"

As the faces of inmates and guards come and go, I can understand the difficulty of maintaining enthusiasm and a sense of purpose for the CO's, the institution and now even myself. Becoming "institutionalized" occurs quickly and it is easy to see how these men eventually get there. I've spoken with older inmates and guards who are afraid to leave. I've spoken and observed the guard clubhouse effect. No one is winning. Oh, the BOP and the "suits" and the suppliers are winning. But we the taxpayers and everyone within the prison system walls are losing.

This was a hectic day which began with the moving of a "broken" refrigerator. The guards had one beautiful stainless steel institutional refrigerator that stopped working. After I convinced them to ask for a hand truck, they located one, and I moved the refrigerator. I suggested before moving it that we check the electric outlet. This industrial refrigerator was one of the most professional looking pieces of furniture in the Day Room. After it left, I was instructed to move their functioning microwave into the refrigerator's spot. Guess what? It was a broken outlet and they had already thrown out the refrigerator, or did they? Who knows to which employee's home basement it may have gone?

While this confusion was going on, the plumber was working on one of our tiers. I have politely become the one who gives the orders and plans without overstepping the tenuous role of slave that I play. The plumber promised me he would come back to finish the list of other cells I am attempting to correct for the inmates. The CO's were laughing because of how the plumber was responding to me and our dialogue was simply not of prisoner and guard. The plumber said loud enough for the others to hear "By the way, why are you in here?" Without any emotion, I responded, "I killed my family plumber because he didn't come back to finish the work he was doing". Guards were doubled over at the double take of the plumber. Once again I defied the stereotyped inmate pattern that they were accustomed.

I wish I could tell you today how many "suits" followed the Warden (about eighteen). Today I didn't wait until they walked by I said, "Warden, I have been here for forty-two days. I have asked your education department and counselors for books, initially for myself but over the past fourteen days mostly for these isolated inmates." "If each of you had only carried up one book each time for the past six weeks during these ceremonial inspections, then these walkthroughs would have been valuable!"

The reactions were to promise me educational department response and for the first time the Warden's blank stare indicated painful awareness of my words. My closing comment was "Am I the only one who hears these men?" The silence of no response stayed in the silent air for some time.

Chapter 53 – Good-bye "Bloody Evil"

I found out today from "Evil" who it is that supplies the contraband the inmates sell and re-sell. He said selected guards have a nucleus of non-snitchers who become their workers. These guards receive compensation or they are motivated by acts of charity or they are sympathetic gang members themselves.

This week Blood gang members are being rounded up out of population because of a danger concern by internal security. Over and over again, I am glad they sent them here. Today I am glad one of the gang members is my friend. I still have difficulty trying to solve my nail clipper problem while these professional inmates have home-made weapons. The real danger here manifests itself repeatedly with events that necessitate this internal need to move inmates. A civil contempt prisoner dangerously housed with murderers. Some system. Some Judge.

Our tier is fully crowded again (sixty-five). My laundry room duties have consumed me from 6:30AM to 9:30PM every night. Washing clothes with soap for this unit requires at least eight to ten commercial loads, minimum, per day. Tomorrow is a shower day so you must also imagine sheets, clothes, towels and the time spent serving them. There are always three full meals delivered and picking up hundreds of trays and running up and down hundreds of stairs while I clean, paint and move perfectly good refrigerators because no one checked the outlet. These are only a few of the tasks as I fill my time daily.

As if underwear wasn't enough, I also solved the sneaker problem which has existed here for five years. When men leave this unit, they leave their filthy and moldy orange sneakers behind. No one ever gets new sneakers. We re-cycle them. Remember the underwear? Well, there were over three hundred unmatched, unwashed smelly sneakers in a big disorganized barrel and we would "fish" for sizes when the inmates arrived. I actually washed, disinfected, matched and sized them all.

Prison life, as mundane as one would have it, has some twists and turns that can rival the society at large. Remember we only have five showers (one is still being fixed). Make that three showers now (two more are leaking or inoperable). Add to that fact, we now have over sixty-five inmates in the hole, Murderers, gang leaders and me (the civil contemptor). But, I can shower at night.

Well, at least with all this unpaid work, I have an assistant to help me satisfy these men with the right size underwear, tee shirts, socks and a jump suit that must be 18 sizes too large. Of course, I have all of the normal sizes but 145 lb. inmates, for prison status, want 5xxx. Not having what they demand requires tact and patience. They will try on at least two jump suits and leave the one they do not want on the floor of the shower because (well, you haven't seen the floor). Where is my assistant? He was fired. With this one orderly job being the only way out of the cell I would think with possible food perks, shower and clothes advantages and intellectually just being out of the cell; one would hold on if they had that job. That's our outside world thought process. "Evil" couldn't lose face with incoming gang members. He had to be "bad" and get fired. "Evil" desperately stole a phone and was belligerently smoking an illegal cigarette, when they caught him. Can they replace him with another? "Maybe next week", they said.

Chapter 54 – Becoming Management

Today the guards have accepted my new welcome wagon policy of towel, washcloth, toothbrush and toothpaste, two soaps, milk and left over food plus (when available) books or magazines to be given to new inmates who arrive. Remember what I had been given when I arrived? That's right! NOTHING!

When three newcomers were dragged into the hole, the first thing they now see is me with their sheets, blankets and new "other stuff'. After I smile, and greet them, the new reaction is remarkable. I have been able to take them from solitary dread to semi-hopeful acceptance. The smell of pine over the smell of urine also changes that dread.

After the initial entrance, they then walk into a very clean Day Room and then their freshly painted and cleaned cell. What a change from 42 days ago when I first arrived. I have angrily cleaned every ward and repainted the steps twice (because the guards *forgot* to walk on the unpainted side).

Although my daily work load has increased, my not having an assistant like "Evil" makes my work less stressful. With "Evil", I never knew what mood to expect, and I always had to instruct him in what to do. I now just do it myself:

The reason I believe "Evil" "changed" was the peer pressure of additional gang members arriving and he was concerned that he may lose respect by being a "slave". In my non-gang mind, I saw this job as having higher status. His criminally taught thought process needed to sabotage it. That decision by "Evil" requires further reflection when one considers prison rehabilitation and societal expectations.

Considering all I am now doing, other Captains and Lieutenants are bringing me additional favors to do for them. Today I received high security wash from the terrorists upstairs including prayer rugs and prayer hats. While I was multi-tasking which included three meal deliveries and three pick-up procedures, I also washed and dried their "favors". After folding and delivering them, the Lieutenant came back and said "Do you think those washes could be done in the next four hours?" I told him they were finished and already delivered. He said, "There must be some mistake. Are you sure you are speaking about what I gave you?" As if it should take ANYONE a significant amount of time to accomplish such tasks.

Today counselors and therapists were actually stopping and speaking with me about their perceived mood transformation of some guards, many of the inmates, as well as a more positive "feeling" around our intimate special housing unit [SHU].

Both Deliverance guards were on duty tonight and they forgot that I wasn't back in my locked cell at the end of their shift. I was working, painting, mopping, sweeping, delivering books and the guards had to rush downstairs and get their keys back, which they already turned in at the end of their shift. One of them said, "I forgot you were an inmate". Now THAT was another breakthrough change in attitude.

Chapter 55 – A "Solitary" Father's Day

The absence of my loved ones hits emotionally hard sometimes when I'm not throwing myself into this survival project, symbolically battling a prison and judicial system which appears intent on damaging, rather than rehabilitating men. How exuberant I would be if I could, even for a short time, show them that their system can be changed. To exhibit that the changes must come from both sides, I wrote a thank-you note to the guard for allowing me to try my phone call.

My "thank-you" note of last night circulated among the officers. You can imagine how infrequently the guards receive thank-you notes.

Fridays are "dress down" days for the guards. In my opinion, it's a mistake on this "front line". The inmates have difficulty with the casual outfits of an officer. These inmates need the uniform and consistent look of authority. I can't recall a single Friday "dress-down day" in the Marine Corps.

Let's address the most recent inmate arrivals. As they came in, I asked them their size preferences and started getting their "stuff" together. One of them said, "Are you that Italian dude here who killed seven people?" I answered, "It was eight". They then accepted whatever sizes I had without criticism and saluted me. How funny and sad is this upside down world?

Sometimes I can disarm these angry men with just a word or two, when they are finally allowed a shower after days or weeks in unpleasant solitary. Obviously, their interpersonal skills need some fine tuning. I often say that our tailor is off on Fridays, or "I'll give you everything I have to make you happy". Remember I am also in orange, and I work for you. Officers observe this salesmanship, and I hope they mentally record the positive results.

"Evil" is very sullen and angry. Since his isolation and firing, I tried calling to him as I walked by his cell. Normally he is festive. I feel sad for him today. He won't speak to me, as he is transforming into his gang personality. For survival, he seems to have a few distinct faces and personalities.

I received a Father's day card today and realized I won't be home with my family on that day. I vent in this BOP analysis diary about one Judge's unchecked power and vindictive actions. I hope it creates prison questions for Senators and Congressmen.

To drive home the point about collateral emotional damage done to family members; can someone tell me how I someday explain to my 8 year old Grandson, who believes that his missing Grandfather is an American Marine hero currently away on a covert mission to find "the bad guys"; when in reality his Grandfather has been unjustly incarcerated without even being accused of any crime. I know he was crying when he was sent off to summer camp, because I wasn't there. Who gives me and my Grandson back those moments lost?

The day's emotions range from hard work, to tears, and to laughter. Make no mistake, I try to embarrassingly shield you on the nights I just want to go home and cry myself to sleep. I repeatedly pray for justice on this case and this issue.

Chapter 56 – My First Prison "Power Lunch"

I haven't looked out my cell window in over two weeks. Some cells have windows, others are blocked or blacked-out. I created a reality that I've become a prisoner of war for my family and shareholders. Everything I do will bring me one step closer to my loved ones and eventual victory. I have gambled my reputation and financial future on exposing the facts that contain the real reasons for the SEC's disassembly of our fine company and my incarceration.

I was surprisingly invited to a CO power lunch today. The invite did not exactly include eating. I just looked at their pizza. They were discussing the pick-up of trays after meals, and I interjected, "I realize that I am only IIC of Sanitation, but if you will allow an observation on how to remember which wards were picked-up and which ones were forgotten; I would like to make a suggestion". I simply showed them that when a ward was finished eating, they should leave the empty cart at the tier cell gates. They could then scan the tiers in an instant and know which tiers were done and which ones were not. They adopted it immediately and they have nicknamed it APUP (Altomare's Pick-up Policy). I'm sure it will be PUP in due time, but under this simple system, the inmates won't have unwanted food in their cells for hours and days at a time. I hope they practice it.

I've watched "Jeopardy" on TV and have yet to see a contestant who said he was a prison employee - so let's go with the percentages here. These are some wonderful men and women who would prefer to rot and work in jail for the job security and camaraderie. There's nothing wrong with it, except America is burning and BOP employees are throwing gasoline on the fire under the guise of doing their jobs, and believing the pails of gasoline they are throwing have water in them.

An inmate who has been here eight days told me that a nurse came to visit and he told her he wanted to read since he was depressed sitting alone in a cell. He also wanted to call home, contact his lawyer, and get a book. (I took care of the book) The nurse came back with 30 Prozac. The young man had never taken drugs in his life! This was the BOP solution to solitary. He took them! They utilize drugs to quiet down the inmates, and this isn't supposed to be a psychiatric hospital. But believe me … it is! Check the number of psychologically damaged Americans who are in these non-helpful buildings.

Rap music permeates this facility from the head phones of the inmates to guards singing themselves. The term "son" has verbally taken over since the gang members arrived. "I'll tell you, son: "Son, I'm saying". From gang hand signals to rap music head phones, this prison culture is being perpetuated and legitimized as it destroys the lives of millions of impressionable inmates. The inmates, their family, their neighborhood, the victims, the next generation, and our society itself are all impacted. We could do so much better.

As I await going out to work this morning, I share with you a brief interlude of some of our newest gang arrivals as they experience their first carefully selected solitary confinement breakfast of one milk carton and one small cereal box. It sounds like this:

Inmate: "Hey, who ate the rest of my fucking breakfast?
        Are you fat fucks eating our breakfasts, Son?
        This can't be all to eat, you fat fucks!"

Guard: "Shut your fucking mouth and stop fucking cursing!"

Inmate: "Where's my food, Son?"

Inmate: "I know you guards eat the extra meals, Son.
You need 20 breakfasts just to fill your fat fucking bellies"
My mundane work will begin in a short time. There's still plenty of my optimistic sunshine to try to spread. One inmate last night told me he liked the top orange shirt I had on. I'm going to wash it and give it to him today. It has DOC on the back. Although it stands for Department of Corrections, I have nicknamed the inmate Doc, and boy does he like it.

Chapter 57 – The Vending Machine Caper

Today I hope to get to begin polishing the floor. We have three polishing machines and polishing hasn't been done here for years. The work may keep me up late but the pain of unnecessarily missing my loved ones knows no bounds. "Saturday night is definitely the loneliest night of the week" - must have been written by a prisoner.

A stand-up head count reminds you of the antiquated and repetitive unnecessary meaningless system of prison life. In this ward mobility is impossible. Yet we count, cuff and multi-lock prisoners not daily, but numerous times throughout the day. During these "counts", nothing is allowed to move through the prison. This emotional stopping and starting of the human psyche damages not only work ethics, pride and productivity; but it creates a dysfunctional thought process which damages all involved. Never forget that the count is modeled after the German concentration camp concept.

This Saturday morning, the count is taking a very long time. Is anyone missing? No. Today is the Summer holiday prison picnic for employees. Those left behind are unable to make decisions because most authority figures are at the picnic and it's an excuse to do nothing. Therefore things halt. Maybe those Prozac offered to that young man is what some "lifers" do to deal with weekend after weekend of the negative energies which occur throughout these punitive walls.

That reminds me, during my legal visits of the past forty-two days, the vending machines have been broken more than thirty-six of them. Seeing snacks, but being unable to get to them is tougher than not seeing them at all. I found out last night from one of the guards, that the guards shut down those vending machines because if the lawyers and inmates use them, there aren't always enough extra snacks for the guards to have when they want them. At night the guards have vending machines on other floors, but these legal floor vending machines are their food back-up. Maybe that breakfast dialogue of them stealing their food between inmates and guards is based on an element of truth.

This Saturday morning I have to listen to that loud cackling and constant laughing of female CO Grant. Her constant laughter and screaming continues. I am surprised they have so much available fun time when they should be getting forms, books or supplies for these inmates. Oh, I forgot the count is going on, so nothing can happen. The longer the count takes the better, and the longer it takes - the harder it is to re-start working.

Not once has there been any professional "dialogue" during their counts, free lunches and dinner meetings. The clubhouse atmosphere is their way of dealing with a penal system that ignores the expected rehabilitation of inmates, the inmates themselves, and the unnecessary and painfully long incarcerations of many who are here.

Neither alternative community service nor emotional closure on the part of the victims is addressed with this present penal system.

Placing the day to day financial responsibilities of incarceration on the families' of the inmates, instead of on the State, would change the popular gang "status" of them being here. We should be demanding a higher level of professional officer who can multi-task and also be rewarded for successful rehabilitation of these prisoners. In fact, last night I asked if I could give an inmate some paper to write a letter home. The CO said "If you want to, do it, all I care about is making sure the same number of inmates are here at the end of my shift - that's all I worry about. I won't lose my job, if they don't have paper".

In fact, Kennedy's Peace Corps Program can be modeled after and transformed into my concept of prison reform. Heck, even if I was one thousand percent wrong, it would solve more than the present system is accomplishing. Society is no safer this way. When we try to reconcile the sixty billion dollar per year costs and the horrific results of the present system, we may begin to examine "counts" and cherish my honest inside the barbed wire observations.

Maybe, if we don't make changes, America should replace the eagle with the ostrich as its National symbol. Burying our heads and pretending to ourselves that our prison and gang mistakes are not coming back to haunt us can be more swiftly accepted when you "See" what I am seeing.

Silly as it may seem, those Thursday walkthroughs represent millions upon millions of wasted dollars of do nothing "suits" with little follow-up execution.  I expressed to the CO's that when the "suits" leave their walkthrough, one feels like a dog trying to "shake off" that wet feeling. But on the day I took over the laundry room and I removed that fifty-five gallon mass of combustible lint in just one dryer, on one ward, not one of the "suits" had ever checked that!  They did see where we could cover over dirt with new paint.  Aren't you tired of covering over this dirt?  It repulses my creative and responsible mind and soul.

It's still Saturday and I'm trapped in my cell because of the "count".  I've got some weekend projects that I want to start.  That also reminds me of what a new guard who was watching me last night said, "Are you a workaholic, don't you ever think it's good enough?"  After seeing these inmates' sad faces and the day to day malaise - "No, I do not".

It's still Saturday and 12:00 noon, and I'm still in the cell.  Lunch has been served and the CO's say "another ten minutes" (this is the fourth 'ten minutes').  One hour later I'm still here.  There have been no breakfast or lunch tray pick-ups!  While the picnic goes on, those having to work want to also do nothing.  Well, I'll wait as my multiple projects remain on hold. Aside from not wanting to be here, I still wanted to complete what I had planned and promised.  That's the problem with CO Ahab (the Moby Dick reader) he's always resting and he's in charge today.  He probably thinks that by letting me rest, he is being nice.  He's definitely going to go far in the BOP.  Heck, in a matter of years he may become a "suit" or even a Warden.

Ahab just came by to pick up the trays and said "Not today".  I replied that, "I have numerous projects to do that I have been told to complete." He said, "I'll come back".  From four "ten minute" delays, to now "not today", dealing with these men can turn a sane man into a crazy one - or even worse, one *of* them.  I must fight becoming uncaring or shutting down.

Chapter 58 – My First Suicide

Today, I appear re-confined to my cell. Since I gave away all my books except the Indian History Book, it will be a long day. Professional communication is definitely lacking in a prison environment. There can be multiple other reasons why all of my plans were stopped today. One reason could be a prison weekend rule to prevent orderlies from being overworked. I have, however, worked over the past few weekends. Another reason is the guards didn't want an inmate to see what kind of a party was going on. A third could be no reason at all - "That's just the way it is" in prison.

This was my first return to total twenty-four hour isolation in 14 days. It really hurts again. I had mentally blocked out the pain of my last solitary experience, forgotten about my legitimate feelings of this unjust incarceration, suppressed my pain, and denied the embarrassment of this absurd event.

It is so frustrating every day to watch some of guards sabotaging my efforts to make the prison a nicer environment for these inmates. I wonder what mess their party will create. Today, the party music from the Day Room is "high school loud". All I wanted to do was keep my promises to myself and the weekday crew to complete some of my planned projects. Well, uncompleted hard work and acceptance of morons will always be a consistent outcome in a place run by broken institutional minds.

The 4 o'clock shift finally arrived, and I'm still in the cell! There's a story coming here. I'm sure this isn't just two shifts deciding not to clean. This could be my first time fired (except of course by the Judge who seemed to have some favors to pay to the SEC). Imagine being fired as a non-paid orderly! This truly is an Alice in Wonderland experience that I have been pushed into. Character requires answering challenges and re--challenges. I can adjust to whatever occurs. If I had to take a prison guess, "Evil" probably "walked the plank" and told them I gave him or ordered him to smoke and make calls. It's so ridiculous; I have to believe these idiots are capable of believing such a fabrication. But who knows? Trying to seek professional approval from a dysfunctional leadership cadre only makes you crazy. I choose to not participate in this exercise. I'll do my best to expose this incompetent criminal justice system, when this temporary stay is over.

Believe it or not, they came banging on my cell at 10:30PM to get dressed. "We need you." As you know, I had been dressed since 6:30AM this morning! The third crew came in and couldn't understand why the place was a mess, and why I had not cleaned up the room of the one legged guy, who seems to have died. Yes, he died during the music party. Died? Or was it a suicide?

Chapter 59 – Soulless in New York

Initially, I reconnoitered the mess and did in twenty minutes, a general cleaning of the Day Room to build up to the real mess, which was, in the cell of the deceased one-legged suicide. At that time, surprisingly, I found out who the "dogman" inmate was. It was, shockingly, one of the guards, CO Fang!

Now I had to once again be locked up for thirty minutes so they could do the "Count". I then attacked the bloodied and defecated cell with a vengeance. They said they had all the protective gear I would need. I imagined one of those Darth Vader outfits, but they handed me two plastic gloves. I did it anyway because I thought if I did a great job of cleaning this mess, I could maybe call home. I finished, and to maintain a PG rating on this diary, it was an Emergency Room kind of mess. I finished. I showered. I asked to make the call. "Can't do, it's after 10:00PM".

I returned knowing that I am still in the worst possible place to be with men whose IQ and sensitivity quotient must be on the low end of anyone's scale. I asked to stay up and work on my projects a little longer, but they said I would disturb their sleep. Their sleep! Now that's a comforting thought as I try to sleep tonight. When do I get to go home? Until I walk out the door of MCC, I am nothing more than an inmate doing work fit for a slave. Could I have assisted the now dead one-legged twenty-three year old if I could have heard his cries for help?

Tonight while showering I found a broken blue part of a shaver. That means an inmate took the whole razor and returned the only blue plastic razor handle, without the blade. One of the inmates has a razorblade! I told the guard. He said, "If you remember, tell the OIC on Monday". Hey, they let it happen, let them try to find it. I wish I could be fictionalizing these dialogues.

You see, if the showers were all operational, the guards could narrow down which cell inmate or tier went to a particular shower. Since there is no shower accountability, any one of the 60 inmates could have that razor and cut a CO, or worse me, as I walk about them or near their cells when we collect their food trays. I still can't have a nail clipper!

Which of the following doesn't belong with the others? This was an old children's multiple choice game. This morning, I was watching the first three cells and then me to be served breakfast. There were subtle differences.

Cell 1    "You Fucking Kidding? This is all I get?"
Cell 2    "Did you eat the rest, mother fucker?"
Cell 3    "Son, give me two!"
Me        "Good morning, Happy Father's Day."
          (Yes, it is Father's Day and my country has confined
          me to a prison.)

As I resist this negative re-education and the bureaucratic "lessons" of being here, I hope to get out of my cell early to undo the missed opportunities of Saturday. There are some regular guards who work during the week who are on duty today. What will be, will be. I must say that the screaming between cells continued late into the evening. It is a scary type of wailing and not understandable to me. There was "jamming" and "corner-side" singing from gang cell to gang cell including many gang fight songs which are very eerie. One would think that discipline and common courtesy during the middle of the night would be enforced by the guards. They were either sleeping, or it is not in their job description.

Cell neighborhood personalities change, and after this prison sweep of one of the gangs due to either a "tip" or supposition, our neighborhood has gotten very "hard". They have empowered these gangs, and make them appear more notorious upon their return to "general population", which is the expression when one sheds the maniacal orange for the coveted brown uniform. What are they allowing to happen to the souls who may slip into this system?

Chapter 60 – Sammy the "Bull" and Me

It is interesting that the fifteen cells I painted and cleaned in one ward have not been used in these past few weeks.  They use those cells to show off to "suits".  I would prefer them to be used by inmates.  That reminds me that Sammy the Bull and John Gotti spent less time in the hole than me, according to "Evil" and Tex, who were here when they were here.  Let's be objective here, Sammy the Bull, 30 or so admitted murders, John Gotti, crime boss, and me.  Both of these men admitted to, and were convicted of crimes.  I committed no crime, had no trial, was convicted of no crime …Yet here I am.  Could I be a Political Prisoner? … In the United States???

This perplexing comparison makes complete sense to me as I sit in my cell waiting and hoping for someone to throw up or die, so I can get out and make the rest of the ward better.  Sammy is out and I'm in.  They really get inmates to shorten their sentences by squealing on others to increase jail membership.  Prison detectives "interview" these inmates.  Inmates can lie, but the BOP doesn't seem to care as long as they can increase their occupancy.  Many are put in prison even before a trial and before any actual legal charges.  The system is a witch hunt and similar to the actions of the villagers in the "Scarlet Letter", by Hawthorne.  These are just some random thoughts while I pass the time until either my long awaited legal visit or a release from this cell to do my projects.

After today's legal visit, I returned to the 9th floor and began all of my projects.  Believe it or not, they let me paint one of the six formerly ugly and stained carts.  It is beautiful, and all of the guards were circling it like men circle a car.  The Brown Population had trouble with their washing machines so they brought me six commercial loads of wash to do for them.  While I was mopping, painting and cleaning up after fifteen guards who just don't respect cleanliness, I spent this Father's Day serving my sixty surrogate sons.

Another suicide event almost occurred today.  A very visibly depressed inmate was brought in to remain in one of our suicide watch cells.  I am in one of these type cells because these cells have a 24 hour television monitor.  Sometimes I think about the camera, but now I just go through the day not thinking about a peeping Tom or Jane. As the depressed inmate stood in front of my laundry cage, he was sadly holding a pair of what seemed like special shorts. Maybe they were his or maybe they belonged to a family member, I do not know. Since he would be changing into our orange maniac squad colors, I asked for his sizes. I also could tell there was something unusual about those shorts. All I did then was wish him a Happy Father's Day. I smiled and asked if he would like me to clean those beautiful shorts. He smiled and said, "Yes, please" and then he said he wanted to go back to his population cell. I told him that I would send the shorts to him. The Captain winked at me and the suicide watch appeared over.

That reminds me of a funny governmental maintenance policy in prison. We have three of these "polishers" to be used for the tile floor, but we can't have an extension cord because of some policy fearing we might hang ourselves. When they mechanically work, the machines have only cleaned a foot or two around each outlet. The guards are trying to get a dispensation for me. Tonight I worked until 11:45PM. The guards were simply napping from the exhaustion of doing nothing, but I escaped another day alone in the cell.

As I was reorganizing the laundry room, some thirty year old female guard said, "Fine job, young man". I responded, "As a sixty year old young man I thank you". She said, "What's your secret, you look young and happy"? I answered, "I never worked for the government". I continue to demonstrate my inability to be reeducated by individuals who should be terminated or prosecuted.

There was a great deal of kicking and banging tonight. It does drive home the personal pain men in solitary confinement can sometimes experience during a holiday memory recall. Father's Day would be such a recall day.

My Wife visits tomorrow and once again I hope it's my final week in prison. I may sound too focused on these cleaning projects, but getting my businesses and lawsuits back in motion are really my priority. Financially, I have taken a "direct hit" by this Judge's fines and his refusal of a trial so that Americans could have realized what this Judge and the SEC were trying to hide.

Tomorrow I have multiple projects plus showers and a visit from my Wife. When she walks away to leave me after that visiting hour, it's so close to what death must feel like. I'm not accustomed to being so powerless, but I'm trying to return to my normal thought processes. Without you there to settle me, to allow me to write to you, and to help keep me from bitterness; you help me to stand up and survive. Today I just want to thank you. My heart goes out to those darkened cells where the inmates try to sleep through the pain and silence. They have been in darkness for much longer than I have been reporting to you.

Chapter 61 – Felix and Oscars (I want to thank the Academy)

I heard that in one of the cells two inmates had a real bad fight last night. Fortunately someone alerted (or woke up) the guards and the inmates are now in two separate freshly painted cells.

I caused a classic double-take today from one of the newer and younger guards. As I handed him the incoming clothes, shoes and bag of toiletries, I said, "We are all out of the chocolate mints for the pillows". After jolting, he smiled and said, "From what I am seeing and hearing, I wouldn't be surprised".

The Chaplain didn't get to us for Father's Day, but when a visiting "suit" asked me how many children I had, I gave two answers, "Outside I have four children and four grandchildren, but until this insanity is over I have adopted all sixty of these men to the best of my ability." I'm sure Prozac will be ordered for me by tomorrow.

What a day! The day was already exhausting, and added to that an unannounced inspection of the medical facility forced the guards to call upon me to clean a less than pristine and frankly unsanitary clinic.

The day started with a typically ridiculous investigation by three "suits". The guards apparently have to initial about one hundred times a day next to each prisoner's name or for whatever other meaningless reasons during their shift. Today the "suits" and Lt. Big Rear End and another Lt. I'm So Pretty were checking to see if the initials were forged. That would mean a guard put another guard's initials so that person may have snuck home early. They love to hurt each other. That's the climate of trust in here.

My newly painted cart was a big hit.

After my Wife's visit, I could feel what this unlawful incarceration and the financial strains are doing to her. I didn't think she would want to hear about my new cart or my plans to humble this broken system.

CO Joker let me stay longer than one hour with my Wife. My God! What happened to the place? In addition to shower day, they decided to try to clean a few tiers and replace blankets and sheets. Coupled with having to also clean the medical facility, I lumbered into my cell at 11:30PM.

Two of the more salvageable guards confided in me that they were learning how to enjoy working here by observing me and they were in awe of my work ethic. It has transformed them into feeling bad for all I have to do, and how pleasantly I go about doing it.

I briefly spoke with eight female prisoners today as they were returning from their family visits. They commented on the condition of my laundry room. They were all under twenty-five and certainly did not appear to be a threat to anyone in our society. "And the beat goes on".

I must comment on the sloppiness of the CO guards. They stereotype uneducated males at a poker game or fraternity party every single day. They really drop food where they eat and simply walk away or step on it. There is no personal pride.

"Evil" now tells me that I have changed because I am exhausted and I can't speak to him while I am working. I explained to him that because of his leaving, I'm alone working sixteen hours most days.

I got a "God Bless You" today from one of the inmates just for answering his questions and helping him to get a pencil and a book.

Extended prison life has today taught me that "Son" according to a few gang members is "Sun" signifying brightness and friendship. Don't ask me to explain I'm just reporting their language as I understand it. The hand signals and code are just amazing.

Despite my efforts, tonight has become a noisy and violent one. After the family visits, the guards left and there were eight orange inmates in the same room without handcuffs. How do they justify this? Why the cuffs and then no cuffs? This simply demonstrates the inconsistency of their security practices.

Today I threw out my milk cartons forever. The plantation dream is over. "Evil" bought me a mug. I had hesitated to get one because I just wanted to leave. It was a thoughtful gift. I think he was touched when he saw all I had done while he was making illegal calls and sitting in the dryer. By intimidating anyone who came near me on my shoe project, "Evil" got to sit alone in that dryer while he guarded his new friend.

I may get a nail clipper tonight.   And I may get a phone call.   Problem is I never know until they actually materialize or fail to appear.

Chapter 62 – Illegally Cutting My Nails

I moved in most of those gray storage buckets, and gave newspapers to a young man who has been here 11 days and is stir crazy talking to himself in his cell. He also was offered drugs by the doctor when he told him he couldn't handle solitary. This is a gentle non-criminal type. But the beat does go on and BOP needs to keep them happy while they charge taxpayers for their unnecessary work.

The CO's have told me today that if I leave, they may retire my cell or name it the Altomare Suite. Today they ate their meals while I catered to the inmate problems, and I only wish I could do more. At today's inmate graduation I received heartfelt appreciation gifts from 4 of the inmates leaving for me little things like soap, toilet paper, books, or an unused toothbrush.

Tonight there were five chicken meals left over and I circulated them to some hungry inmates. I've made a difference. I've changed the climate. I am exhausted and I am dying to go home. The power of a Federal Judge is dangerous. I am living proof. If he had questions, they could have been answered in a courtroom. Shame on this man and a penal system that both need to be exposed.

The CO's consist of some who care, some who don't, some who used to care but don't anymore and some who never cared at all. Their job is disrespected like a flight attendant not a pilot. They should be deciding professionals not on the lower end of a "suit" hierarchy. I repeat that the system also incarcerates the minds of its employees. The costs do not justify this system and inmate quotas between Judges and the BOP. Their State financial bonds and other funding are more important than separating the gang leaders or institutionalizing poor non-violent young offenders with the violent ones.

Time is ticking away, and my phone and clippers may not appear again tonight. I hope they do. Remember I still have not made one phone connection in forty-two days. No phone tonight again. Those on the "lists" get nowhere. Those sitting in dryers with illegal phones speak to their families. You figure out which prison behavior is reinforced.

Wait a minute, it's 11:00PM and CO Joker brought the phone and nail clippers. I actually spoke to my wife for three minutes while I cut my nails. I can't express the feeling of now having 1" nails and hearing my wife's voice. Believe it or not, I again wrote a thank-you note to the officer. He choked up. I'm definitely not changing - but they are!

I regained my prison "center" today long after my Wife's phone call. I must just stay focused on defeating my opponents on their home field.

Chapter 63 – The Tail Wagging the Dog

Today was another busy day, I was awakened at 6:30 AM because the Officer in charge (OIC) ordered a steam cleaner, and he had me supervise the trustee inmate who worked it. This has to be done through bars because, if you remember no two inmates can be in the same room if one of them is the maniacal orange guy. (That's me!)

As I await tomorrow's now steam cleaned showers, I have to carry out sixty to eighty jumpsuits, underwear, shirts, towels, and supplies of everything we have so the inmate's showers and cell clean-up can continue, to allow for the making of a new regular mess every two days.

All of my equipment supply requests are on hold, so I washed the mops in the washing machine because they just couldn't be made clean without supplies and bleach. Like those forbidden extension cords many effective cleaning products are not permitted for us. We apparently might drink these supplies. The beat goes on.

Yesterday two CO's told me they were applying for jobs elsewhere. It is refreshing that they speak so openly with me. Morale is simply not the greatest amongst the staff. Complacency of their tasks and criticizing each other appears to further set the negative tone at this prison.

Food remains inedible, but today I was given another piece of chicken from the Officer's lunch. It is no wonder they supplement their meals by sending out for civilian food deliveries.

In defense of the CO's, and a further attack upon this system, the inmates always want more than you can do – whoever it is "you might be. That's because they ask for the same things over and over again and they don't get it. From phone calls, to toilet paper, to pencils, to books, to visitors forms; they are frustrated. It would be so easy to create a professional prison for the small percentage of violent inmates who really should be here. Many of these inmates are not criminals. They are emotionally ill or in need of family (home) detention.

Tonight one of the new arrivals refused to get out of his 4 x 4 holding cell. He went to sleep on the floor crying and screaming. After three hours I walked by and spoke to him. I gave the "salute" and I said "(Son)" or (Sun) my name is Mr. A. and I'm the orderly. Can I get you some dinner? I have a few left over. He ate what I gave him and, was up and in his cell in 10 minutes. The guards were content not to engage him.

Listening to the Lieutenants and Captains talking to these prisoners indicates a less than sophisticated English speaking dialect. To be accepted by the inmates, the guards speak and "play" and "respond" in the prisoner's language. The tail wagging the dog really exists here.

This diary may have only a few more entries. I expect to leave soon. I'm told by "Evil" who today likes me, because I got him some toothpaste and a tee shirt, that there may be a physical incident during showers. Hopefully nothing will happen because I can't warn anyone. I may have to move my cell again today. I hope my new cell doesn't have night visitors. I'll keep the lights on.

Chapter 64 – Book Brigade

The CO's are going to an emergency CO meeting to finally ask for books! They have every inmate asking them. I wonder why that's happening. This is progress. They have never asked for books before. I am proud of them.

The present educational book system requires asking for a specific author or topic from the inmate's counselor. After the counselor submits your request, then within fifteen days in solitary they will try to send you the book! Most inmates have left solitary before the books arrive twenty days later. An inmate can't write home for anything until he gets paper, stamps, pencil and an inmate PAC number, all from a counselor who never shows up. My suggestion of a book cart for us to trade or give the inmates books every day was responded to as follows: "These inmates don't respect books. A few years ago one used the Bible to keep water out of his cell - the Holy Book". How do I respond? If the plumber can one day fix our 3 showers, books and towels won't have to be used to block flowing water. But none of these current inmates built that one Bible Dam (is that permitted to say?). I hope the CO's can knock this book hating stereotype wall down tomorrow at their meeting. I wish I could attend.

You should see my professionally organized line-up of clothes for the shower. In the past everything was in a pile without sizing. It looks like an orderly shower procedure will occur tomorrow. Let's see how smoothly it goes. I hope "Evil" was only kidding about the incident.

I just got released from my cell and believe it or not one of the Lieutenants ignorantly pushed everything which was organized into one pile again. The time spent searching for sizes of clothes, which are now unmarked, adds hours of confusion to the showering project.

For the first time, this slave threatened to quit if a "suit" or Lieutenant didn't at least ask me before they messed up my work. I am improving the jobs and appearance of all, and these hillbilly guards don't understand cleanliness or the value of order.

They are rounding up a number of prisoners this morning to bring them to Court. The music head phones, which are purchased in prison, are being listened to so they can hear selected AM stations. They are "carrying on" while they listen to some gang related comedian. It's like listening to a laugh track, but hearing none of the reasons for the laughter. Head phones just don't seem to demonstrate the behavior prison solitary should strive to accomplish. Yet rather than rehabilitate or mature a head phone user, the broken system sells them headphones and allows violent programming.

Chapter 65 – My Fans Speak

To better understand this institutionalized thought process, picture this morning's breakfast. Remember, normally we receive our 4oz. milk carton and one paper cereal box. They deliver this at 6:30AM and then come to pick up the plastic holding box/tray that the milk and cereal were delivered in, thirty minutes later. Today they delivered and wanted back the brown box/tray at the exact time of delivery. This way the guards don't have to come back a second time to pick it up. On the surface this may be an efficient move, except today with cereal being the meal, there was now no box/tray in which to mix the cereal and the milk. When the inmates don't possess the ability to use the plastic box/tray to eat the cereal from, the efficiency of the one tray delivery system loses its allure. This process obviously can only be done when there is an actual box of cereal. I'm listening to the prisoners trying to figure out and strategize on how to eat their cereal without a bowl. The tray is their bowl.

"Yo, what up"? is an expression that permeates these halls. Gang and slang English certainly have taken over as this prison's primary language. The entire staff does nothing to return these inmates to our English speaking and homogeneous world, but it only prepares them to go back to their gang patterns which brought them here in the first place. That's BOP built in obsolescence, and prison loyalty.

Prison life has extreme frustrations and also some personal satisfaction. After trying to rebound from the Lieutenant moving all of the organized shower clothes into one governmental pile of mixed multiple sizes, I have been staying ahead of the continual mess which frankly keeps coming at me.

While I'm writing to you, guards are sitting outside of my neighbor's cell on suicide watch for a new inmate who just arrived. I had to clean the cell. The previous inmate had mounds of cheese in the corner of his cell with paper on the floor to feed the mice and rats that live in the walls! How lonely must he be for companionship?

Please, think through with me, this idiotic governmental action: We had showers and clothes changes today. More than fifteen inmates were leaving solitary at 4:00 PM. All of them changed into clean "orange" outfits at 2:00PM and then all of them were instructed to give everything they were wearing back to me after wearing them for only one hour. They were then instructed to don their general population "browns", discarding to the floor all the orange clean outfits I had just given them – now requiring a complete re-wash. Why were they not instructed to change into the "browns" just one hour later? I had eleven (count them) eleven commercial loads of wash tonight. Add to that all of the cells I had to clean and clean again to prepare for eight newcomers. Nothing here is planned, organized, anticipated or scheduled. It all just "happens", with no regard for human effort or institutional cost.

While I was cleaning the cells of the inmates who left solitary, some left me notes of appreciation with an orange as a gift. The notes said Thank You, Rich for being so nice to me. GOD Bless you. Or another note said, "Yo, Rich you are the best." While I was mopping, another inmate pushed a week old paper under the cell door to give to me. A black guard told me I cannot take presents from the inmates. I really didn't want the paper, but the inmate said to me "We "niggas" are behind you and tell that black mother fucker to give you the paper. You are so good to us, and you work all fucking day for them".

Chapter 66 – Choke on those Pretzels

Today the Warden sent an education representative to give me the forms for all of the inmates because the inmates have been telling all visitors that they wanted books. I will fill these forms out on the inmates' behalf tomorrow, and get those books here before I leave. These prisoners don't know authors and titles. The present system is simply not relevant for them.

I watched Andrews' counselor replacement ignoring screaming inmates while she sat with the CO's eating a large plastic container of pretzels. I told her that some inmates wanted to speak with her and she said "Too bad, I'm busy". She sat there another hour, and then went home. The beat goes on.

I got the guard to get me supplies and a big roll of paper towels because there is a big paper towel rack holder behind the officer's one desk in the Day Room. The holder unfortunately is for "show". It is not able to be opened for anything! The beat goes on.

Showers today were pleasant and I heard a great deal of laughter coming from the inmates. That was good.

Tonight I did have a new idiot officer in charge. He locked me in my cell at about 7:00PM instead of allowing me to work in the laundry so I could have finished the over six hundred dirty pieces of wash. Remember this means sheets, blankets, towels, wash cloths, underwear, tee shirts, big jumper outfits plus whatever may be needed for new arriving inmates. This same CO then went into the laundry while I was locked up and viciously messed up everything because he is incapable of keeping things in order. Some CO's seemed threatened by my attempt at order.

The guards are buzzing because the Warden sent an Education representative to see me. Neurotic governmental insecurity adds to this less than creative atmosphere.

Not much is ever said about the twenty-three year old inmate who died. I'm glad at least I gave him a book and some human friendship, but I don't even know his name. These inmates all need so much more than they get from this system.

The guards assigned to tonight's suicide watch continue to wait until the drugs that were just injected into the inmate make him fall asleep.

I've become friendly with the more mature and "intelligent BOP workers" and continue to be very silent around the ones I would love to tell off. But with the UCMJ and the Judge hoping I do something wrong, I'll save my comments until after I am out.

Chapter 67 – Napoleon meets his Waterloo

Today I was touched by some e-mails my attorney showed me during our hourly visit. Boy, did my shareholders go after the Judge. This is either good or bad for me. They also sent the facts of this story to hundreds of news outlets. I was asked by a French TV station to be interviewed in prison. The prison rejected the request as expected. With you listening to me, and my working to exhaustion, plus now my wife's inspirational notes, the evenings go by quickly.

I had a number of discussions with the Officers today because I complained about last night's OIC. This was CO-Napoleon (as the guards call him). He was a Lieutenant and was busted back to CO – Corrections Officer. Can you imagine how bad one has to be to be reduced in grade here? Believe me, he hates everyone. He is an angry pressure cooker accident waiting to happen.

Some additional thoughts occurred to me about the boy who died. Remember I was ordered to clean his room without safety equipment and not to throw out his sheets and linens which were soiled with every imaginable bodily fluid.. I was instructed to simply wash his clothes and reissue them to the next inmate. I wonder what he really died from, and if any prison rules were violated. After I get out, someone should investigate.

"Evil" now has a very mean room mate who is also a murderer. He wants me to get him things like plastic bags or gloves. All of which are not allowed, and the last thing I want is to end up like "Evil". The issue is that he has threatened "to mess me up" if I don't get it. I'm not going to get it, or I'll have to rely on the Cracker Jack security of our CO's. Plastic gloves can be used as prophylactics. Plastic bags make moonshine. There are numerous moral issues to assimilate with this request, including my own safety.

I cleaned a cell today where I found two disposable razors and a straight edge razor! The inmate was moved unexpectedly, and I found these items AFTER the CO had finished his inspection. I found them and the guard did not!

After I openly expressed my displeasure about CO Napoleon, three officers told me that everyone wants me to be the orderly, so Napoleon has been reassigned.   How's that for progress?

I'm now personally reading three books.   One is in my cell, the second is in the laundry, and the third is in the law library.   These are places I am locked up throughout the day so I don't become a prisoner in waiting with nothing to read.   I escape to "Marine Sniper" (laundry room), Cradle and All, about the second coming (cell) and a GED English and Social Studies Review Book in the law library.   Reading, working and writing has enabled me to get to this stage of solitary and "master slave" status without a great deal of depression and typical prison self-destructive behavior.

Today from the commissary they delivered to me a box of Matzos and Velveeta cheese.   I could live on it.   Unfortunately, I don't get much so it will be gone by Sunday.   An inmate today left me an extra pair of shower shoes.   I washed them and now I have three pairs of shoes in a one shoe world.   My worn original blue shoes I use for painting, mop ups and diary delivery, my dress orange sneakers with a large 12R and a 12L written on each are for every other demeaning job and now my lounging slippers are for the thirty and forty minutes I spend before I fall exhaustedly to sleep at night.

I really have emotionally blocked out my family separation and societal isolation and like a true religious believer, I simply place 100% confidence that there will be, without doubt, a reversal of these injustices due to the unwavering faith I have in One Nation, under God, Indivisible, with Liberty and JUSTICE for ALL.

## Chapter 68 – Fireside Thoughts

Tonight we accepted eleven new orange brothers. We graduated seven to the Brown. One of the new orange inmates turns out to be the Illustrated Man - with hair! I've definitely been in prison too long, when I start seeing inmates I already know, repeating this process.

I didn't see my attorney today, and I wonder how those e-mails were received by all involved. After the deposition, the Judge has to end this unwarranted punishment. Only an Appeal or Supreme Court victory can force someone to pay for this time illegally taken from my life, society and family.

They moved a crazy kid next to me today who sings rap and yells with his head phones on all day long and even into the late hours. I hope I can sleep with his undisciplined carrying on. I can say nothing due to the hostility levels of these young men, and prison etiquette dictates silence, at least for now.

At today's inspection by the "suits" at least six of them came to me in the laundry room to remark that I have done alone what other units with three or four orderlies have been unable to accomplish. Even the Warden tried to endear me today. I'm not "re-upping". Get me out of this place"! I held my tongue due only to the UCMJ.

I have a real problem with the guard Deliverance. He has decided that he doesn't like the semi-respectful manner in which I am treated by the other guards, so he has stopped talking to me. He is an interesting psychological study of passive aggressive behavior. I am going to endear him or at least keep trying to soften him until I leave. This young man could keep an entire psychology team engaged for months.

Books are finally getting into the unit. During the walk-through today the book lady said she was amazed at how animated and desirous of books these inmates were. Noise levels have gone down. How remarkable! Not surprising, but pleasantly remarkable.

Since I've also been working with the plumber, we have had no leaks and no inmates are in cells that have broken sinks or toilets.

I'm working on a prototype of a "rules, regulations and procedures" sign to be placed in each cell explaining ward procedures and time guidelines to avoid the hysterical screaming and officer avoidance that existed when I first arrived.

The solitary prison power of the laundry room is like running the kitchen in general population. The time alone from the ward far outweighs the wash loads. I have pretended the washing machine is a fireplace and sit in silence and I read watching and listening to the clothes spin (like the fire in my imagination) instead of listening to the injurious surrounding noises that permeate the prison.

There are times in solitude that any reasonable man must ask the question - what if USXP and I had issued shares improperly? Disregarding my past defenses of 68 certified quarterly reports accepted by the SEC, no questions raised until literally days after I had the audacity to sue the SEC, and ignoring the continued assurances of my attorneys that we are correct … what if we were wrong?

Nevertheless, what if the company and I missed a small printed loophole, and the SEC, on paper, not in reality, were right - why then no trial? After all, two Florida juries heard the same issues and awarded us over $700,000,000.

This case was fast tracked because the company, not I, owned that now smoking gun of regulatory malfeasance. The company had to be silenced by the stereotypical rogue agents we have seen countless times in movies - exposing governmental wrongdoings.

In short, the defendant (the SEC) murdered the Plaintiff (USXP) and silenced (in solitary confinement) the lead witness (Me).

If we ever went to trial and our motive and actions were proven illegal, even then, USXP should still be operating. Seizure? Shredding? Closing the doors? Oh, come on! Reality check - PLEASE!

<u>Chapter 69 – How do Urine and Feces Feel?</u>

Well, I received my first prison pre-birthday gift. Tomorrow I will be sixty years of age. Tonight after I finished all of my work, I showered and changed into my clean clothes and was going to my cell. A disturbed inmate had been banging and screaming all day. Outside of his cell were splashed milk and various concoctions that he put in a milk carton and stomped on it to shoot the contents under the steel door, hitting the door and wall across the way. Let's call him the Screamer.

As I looked at the indescribable twelve hour mess he had made, there were two reasons I wanted to wait until tomorrow to clean it up. First, it would assure me getting out of my cell over the weekend, and secondly, I was freshly showered with no change of clothes and I didn't want to return to the prison filth before sleeping.

The cracker jack Deliverance said, "Do it now". As I went down to the tier and said hello to the other inmates, who were being verbally victimized and intimidated by this inmate, I began to mop up the mess and talk to the inmates. Then the swift milk carton machine gun attack was directed at me! I was completely covered with "stuff'! Guard and inmate reactions were violent. Some inmates were outraged that he could "do me". The guards rushed into action spraying him with a fire extinguisher surprisingly coupled with their sympathetic concerns and apologies to me. Think about it. Should I have gone down to this active situation while this was still an ongoing (fire fight) of urine or defecation or old food being thrown at others?

They hastily brought me to my cell while the Darth Vader Team will deal with the Screamer shortly. The troubled inmate made no distinction between the intended authority figures or his own orderly. The hysteria of the inmate is more of a concern to me than the memory of my unusual birthday fragrance. No, I didn't get another shower tonight. I washed in my sink while the guards disregarded their responsibility to get me re-cleaned.

Let's go through the events and conversation of my final day in the 50's decade because tomorrow I turn sixty years of age smelling as I may have at birth. This obviously is not my initial plan for a milestone birthday. Thank you, Judge. Your poor decisions continue.

Chapter 70 – One-legged Suicide Solved

My daytime favorite guard is CO Rutgers (flawed as he is) but he is still my favorite. Watching him orchestrate and cause organized pandemonium within his staff all day is exhausting. He forgets more than he remembers, but his interpersonal strength is that everyone likes him, and he is more concerned about that than "the job" and required daily task completions.

I told CO Rutgers about the threats by Evil's roommate if I didn't get him plastic bags. Rutgers planned to have me give the bags, and then catch me, so the inmates would think I tried, and the guards would pretend they were angry at me. I gave the plastic. He forgot to do anything. The inmates are more organized and intelligent than many of the CO's. I'll not include the COs in any of my future moral conflicts.

Another case in point in trying to explain the faulty thought process and lost pride occurred tonight. I had finished showering and I carried all of my soiled clothes in a pillow case for my wash tomorrow. They forgot that five new inmates were arriving. They asked if I could organize what they need before I go to my cell. I agree to anything they ask without comment. When I returned an hour later, all of my soiled belongings were laying on the floor next to the guards' desk because they needed a pillow case. They were fifteen steps away from a hundred clean pillow cases. They simply threw everything on the floor and utilized a dirty pillow case. It astounds me.

Watching the daily dysfunctional ballet of showers and movement of prisoners while I am trying to get some projects done makes my head hurt. There is neither consistency of work distribution nor consistency of rules and expectations. It's a disorganized men's clubhouse, and the inmates suffer. Organizing it would be so simple thus creating more calm and order amongst the already stressed prison population.

The totally tattooed Illustrated Man still loves me. The problem is that due to medication he now speaks as quickly as an auctioneer. He is on some medication that actually requires translation. He shaved his head in the shower without a mirror and now his head looked like a bloodied typographical map. He then said "I'm so proud you have become a man of the people" (imagine it being said at two seconds or less). Psychologically what gnaws at me about last night's milk carton incident is that just today I gave Inmate Screamer that lounging pair of shoes I had received (because he was quiet and sullen). He was so hysterical I don't think he even knew it was me. If he did, I forgive him anyway. As I put a fist on his window, he awkwardly met mine. All he said was that he was sorry. I know he is responding to the caging. I must forgive him.

Today another inmate told me that he was the bunkmate of the one legged Inmate who died last week. He said he called for help on the inmate's behalf for at least three hours before the boy of twenty-three lapsed into unconsciousness. He believes this unfortunate death was caused by negligence, through indifference and the lack of even the smallest amount of extended humanity. And why would there be any? There is no accountability here, no reporting, no true reality - and we may never read about these events or of his life and his family's pain?

Over the weekend, I'll write some more penal suggestions and recommendations. I may be out of my cell early because of the weekend mess, but I must accept that the mess may not get addressed until Monday. I have only one book left. I gave the other two unfinished books away to inmates who just arrived and needed them more than I do.

Chapter 71 – Happy Birthday First Timer!

I didn't think I would let my birthday be a reflective day in this diary. All I want to do is win that Appeal and then this Judge will be responsible for the size of the check our government will have to write.

My 60th birthday is also my 50th day in captivity. I hope my breakfast meal was a symbolic sign that I received this morning. First, last night's milk carton attack has not enticed me to want to rush to work, so I thought that if they didn't call me to work, I won't make myself crazy about it. I'll simply observe the activities from my cell and write, read and sleep on this chronologically important milestone birthday.

Our ward has filled up again to over seventy. They also had a suicide watch on the milk carton screamer guy last night. And to think I foolishly was going to waste these potential weapons as orange planters. One can see how ill prepared I was for prison life.

That reminds me of a question I often hear and am asked a great deal in prison. The question is "Is this your first time here"? When I answer that it is my "first time in any prison", they respond with shock. Obviously the expectations of those who have experienced multiple prison stays and the faulty thought processes and gang status of repeat offenders, as well as current inmates   need some adjustments.

The guards are like journeymen in baseball. Many have worked in multiple prisons and some of the inmates actually endeavor to follow their favorite guards. Counselors can, with justification, recommend prison changes for these reasons.

Many are lost "boys". Many are emotionally "needy". All are emotionally dependent. That's the guards I am speaking of. Some of the inmates are truly deserving of their incarceration, but a percentage of them are not. It is what happens to those within that percentage, after they arrive in prison, which I see as faulty, and in need of a Special Investigator and a Prosecutor too.

You're probably still waiting to hear about the birthday sign. I arrived some fifty days ago and I'm pretty sure I have told you twenty times or more that one milk, one cereal, and sometimes a piece of fruit is always my breakfast meal. What did they serve today? On my birthday, (which they do not know, nor have I discussed), it's not "prison cool" (PC) to expect the singing of Happy Birthday. They served chocolate cake for breakfast! I swear it's true. First, I thought it was a surprise for only me. How naive and foolish I am. These men to quote Holden Caulfield in "Catcher in the Rye" have as much sensitivity as a toilet seat. It's really not their fault because what you see here is what you get. They must become the culture or the culture spits them out. It's the prison culture from which I heard only one comment that told me I wasn't the only cake recipient. That inmate said, "Chocolate cake for breakfast that's ass backwards!" After acknowledging my ass backwards birthday to myself, I ate the cake and went back to sleep figuring that they would not want me to work early if at all today. The dream I had was another birthday gift. Everyone I love and have been loved by appeared pleasantly in my dream and with some clarity I feel it is yet another sign of my impending release.

Many religious or political leaders have been forced to do things that were unpleasant for longer than fifty days. Their outcomes faired pretty well (other than one crucifixion). So for more than fifty days I have been watching and studying this system. Events continue to show me how damaged our prison's soul has become.

On Passover the Jewish people ask the question, "Why is this night different from all other nights?" Remember my belief in "signs"? Every Saturday and Sunday we have had the mystery meat with potatoes and some sort of mush. On my birthday we received, eggs and bacon with bread to make a sandwich, plus extra butter for my matzos. It's a miracle and my birthday celebration, humble as it may be, continues. These two food changes really have amazed me. Could this day be different from the others?

This day did become different than any other. My attorney brought me a cookie because it was my birthday. They threw him out, and he may not be permitted back until I myself leave. I'll know on Monday, if he is allowed back. When I visit with my Wife on Monday, she will know what has happened to him. I hope.

Chapter 72 – Mr. Clean

All three shifts let me out of my cell to work today. My reaction may sound crazy, but the day goes by more quickly and I get to interact with the inmates and the guards when I am free to move about the ward. Today I even broke down Deliverance. He observed three new guards who liked what I was doing and the way the place looked. He then asked me to help him clean the cells. This is a cleaning procedure unlike any other cleaning one can imagine. The inmate's cell slot is opened and we put through an envelope with some comet and a toilet brush. After these items are returned, we give him a green soap bottle and a cloth. Then I pass them a broom and dust pan and then the clean mop. Now comes the exchange of linens, and anything else they may need. Deliverance left after the second cell as he saw how the inmates did anything I asked. I didn't really have him on my side until I finished thirty cells (a big number) and I then energetically started painting the red ceiling pipe which had never even been seen or noticed by most of them. It was when he saw I had painted the mop sticks and dust broom's red that he just gave in. He said, I heard what you did to the inmate that threw milk and stuff at you yesterday - I am impressed. "I would have never forgiven him", he said.

To review, all I really did with that inmate was go back to clean his tier and when I came to his cell he looked at me. I walked over to the glass window and put my hand to the glass and said, "I forgive you and I'm sorry you are so sad". He cried, and thanked me for not being angry with him.

I don't know if I'll get out of my cell this Sunday, but whatever happens, today, Saturday was one day that I got to spread some positive feelings of humanity amidst this negativity.

I spoke again with the Illustrated Man today. "They think I'm crazy", he said, "They put me in a solitary plastic box for twenty-one days and they are moving me to a psychiatric ward this week. "Do you think they are making me crazy?', he asked. My tearful eyes prevented an answer. His sentences were said in three seconds.

## Chapter 73 – I'm Not Here?

Today I met at least ten new inmates and helped each of them to feel welcome and not alone. One of them gave me the History of Salt book back and said, "Who could read this fucking book"? I said, "In a few weeks, you'll love it". He laughed and kept the book.

With the exception of possibly losing my daily attorney visits it was a fast moving birthday weekend. On one tier many of the inmates sang "Happy Birthday" while I mopped. It was quite memorable and touching. Sure, I cried. Them singing for me touched my tear ducts. I have so much to do for them once I can get Americans to hear their songs.

Sunday however, was a difficult day. First, I was confined to the cell since it was Sunday and some of the weekend crews prefer to be left alone without a witness able to observe what they actually do during what are supposed to be their work hours. The loud playing videos and fraternity yelling and laughter made me understand why I was left alone in my cell. My efforts to improve the place are simply threatening to some, and I am now at peace with that. The guards are simply more comfortable with many of the more hardened inmates, but unable to understand an individual like myself who they could never hope to become. On the surface that may sound a bit egotistical, but you haven't seen nor heard nor watched these men in motion. I pity these prisoners sentenced to years and decades of this establishment's consistent insanity, laziness and discontent occurring without outside supervision, or even a review by someone entirely outside the prison system.

One cell away from me today I heard an inmate yelling all day for a wash cloth and towel. Since he came in late last night and he still hadn't been given one, the guard said, "The guy in charge of these items is not in today". Hello, I'm here! "Put me in Coach, I can solve this in one minute and return to my cell". Going to the laundry to get those items requires two locks and thirty steps. That's why the guard said "the guy isn't in", because he is too lazy to open 2 locks and walk 30 feet to let "the guy" do his job. That guy is me!

Chapter 74 – Cookiegate

This was another difficult day because I now think my attorney may not be able to visit me anymore because he tried to give me a Birthday cookie. Those vending machines never work, but delivery by my attorney of a sealed vending machine cookie product caused him to be unnecessarily accused of smuggling an item into the prison.   All they had to do was plug in the vending machines.   So he could have bought my Birthday cookie right there and contributed to the prison system economy.   After all, this non-criminal should, at the very least, be trusted to use the vending machines.

I am listening to two black gang members yelling at each other. I know they are using a form of English, but it won't be understood in the business world.   There seems to be a great deal of bantering and happy laughter between them for being in prison.   Could they really feel happy and at home here?   Some of these inmates may consider this lifestyle a way to beat the capitalistic white system and they seem to prefer prison dependency over having to perform in the outside world.   How sad is that?

Oh my goodness!, that gang dialogue I was just referring to, was between a guard and an inmate.   Not two inmates!   Remember the system changes almost everyone in here.   "And the beat goes on".

Chapter 75 – Trust Our Military

Let's get back to some other thoughts on reducing the number of prisons, costs and the perpetuation of a system that society would rather ignore than change. At 60 billion dollars a year we owe it to our children's long term debt and our reoccurring and increasing crime rates to have the courage to examine creative changes to this broken system.

Many of these young men should be put into our military instead of in jail. Others could be rehabilitated by a prison peace corps type program of National repair and revitalization. Failure to perform their contract satisfactorily will result in a return to jail. They themselves would be choosing jail by not performing in this program.

The costs related to prison life should not be borne by government and its taxpayers. With the massive workforce that exists within our prison system, why is it that this system is not made revenue neutral by using that workforce to pay its own bills and improve the public infrastructure in the bargain?

Until such logic is acted upon ...prison terms should be shorter and food, clothing and overhead should be paid by the prisoner's immediate family. There is no stigma within the underbelly gang community for going to jail. In fact, it is a badge of honor or rite of passage. This will "bring home" the consequences of their crimes and impose responsibilities upon their families, who the prisoners love and would regret adding additional financial burdens to, by their illegal actions.

Last night a guard asked me, "Why are you nice to them? They are garbage". I responded, "Someone loves them and God doesn't make garbage. Sometimes we all get lost". His "whatever" and the abrupt end of the dialogue defined why a thinker can't communicate with a governmental guard. It's remarkable how pristine I left the place when I went into my cell Saturday night at about 11:00PM. I am always amazed at the lack of cleanliness habits of some who work here. They show their hatred of themselves and contempt for their work environment, by taking no pride in their surroundings. Last night one of the inmates said, "You're as neat and polite as a butler". I guess I am. I will continue to try and maintain that standard and I will never adopt these lower governmental standards as a way of living or being.

I would like to continue addressing some additional thoughts on prison reform. To raise the overall standards and accountability of prison life, I would place management directly under an existing military organizational structure. A higher competency standard for Corrections Officers (CO) would be mandatory and the present support overhead for "suits" and other unionized civilian executives would be eliminated. Regular rotation of guards, rather than the existing familiarity, would standardize the punishment and insure consistency of actions. There are too many creature comforts such as commissary, head phones, telephones and prisoner rights. Prison should be stark, but it should be time sensitive. I am against long term "stays" without restitution to the victims. There can be any number of alternative forms of time served that will benefit the victims, as well as aid in restructuring the criminal's life. Rights of prisoners should never be more important than the rights of the guards, our society and the victims. I've been thinking of the Coast Guard and Marine Corps. Those Generals, Admirals and their Officer Corps can better organize and mold inmates than the BOP is presently capable of accomplishing. Look at the return rates of prisoners. The way it is now just doesn't work.

## Chapter 76 – The BOP's Statue of Liberty

Tonight I was surprisingly "taken out" of my cell to work after 10:00PM. During that time I spoke with a female Lieutenant heart to heart. She told me that the BOP now has begun filling their buildings with non-criminals, homeless people, psychologically damaged individuals and basically any warm body to help fill their quotas. The BOP denies these actions and the quota system. It has become a business fueled by human suffering. From public bond issuances based upon guaranteed revenues that support each prisoner in the population, they just keep building more and newer prisons … it's no wonder that the prison system is an outsourced and politically influenced growth industry funded by you and me.

How interesting and even ironic is it that the Statue of Liberty, so near this prison, bears an inscription on its base, which seems to mimic the mantra of the BOP: "Give me your tired, your poor, your huddled masses yearning to breathe free".

Tonight's crew was eating pizza, donuts and ice cream. I'm definitely getting a slice of pizza before I get to the airport. This week there will be a deposition, which could have been done months ago at no expense to taxpayers. This deposition is nothing more than an SEC ploy to justify putting and keeping me here. Well, let's hope justice doesn't stay blind and my loyal shareholders are compensated for our company's illegal seizure and attempted silencing of their CEO.

It's important for you to see cascading examples as they manifest themselves to me, so that you can better understand why prison life is not the properly run rehabilitating process that most of us assume it is. It is not … and this needs to be investigated.

As I was speaking today with another young male officer about my ideas to change the BOP, he was engaged by the idea and added that there is no job or societal re-entrance training for departing inmates. Only past crime and old neighborhood behavior are what the inmates can hope to repeat, once they get hungry or bored after leaving prison.

Definitely a more professional and happier mood now exists around here. As I mopped all six tiers twice today, I could judge the mood. There were voluntary book exchanges, item requests and good natured laughter from the polite inmates and even the CO's have remarked that the place feels better than it has in years.

One twenty-two year old inmate who has impressed me with his wit, maturity and sensitivity received a life sentence today. He was sadly sleeping at 4:00PM, so I'll report after I speak with him. I am devastated for him. That poor soul. He has no money to even appeal the non-jury verdict. Sound familiar?

Chapter 77 – I'm not eating garbage … Yet

Today my Wife visited and we both cried when we saw these young men saying goodbye to their children after visitation was over. It's not natural.

While collecting garbage, I stole a few old newspapers and I almost went for some uneaten hot dogs thrown out in a sealed Styrofoam box. After all, I had just changed the garbage bag. I removed the box quickly with only the hot dogs - but still I couldn't eat them. I'm still winning! I haven't yet become what they strive to create, a prisoner in my own mind.

I got a great book today and started reading it in the laundry. Just then a new inmate arrived and asked for a book, and I gladly gave it to him because I have you and this diary. He may not even have a pen and paper.

Tonight my surround sound banging and continual gang communicating coupled with their annoying rap singing creates a cacophony of sounds that are very unsettling to a clear mind, and it continued unabated until morning.

Another man with whom I have had a good friendship went into suicide watch tonight. I don't know why, but he seems so upset I will have to try to find out.

My non-stop therapeutic working has created an unbelievable appreciation from most of these inmates. Normally the orderly only does what the officers "see" needs to be done. Hence, the great difference in my actions. I have raised the "bar" to improve what *I* see needs to be done. Inmates' lives are in disorder. By giving them order and consistency I can see and feel a positive emotional impact.

We cleaned another twenty cells again tonight replacing all of the linens, while I continued sweeping, mopping and disinfecting the hallways. Never before, and as a result of my supply list requisitions, have the cleaning utensils been so clean and so user friendly. Unfortunately that means that I have been working some nights until after 11:00PM. Tonight it is worth it, when you can smell the pine cleanliness and feel the personal pride that the inmates are taking in their surroundings.

Chapter 78 – Turning Grey without Sunshine

Today I helped create a new policy for the MCC. With the exception of me, who has never seen the sun for my entire stay, all the inmates exercise on the roof, and they join inmates from all floors. Most of the CO's have to go through a great deal of prisoner preparation for this one hour movement. Frankly, in my opinion, it should be more than an hour and it should be scheduled without the other inmates to minimize tension. The CO's were complaining about the problems and that they would prefer organizing recreation time throughout the day instead of early in the morning. I said, "Do a cell check on the next three inmates that go to recreation. No one else will want you finding out what they have squirreled away in their cells." I have also suggested creating a special three hour per day (instead of one hour) recreation and education program that may afford the inmate more constructive use of the facilities as they presently are too crowded and nonproductive. After the inspections, no one went to exercise the next day. They decided to stay in their cells instead of being spot inspected. We were then able to petition for the three hour exercises. But that never happened.

To further define the feelings of prison life I have another relevant story. I now have three repaired polishing machines but no electric outlets that work on the entire unit floor. We are on the "electric repair list" (remember the refrigerator). And the beat goes on.

Another relevant prison event defines why I don't want to get sick here. I watched a CO take ill. I was locked in the library cage when it started. I tried to talk the other CO through what to do because it was obvious the older guard was about to pass out. The healthy CO was frantic and acted like Ralph Kramden from the "Honeymooners" and could do nothing that I calmly told him to do. The older CO finally passed out, threw up and after "Ralph" finally followed my advice, we called in the medical team and stabilized the older guard. I, of course, was then released to clean up the vomit.

Well, the cookie incident didn't lose my attorney his visitation rights. He was able to visit despite the incident, but we are on a short rope so no snacks or letters are to be exchanged. I will still continue to sneak out these entries because they would never ever allow these to leave with me, when I eventually walk out of here.

One of the Lieutenants asked me if I would consider teaching the orderlies on other floors how to work. The logistical problem of me in handcuffs is still being discussed by the "powers that be". Would I be permitted to speak to the other non-cuffed inmates? It is probably not possible in this inflexible system.

Frankly, this place is not the same unit as when I arrived. It smells pleasant. Urine does not permeate the tiers. Clothes have been washed with detergent and inmate cells have been improved drastically. In the past, wet clothes were only dried but not washed. No water or flooding problems have surfaced in the past 3 weeks. CO's are not yelling. Inmates are still without many things, but I'm able to verbalize their needs and reasons for delays. They seem to believe me. I live between the two worlds. Today the Guards were upset because a guard was killed in another jail. He was stabbed as he opened the slot to feed an inmate. There are over 1100 prisoners in here. I am told we only have 200 guards. Most general populations units are without firearms and handcuffs. Someday under this system you will read of an incident in this jail, if they ever write about it. No one wrote about the boy who died last week through neglect. Prison deaths, I guess, don't sell newspapers unless it is riot related. Riots are normally followed by pay raises, union demands and increased inmate commissary prices.

The night before tomorrow's eight hour deposition should be one of apprehension. It really is not. Although I do not believe my answers will determine the Judge's release of me from this ridiculous incarceration, the truth remains on my side. (If that even matters in his Court).

Chapter 79 – A Rose by any other Name …

After I returned from that deposition, some unexpected events combined into the worst night of my short orderly career. Picture the following: Twenty-three inmates were scheduled to leave. Fifty-nine inmates were required to shower and to change clothes. Twenty cells were selected for me to change their blankets and sheets. Then six new inmates arrived. Over thirty meals were dropped and walked over for three hours by the guards. In addition, two inmate suicide attempts now prevent me from getting unlocked to begin cleaning up the guard's mess. I have over thirteen loads of wash still to do! I have done nine loads tonight, and tomorrow I have to once again leave to attend the continued deposition. The Warden and his "staff" also inspect tomorrow. Tonight's crew wouldn't let me clean the showers and we have the "suit" inspection in the morning. I won't even be there in the morning to help out, and remember I still have no assistant.

Then an inmate tried to "cut" a guard. It required more people than the United Nations to gather for a summit to stand outside of his cell. I was still confined until a BOP resolution of this incident. I spend more lost time while doing time in prison than the loss of my normal life time while I do this time in prison.

"Gang language" is a code known only by the gang members. It sounds like nonsense, but it's similar to radio operators in a war with a non-breakable code. Many of these inmates are at war! We just don't acknowledge it! Hopefully it won't be too late for us to change our acceptance of an urban war and our desire to win it. We need to win it for the young men and women yet to visit these places. We must phase out these 18th century penal systems.

At least nine inmates have asked me for employment help or advice when and if they come out of prison and go looking for a job. Shouldn't counselors be doing that?

It's after one o'clock in the morning, and I want to be ready for an early morning wake up for cleaning and the deposition. I'll tell you tomorrow how I thought the deposition went.

The prison feeling of disorganization tonight must be written about for you to grasp this place even deeper. Along with the four CO's, I had to prepare for the twenty-three departures, serve meals to fifty-nine inmates, pick-up dirty trays, accept the newcomers and then clean empty cells. I also had to carry hundreds of pounds of wet wash from the showers to the laundry. The disorganized confusion coupled with the burn-out inactivity of two of the four CO's, enabled me to watch their "ballet" of non-performance. I got to observe them because there were brown suited inmates on the floor, so I had to stay locked up. One of them started delivering mail because that was less strenuous. Another just sat down and stared. The inmates were screaming and pounding on their cell doors for food which had not been delivered until after 7:00PM (cold). That food arrived warm at 4:30PM. The different shifts do not communicate or have common goals, or even dialogue with each other. Tonight's crew didn't care about the inspection tomorrow and the day crew leaves all of the dirty work for the evening crew not caring about their other work responsibilities. There is a clock in the Day Room, so when I am out of my cell I can often post accurate times to my diary.

The day crew didn't care about the amount of mess such a twenty-three inmate graduation change-over would cause. We could have prepared for it before the night crew came in. I watch and feel the frustration of some very caring officers trying to complete a thankless job made more difficult by BOP rules, locks and antiquated procedures.

During the graduation to brown uniforms, inmates are laboriously handcuffed to walk ten or fifteen steps and then they are let loose in the same holding room. Instead of this hour long unnecessary procedure they could open each of the fifteen cells and let the graduates walk unaided. It would save a good ten minutes of worthless cuffing activity per inmate.

Even more new inmates came today. Our total is now seventy (with one orderly). Most units have one orderly for every twenty-five inmates. The loud surround sound rap singing continues. These young men are so confused, and this type and length of incarceration accomplishes nothing, except to add to their desperation and depression.

My multiple jail names have expanded to the following: 1) Mr. A.; 2) The A Man; 3) Rich the Concierge; 4) Rich the Butler; 5) Richie Rich; (they believe me to be a tycoon)(the Judge thinks so too)     6) Orderly Man; 7) IIC (Inmate In Charge); 8) Rich; 9) Lord Baltimore; 10) Son (Sun).

I look forward to meeting our newest arrivals tomorrow.   It will be at their first shower.   Oh, the shower door was finally delivered.   It didn't fit!   It will be business as usual tomorrow without that shower.

Chapter 80 – Sign-In, Sign-Out – Who Loses?

I came face to face with the Warden while he was escorting some BOP executives around. He said nothing. Outside of his walk-through inspection game that he performs, he really doesn't care either. Tonight I watched three counselors "sign in" and "sign out" at the same time and I heard them say they were going home. The sign-in book reflects hours of time spent. I watched them sign in for time that was not spent with the inmates. Those inmates need someone to help them. What a disgrace! They signed in for two hours and simultaneously signed back out – and promptly left the floor.

The deposition was conducted today. I was very happy with the questions and the answers. To think I waited fifty-six days for their meaningless attempts to pretend that their seizure and liquidation of our company was and is based on something they can explain or justify. How can the SEC get away with this cover up? Oh, I forgot they have that fair and insightful Judge.

The deposition took most of the day so I had to train my new assistant orderly Tom, and his attention to our responsibilities made it much easier today for me. He is a gentleman and does not fit the prison stereotype we might imagine.

In addition to our daily work load, another eight inmates left our ward today. We have sixty-two now. Tom may make my last few days easier before I am allowed to tell off that Judge and get on with my life.

Each inmate's story makes me feel guilty for complaining about my incarceration. From scrubbing off "Life Sucks" on the cell wall of a twenty-two year old, to giving an older inmate my more comfortable shoes, to giving my meal to an inmate on suicide watch; every day reminds me of the need for humanity in this broken prison system.

We've been without razors for two weeks so our beards seem a bit long. Maybe this is a test by the guards to ascertain which of us have illegal razors. Those with clear faces are suspect. Those with fourteen day hair growth obviously can be trusted.

I will not think or act like a prisoner. I must re-affirm that unusual affirmation hourly.

Watching the clean and happy orange graduates and their smiles today made my humble efforts seem worthwhile.

I still regret my lack of phone communication. I so wanted to tell my Wife or someone how I did in the deposition. But then again, since all phones are monitored; I probably wouldn't have been able to speak freely. I'm going to write to her tomorrow during my legal visit.

Today my new next door cell neighbor (that suicide friend) was quite talkative. His story was tragic. His two brothers are FBI agents, and one of them arrested him. His father committed suicide over this action by the sons, and the rest of the family is in turmoil over this son's recent incarceration. With no money to defend himself, this time, his drunk fighting sentence was longer than a competent attorney could have gotten him.

Today I had to remove more feces from a cell. I tell you that to try to give you the harsh realities of this lifestyle day to day. I don't always tell you everything I see and clean. It's hard enough to believe the other stories, and I try to block out some of the sights and smells of this system.

Putting a civilian into this environment without him having committed any crime speaks poorly of this Judge's irresponsible sentencing. When I eventually expose the wrongful actions of the SEC, I will sue the Court for this illegal incarceration.

Tonight we had an entirely new substitute CO team. Boy, did they work well with Tom and me. They were very professional and caring! The inmates are peaceful and contented. I am sure they will not be back. Sure enough, they were unhardened trainees and they never returned.

I received sixteen books to distribute and trade and another thirty new pairs of socks to give out which made my evening "rounds" a delight.

Chapter 81 – Missing Picture

I now believe I should be out of this place by July 2 or 3rd.   The next few days will begin to clarify that opinion.   Today, when I went into my legal visit, I could really see the "rehabilitation" that goes on here.   There was always one motivational poster in a glass frame on the wall of each room. An inmate, obviously with an attorney watching, stole the picture and left the empty frame hanging on the wall.   It's a funny visual of the rehabilitative progress being made here.   Then again, a guard could have needed it to go behind that "broken" refrigerator.

My new assistant Tom is an effective multitasker.   His story, like many, explains why China has fewer prisoners than the United States.   We're doing something wrong.   In fact, we have the highest prisoner percentage of any country in the world and we incarcerate over 25% of the entire world's prisoners.   Chew on those wasteful facts.

If there was a good time to leave, it would be now.   The physical appearance of the place is the best it has ever been, according to everyone who speaks to me.   The camaraderie of the inmates was evident today at showers.   Respect, courtesy, appreciation and respectful comments of "thank-you" and "I feel better when I talk to you", comments flowed easily from my orange friends.

My attorneys tell me that I'll go home in a few days.   But the SEC and an arrogant Judge may feel differently.

One of the new inmates asked for three pairs of socks and "fuck the world" if any other inmates want any of those socks.   I told him I was going to call him FW for Fuck the World, but I would only give him one pair of socks.   He was pleased when others started calling him FW.   They love nicknames.

As the officers grow more comfortable with my presence and efforts, my daily insanity of prison life in solitary has been somewhat neutralized.

Yet Tom, my co-orderly has a brother on another ward.   Tom has never been in prison and was put here due to a new Patriot Act catch-all phrase which further eliminates American rights.   It is called "conspiracy".   If nothing happened, but someone says you were considering committing a crime, you can be incarcerated. Tom has been here one year and is still awaiting "sentencing". How tragic!

I will once again this weekend (maybe my final one) try to polish the floors and make a third list of supply items they still need (they have lost my last two lists).

To a person without a family, prison guards and inmates substitute for each other's needs in this unusually dysfunctional governmentally created sub-culture.

Chapter 82 – Being a "Lifer" – On the BOP Installment Plan

I learned today that the inmate leader of the tan suitors (trustees) sells food products and services to the other inmates through air vents and with the help of some of the guards. Some inmates eat better food. I certainly hope so, because my commissary snacks have become my only daily eating. For example, today's multi-meal feast included: frosted flakes (with tartar sauce) hot dogs (with sugar) and burned fish with frozen macaroni and cheese. Without my commissary granola bars, cheese and matzos I would lose more than the twenty pounds I estimated. (I lost over forty pounds when I finally weighed myself.) Tonight I had to carry ten especially heavy boxes for a young strong twenty-five year old guard. Those boxes were hundreds of pounds each. My daily "master slave" life continues even with this regular humiliation. Carrying those boxes while he lazily sat by without an ounce of guilt or compassion will always be engraved in my mind.

Yesterday an inmate attacked another inmate with a medical scalpel. He received over two hundred stitches and the inmate is still in critical condition. You tell me how an inmate gets that when we are searched for a pen or paper clips! All that the attacker will probably get for his actions will be a longer stay which will be paid for by us and the attacker "gains" in status in this upside down prison world. Can I cut my nails with a scalpel?

I am told that when this prison was new three inmates tried to climb out a non-completed ninth floor window with tied blankets. The blankets ripped; one died, one was paralyzed, and the third is still in here (or in the system) for the attempted escape. Yet, we continue having counts even though this has been the only escape attempt in the prison's history. The "Count" still continues four or five times daily. Holding on to these inmates has become more of a priority than "fixing", or" helping" them!

Well, I really got my next door neighbor, (FBI brother) really upset today. He was the one whose brother arrested him. When the lunchtime meal came today, it was mystery meat with eggs. He was telling me how hungry he was because he had lost thirty pounds since he's been here. I asked the guard to give him my tray. The guard said, "OK", but didn't give it to my neighbor. My neighbor is absolutely ballistic with anger. He's not mad at me, but he's going to tell off the guard who "disrespects him". He's been screaming and pounding on the walls. I'm afraid that I caused an incident which is about to occur. He's poised to explode. They are arguing now. The guard is trying to explain that he didn't disrespect him. It's not working. The inmate is in free falling anger. I'm sure they will "write up" his anger actions. He has an alcohol and drug addiction problem and he will be in prison for the rest of his life. There is no effort to rehabilitate him, only to keep him as a life time customer of the BOP. He's a "lifer" on the installment plan.

He's silent now. He's been speaking to me non-stop since 7:00AM. Thank God for the quiet relief. Responding to this inmate's faulty mental thought processes becomes an exhausting exercise. One cannot discredit these inmate's faulty thought perceptions without creating additional tensions with them. It's frustrating that most inmates do not make much sense in their conclusions, decisions or basic suppositions. My neighbor thinks that I have to run my hot water for him to get hot water. This is another job for me to do whenever he wants hot water. That plumbing crew should be franchised out to unfriendly countries. After this plumbing team fixed foreign toilets and showers, the country itself would have a revolution.

All is well right now. My neighbor has gotten his hot water and forgotten about the food. I await my legal visit where I can rest my ears and my head after listening to four hours of his justification of his ten fights and multiple lost life opportunities. I count the moments until I can be called to the silence of the legal visit.

Chapter 83 – It's your desk, Deliverance

After I returned, I polished all of the six tiers floors and varnished the one officer desk. The day shift officers loved it. Deliverance however came in to work at 4:00PM and erupted violently. He actually put tee shirts on top of the wet varnished desk before it was dried. Then he embarrassingly yelled and returned me back to my cell in disgrace. He has become the antithesis of everything I represent. He has literally "sent me back to my cell" for attempting to improve the unit. Maybe I should request a meeting with the Lieutenant tomorrow regarding Deliverance's behavior and attitude. Being so close to the end of my stay, I should be careful not to make public comments directly to or about him until I have left.

We have prison celebrities in here. I saw a Columbian magazine article about one of our other celebrity inmates. He was a General arrested for drug trafficking. Fortunately, I have always been nice to him. Maybe, after this demonstration of justice, I can move to South America. With American Judges like mine, I don't see the difference between dictatorships and this Judge's definition of judicial democracy.

Now Deliverance came to my cell to apologize. Apparently all of the other CO's sided with me. So I redid the desk and it is now drying. Then Tom and I cleaned thirty more cells and washed their sheets and blankets. While we were about to finish the wash and rest in our quiet laundry room with a sense of accomplishment and satisfaction and then eat the two extra chicken meals given to us by Deliverance; two inmates were dragged in. They were bloodied far beyond any combat visual. Our night mood changed forever when one of the bloodied inmates saw Tom and said, "your brother is fucked up - he may be dead".

Poor Tom physically collapsed at the concern of not being there to help his younger brother. He is immobile and almost in a fetal position. I am helpless and trying to absorb this horrific and unexpected situation.

As we waited hoping that his brother was coming through the door, about six more officers came frantically running into our unit and sent us both to our cells immediately. I was told that there were many inmates coming to us tonight.  By the looks in the guard's eyes this was not just a fight.  It seemed like a most serious situation.

Tom wanted to know about his brother, but they dragged him reluctantly, without responding, back to his cell, and then very quickly sent me to mine.  All I wanted was the leftover chicken.  The other inmates already knew something "big" had happened.  It may have been planned because as I was walking in, one inmate yelled "It started, look at them trying to keep it a secret".

The multiple inmate arrival activity is ongoing as I write to you.  Remember once before I said to you that "Saturday night is the loneliest night of the week"?  Earlier tonight when cleaning cells I observed an officer find fruit, bread, sugar and water fermenting in a plastic bag.  The inmate had made a cheap form of "moonshine" to create a Saturday night "jailhouse high".  Saturday nights are a tough one in this setting.  There may be over twenty new additions tonight.  I wish I could be there to help check them in because the guards make such a mess when they are left alone to do anything.

My crazy next door neighbor wants to remain alone in his cell and he is already angry that one of these fighters is going to be put in his cell.  It's not going to happen because tonight he said to me, talk to me, or I'm going to commit suicide".  I passed that information on to the CO's.  They don't like him, so they'll keep him alone until he commits suicide or some act of stupidity.  It's only a matter of time that he will self - destruct.  They will leave him alone in that cell.

When I find out more about the "fight", I'll let you know about it.  Sometimes I get the whole story, but prisoners are not always like retirees in Florida, they don't talk or pass along gossip, or even facts.

My crazy next door neighbor is still screaming and banging on the door.  He doesn't want a roommate and he has worked his crazy mind into believing that he's getting a roommate.  While he's carrying on, the screaming "gang code talk" has begun about the fight.  The forms of communication that move the prison world are telephones and "tell an inmate".  I hope my next door neighbor stops screaming.  His insanity is quite humorous. No one has said anything about a roommate, yet he has worked himself beyond a tantrum state. What a sad character. I wish I could do more for him. Hopefully this book will help many of them.

After many hours later, the CO's came to offer me a shower after working. Unfortunately, there is no hot water. So, I took an ice cold shower tonight. Since the Marine Corp in 1969 and two other prison showers, this was a most painful shower. It was better than no shower at all, but not what I had in mind tonight.

My hysterical neighbor has just now asked me for cheese and crackers because he is starving to death. Of course, being in a world of narcissistic cons, I know when I am being taken advantage of, but I'd rather have that happen than feel selfish or regret a possible act of charity.

After I gave the food to him, he has been quiet. I wish I had more to give to him. Unfortunately, I have none left for myself and I am also hungry, but at least not suicidal.

Here's the updated scoop on Tom's brother. He's here. He's not dead. I heard him screaming while I was trying to muster the courage to walk into that cold shower. He sounds like a hardened black gang member but he is blue eyed and white. Prison life can alter one's view of self. He is very loud and very angry. Even other inmates are telling him to "shut the fuck up". It's close to 11:30 PM. By the way, two officers were looking at the varnished desk talking about how great it looked. Deliverance had his feet up on it.

Chapter 84 – Strip Searched by Little Richard

Sunday is sometimes a long day. There are no legal visits. There may not even be work to do. It may be a good time to write a little more in anticipation of my leaving solitary confinement. If I am not released, you will know firsthand how sad and disappointed I will be. However, I will continue writing to present this place for what it really is.

Tonight they *let* me clean cells and I moved the bar of cell clean-up a bit higher than ever done before. I had the inmates actually clean the inside door window in their cells! After polishing their floors and now cleaning their cells so thoroughly the laughter and good natured friendship was quite unusual and commented on by the CO's. One of them said "Altomare, I don't know how you did this, but I've been here five years and you have every one of them treating you like you are their father and mother". "It's remarkable and some of the other COs have even been cleaning up after dinner". They appear to like this new prison "feeling" of freshness and cleanliness. I am exhausted.

I almost forgot to tell you about the follow-up and fallout on the missing picture in the legal office. Remember an inmate (or a guard) stole the picture, but left this large frame hanging on the wall. Now complete strip searches are mandatory after every inmate's legal visit to further enhance the joy of meeting with your attorney. It adds yet another strip search to my already mandatory two daily strip search experiences.

For today's legal room strip search, I had to go into a little 5x5 room with a guard whose hairstyle and mannerisms look like "Little Richard" from the old rock and roll days. He was a bit too "interested" in my strip search. Fortunately I didn't have a four foot by three foot poster hidden anywhere which required coughing or bending. Probably the poster is in the vending machine jamming and preventing it from working.

Because I think I am going home, I enjoyed a mental victory lap in my cell. I hope I am finally leaving, but I am doing all of the activities which maintained my sanity and emotional edge during my first thirty days allowing me to rise within the corporate orderly world of inmates. Such activities as Bridge, push-ups, exercises, scrabble, reading and writing to you were that victory lap.

I am told that sixteen new inmates came from the "fight" and four more are in the hospital. Also, I'll find out more tomorrow if Tom is still permitted to work as an orderly. They may not allow him if his brother is also here on the ward. Don't ask me why. Rules supersede logic in governmental buildings.

A female guard who calls me "cookie man" because of the time they sent my lawyer away (my birthday) for bringing me cookies, delivered my breakfast today. She was wearing sun glasses in the darkened tier. I couldn't miss the opportunity to ask if she was wearing sunglasses because of the glare from the polished floors and polished desk. She's still laughing, but she said, "This place is starting to look like a hotel. It also smells cleaner than a hospital." Then she added, "I miss the smell of urine." How do I overcome that?

Because I gave my neighbor my lunch yesterday, he now believes that when every lunch comes - it's now his. If it's the mystery meat, he can have it. But normal adults like us would not say, "When MY lunch comes don't forget to send it to me." Emotionally it is quite easy to understand these damaged souls. It is also revealing to grasp why officers emotionally turn off when sixty of these inmates all continually want and want and want.

Last night, Tom said, "Stealing cars is not really a crime. Everyone does OK. The insurance company pays the owner and the owner gets a new car to drive, and we get to market cars to new buyers who don't have good credit." How does one begin to respond to this thought process and that guard's problem with urine withdrawal?

I don't want you to think that I've gotten soft in prison. I still haven't cut my nails since that one phone call. The guards are working to get my ward on the nail clipper "list". They have scalpels cutting inmates around the rest of the jail and yet a monitored nail clipper at shower time continues to be beyond their task completion. I'll put it on my third supply "list" which I will give CO Rutgers tomorrow.

Some of the guards who resist structure and self-improvement are exemplified by the fact that Deliverance initially violated that newly varnished desk. As he puts his filthy shoes on the newly varnished desk, he obviously is more comfortable in an unchanged filthy prison atmosphere.

This crazy guy next door is now screaming that he has no hot water again. He is calling to me to run my water so he can have water. By the way, he is incapable of thanking me for last night's crackers and cheese. A socially educated person would show some appreciation. He's a taker. That's what the criminal addictive mind of entitlement without social responsibilities appears to become. He dropped out of school in the eighth grade. He has been arrested over eight times and he can't write or speak as a forty-six year old would be expected. Yet, he continues to blame others for his plight. Not one counselor has visited him during the three months he has been here. He says other prisons have better food and more outside activities. Prison attitudes he says are the same as here except, in other prisons he has seen guards beat and kill inmates. He prefers to be in solitary because he is afraid of other prisoners and guards who beat him. Some life? Think about his diary, if he could write one.

Chapter 85 – Papa John Delivery

Apparently one of our new sixteen inmates is a "Booty Bandit, (BB). I am told a BB is someone who rapes other inmates. That's one good reason I remain in isolation. On the other hand, my crazy man next door has just begun to hyperventilate that they better not put that BB into his cell. It's amazing that he gets so angry over any possibility without even any indication of such an event happening.

I gave him today's mystery meat and believe it or not - he's now threatening to commit suicide once again. He wants to commit suicide because he's too full, and I have to continue talking him out of it, as long as I remain in this prison psychiatric ward.

Remember (the BOP) are more interested in counting and holding on to these customers rather than attempting to fix those lost souls that are sent to them.

After years of this alternative prison world many lose their survival qualities on the outside. Isn't it the same with wild animals when we rear them in captivity? They can't provide for themselves in the wild. So the BOP is not only modeled after the German Concentration Camp concept - it is also modeled after a Zoo.

A short time ago a seagull would fly elegantly out into the ocean for fish to eat. Then man created garbage dumps, so the seagull got accustomed to the easy eating. Now the seagull has lost its uniqueness and has been branded a "garbage-picker". Is not a prisoner (or prison employee) affected by the same circumstances? Prisons are those garbage dumps which provide an alternative to fishing and working for young inmates, and thus, they settle for the left over scraps of prison life.

Today my crazy neighbor was talking to me through the wall about movies he liked. His favorite movie was "Papa John". I had never seen it, but he began to describe "Pappion" the prison escape movie. I dared not tell him his mistake

Tonight I had once again wanted to get out of my cell to clean ten of the cells and wash about eight more loads of wash including the organizing and preparation for tomorrow's showers. Tom was, as expected, suspended as an orderly because of his brother's entrance into the unit. So I'm alone again.

As I was looking at the newly varnished desk, I couldn't help but ask a young guard, CO Arab, if he liked how the desk looked after I varnished it compared to the past twenty years of neglect. It's important to review that this is an 80 x 80 ft. massive room with only one desk, four chairs and two garbage pails. His response was "what desk"? When I tried to respond politely he defensively said, "It looks the same to me". I am sure it does. Therein lies our problem. Those who work here do not see what's wrong here.

Whenever I come out of my cell, I immediately pick up all of the thrown about pieces of clothing, food, garbage bags and even used blankets on the floor. After doing that tonight and washing those eight massive loads of wash, CO Deliverance came into the laundry trying to find a tee shirt that he had thrown on the floor near a garbage pail. He was upset that I had washed off some blood evidence he had saved. If it was important, it should have been protected and not thrown on the floor, but in this prison world, clutter and disorder become the work ethic of many of these men.

"Evil", who has now changed back into an acceptable gang leader and his psychotic looking friend make returning to my cell a stressful occurrence. Remember they are both "lifers" at the age of twenty-six. They have decided that I think I can change their prison, and since I'm not prison worthy they don't want me to soften the other inmates or make the prison nicer.

My to-date functioning and handling of prisoners as an Orderly often upsets some of the traditional prison leaders. Some like to bully and intimidate those of us just "passing through". It's easy to threaten inmates when you never have to physically act upon it. So, only in solitary confinement, I take whatever is said without response. If I was in general population, I would acquiesce or risk physical harm.

I was told today that in Florida there are almost forty prisons and eight of them have become totally psychiatric. If we use the Florida stats and we find out the number of total prisons in America, we can then estimate the number of psychiatric prisons nationwide. We are making a huge societal mistake with these psychiatric patterns of internment.

I did get a hot shower tonight. Tomorrow I will begin to get concerned again about my imminent departure.

Nothing good can come from not leaving this place as soon as possible.

Chapter 86 – Booty Bandit & the Broken Washing Machine

Today our unit got actress Ann Hathaway's boyfriend, more Columbian Drug Generals, Conspiracy Detainees, Gang Members, Murderers, Booty Bandits and Me, the only guy still looking for a nail clipper and a hair brush.

As I return to my cell tonight, I must honestly say that today had some prison "highs" and "lows". It's 11:00PM and I just stumbled into my cell. Let's start at the beginning. At 7:00AM they needed me to start the showers. They are using all six showers today even if three of them leak badly and have no doors so that the streams of water will cause additional cleaning and multiple safety issues.

"Evil's" roommate "Mean Face" has decided that I am his new person to hate and stare at and even attempt to threaten. Most are intimidated by this psychopath and under our solitary safety I can just ignore his petulant banter. All was going smoothly today until the washing machine broke down. Fortunately, I'm on the plumbers "list" for next week. The daily wash needs will cause piling up of the soiled clothes and linens from the showers and cell cleanings. I will run out of replacement clothing and linens without continual washing. No one cares but me. It is quite frustrating.

Another fight started in the general population. Ten new inmates were being put in our cells. I am somewhat prepared for them but I also need to pick-up from today's showers. Cleaning the showers takes about fifteen minutes but it requires the opening of twelve locks (two per shower). No one would accommodate me, so tomorrow morning I will be met with "disappointment" by the early crew at the condition of the showers.

The surprise of the day was my Wife's unexpected visit. She doesn't believe I'm getting out and my greedy Florida lawyer has threatened to quit over his as yet, unpaid fees. He's not willing to wait until I can get out of prison to pay him. Legal extortion is allowed if you are a lawyer whose poor performance put me in prison in the first place. Now, he can charge more to get me out. Seeing her so worried about money hurts me deeply as I am not so concerned - believing in the eventual positive legal outcome.

One of our newest inmates got into a fight and used his cane (yes, cane) to really wound his victim. I spoke with both of them and they seemed gentle except the surrounding world of prison makes them crazy. How one had a cane and I can't have a hairbrush remains a mystery to me.

My next door neighbor is already pacing and threatening to kill himself if he gets a roommate from one of these new fighting arrivals.

"Evil" and "Mean Face" may be leaving tomorrow to another prison or to general population. I hope so. They seem to create a more hostile mood around the unit and certainly on this tier. They have become loud and angry. I don't even recognize "Evil's" appearance and voice.

Our unit has over eighty inmates again. Without a functioning washing machine and an assistant, I pray my wife is wrong and I can leave before the daily cleaning needs explode. Yet, the CO's will wait until it's too late to manage the running out of clothes problem reasonably.

Apparently my Wife believes recent internet postings by my shareholders have angered the Judge. I only wish I could go home and straighten out all the financial and personal problems that are immobilizing my distraught Wife. How do other prisoners deal with this? My sons and grandchildren also need me, and it's killing me to be away. I can't help them while I remain in here. I must detach and survive in here until I am released. Remember, my grandson thinks I am on a secret mission for the government. Maybe I am.

Looking outside my fogged window, knowing my loved ones are living out there, yet I am forbidden to be with them by an erroneous Judge's order, makes me quite frustrated and angry. Wouldn't you be?

Until today's visit I never considered not being home for the Fourth of July. Seeing her so worried makes me feel powerless. Hearing of my sons financial travails gnaws at my parental heart. Hearing that my grandchildren are crying for me makes me hate the system that empowered this one Judge to have such power over the innocent.

It's possible that the staff of this prison are not as professional as they should be because the system prevents excellence and simply rewards mediocrity like most governmental organizations.

Four Counselors and Case Workers visited us today. The same phone, book and food needs that I have requested go unanswered for all of the inmates.

Losing confidence in your legal team while in prison, is an almost impossible problem to detach from, overcome or solve. With no phone call access, an inmate is totally dependent on his visiting outside contacts.

Food has continually become less tasty, and the portions smaller, if either of those are possible.

If my Wife is right, this will be a very emotionally difficult weekend for both of us. May, June and now July in here?

Chapter 87 – One Minute of Freedom

This morning I must be reacting to my limited sleep along with my crazy neighbor who has now heard the crackling of the plastic paper as I open my box of matzos. He heard the noise and asked me what I was eating, and could he have some. I have now begun trying to eat quietly because of this neighbor. Of course, I asked a passing guard to give him some of the matzos.

I felt so violated by his intrusion into my meal that I told him I had hot water when none of us really did. He just started screaming at the window to the guards for his hot water. Everything psychologically in prison belongs to or is rightfully due to the inmates. They have faulty entitlement issues along with a thought process of incorrect suppositions. The jail has rights and rules which further confuses me as to why such a system imprisons all sides (the inmate, the guard and the taxpayer). Terms should be shorter and inmates rehabilitated with responsibilities. Today's responsibilities are only to stand up for one or two of the "counts" and the rest of the responsibilities and costs belong to us and our families. Remember this place represents only one prison of their sixty plus billion dollar budget annually. Divide that by 300,000,000 citizens. How much could they refund to each of us? How much could be spent on education, infrastructure or child and health care?

Don't pretend you are safer because of prisons. The current prison systems are fueling more dangerous inmates with zero chance of rehabilitation. This is a dual welfare system and a substandard psychiatric budget. Want to know why we don't legalize drugs? The BOP couldn't afford the lost revenue.

If someone were to trace the connections and financials of the prison contracts for food, supplies and construction, and add the costs and arrangements for staff, salaries and pensions, and then further consider and add what will ultimately become the second, third and fourth generations of not only prisoners but all support and functional staff to run and supply these prisons … there can be no doubt that what will be discovered is a system run by lower class Americans that maintain the system to forcibly house lower class Americans. How can this not ultimately implode?

This is day number sixty-one. There is much to say tonight. I still believe that it may be the final night. It may be close to the final night or it may be the last night before more severe disappointment and concern if that Judge doesn't follow proper legal or moral procedures again. Let's not think about it and let me share some unusual prison events which happened today.

Initially eleven inmates left including "Evil". "Evil" was cordial before leaving because his peer pressure friends were not with him. The memorable and thought provoking scene of this particular "graduation" after weeks or months from solitary to finally graduating to phones, T.V., more food and more freedom deserves mention. As I said goodbye, one of the graduates tripped on another inmate's foot and a fight broke out returning the two of them back to orange land after only six seconds of freedom. You figure it out. I've stopped trying to impose my values on these damaged entities called inmates. It was a testimony to this system of false repair. They are both being carried in and cuffed as I write this to you.

Today I miraculously fixed the washing machine by simply asking a stranger in a repair uniform on the elevator to please look at it. He was terrific and I was back in the washing business again. I needed to fix it because one of our psychiatric patients (inmate) blocked his toilet and started flushing until the entire tier was flooded including four prison floors below. It took the CO's over one hour to realize that all of the inmates screams were real. The scene was out of a comedy or a macabre novel. While this crazy inmate was pushing the water under his door, a CO was pushing it back into his room with a broom while trying to make a dam of wet blankets and clothes around the cell door. The piercing screaming while the inmate was urinating out of his food serving slot added to the unique start of a visually memorable encounter. The Officer in Charge told me to get one of the wet vacuum machines to try to pick up the water easier than the hours of my mopping and bailing would require. Two Wet-Vac machines started and began smoking and one actually caught fire. The inmates were hysterical and pounding on their cell doors watching this Three Stooges type TV scene from their windows. With the pushing of water between the inmate and the CO, along with the smoke coming from both machines, a true prison memory was created. Sadly, I bailed and mopped for four hours.

This became a four hour laborious and unnecessarily messy exercise. I was soaked from my sneakers up to my waist! When they finally handcuffed the crazy inmate, they let him go and take a shower, get new linens and they sent me to get him new clothes. You figure this reward! I remained in wet clothes and he was given new dry clothes.

While I was cleaning his cell, this twenty-six year old black inmate taunted and called me "his slave" and told me to make sure I cleaned his cell properly. There were no consequences for what he did. I felt like a fool for my proper societal behavior, but this place doesn't have well thought out behavioral standards or consistent enforcement. Some of the guards have adopted their inmates as pets. Some of the guards seem to dislike the ones who do what they are told. Hence over time, they re-condition the good ones to become difficult, and to remain with them longer. Leaving seems abnormal. Remaining is acceptable.

At least five wet loads of commercial wash (about ten loads in a normal washer) were still piled in front of me from this episode alone. The geniuses now decided to change linens in twenty more of the other cells creating another seven loads of wash. I wish it were only washing. It's drying, folding and storing away. Of course, tomorrow is another shower day so I have to set up for the forty-five or more showers along with tomorrow's regular mess and garbage. All of this is done by one orderly, one machine and no consideration for the fact that while I was doing this they ordered me to sanitize the six showers and clean-up whatever the inmates left behind (clothes, paper, and you wouldn't believe what else). All of this is being done, while the guards were eating pizza and playing on the computer. These same overpaid guards couldn't find the time to even pick-up food trays. These are only a few reasons why I need to get out of here.

The food trays have a hard plastic top. As of today the "suits" have decided that the trays are now not allowed anymore because (hello!) the inmates can break the plastic top and use it as a weapon. They can slide these covers with messages or supplies from cell to cell with their ropes. The prison, however, still uses them to keep the food warm. We now have to remove the tops at the time of delivery. The mice have won again and this unnecessary procedure adds mess and wasted time.

This institutional eight hour shift concept creates the appearance of a well-run military type operation. Remember water (sorry, I'm still thinking about all of the water today) seeks its own level and this organizational shift plan just doesn't work. Being a guard is a "job for life" mentality. Twenty percent of these employees are terrific until the corporate malaise sets in. Twenty percent should be terminated immediately and the remaining 60% go through the motions offering very little effort beyond what they absolutely have to do. Thus shifts add to cliques and three separate fiefdoms. They do not coordinate with each other.

Chapter 88 – More or Less … I'm Chillin

I'm listening now to new inmate gang codes and dialogues. There is a phrase called "more or less". Most old timers seem to use it twenty times in ten minutes. Along with the term "Sun", inmates use these two words repeatedly.

I don't remember if I told you yesterday that I found a weapon for a handmade device to remove handcuffs that was hidden in the legal consultation room. Well, today in cleaning a cell, I found another hidden knife. Again, this discovery occurred after the guard had inspected the cell. Obviously these cell inspections are as thorough as everything else I have observed here.

If I could leave prison tomorrow, I beat the system. I changed it. I just remembered to tell you that the education department now sends a man around daily to give the inmates books and magazines. I didn't acquiesce to their pace of nothingness. If I hadn't gotten the washing machine fixed, we would have had no clothes for the inmates. We would have had over twenty loads piled up and no new linens to give to those prisoners arriving tonight and tomorrow. All of the CO's went home without caring for the consequences. The fact of total sanitary breakdown was acceptable with them, or they were in complete denial. This denial fact astounds me, but it is true!

I started sneezing over twenty times tonight. It must have been caused by no air conditioning and the dust and slime I work with. It is almost unbelievable that sneezing will be the only negative physical result from this travesty.

The funny part is that my sneezing has woken up the crazy guy next door. He said over and over again, "If you keep sneezing, I'm going to kill myself". I have never had such pressure trying to suppress a sneeze.

I don't know if the Judge has honestly decided yet that he made a mistake and plans to release me. I may know in the morning. I hope I get out before the July 4th Holiday Weekend. The thought of Independence Day certainly has changed for this non-criminal in America's new justice department.

I worked another seventeen hour day. That's probably against some rule, but my sanity is sustained by working despite the drudgery of the work. In a day and an age of immediate communication, I remain "in the dark" and do not know if my Wife is happy or sad. Since I can only make one call every thirty days I opted to make the call to find out tomorrow night. I didn't want to "waste" the call and then not be able to speak tomorrow; if I am still here then she would need to hear from me.

While I wait, let's now go to the events and experiences of my prison life on day number sixty-two.

Do I talk about the guy who urinated all over his cell and I had to clean it? Not him, me.

Do I tell you that my crazy next door neighbor was one of eleven inmates who left tonight? Fortunately, they all left and remained away unlike last night's last second fight and immediate return of those two fighters. One of the eleven inmates who came in tonight has them running in circles. He has a doctor's note which requires a special bed and protection for his back. I am told that he pretended to commit suicide and left his car on a New York bridge. They do not have provisions for him.

Throughout the day I continued working on inmate showers and the washing of cells, cleaning of the floors, and painting of all newly vacated cells. Same old stuff: but I continue trying to scrape away layers of institutional filth while I hope to hear my release call.

The entire "brain trust" of the Education Dept. arrived today. The inmates' interest in books has been a revelation to all six of them. The head executive in charge of books walked into the unit and remarked that the laundry where I work was not there the last time she visited. It has been operational over six months! I'm glad that I brought about this visit. She has not been here for six months! How tragic.

We received cleaning soap today, but we're going to hide it from other units. I am not allowed to use it for a few days. If I leave, the supplies probably won't be used for years. We now even hoard soap here. We are cleaning with water and we hoard the soap.

Deliverance got promoted again! This officer should be removed in hand cuffs. Yet, in here, why should I expect anything different?

One of the truthful CO's told me that just in our unit alone over fifty percent of the inmates qualify as psychiatric with depression prescriptions administered and paid for by the taxpayers.

Tonight is when we must order our commissary supplies before 10:00PM or wait until next Wednesday night. I ordered just a few things which I will gladly give away, if I leave tomorrow.

Tonight I wanted to try to tell you more specifically about a few physical "areas" that consume my prison days. If I had remained only as a solitary inmate we wouldn't have seen many of these things. Before I do that, let me tell you of the visiting trainees who were "observing" today. It's important to remember they look about fourteen years of age and have staring eyes that look like a frightened animal at night.

When these five trainees walked in, our recent "flooding psychotic" had just started one of his temper tantrums which adds a surreal piercing sounding to the already stark surroundings. His horrible screaming and banging on his cell door, along with the clanking of cages, locks and handcuffs set an ominous background for the trainees to observe.

I happened to be waiting in the library cage (it was unlocked so the CO's wouldn't have to keep locking and unlocking me for this "camera" they always pretend exists). I'm sure there's no film, or our unit is on a "list" to receive new film for this camera.

I waited until three of these training officers were without an officer nearby and I stormed out of the cage and scared them so much that they screamed. When their fear subsided, I was able to endear them.

I asked the officer escorting them around to let them spend some time on the inmate side of the cell to better understand what an inmate may feel during a twenty-four hour solitary incarceration. It would be illuminating for these trainees. Unfortunately, it did not happen.

I told two of these newcomers to consider quitting before they evolve into the officers escorting them about. Unfortunately, it's tough to compete against union job security and a governmental uniform. I had no success at changing their careers and outlooks. Years from now, as they blankly stare into the emptiness of boredom, they will know it was too bad that they didn't listen. Except for Deliverance, each officer appeared to genuinely hope for my anticipated departure and all had the kindest comments of our time working together.

One guard said, "Tonight, I'm going to try to pretend you did something wrong in prison, so I can write a "ticket" and get to extend your stay longer." "We will turn this place back into a shithouse within a few days", he concluded.

Chapter 89 – Roaming Around My Ponderosa

Now about those physical descriptions I promised. You already know what my cell looks like, so I'll not re-describe the un-describable. That slop room requires my constant upkeep and maintenance. I have three mop pails always cleaned and filled with water and disinfectant and ready to go. Most supplies and orderly activities begin from here. This 5'x7' room was the guard's unkempt urinal before I arrived. It is now a pristine slop room that actually shines and all the supplies are organized and lined up as if an inspection was imminent. The walls even now have supplies hanging neatly in order.

My home base and laundry room is 15' by 12' with two machines, a folding table and unfortunately I am completely caged in like a zoo animal. I am on constant display. This is across from the only entrance and exit door and literally hundreds of guards and inmates come and go by it daily. It looks like a well-kept postcard now, and it's gratifying to see guards showing the room off to others. All I want to do is to leave, but it is frustrating to know how it formerly looked and how they will ruin it after the constant attention needed to maintain this appearance is forgotten. I hope it is not, but they have not let me train anyone to maintain its appearance.

Tonight I discussed with a few guards how ineffective this prison system performs. They embraced writing my book and actually wanted the whistle blown on the BOP. They feel that they are doing very little to help anyone and are as frustrated as I have been during my stay. It was encouraging to hear them validate some of my observations which I have shared with you.

My work ethic has won over many who I have not been too kind to in my earlier observations and writings. It's easy to like many of these guards when you get to know them, but I must stand behind my initial observations because those initial thoughts were honest and objective. After becoming the head slave, it is only natural that you will bond with your captors.

CO Rutgers, who "hired" me (I don't get paid), and who has some multi-task issues is also being promoted. He's a terrific guy and I hope he can utilize his personality to make things change in this system. He probably won't however. Somehow he's too concerned with not rocking the corporate boat. I, on the other hand, have rocked the boat of the USA's Regulatory Agency. Rutgers and I worked well together. I worked, and he pretended to be busy. I will miss his persona. After he reads this book, he'll definitely come to my book signing.

It's a little past midnight and I have to prepare for hopefully a great or God forbid, more disparaging release news tomorrow. Good night. We'll speak tomorrow.

Chapter 90 – What came first?   The Chicken or the Bone?

I'm still writing, so sadly I am still here.   I tried to call my wife and I got her answering machine.   It will be another thirty days before I can try again.   There is again much to share with you today.

I was given another new orderly assistant.   What can I say about a guy who comes on his first day to the job with a pillow case to take extra food, a deck of cards and a book to read?   He has been in jail four and a half years charged with a $12,000 tax return issue.   He has three children and for four and a half years the government has spent more money than he originally owed the IRS on this non-violent inmate simply by holding on to him.   He shared some interesting stories of guards stealing mail, his lawsuits against guards and he really knows the rights and privileges of inmates.   He spoke with many of the "suits" and was complaining about the food, the facilities, and he stated the multiple inmate rights that are being violated.   He also brought a mug to make iced tea, and we played cards intermittently throughout a very slow work day.       I won't name him yet because he may not be back.   He asked to go back to his cell at 7:00PM because he likes to unwind for the evening.   The CO's were talking about him and his ongoing prison legal issues.   They may not let him come back.   I hope he does come back.   He has a great deal of prison information.   For example, he told me that America has one citizen out of a hundred in prison.   That's 2,000,000 prisoners at $200 per day average. That's $400,000,000 per day or is that $146,000,000,000 annually?   He received direct letters from Judges regarding his cases against the BOP. He was writing administrative complaints.   He may become a barrel of fun for this diary.

By the way, that inmate last night who needed a special bed was, I am told, all over the news today.   He allegedly stole $450,000,000.     They sent him to suicide watch in the prison hospital.   I guess I could have stayed in the hospital.   This is some system of reward and punishment!

Before "Independence Day" the guards dressed down.   Without uniforms and carrying their bags of McDonald's lunch, the prisoners looked better than they did.

The Judge hasn't signed the release. I hope, after I get out of here, that I can become an effective prison activist. This is a system so broken and so costly to every American, that only together can we improve our country's financial problems and simultaneously repair this ever increasing societal malaise. I can only hope the American people will stand up and demand change when they know more about this ongoing travesty. Keeping it as an "out of sight – out of mind" issue will actually affect them and their pocketbooks directly.

While I waited in the legal conference room, I met some of our recent orange "graduates". They looked good, and the hellos were of old friends meeting again. Of course, we can't speak but our gestures, smiles and "salutes" made me feel good for them. They had made a friend, and they remembered. I am pleased about that.

Over forty percent of the prisoners should be released to their own home incarcerations. I am told by my new orderly that the BOP website is a pack of lies. These inmates would crush the BOP propaganda if they were permitted to be heard and testify before Congressional hearings. Five years of prison for $12,000? This is a non-violent, law abiding citizen whose family and children are weakened by the system. They have unnecessarily imprisoned their father. Because he regularly fights the system, they move him far away from his home, extend his stay, and even prevent family visits.

The guards could tell that I was a little disappointed about my not going home tonight (hell, I was fit to be tied) but I'd be damned before I gave that smug, insensitive Judge the satisfaction of ever acting like what he is - petulant and ignorant - so I remained quiet and pensive.

The CO's were quite supportive. By the way, my new assistant urinated in the laundry room drain and slop room within the first hour of "working". Remember I said they will turn this place back into a pigsty. The other inmates however seem to be in the weekend holiday spirit. They seem at peace tonight. We are only at about forty-eight inmates now.

This is my saddest 4$^{th}$ of July because of the helpless injustice and my personal financial concerns caused by a governmental agency and a Judge who accepts the SEC's lies and requests, "hook, "line" and "sinker". Time will prove to all involved how incompetent and mean spirited this agency is.   (Only after my release did the Bernie Madoff scandal expose their duplicity, fraud and incompetence.)

I don't think my attorney is coming until Monday.   He knew how upset I was today about not going home, and he ran out like a coward with "I'll see you on Tuesday".   Before I could question his comment, he was gone.   I guess those attorneys that are responsible for my incarceration should enjoy their weekend.        I hope I heard it wrong.   I'm hopeful that I will not be rotting alone in here throughout this long weekend.

The barber came tonight.   This barber is an inmate and also a passer of unauthorized goods between inmates.   The COs had to cancel haircuts because he's also the electrician and plumber and he was needed on another ward.   I guess they were lucky they arrested him.

The warden's inspection report on our unit was "outstanding" except the report said that the showers should be steam cleaned.   This comment resulted because one of the guards urinated in the shower minutes before the inspection without running the water to clean away the odor.   I told the "suits" we have to retile and renovate these showers.   The water damage from these showers regularly rots the infrastructure and feeds the rats.   Many of the newer prisons have showers in each cell.   Is there something crazy going on here?   No one cares to deal with the "rotting" and structural problem.   Now, showers inside each cell?   Do Americans really want to create long term life motels for their inmates?

Today was the Fourth of July!   The day began uneventfully with showers planned and my new orderly helping me.   Until lunch time, it appeared to be an uneventful Friday.   The food came at 11:30 and there were *two* meals delivered.   One was a sandwich with the mystery meat (low grade baloney) and the other a more palatable Fourth of July hamburger and chicken meal.   One of the officers decided that the chicken hadn't been deboned.   We aren't permitted bones because inmates can make a sharp weapon out of a bone.   Of course, I could see nothing good happening if we returned the meals. I suggested keeping the baloney sandwiches while the inmates waited for the actual holiday meal. We could, I said, simply remove the chicken and we could wait until they redelivered it. All of my ideas were rejected, and the entire cart was returned for the "deboning". When the cart finally made it downstairs, the culinary inmates had one hundred meals to re-sell, and they told the mess officer that they threw the meals out. By 2:00 the inmates were pounding on their doors and screaming for food. By 3:00 some of the inmates were hysterical. I was in the laundry eating some vegetables that my orderly had stolen before they sent the cart back. By 3:30 they sent up only the cold sandwiches. One inmate reacted honestly by saying, "I would kick the door, but I don't have any strength left". By 6:45 the same cold deboned chicken and hard hamburgers made it to the now sullen inmates. Happy Independence Day!!!

Chapter 91 – How does a "Patriot Act"?

As the next crew came in, Deliverance was there in full glory and temper. As expected, they sent the new orderly to his cell, and they asked me what projects I wanted to work on.

To set the scene, I handed to Deliverance a finished personal sweatshirt that one of the inmates had asked to be washed. Deliverance said, "Have the CO who approved the washing give it to him tomorrow". Bizarre, but I obeyed.

I then started my painting project, and it was easy to see how pained Deliverance was that I was working. He simply doesn't like me or any inmate. When that inmate asked me where his sweatshirt was, I told him that he had to wait until tomorrow because that's what the Deliverance told me to say. Deliverance went as ballistic as he did on the day of the newly varnished desk. He enjoys his explosive and deranged "time out" temper tantrums. He sent me to my cell once again in supposed disgrace. I don't care, but the Officer in charge not only cared about his actions, I hear him arguing with Deliverance about sending me away. My defender came to my cell to apologize and asked me to return to painting. I told him that he had to work with these people. I was fine with the uncontrollable anger management issues of Deliverance. I would go to sleep and the projects would simply not be done tonight. Institutional mind set creeping in or not, I was not going to genuflect to an incompetent.

Earlier tonight, I spoke with an alleged foreign arms dealer who is threatened with a life sentence, and has been in solitary for 125 days. In an attempt to lighten his overall sentence, he became a cooperative USA informant, visiting numerous countries to help the US identify and apprehend other arms dealers. So, if I understand this correctly, at the rate of $200 per day (prison cost) for 125 days, our costs were $25,000 plus goodness knows how many tens of thousands of dollars were spent on his "visits" for the sting operations that simply added more prisoners to this system. Have I got that right? This refined British seventy year old estimated he completed fourteen country visits, adding some 34 new inmates to the US prison system. He believes he is still receiving a life sentence, despite his cooperation. I hope I can be there to ease his pain when he is sentenced, but I also want to leave. Can you understand what happens to prisoners in jail and how friendships occur?

My new orderly previously worked in the kitchen at another prison. He swears he saw 10 year old frozen chicken from the "Gulf War" served to the inmates. He also swears that "not fit for human consumption" was on multiple packages they gave him to prepare.

It's obvious during showers I have changed the attitude of this previously somber and quiet mundane exercise into a more respectful and relaxed one. Here is an example of how I speak to them. It is important that you understand that most inmates are appreciative of this courtesy, but a few hardened prisoners are not softened in any way. The majority appreciate what I have done to make them, for only a few minutes, feel a bit of "being special". Here's an example:

Me - Good Morning, how may I help you today?
Inmate - Give me a 4x jumpsuit, 3x tee shirt, 42 underwear, socks, towel and soap.
Me - I'm going to bring you our latest model jumpsuit and some special gifts because we appreciate your shower business.
Inmate – OK.
Me - I have given you some soap, toothpaste and a toothbrush. I have given you two tee shirts and two pairs of underwear for day and evening wear.
Inmate - (laughs) yeah, for nightwear.
Me - In addition, will you be shaving with us today? We hope you like our shower and we hope you come back and choose us for your next shower.
Inmate - Like I have a fucking choice! (laughter)
Me - Tell your friends the BOP needs your business and Happy Fourth of July!
Me - In addition, we guarantee the clothes until your next shower. So thank you for showering with us today.

The smiles and relaxed mood makes me feel like I'm helping these individuals to smile in a place that has forgotten what men need. The old showering experience was done by the Officers as follows: The inmates were given whatever un-cleaned and un-wanted sizes they had. Nothing fit. There was no interaction, and we often stood for hours waiting to be returned to our cell. When they finish showering now, I talk to them until the COs come to take them back to their cells.

Tonight I'm feeling the emptiness of prison life. You see there is a difference between an inmate (me) and a prisoner, (10 years or more). This inmate (me) is not allowed in our civilian world because of the actions of one Judge and the silence of others afraid to question an improper system of justice. I don't really belong in the prison world of pull-ups, "respect", gang language, dysfunctional thought processes, governmental ignorance and non-creative thoughts. So due to a corrupt governmental agency, I have been put in this purgatorial abyss.

Before this holiday, I thought my stay would be over soon. As a military patriot and political candidate, I have now lost all confidence in the integrity of my country's Court system and our supposed system of checks and balances.

It appears that I'm going to be in my cell this holiday weekend. My attorney is not coming to visit so it will be a long weekend of mystery meat, sadness and a time to fester. I am going to try to remain creative and optimistic while I listen to the frightening thoughts, sounds and gang dialogues from my neighbors.

The Officer in Charge (OIC) tonight came and ordered me to get a haircut, finish my painting and take a shower. Deliverance was put at the computer and told not to speak to me. The OIC apologized and asked me to try to forget Deliverance's behavior of last night. This only makes me a target for the next time Deliverance is in charge. They change roles of command here to further confuse the inmates ... and themselves.

"Evil's" roommate stuck up for me when he saw Deliverance bringing me back to my cell last night. He said, "He may not be like us because he's never been in prison, but I respect that he tries to help all of us". When I walked by his window, I put my hand to the glass and he touched it. Now we're apparently friends for life. This turnabout of affection was a surprise to me.

Independence Day was also sad because I could hear the fireworks outside, but I could not see the celebration. Thinking that everyone I love can't either speak to or see me while I await the broken wheels of justice make it a little hard for me to celebrate freedom.

I got a second hair "trim" tonight. The barber said, "The young men here all like you". He said, "you make them feel good about themselves, and you stand up and fight for what they need". He couldn't believe this was my first prison at age sixty. He also thought I had lost a great deal of weight since he first saw me.

Chapter 92 – Did you read my letter?

I wrote the attached letter, which I sent through my Attorney, to the editor of the New York Times on the Fourth of July holiday. They never printed it because it may not qualify as the news fit for them to print and for us to read.

> For 60 years I have been proud to be an American on the Fourth of July! This Fourth, I am in a Federal Solitary Confinement Prison without having been convicted of a crime. I have been here for over 62 days, and my "Independence Day" is to me a little different than I ever thought I would experience on my country's Birthday.

> I also spent my 60th Birthday a few weeks ago in this same cell because one Federal Judge believes he alone defines our Constitution and has held me without legal precedent for unwarranted civil contempt. His definition of civil contempt is my inability to pay a fine which he arbitrarily levied without a jury trial and his incorrect decision is under appeal.

> America deserves better than the loss of any of our freedoms on Independence Day. As a former Marine and CEO of a public company which was closed and seized by this same Judge (These actions are also on appeal), I don't support our present life appointments for Judges. Originally what was our Fourth of July holiday to celebrate? It was the birth of a new nation conceived with a belief in individual freedoms and the elimination of demagogues and tyrants appointed for life without the due process of its citizens. As you watch the fireworks and celebrate with your families, please remember the significance of the day, and those in this country unable to celebrate with you. There are over 2,000,000 Americans in prison as well as their ten million suffering family members. Many inmates should not be in prison. One of us is too many!

> After 60 years of respecting my country and its laws, I may be observing my last Independence Day as a respected and dutiful

American. If this atrocity can happen to me, your family's freedoms are also much too fragile to really celebrate.

R.A. Altomare

Chapter 93 – Incoming!

Without a window in my cell, I have not seen the world for most of these sixty odd days. My improper punishment for a lack of a crime continues to mystify my sensibilities and disrupts my clear thinking.

This orderly, as you know by now, infrequently gets out of his cell on Saturday and Sunday, so those days create more time to ruminate on the situation, the characters and the possible outcomes of my case.

I have limited books to choose from because I have been giving them to other inmates since they live this isolated silence every day while I am selfishly cleaning up urine, vomit, as I follow the directions of unqualified and unmotivated leaders.

Not all guards are unqualified. Yesterday during the 4th of July holiday, one of the Officers refused to eat until the inmates finally ate. The other five officers ate their specially prepared luncheon at 11:30AM because despite their own easily observable emotional deficiencies they can have chicken with bones. We didn't eat until seven hours later.

The funny part of that inconsistent "Bone" issue is I have been here for almost sixty-five days and I'm sure you remember that never once was it deboned before. Thus, there may be a set of cutlery in these cells from past chicken dinners. Not being of a criminal mind, I didn't even know that weapons could be made from the scraps of chicken bones. I hope that I may never begin to think of all objects in our world as potential weaponry making resources.

I'm enjoying a much needed day of rest from working and dealing with intellectually deficient "Corporals" who think of themselves as "Colonels". Most of these uniformed men are intent on doing as little as possible to get paid at the end of the week. Never once did I hear them trying to assist one sad inmate, improve prison daily procedures, to simply not urinate in our showers or slop work rooms, and to improve the initial urine stench upon entering this Special Housing Unit - SHU.

Because of prison overcrowding only one or two officers are assigned to general population units with hundreds of uncuffed inmates. To avoid prison overcrowding, the BOP has recently adopted a "half-way house" early release program. I hear the prisoners discussing these houses. There are not enough of them and they are more poorly supervised than this prison has been. This is just another financially wasteful BOP activity blindly paid for by us.

Eventually when society begins a prison investigation, we need to rethink modified privately run prisons, military service, retribution to the victims, elimination of Justice Department quotas and allow my peace corps prison program to be introduced. I have found most inmates to be emotionally childlike because abuse, alcohol and drugs normally regress the individual's development back to the time of their initial abuse. Some are "doing life on the installment plan", which means they may get out, but they are destined to return. Local cops see to that when quotas or new State Prison Building Bonds are called for to be financed.

Without planned careers, trainee job placement services, non-drug induced psychiatric services, or self-esteem training, this is a containment center for most of them and for the welfare-type salaries of those who watch them. No well-balanced individual would repeat gleefully year after year these types of emotionally difficult jobs. Those CO's should be counseled and rotated because when a guard is subjected to daily prison thoughts he becomes like one of the prisoners. It's just a different gang to which the guards belong.

My weekends are centered on eating matzos and granola bars. I didn't purchase that much from the commissary this week because I thought that I was leaving.

Yesterday the pregnant female psychiatrist who treats the crazy "waterfall maker" asked to speak with me.

"Are you Richard Altomare", she said. "Yes", I responded. "I am supposed to evaluate each inmate every 30 days, are you feeling OK?", the very pregnant woman continued. "Should I tell you I'm OK or shouldn't you ask those who work and interact with me? - After all, if I think I'm Napoleon and say that I'm OK - how could you evaluate that?" "Do you want to kill yourself at times?" she now asked. "No, I quipped, but do you spend any time with these officers?" "I only work with the inmates." "Does anyone work with these guards?", I said. "I can see that you are fine, she concluded.

The fact is that thirty days have passed by twice and I've never spoken to her before. I'm glad my disciplined mind and having you to speak to have prevented me from stuffing my toilet bowl, pounding on doors or getting free drugs from a government which outlaws drugs. Only then would I have met the counselor within the first thirty or even sixty days.

Exactly what is normal in a world of created abnormality? In addition, the negative energies of prison are no place for a pregnant woman to subject her unborn child to absorb. That's a study I would suggest.

At 5:00PM tonight they called me out to the weekend clubhouse party show run by Deliverance, the officer in charge. Deliverance wanted to watch me clean forty cells, while he and the officers ate Chinese food.

As expected, they want to phase out my other orderly because they think he's a problem on many levels. Tomorrow they are going to give him the showers to clean. I hope he does it to their "high" standards, but I think he's being set up to fail. They are concerned that he will file a prison case against them.

The real nightmare of the night was a CO Powers who was filling in on overtime. I'm embarrassed that he was a former Marine because from his sleeping on the job to his crude behavior; he is a disgrace. To embarrassingly describe this man's actions while he guards prisoners is difficult even for this diary. He sits on the chair around the desk while I am mopping, and like a 9th grader lifts his leg and yells "incoming" and continually passes wind to the laughter of his fellow officers. Think about the emotional quotient and then think about how I feel being deemed unworthy to enter society while men like this are worthy to walk our streets and guard our inmates. My Judge and his cronies are responsible for men like this CO Powers. All names, you recall, are fictional - but close enough for the officers to know of whom I am speaking. If the BOP tries to deny this, check the visual tapes of SHU 9 South, July 5, 2008 from 5:00PM to 10:00PM and tell me who is sleeping and who's performing to the standards of an Officer of the Court.   Also, tell me which guards were getting free haircuts while the inmates were not allowed to get them tonight!

Being locked away from society while idiots like this are actually playing ball in the day room and disregarding their sacred duties awarded to them by our own public to help mend these troubled humans who became criminals, and now inmates, just infuriates me.   Yet, that Judge incarcerates ME!   Shame on him!

Chapter 94 – My Exercise Class

Last night, while I was trying to go to sleep, I heard the various voices of my cell neighbors. Most inmates on my tier are alone in their cells. There are, once in a while, two inmates in a cell. But at this time, we are all alone. Since I've forced the Education Department to deliver self-help books from the psychology section, I've read them and gave them to the inmates. One is the "Self-Esteem Companion" (most who know me believe I'm skimming this one), "Honor your Anger" (I gave this to Deliverance and he threw it on the floor), and "Who Is Man" (I've read this short religious thesis twice and am still trying to fully grasp its religious message). Nevertheless, with all these thoughts going on in my sleepy head, I heard the inmates trying to exercise together. How successful I felt my books had been to have them exercising together. "I'll do forty push-ups and then you do a set of forty, OK?", said an inmate. This now involved four cells. When one finished his forty push-ups, which no one can really see because of isolation, one of the other cell mates accused him of not counting properly. It was a discreet non-attacking and yet maintaining self-esteem suggestion. "You're a fucking liar, you didn't do forty!" The other inmate, comfortable in his self-esteem and recently schooled on anger management from our books, digested the ill-thought out criticism and tried to embrace his friend. "I'll stab you in the fucking heart, you ugly mother fucker, and I'll fuck your sister, you scum bag". As the dialogue reached a calming status, the original accuser retorted, "You've been lying about exercising all week. You probably are jerking off while you're pretending to do push-ups. You can't do ten push-ups with those bony arms you booty-bandit and suck my dick!" (This I am told is one of the greatest prison disrespects). (It may even be worse than the food).

The barrage of their hilarious and bizarre yelling and uncontrolled banging that followed may have been more exhausting and physically challenging to these inmates than another set of forty push-ups. Well, our SHU 9 South friendly exercise session seems to have ended. Maybe my self-help books need some follow-up lectures for the inmates.

What fascinates me is that tomorrow or soon after, these angry words will have been put aside (maybe not forgotten), and the inmates will continue on as if nothing happened. The storing and proper release of anger in prison might be transformed into a beneficial exercise, if they had lectures or classes or films or anything to educate them on how to discipline their own minds. Something other than nothing would benefit inmates.

I've been living in a dysfunctional ghetto family setting, the same as an innocent child helpless to prevent abuse, and subjected to listen to those broken authority figures. Unlike such a child, I may choose to not permit some of these thoughts or actions to appear as normal. The guards have not changed the inmates. The inmates' thoughts and beliefs have easily changed the expectations of the guards.

Need we only remember CO Power's, "Incoming" actions and more importantly the childlike acceptance of the other four officers, because to act differently and to be professional in their "officer world" invites isolation and the loss of camaraderie.

Guard tattoos are another dead giveaway. The Officers Corps in prison have more tattoos than most law enforcement agencies. I have seen entire arm tattoos on the women officers. One or two isolated and respected guards are without tattoos, and they coincidentally are not part of the "in-crowd".

As the Sunday morning Day Room CO "music playing" continues, I was personally moved by some songs played. In between some Country Music and some rap sounds, two Sinatra songs were played. These two have always been my favorites, but today they were emotionally meaningful as well. In "New York, New York" there is a line which always had a powerful meaning for me. "If I can make it there, I can make it anywhere". My prison cell is in New York, and I can "make-it" here so I can make it anywhere! Then came the song, "My Way". The line that caused tears to appear was "and not the words of one who kneels". Yes, my smug Judge; I'll not "kneel" - no matter what you and your governmental cronies try to do to me. Right is right, and it's still my America and your America, my dear diary reader. We will one day see those who prosecute, being prosecuted themselves, and we heroic victims will be recognized for our honesty and courage. Being defamed is initially painful, but knowing that it is not true can sustain one's efforts to reverse the hurtful innuendoes, lies, embarrassment and even financial distress.

The Chaplain visited the cells this morning. He now runs away from my gaze like a child who knows he has been caught with his hand in the cookie jar. I find that the Chaplain's need to visit only those who don't see his phoniness and duplicity quite revealing. One day I'll send a letter to his Superiors. It won't matter, because "the beat just goes on here". There are a few staff members and CO's who outside this prison go door to door preaching "Born Again" religions. This prison venue affords them free access to their beliefs since they preach to these inmates without any consideration for the separation of Church and State. Listening to the unsolicited and unchecked force feeding of their religion on this "captive" audience adds to my angered observations of no disciplinary controls throughout this institution.

Chapter 95 – Two-Ply Forever!

CO Tiny is on duty this morning. His yelling and loud non-stop laughing becomes so annoying and upsetting to the inmates who are today quiet and reflective. His chatter is continual and unabated for the eight hours he eats and rests. It only stops when this almost 350 lb. plus frame consumes his own lunch and as many extra meals that may be sent up from the kitchen. Personally, I like this CO, but he is unqualified for the physical needs of this isolation unit. The other guards are conflicted working with this CO. All may like his friendship, but they find working with him difficult. He is a food dropping slob. He has some prison family connections which serves to protect his presence here, but he creates confusion and does very little to justify his position. An inmate today made an airport type sarcastic announcement. "CO Tiny, please step away from the food cart." Laughter was everywhere, as Tiny was at that time circling the cart for leftover food.

My attorney visited today and told me that after we win our Appeal, we can sue the Judge for my illegal incarceration at the rate of up to $2,000,000 per day. Maybe I shouldn't push to leave too quickly. Believe me, even at that price, my head and psyche still need to leave soon.

After today's legal visit, I was asked to pick-up after CO Tiny. Imagine me in an orange jail two piece suit following this 350 lb. CO around with a broom, mop and dust pan like a circus scene of an elephant and a clown. This obviously brought laughter from the other CO's. Tiny is such a sweetheart, and he seems to care about these inmates. He should be a counselor. Moving and working around quickly may be beyond his long term physical capabilities. He is just too fat and too tired to work.

As I set up for showers, wash the mops, and clean each tier, I tried to get the CO's to take the other orderly out to clean the showers. That orderly is really outspoken, so I believe the CO's will eventually move him out of his position. He's a very fine inmate (actually, sadly, he's become a prisoner). The difference can best be described by our toilet paper delivery of today.

Solitary confinement and toilet paper use are more important partners than I used to think. Toilet paper becomes something inmates begin asking for weeks before they need it. The past inconsistent delivery system and rodent problems tend to cause this created "need" for toilet paper hoarding.

You would assume that one-ply commercial paper would be the choice of prison toilet paper. We have hundreds and hundreds of rolls on a multi-tiered rolling cart for distribution. I fill the cart weekly. I don't know who could actually use as much as I deliver, but we really go through that much toilet paper.

Today one of my new supply friends gave me a case of "two-ply", "real people" toilet paper. I was planning to give each inmate who showered tomorrow one of these softer rolls. My orderly who we will now call "Two-Ply" hid the case so only he and I would use it. Based on the size of the carton, I will have to serve 5 to 10 years to use it all. Nevertheless, Two-Ply was like a giddy first time millionaire as he squirreled away his first two rolls tonight. That's a prisoner. I still want to give it to the men. As soon as Two-Ply is fired, I'll distribute the two-ply paper. If I leave first, he'll be selling the two-plys within hours of my departure. That's an opportunist. That's a prisoner. FW (Fuck the World) would be proud. I still think in life and in prison we are defined by what we give and do for others.

The "squealers", from the witness protection tier, are getting haircuts tonight. The other inmates including this orderly, are not permitted to be around when they come out. The inmates therefore know why I'm in my cell early tonight. They are screaming "Big Rats". "Cut their fuckin' throats". "Big Rats". "We get you soon". (Not, "we'll" get you soon).

Two other prison events occurred tonight worth discussing. As I was mopping the tiers, some cell inmates wanted to talk and we obviously speak a very different language. So tonight as I came to the tier, I said, (in their gang language) "You heard? Yo, more or less, Suns, I as tired as a .25 cent whore, more or less. So no fuckin bothering Richie Rich, you heard? Word of my mother."

As nonsensical as that sentence sounds, they are still laughing, including today's newest friend Deliverance. His sugar level must be high tonight.

Deliverance said "hello", "good evening", "thank you" and "great job". Someone must have said something to him. He was even likeable. These are extreme mood swings of a multi-personality psychopath, which like an abusive alcoholic, wreaks havoc on these prisoners.

Tomorrow the pressure begins to find out the newest Judicial game being played by the SEC and the Judge of delaying and keeping me here. After I meet with my attorney tomorrow, I'll know more.

Chapter 96 – Yes, Blind

I made a basic "Solitary 101" mistake tonight. Because I was physically exhausted, I fell asleep too early. I just woke up and it's the middle of the night so I'll report two other events I saw today. The first came from the elevator operator. This was the Russian guard who told me to paint the door locks a while ago. He's been assigned somewhere else in the prison (probably maintenance). He said, "you have changed the whole feeling on the prison floor. I don't know how, but everyone is acting differently". Another unsolicited comment came from a regular CO Tom Tom. He said, "Mr. Altomare, you definitely are inmate of the year. No one has done for us what you have done". That just doesn't change the fact that it's the middle of the night and I can't go back to sleep. I'll force myself, but this was my mistake of poor sleep management – (PSM). I'll read - I'll exercise - I'll play some games - I'll ruminate (I don't use that word around here) about my future plans after I get home.

Tonight I will count the days until justice reappears and these governmental bullies are repaid in spades. (I must be playing too much Bridge.)

As the morning finally arrives, I am another day closer to my freedom. When is determined by a conflicted Court, why is determined by the facts, and how I spend those final days is only determined by myself.

By the way, when you add a two-ply to a one ply you exceed the toilet paper that the Judge probably uses. I'll continue to be a "three-ply" user until I depart. From my existing supply I can outlast whatever inappropriate time the Judge attempts to smugly order. I would like to have this Judge's hubris cost the Judiciary money. That's the only way to remove his arrogance from doing this to others. There's been enough "lynchings" to last a lifetime.

I found out that Two-Ply has been making a chess set out of toilet paper! In his last prison he was working on a castle built with toothpaste as mortar and the bricks were made out of toilet paper. The human spirit thrives in the least stimulating surroundings. Watching grown men use toilet paper to pass time, speaks volumes. Can you hear this?

My wife visited today and to see what having to deal with my two lawyers and the rest of this emotional and financial upheaval have done to her was upsetting.

I'll wait until after the Appeal to make a decision on possible legal actions regarding my representation throughout this matter. Something is wrong here, and despite my flourishing career as an orderly; I wish to return to correct this violation by the SEC and their handpicked Judge. As an American, I am appalled by what our government can do to destroy a citizen. Let's see who eventually wins this one. I can only hope that my lawyer in Florida will suffer more than my wife has in these past months when I complete this process.

The outside world goes on while these vengeful bureaucrats continue to attempt to destroy my reputation and my ability to make a future living. Hearing of my sons struggling lives and my distraught wife only raises my resolve to defeat such an abuse so that other innocents may never suffer as I have. Somehow, I thought that is what was intended with the passing of the "National Whistleblowers Act". I must have missed something in its translation into English!

Two-ply is really not a great worker, but he's a fine individual who has been turned into a prisoner by his incarceration. Watching him steal uneaten lunches and squirreling away food in various storage bins was revealing and quite sad.

I was approached by a prison photographer who said, "I have been taking pictures because this unit is the cleanest of all in the prison". My Wife's visit reminded me of her troubles that only I can fix by returning to work. Without money, fighting a beast like the SEC becomes more difficult, even though we were the cleanest ward in this ineptly run institution.

Tonight I planned to paint ten more cells. I sat inactive for three hours because the guards simply couldn't organize moving one inmate to another tier. It's not possible that it couldn't have been done quicker. "We'll do it on the weekend". Then on the weekend, "We'll do it during the week": is the double thinking dialogue I can often anticipate.

I hope the same governmental think tank exists in the SEC that exists in the Court system. Then my victory is only a matter of time. My poor Wife has been hurt by these bullies.

Tonight I can't find much humor in prison life and I dejectedly no longer believe in my Country's moral sense of right and wrong.

I have continued to find hope and optimism amidst the stark and often bleak backdrop of this institutional prison. I miss my company, family and friends.

As I approach seventy days which is more than Christ was asked to be in the Garden of Gethsemane I couldn't help but compare the devils temptation to that of the SEC's.

In the case of the SEC, the location's name may be "GET SOME OF THAT FOR ME" instead of Gethsemane, since they are paid for every illegal naked short trade, and the public still hasn't demanded an investigation.

Well, the summary judgment was wrong! The seizure and liquidation of our companies were wrong! The fines were wrong! My illegal incarceration was wrong! Our positions remain correct!

What is really right is our resolve, our tenacity and our discipline. We will outlast them. If not us, then who?

Although I've lost some weight, and had my hair cut by an electrician, but fortunately, the lights in my cell have been repaired by my barber. Yet, my enthusiasm and desire for the truth has not waned. Fighting against such pure ineptitude empowers me to continue.

Financially they have attacked as I anticipated. In the long run, finances and reputation will be resolved in our favor. The funny thing about the truth is that although it may stay hidden for a while - the important truths always resurface at the appropriate time. I'm still Chairman and CEO of my company. I will recapture our ideas, goals and the company itself.

Today was an uplifting day. I received two positive letters from my Wife which made me feel like she'll get through this ordeal without too much more pain. I can only hope that is the truth.

I did catch another bad break tonight. My next door cell has been unoccupied and tonight it was filled by a loud yelling inmate. He has a few friends down the hall and he's going to be yelling all night. I saw his size when he was brought in. He can yell all he wants. That's prison survival skills "Word of my Mother"! That means, I swear to God it's true. Listening to Two-Ply today was informative. The rules and procedures of living in prison and fighting disciplinary matters seems to be a case of futility. They have been withholding privileges from Two-Ply because he "wrote-up" a CO for touching his private parts. He lost that case and he has been unable to win one of the subsequent twenty cases he has filed. They continue to move him from prison to prison for his own "protection" from the guards.

He was teaching me prison hand shakes and hand signals while he folded and organized the underwear. I hope that they let him stay.

Tonight a rumor spread throughout the unit that I was leaving. I hope it's true, but there was a surprisingly sad reaction by these lifers and long term convicts. I learned today that a "convict" is a term of respect. An inmate is a novice, a prisoner is respected but not like a convict. A convict has been in multiple prisons and has numerous charges. What a goal!

I really like this one convict, who is in prison for life as an accomplice to a murder. Tattoos give some of the signals in this world. Barbed wire means you've been in prison. A tear drop tattoo represents "only" one murder. Carefully count the tear drops of a nearby sunbather the next time you are at the beach, and move your blanket. Multiple teardrops, multiple murders. Two guards also have barbed wire tattoos!

This lifer convict is going to general population tomorrow. He appears to be a changed man despite his one youthful mistake. He was in the car of someone who committed a murder. He's going to leave me some of his writings tomorrow at his graduation. I'll share them with you, if I get them. (The guards prevented the transfer).

My cell neighbor screamer says "Ya heard" at the end of every sentence or phrase. He just came back from the street. He's been home for thirteen months and he's filling in his gang friends on all of the gang members and neighborhood events. These "events" don't sound like typical block parties. There's guns, drugs and "POE-LICE" problems.

Let's get back to them missing me. This astounds me. If you knew how differently I speak, act and interact with everyone, you would also understand my reaction. I will miss many of these lost souls. They will be invited to my next Memorial Day imaginary golf tournament. I am haunted by their eyes and life stories.

Tomorrow I should know if there's a signed Judge's release. I would like to be surprised. I'm prepared to continue fighting, if there is no release.

Again tomorrow offers showers, painting and cleaning. I'd like to be going home now that everything is in order. The timing is again right for me to leave.

I am so bored that I'm going to do this diary entry backwards. They asked me to stay working until midnight. That's from 7:00AM in the morning. The other orderly went back to his cell at 7:00PM. He had had enough. I think they may fire him tomorrow. Let's start at the late evening and work backwards to the morning. With apologizes to Seinfeld who once aired the backwards "India wedding" episode.

Twelve new inmates arrived after 9:00PM. They were greeted by my new special blanket rolls which contain everything they need. One of them was blind – Yes, blind. What's the punishment of solitary for a blind inmate? What is wrong with the BOP? What is wrong with America? I was embarrassed that this helpless man also requires solitary incarceration. Hey, that's me too! The logistical nightmare of a blind inmate is beyond your wildest imagination. Cuffing a blind man insults even the intelligence of this place. Where is he going to run?

Speaking of institutional intelligence, a CO Sang was in charge of my orderly efforts tonight. I volunteered to stay late because they obviously were overwhelmed to accomplish the multiple tasks without my help. Can you believe that at 11:50PM CO Sang said, "It's too late we have the count in ten minutes - so you can't take a shower tonight". If you saw what I looked like from all I did today, you would marvel at his insensitivity and pure ignorance. Fortunately the same OIC who has stepped up repeatedly CO Labrador "righted" that selfish and incorrect governmental decision of CO Sang. I showered.

In addition to the blind man, they also delivered many French and Russian speaking prisoners. Our Feds are capitalizing on this Patriot Act and a disinterested citizenry to fill the BOP's cash burning machine.

My Wife is so distraught about missing me and our weakening finances that it rips me apart at the core of my existence. I must remain distant to her problems, or it will eat me up while I am in here. There can be no doubt that surviving in prison, any prison, is a matter that can only be handled by an individual's normally buried subconscious instincts for survival. My dilemma is that I can see both the need for turning on my innate survival mechanism, and also the need to reassure my Wife. But these two are mutually exclusive in the brain. I cannot allow myself to "feel" her sadness (and then react to it) if I am to be in survival mode for my own sake in this hell hole. This is most likely the worst part of this entire series of events.

"Two ply" and some of the convicts sat me down to discuss "Jailin" which is speaking jail language". "Yo, What you hear?" is my new greeting. When one adds butter to anything, it is to improve it. If I insult someone and then try to correct it, I have "buttered" my comment. They buttered Ritchie Rich and have re-named me Lord Baltimore. Don't ask me to explain. I'm only trying to learn and report on this language.

Let's discuss "Rent" and "Currency" in the jail world. First, I'm going to sleep, and when I wake up (because it's 1:00AM and I am exhausted) I'll continue backwards to the Judge, my lawyer and other earlier events of the day.

It's quiet tonight because the CO's moved me to a new filthy cell and moved all of the talkers to another tier.   Cleaning my new cell at this hour also added to my fatigue.   Let's talk in the morning.

Chapter 97 – Rent … Not the Play

"Rent" is the price some inmates extort from other general population inmates simply for them to stay on their tier or unit. Two-Ply had to fight not to pay this extortion. It is often done by those physically superior or gang strong as they decide who is "weak" and who is "strong". One young man here was sentenced to two years and while in a Federal institution got into a fight to avoid "rent". The other inmate died. He is now sentenced for thirty years! This is only one of the Fed's black-eyes. In fact, the number of deaths in Federal prisons is a number that would shock America. The currency permitted in prison since money is not permitted and yet "business" flourishes; are stamps and "Mac's". Mac's are a $1.15 fish meal of Mackerel. These currencies move around prison life. Since putting money into your commissary account can be wired in by anyone, those with commissary privileges supply those without. Those who want to "pay" for laundry services will buy a $1.15 "Mac" and may sell it at $1.00 or $2.00 for that same extorted "Mac" package due entirely to whatever service they might be paying for. Inmates have no financial limit on amounts permitted into their accounts. Some have tens of thousands of dollars in their accounts! A prison magazine even has companies advertising to purchase books of stamps at $.65 on the dollar. How many inmates would pay $1.00 and then sell at $.65? I am told that prison businesses even charge for protection, sex, food, use of gym equipment, phone call usage, and the list can go to whatever is within your imagination. It's as if the BOP wants to create a class war inside their classless society.

The blind man of yesterday night was made blind by the BOP's medication! During the past two years he has been "dieseled", which is a prison term that means he has been moved from institution to institution to make his lawsuit and venue nearly impossible to file. With no Constitutional rights the defendant (BOP) moves the plaintiff so he can't sue them (BOP) properly. Isn't that similar to the shenanigans of the SEC and myself?

The lack of sensitivity of some of the COs was painfully apparent when this blind prisoner celebrity (most know of his story) came into the elevator with me today.   The insensitive CO said, "My God, a blind guy - what did you do?   Did you drive the getaway car?"

Today again there was no word on my release and I couldn't contain my frustration at the stupidity and mean spiritedness of what they are vindictively trying to do to my family and myself.   Like the blind guy, I have been wronged, and then they are trying to discredit and further victimize the victim.   What a travesty!

Believe it or not, I got a polishing machine and an extension cord this afternoon.   That may mean I'm near the end of this illegal incarceration, because I have wanted to finally polish my way out of here.

In addition, "Two Ply" got caught selling a book of stamps in exchange for some commissary products.   I think tonight may be his grand finale as an orderly.

As I was walking about a very clean unit (Warden said the cleanest unit in prison), the inmates were especially receptive and friendly.   Our number is sixty-seven, but we are scheduled to release twenty tomorrow.   I hope I leave because the anticipated work will be massive tomorrow with showers and twenty or so cell clean outs.   Tonight the FBI is bringing in four more inmates after 11:00PM.   Fortunately Two-Ply had a kidney attack so they reluctantly sent us back to our cells and allowed us to shower early.   They are mad at "Two-Ply".   Tonight I can use the time to catch up on my diary entries.

While walking and working about, one "jailing" inmate told me that all I have to say to silence the fifteen inmates that all start speaking with me when I walk onto their tier is to "Tell them what they are talking about is DOA".   Apparently DOA means I don't want to talk about it.   The reactions tonight to my DOA statement (Richie Rich is DOA!) were better than expected.   I never curse which amazes them and I have tried to become a calming parent image for many of them.

The inmates want to talk to me and the CO's are amazed at our developing emotional bond, which touches my heart despite my pain of being here. Today when one of the younger fresher inmates started "talking some stuff" (without butter) I responded, "That's DOA, sun! Ya Heard!   The entire tier including the COs who never expected me "jailing" a complete sentence laughed for a very long term, and I gained prison respect for politely and respectfully utilizing their language. Get me out of here before this language becomes normality.

I will miss Two-Ply when he goes. He is filled with BOP perceptions. I am overwhelmed that he has a lawsuit going with over 20 CO's at the same time. Here's the nutshell of his story. As said before, he was touched by a CO in an inappropriate manner. He reported it. They locked him in solitary for his own protection and refused him any hearings for over 60 days. During that time his cell was searched and they found an orange and one container of milk and took away his early release time and transferred him to this jail where he remains in solitary confinement. This is a maximum security prison and he should not be in here due to his non-violent crime. Hey! What about my no crime at all? The emotional strain of canceling his early release on his family and himself indicates that the BOP makes too much money to let convicted prisoners go. "Write Ups" extend inmate sentencing which, he claims, is still against the law. Most inmates cannot retain attorneys to fight their system. If they do, there is retaliation.

With over 2,000,000 prisoners presently incarcerated, I started thinking about commissary and phone revenues of this unchecked and non-audited prison bureaucracy. Investigators and reporters please take note. Do the math!

To add to my poor Wife's pressure, now the sister agency of the SEC, the IRS is trying to harass her over my last five years of tax returns. Those harassing civil matters mean very little, but at this time, it's really overkill for her frayed nerves.

If I go home tomorrow I will miss 21 graduates. Since 21 is my lucky number, it would be a great ending to this horrific experience. I do hope there is a legal basis to sue for this wrongful incarceration. Thinking that one Judge can arbitrarily do this to any American citizen without any definitive facts, is upsetting to me and I hope some of these financial issues can be rectified with my governmental malpractice suit.

The inmates continue to speak privately with each other. Despite my few words and learned sentences, I just cannot understand most of their coded dialogues.

My Commissary order was either botched up by the BOP or by my Attorney for "not putting the money into the proper account". In either event without the commissary order I have to subsist on their food alone for the next week. Today, the prison food was not even edible. I am looking for a snack, but I am not going to participate in the underground barter or "transfer of money into my account process." I'll do without it! I would rather lose weight than lose my dignity or be written up for some offense.

They moved me into another cell and my new cell has a window! I want to begin living again. I am ready to graduate from Orderly College or BOP 101. When is my graduation? How will they release me?

My writing was disrupted by a noise at my door. Believe it or not, one of the inmates heard that my commissary order didn't come and he sent me a "fish line" (It's really just threads from a blanket or clothes with a battery or weight at the tip. (He sent me a candy bar!) I'm really a prisoner now. Do you think I belong to him? Thank-God I'm in solitary. How touching that this delivery of candy was from someone who will be here long after I leave, and he thought of giving it to me. I am touched. (I mean moved.)

As the monotonous days lumber by, I begin to feel the absence of society, family, stimulation, a kiss, love and countless other previously taken for granted emotions.

Inmates are not supposed to write their name on prison walls. The superstition is that if you do write on the walls, you will return. Based on the graffiti that I see inside these cells, many do not heed the warning. I have written some names on my cell wall. Let's see if the superstition works. How do you spell Judge?

One inmate simply refused to leave the shower and taunted the guards to send in the "goon squad" (those are the Darth Vader guys in black uniforms and a filming crew; they walk in scary German (what a surprise) high stepping style.) He was writing on the shower wall for almost 2 hours while the water was running. No goon squad was called. This was just another BOP day camp experience for those of us to watch and those disobedient or psychologically deranged inmates to avoid prison consequences.

I am told that gangs control TV's, weights and many food privileges in general population. During certain times of the day only gang members can use these services. Failure to follow these time rules results in gang retaliation, which is not normally a warning or hand slap.

Last night Two-Ply stole a newspaper from the garbage. How pathetic we appeared being reduced for no apparent reason to secretly reading about our society. Are they preparing the inmates to return to society or not? Are they trying to procreate their own prison society, so that the inmates will be addicted to the BOP?

The relationship between inmates and guards is not healthy for anyone involved. It may get them through the day, but it is neither productive nor beneficial for the long term needs of either side.

Although these guards are quite likable, their level of professional sophistication and intelligence begins low and advances lower as the shifts (8-4, 4-12, 12-8) take their toll on their minds and actions.

Two-Ply was fired. My attorney couldn't see me, and I didn't go home. However sixteen inmates did graduate! Five new ones arrived. I was the only one working shower distribution. I worked from 7:45 AM to Midnight again for no money. All I get is just a shower and the short term satisfaction of forgetting about how sad I am in being here. I felt sorry for Two-Ply. He pretended that he doesn't care, but to be fired by men he really doesn't respect must infuriate him. On the other hand, this idiot (me) by my efforts is making the system look like they know what they are doing.

Tonight was a goodbye love-fest from some of the graduating inmates. They really have discussed this and I guess they are happy with how I have worked for them. I need to return to the outside battlefield of life to generate the money my family will need until we finally file the legal actions against those who today feel themselves invincible.

I'm not going to worry unless my attorney doesn't come tomorrow. I hope he's not ill. What if he died? What if my parents died? Would anyone be able to tell me? Would I go to their funeral?

Our food has gotten worse. My commissary order and about twenty-five other orders were botched up by either our COs or the institution itself. We are without these commissary food products which supplement the inadequate food.

Two-Ply expects me to keep doing his laundry as if he was still working and to get him two-ply rolls every time I return his clothes. Prisoners have a sense of entitlement that we would never expect. Of course, I will do it. I'm now doing over fifteen personal washes weekly. If I stay much longer, everyone will have me as their valet.

Chapter 98 – Chillin' in the BOP

Yesterday night one of the younger inmates (Tom's brother) wanted to move his cell because his water did not work. The inmates have some printed rights, but just like the vending machines - the CO's only care to help the inmates they choose to help. Telling the guards that you have a right to anything normally results in a "ticket" or delay. Last night was no exception. By the time the dialogue was finished both the inmate and the CO "disrespected" each other. All one could hear last night was pounding and screaming because Tom's brother wasn't going to "lose face" in front of the other inmates who were following and recording the drama.

Once the initial cursing and threats began, it means an "extension" to your original term or an elimination of the "good time" earned by not getting beaten up, robbed, abused or disregarded in a system which clearly does nothing.

"Chillin" is a term in prison that means everything is OK with you. There seems to be different interpretations of similar phrases by different gangs just as "DOA" may mean different things between multiple "gang dialogues".

No matter what it means, the creation and perpetuation of these dysfunctional life styles and languages are not beneficial to the society, the individual or the prison itself.

What happens with governmental agencies is that they require self-perpetuation to justify their budgets, pensions, salaries and unfortunately more prisons.

The Judges make it very difficult (look at me) to get out of prison. Imagine if there had been an actual violation of a law with a "sentencing guideline" of decades. The length of time for a crime is not a deterrent. Society pays for those it should not have incarcerated. I recently listened to CO Tiny tell an inmate, "If they offer you a deal of ten years - take it because the Judge ninety-five percent of the time sides with the government, and then for going to trial they will throw a term of thirty years at you.

How tragic was that advice because he then proudly said that the Federal Court will now allow an inmate to make a tape of his reading a bedtime story so he can "play" a bedtime story to his child. And we question how we "seed" future generations to crime?

The BOP also limits the amount of food inmates can purchase from the commissary. For example, an inmate can only purchase 3 tuna or "mackerel" packets weekly. Since many of these inmates physically "workout: to defend themselves from other inmates, they have to purchase other protein meals from "stores" (private inmate businesses), "stamps" or steal it from others. In other words, the BOP causes prison problems with food quotas". I wonder why?

As I was discussing questionable BOP policies tonight with one of the COs, I pointed out a few of my favorite improperly printed prison signs. One Unnecessarily says, "Remove clean clothes before throwing dirty laundry into this cart". Another says "Always ensure "accurated" number of meals - details are important". Signs can say a great deal about an organization. Such stupidity and lack of attention to detail should speak for themselves.

One guard actually told me tonight that this system is designed to be a revolving door. The revenues received for each inmate and the prison employment needs require more and more inmates. He even said that they like "when children visit their parents in prison because it adds to their propensity to enter prison themselves." It's important to note that he didn't use the word propensity. I added that for clarification of the dialogue. He said, "fucking end up being here."

I had a true "governmental" example of "this is why I am in prison" experience today. For some unexplained reason stripping the floors seems to be the pet project of the daytime OIC Rutgers. We neither have the equipment nor the supplies, but despite all of the really important projects needed to be done, this one is "manly" and so repeatedly selected. Stripping of the floors creates an unnecessary mess. Real men like mess.

I stripped one tier, but I have no polish to make it look good again. I can guarantee they won't even notice the difference. (They didn't.)

My attorney visited and told me that the arrogant Judge will now decide next Monday. I hope I get to put him in his rightful place after my wrongful incarceration lawsuit is decided on, hopefully by impartial Judges.

Tonight I got paired with CO Charity to clean cells again. He's another "born again" ready to preach his self-appointed form of Christianity, when the inmate opportunity presents itself. He said that there were two prisoners he was ever impressed with and I was one of them. During our twenty cell cleaning experience I studied his reaction to the inmates' dialogues with me. My real purpose was to change the prison system and not to allow it to change me. I spoke to one of the younger inmates who I call "Sun" and he said he was happy I was staying one more week because no one here wanted me to stop being their orderly. He said, "This is the most I ever cleaned my cell. The mops are clean, the tier feeling is happy and my cell smells like home". That has been a chore to create; but I am glad I have moved ever so slightly towards accomplishing my goal.

Two-Ply's legal request was given on to my attorney to mail after he researches it for him. Two-Ply then put a tuna fish meal and peanut butter stick in my laundry bag so I guess I have been paid for a prison service. I'm really getting to experience every dysfunctional activity this BOP creates.

No Commissary deliveries continued again this week, so it's a very "long" non-eating weekend. I hope there are some extra meals left over tomorrow. Deliverance has been as nice as one can imagine. I wish he'd leave me some of the outside food they order. However, I'm going to not get a "ticket" and have to stay one minute after that Judge's order to release me finally arrives. So, I'll not eat unauthorized food.

It's quiet tonight. Remember that screamer last night? They moved him! Normally patient inmates get nothing, but if you "act-out", they will reward you (after they extend your stay). They moved him nearer to his gang members. You figure.

Let's conduct an investigation into companies that the BOP uses, supplies that they purchase, and where the commissary monies go. This would make Watergate and Iraq look like child's play. The BOP makes the USPS appear to be an efficiency expert in comparison to the BOP's inefficiency. Such an investigation could make a politician or a reporter's career.

Is it possible that the BOP has created a self-perpetuating business with no actual desire to rehabilitate its victims but only to addict them? Remember I said if the BOP was an automobile repair shop with as many customers returning for the same problem or worse - wouldn't the Better Business Bureau and the Attorney General investigate those claims? They would be closed down! Physician heal thyself!

There are creative alternatives to prisons with a higher probability of success. Let's demand them.

If I win my wrongful incarceration lawsuit and collect what I will be suing for, I would like to create an inmate credit union (ICU) to help them start their own franchise companies after leaving prison. They really cannot find an entry job because of their felony convictions. They are often treated worse than they have been in prison which simply "re-marches" these men and women back into a world where they are wanted and accepted-that's prison not Main Street.

Tonight a guard was explaining to me and the rest of the guards about how an inmate hung himself years ago in the slop room where I work. He electrocuted and hung himself! The description of his body seemed to have missed the newspapers. Prisoners have been telling me of countless other unpublicized stories. Shouldn't those of us who i regularly pay the "bills" put an end to this cash cow for friends of our democratically elected representatives or their contributors and demand to be told what is going on inside?

Chapter 99 – Spanky and His Gang

From theft to murder to stealing away the hopes and dreams of millions – perhaps, there is a more devious and overlooked set of criminals here, namely the BOP and the oversight elected representatives entrusted to supervise them.

Unicore is an "independent" BOP business that hires and pays the inmates. Some inmates are paid $1.00 per day or less!  Yes, in America!  When these men and women finally get out of servitude they have put all of their monies back into the General Store (Commissary) which charges more than you or I pay for the same products.   Do any of my readers pay more than 24 cents per minute to make local phone calls?   Incarcerate and rehabilitate?  I think not!   Investigate Unicore!   Investigate the BOP!

Because of a failure to receive a commissary delivery, I am functioning without any supplements of cheese, matzo, cookies or granola bars.  I only get the regular meals served.   Today's breakfast was the same. Next meal is in four hours, but I'm on the "list" for the Warden to sign off on their commissary mistake while they earn interest on the dollars in those accounts.   Someone should study those interest thefts as well. Prisoners in our society are without a collective voice.   Their families must helplessly sit silent.   For those non-violent criminals that this system turns violent or agoraphobic, are we not, in part, responsible by our silence?

Anger creation and gang recruiting are two of the results of this present system.   When an inmate yells (and I can't understand why that is permitted in a day and an age of electronically monitored communication) "I'm bringing Tommy home", that means he has joined their gang.   To survive in any prison institution long term "friends" are required.   When one guard is ordered to supervise over one hundred inmates without handcuffs, tell me how strict he should run his eight hour shift?   The tail is wagging the dog in here.   The guards are compromised.   The "suits" and the system are the problem.   They need measurable programs, on the job placement, self-esteem classes, orientation back to society, how to dress, how to interview, how to raise a family, how to handle anger and how to eliminate the desire to re-visit prison.   At this time none of these exist. Counselors like Ms. Black ("Et. Al.'s" replacement) was a secretary before her recent promotion. She hates what she does, and she hates the inmates she serves.

My unit is run like "Spanky and Our Gang". To survive the negative feelings and being so overwhelmed by their tasks, they shut down. Yes, they mean well. Yes, they serve the food. But it's a non-functioning club-house to "count" inmates only. That's the bizarre relationship of being "kidnapped", but being fed by the one who prevents you from leaving. You hate. You need. They become a surrogate family to those in need of much more. Like a dog, you respond to the clatter of Keys not to go "out", but to be "fed". No wonder the hostility festers deep inside men who have had their ability to "hunt" taken away.

When monies are transferred into inmate accounts, Western Union charges fees. Does the BOP get those or any percentage of those fees? Who benefits from the 24 cents per minute phone system? What about the profits from the general store?

Although I have been dropped into a make believe world, I have unfairly paid 80 days of my life for those injustices. Together we can ask enough questions to prevent this from happening to someone you care about. Believe me; if one Judge without a hearing can do this to me, no one is safe in our America of today.

On this day my spoon/fork began to show signs of old age. One of the tiny teeth bent. Was it the boiled potato? (not boiled) It wasn't the mystery meat that resembles a human tongue. Symbolically the BOP has captured America's tongues. Maybe this expose' will begin an inquiry that goes somewhere. Back to my damaged spoon/fork. It has served me well. I intend to retire it when I leave. It may become my comb as I'm still not allowed one. My nail clipper also hasn't appeared since the one illegal cutting. Some inmates who are here for over 130 days have begun chewing their nails. They have grown tired of asking for a nail clipper.

The Sunday meal without my ability to supplement with commissary food reminds me of the nausea feeling that I had when I lost my first fifteen pounds. Most people brush their teeth for hygienic reasons, but I do it to remove the taste of this food. In this prison I brush my teeth to eliminate the feeling of impending indigestion.

As you know by now, on weekends I have to wait until one of the guards can't stand the filth they have made, or they remember that I have work to do to make these incompetents look like they function. The criminal justice system has little room for creative and individual thought. My tier is so quiet. All of the "characters" have been moved to some of the more talkative tiers. At night, I appreciated that. When being confined I must confess that, I do like to observe the insanity that I hear and see going on in the other tiers. It passes the time between the pains of silence.

Until yesterday I couldn't understand why the CO's took the outside wrapping paper off of the toilet paper rolls before "displaying" and "issuing" them. One of the inmates told me that the inmates smoke the paper using the paper to roll "whatever". How they get the matches into here is a prison secret I won't reveal.

I am furious as this soon to be eighty day incarceration continues. I also sometimes get exasperated that I have to work for idiots, without pay. All of Sunday slips by while I sit in my cell without commissary food products, due to their ineptitude. I know the amount of work that has to be done in here every day. I could handle it in a fairly comfortable manner and get it all done – if the COs would let me out to do it every day and not make me wait hours for them to simply get up and unlock a door to allow me to move from one work area to the next. It's as if getting up to open a door for me is too much effort. Because the schedule of letting me out to clean is intermittent and unpredictable (as are their door opening skills) I am forced to work until midnight each day trying to finish while the rotating crews ignore their paid responsibilities.

I am the only one who sees the problems and I can't change the thought processes of an organization backed by the same government which has attacked and hurt myself and my loved ones. There are times when I think that the "deck is stacked" against my righteous position. Then despair and hostility begin to boil within me. Until now, I cool it down with my belief in justice along with the knowledge of our moral and correct stance.

CO Sponge Bob (a female who looks like the character Sponge Bob) came around to give advice.   Listening to her is like watching a sit-com.   This is a woman with no sophistication telling the ways of the world to men lost in its BOP circular roads.   The BOP roads go nowhere.   She said, "You have to yell so I can hear you", as I tried to speak to her.   I haven't reached the depth of insignificance to scream and then to be intentionally ignored by her.

Picture your obviously gay male hair stylist sauntering around the prison with a long chain of keys on a black outfit, and you have the "acting" Chaplain.   As I ignore him and he me, I listen to his attempts at being an understanding priest.   There are some issues here that should be examined before a Boston-type priest inquiry is initiated.   What better place to hide someone who may never be exposed then in a prison?   Am I the only one to see it?   Many CO's just smile when his name comes up. This is one lifetime employee who may like his job very much.   He may like it much too much!

One of the older refined European inmates has been arrested because he is a Muslim.   Seventy days ago I wouldn't have believed his explanation. Today I leave open the possibility.   Do you think they think my Italian surname is Muslim?   Is it AI-Tomare?   Maybe the degree of intelligence inside our walls of government broke down for a few minutes.   A few minutes?   Hell, it's been broken for decades and our citizens don't raise the outcry necessary to change it.

Nevertheless, the refined European inmate with fear in his eyes asked me what he should do about mice or rats in his cell.   Since no one had responded to his previous requests, I tried to ask the CO I was working with.   He said, "If you have mice or rats, you have to leave the cell until our traps catch them".   "If that were true, no one would be in their cells", I thought.   So I asked when my friend could be moved.   He put him on a "list" to be moved.   I felt terrible that I had to leave him to stay in that cell until his name comes up on the imaginary list to move.   If he started to kick, scream and curse, like the other inmates, he'd be moved in an instant.

Prison is not for the gentlemen in our society. It is designed to make you "theirs". Prison is prison, but as I listen to now the evening crew laugh and play in the Day Room; I know one of the officers on duty tonight is that previously mentioned "Incoming". Hopefully I'll be left in my cell all night. To try to prepare the ward professionally is beyond the capabilities of twelve "Officers" during the entire day. Tomorrow there will be no wash ready for cell clean up, no mops cleaned for general maintenance. They sadly like it better that way. Trying to treat prison like a functioning job creates defense and resentment. There is more resistance from the staff than the prisoners.

If I knew definitely I was leaving next Monday, I would simply stay in this cell until my release. Because of the corporate and moral idiocy of this entire experience, I have to acquiesce to little men and women not even worthy of ever working for one of my companies, let alone me being their "Master Slave".

My entire calorie intake today had to be 800 calories or less. What annoys this hard worker is that when the commissary botch-up occurred, one of these governmental drones should have "stepped up" to help the one who works so long and for nothing except to add a degree of professionalism to this dead-headed organization. They remain immobile at challenges or obstacles.

I fight this broken corporate culture and damaged work ethic here on a minute to minute basis. Once again thank you, for being there. Between you, Bridge and my word games; I have nothing else. I used to have books, but I gave them all away to the other inmates.

Knowing that sometime tonight or early tomorrow morning one of these security guards will come in hysterical to try to solve partially what could have been done properly and timely makes my stay in this institution even more unbearable. This institution is to stay as is, but our fine company was closed by this Judge to protect a governmental agency. He can say and write whatever he chooses to, but the truth will always remain with me. Tonight I am angry. Shame on our society for what they did to one of us (and hundreds of Employees) (tens of thousands of loyal and deserving shareholders) and they leave one institution like this untouched. Shame, shame, shame.

Chapter 100 – Into the Secret Prison

This day started as predicted. At 6:00AM the new crew was banging on my door saying "the place is a mess, and there's no shower supplies out! What did you do all weekend"?

I smiled an inmate smile and went to work cleaning up what looked like an unsupervised fraternity party. I proceeded to work and serve the inmates and by 7:00AM the showers began. A little later CO Left Handed asked me to deliver food to the terrorist inmates upstairs in the secret prison within the prison.

At about 8:30AM, when I was still trying to think of how to express my weekend frustration, and to whom; the opportunity finally arose. Lieutenant "Suit with a Uniform" told me not to talk to the inmates because they all wanted my attention, and he had never seen that before, and it bothered him. He told me this unit (the MCC) is the most secure prison in the nation - and the terrorists' cells, (the secret prison within the prison) were the most secure prison units maybe in the world. As I listened to this self-aggrandizing garbage, I walked up the stairs, picked up the phone near the door as I had been told by one of the keystone cops in the past few months, gave the code and the door buzzed me in. Lt. Suit went out of his mind and took me outside to talk to me. He wanted to know who gave me the code. I told him I figured it out on my own because I didn't want to have a guard lose his job. Entering this "secure" unit so easily helped me redirect my anger at how ignorantly I was treated this weekend. I did see a slide projector and garbage pails filled with party foods and drinks, so I better understood why I couldn't work because we are in one of the most secure units in the Country.

Today I distributed over two dozen towels, socks, shirts and jumpsuits to those inmates who had asked for them. To remember their requests and to make the inmates feel special is important, but to actually deliver them is "priceless" and difficult to achieve because access to a tier is often not available without a disinterested guard using many keys to open the maze of locks and doors.

One of the inmate's reactions was really memorable. "Evil's" roommate called me over and said, "I didn't like you because you were different, but man, you're a "good different" and we're friends forever, ya heard?" When his gang members got the word, I became "his protégé". It was interesting to see them now treat me as I have treated them - with respect. I was then made an honorary gang member. The ceremony was secret and I felt protected inside the prison with my new gang nickname, RT. Even I had to join a gang in this quagmire called MCC.

A number of incidents flew at me today. First, a very mild former orange graduate returned to us being carried in by four CO's. He was hysterical. After they left him to calm down in a holding cell which was next to my laundry; we then spoke. He had asked not to be sent to a particular unit which was headed by a "suit" named Mr. Mansion. He and Mr. Mansion just didn't get along no matter how hard he tried. Of course, that's where he was sent. That was Friday night. This is Monday. Mr. Mansion broke the inmate's finger and they carried him away after he complained about his finger. He has called for all of the psychologists, and he has gone on a hunger strike to protest this action by the BOP. Last year he went on a four week hunger strike until they force fed this 25 year old, who was planning to get out next month. They have put him on suicide watch. His time will be extended. This boy should be permitted to go home. He makes more sense than these "suits" and uniforms.

I was told today "This bleak place has only one light and that is you". (My older English friend) "You're the best and hardest worker in prison". Four inmates asked to be orderlies with me. I had a sandwich I saved from lunch, but I gave it to an inmate standing at his door tonight as I cleaned his tier and he was looking very sad. That sandwich could have been a seven course meal due to his reaction of appreciation.

My Wife visited tonight. Our finances remain bleak until I get home. I will rebound our life, but with repossessions and foreclosures being threatened, she is distraught. I will solve it. We will win our cases to teach these bullies a lesson.

I gave out the two-ply paper today to the inmates and I must add that there was a woman CO today (CO Favor) and she was terrific. She was competent and she stood out. Her sense of humor and intelligence added to the morning. Working with and for her was a pleasure. When I asked an inmate who had asked for toilet paper, "did you want one-ply or two-ply" - only she got it. The rest of the CO's were unable to understand the humor. Humor and intelligence co-exist, but in here many are without either.

One interesting dialogue transpired today between the broken finger hunger striker and his prison's case worker. She lost it! She said, "I can't take this anymore. I want to go home and not think about all of this craziness. I don't know how to counsel you. You are right, OK? But there's nothing good going to happen "here".

An Assistant Warden walked by the distraught inmate and told him to put ice on his finger. The inmate had been contained in a 4' x 4' box at the time. He waited there another three hours before they moved him (with no ice).

Mr. Mansion sends at least two inmates a week to us. He's good for BOP business and not one inmate benefits from him and his sadistic counsel.

Tonight was spent cleaning up after the three leaky showers and the washing of clothes. In true governmental style I was told tonight that before I was the orderly they never ran out of towels. I responded, "There are two reasons: one, there were infrequent showers and the inmates wouldn't walk into the showers with mice, the other was that you just didn't give them any towels! Instead, the officers should be blamed for not getting the towels back from the inmates when they leave the unit. It's easier to blame the orderly".

Tonight I was given extra time to visit with my Wife. To thank them I cleaned their visiting room and bathroom. The CO Joker responded by thanking me for cleaning something which had not been cleaned in years! Imagine, years!

The funny conclusion to that "protégé" story is that when you are "sponsored into a gang" the individual who is sponsored may often take a part of his sponsor's nickname. Move over Lord Baltimore. I am now being called RT, after the gang name of "Evil's" roommate which had a "T" in it.

Today I was "forced" to have a day off. Don't ask me to explain the reason why. It could be that they think I'm working too hard. It could be they think I'm enjoying working too much. It could be the problem of yesterday with me breaking the security and refusing to give the guard's name who gave me the code to enter the high security area. It could be any number of things. Without commissary food in my room, it's a punishment. If they intend to continue to use me after today, the extra work created by them after my being off does not help me. Trying to understand their thought process in prison is difficult. Nevertheless what are my options ... bang on the door and get promoted? Sleep all day without extra food is another option. My legal visit will last a long time today. I will stay longer than usual. I should not let them upset me.

Last evening I counseled the brother of Tom. I have convinced him to stop playing into the CO's attempts to upset him. He said, "If you say not to do it, I believe you". With all of the counselors, psychologists, CO's and higher ranking officers, I'm glad simple human kindness worked with him. Being off today extends the length of the day. Whether I am being rewarded or punished is still in question, and that confusing thought helps one to better understand prison thought. That I do not know whether I am being punished or rewarded is a good description of the mental games played in places like this. Consider this impact on unsophisticated inmate minds.

I am told that the Lieutenant decided I should not work today. If I reacted, I would play into their hands by going to the Captain. I don't care. I can rest for the day. The evening crew may let me out of my cell to prepare for showers. If not, I'll let the Lieutenant do it himself.

My instincts were so right on that Lieutenant - a suit in a uniform. He is threatened by my efforts and results. Insignificant men like this gang language speaking, "quota" Lieutenant make wrong decisions that can hurt an organization. Only in here can he get away with it.

For diary material alone, I am considering having a meeting with the Captain and the Lieutenant. It may be a valuable exercise to see if I "retire" in prison over stupidity or just the injustice of one guard.

My commissary "partial" order just arrived so staying in my cell is not as painful. When I consider this behavior by the Lieutenant, I have to wonder as to his alternative plan. With showers in the morning and a shortage of tee-shirts, towels and the regular scheduled cleaning of tiers and cells tonight, who will do their back-up work? Anyone can be an orderly, and it's not that anyone is irreplaceable, but they have no one in the wings. For the sake of the inmates, I hope they do. Are they trying to chastise or confuse me? The silence of the officers as I sit in the cell makes me wonder if unjust orders when followed affect the psyche of the officers themselves. Just ask former German soldiers.

One of the CO's just confirmed that I have been officially "fired" as their orderly. Even before I could resign, I was fired! It's quite funny, when one looks at it though the words and entries of this diary.

Chapter 101 – It's Deja Vu, all Over Again

Well, I was previously "fired" by the actions of one other governmental agency and one Judge for doing everything right with my company, and now I'm fired in prison for doing everything right once again. Being fired for doing everything correctly is what happened, starting this entire trip down the BOP "Alice in Wonderland hole"? Why should my second governmental firing be a surprise?

It appears that in the following weeks it will be just you, me and my window again. I can use the rest, and I can watch them return their tier and unit to the condition with which they are most comfortable. Returning to non-prison orderly status may be a good way to wind down my prison sentence for no crime having been committed in the first place.

Think about that! Being put in prison for no crime and now being replaced as an efficient orderly for no specific action seems at least to be consistent Justice Department action.

Let's play a game. Before I officially know why I was fired, let me list some possible reasons and then if and when I actually find out, we can see if any of these were right.

1.  Simply a time issue - like cell movement, I had been an orderly too long

2.  Too friendly with prisoners

3.  Giving prisoners towels

4.  To protect me from a threat of some sort

5.  Not respecting the security of the terrorist unit

6.  Becoming too independent of an insecure Lieutenant

7.  Being disrespectful

8.  Giving food to prisoners

9. Seeming to enjoy myself too much

10. Simply no explanation given

11. Writing a book

12. Knowing too much

13. Poor performance (I have to put it in)

14. A lie of some sort was told about me

15. Talking to the Inmates and making the prison too humane

16. Using too many cleaning supplies

17. Being too neat and orderly (no pun intended)

18. Threatening authority of existing cadre

19. Moving around too freely

20. Following the order of an officer by delivering food up to the Terrorists' cell

Another CO just came by to tell me that the guards are trying to get the Captain to reconsider the recommendation of the Lieutenant. Let's see what transpires. The real issue becomes, "do I refuse to be rehired, or do I just accept this as another reason the prison system is even more broken than I previously thought".

My first responsible thought was, "Do they need someone to help train or replace me?" The CO on duty said they have no replacement. They just fired me without thinking of the consequences. Like the old ballad "What will be, will be." How funny really is this episode? If I did something worth being terminated, why would they not have an alternative plan in place?

In reality, they are hours away from an organizational shower and inspection nightmare, and why wouldn't they have discussed it prior to an impulsive decision?

Because I'm hoping to be released from this crazy house this Tuesday, I will go through the necessary steps of reconciliation. If the prisoners find out that I am fired, I'm curious as to their reactions. I can hear the prisoners calling "orderly" or my various names because they think I'm out there doing whatever it takes to maintain the cleanliness of the unit.

The real issue is "the suit with a uniform on". Without the facts (just like the SEC) the Judge (the Lieutenant) makes the impulsive and corporately approved decision until reconsideration by an objective appeal Judge (the Captain) is heard.

To quote the ballplayer Yogi Berra - "it's deja vu all over again".

Let me nibble on my snacks and wait for some rational judgment to surface. It may have to be ordered from an outside source. For the sake of my story, if given the opportunity I will go back to work to prove the stupidity and irrationality of this firing decision. If his original decision stands, then I will have been victimized twice by an agency's (or officer's) fear, which had neither the facts nor best interests of the general good in mind. Governmental employees simply have their own personal causes or agendas to carry on.

As the "reconsideration" goes on, they continue to begin creating confusion and more mess. Without someone in the laundry room, it will return to its original filthy condition. I am reminded of a poem in which a pail of still water no matter how energetically it is spun; when stopped, the water will return to its original still position. Unfortunately, that is what will happen here. The silence of the officers on this obvious injustice also speaks volumes on the condition of the human spirit. I don't expect mankind to strive, as I have always done. I simply find it painful that when presented moments of courage or silence, they genuflect to power alone without regard for the greater good. I guess water seeks its own level and the following of a mistake, even when you know in your soul that it is a mistake, seems to be far too common in today's Patriot Act inflicted fearful society.

I have to get myself ready for a shower tomorrow. I hope the new orderly can find everything and can make the place good for these inmates. Tonight again ignorance defeated the positive elements of the human spirit. Power alone without consequential thoughts results in backward movement.

I marvel at what thoughts go on in institutionalized minds. How do they rationalize their actions? Well, there seems to be movement "out" tonight. Two-Ply was yelling because he wanted to give me his forwarding address to receive his legal brief. He left tonight.

Well, I had a good run in a broken and dreary organization. Like an athlete with a good season followed by retirement, I left on top.

Some inmates may wonder why I left. I will miss some of the freedoms even though the physical price was a costly one of lost writing and reading time, thankless and redundant activity and additional weight loss.

Wait until my attorney, family and friends find out I was fired as "head slave". Like this trumped up contempt charge, I believe that everything works out for the best. In time, the truth always wins out. I wish I could have actually done something wrong or against some rule to justify my firing. But I guess symbolically, I had to be treated poorly and unjustly to make it an appropriate firing for me. I am relieved, and I will enjoy my quiet time until my release; whenever that may occur. Closure comes in many ways.

## Chapter 102 – Bottom of the 9<sup>th</sup> – Two Out

I just heard from the inmates' banter that the last All-Star game in Yankee Stadium was going on. I must confess that touched me more than some of the things that have hurt me during this incarceration. As a young boy and adult, my sons, my parents and I have followed baseball. Knowing that I was not to participate or view the final All-Star game at the Stadium while a wrongful government had their way with me did activate my feelings of anger and sadness. Adding today's firing to my unaccustomed feeling of helplessness with the gang banter going on makes me a bit melancholy. When such ignorance is prevalent, something is wrong with the world I knew.

The inmates have been yelling about my firing and have started flushing and clogging their toilets to create a protest with flowing water. Imagine thirty or more inmates banging, yelling and protesting the guards' ignorance. It is gratifying to hear them defend their orderly and to stand up for their own dignity.

A few of the CO's came by my window to wave. They feel badly and know that my firing is not even remotely the correct decision for all involved. They really appreciate that I refused to give up the name of the guard who gave me the access code.

Like my plan with this appeal reversal, it is better not to be a "cry baby" during the "wrong doing" period. I will remain steadfast, but maintain my dignity.

The inmates are yelling about a sudden outbreak by mice in many of the cells. It's a night-light night and a tight tucking of my sheets.

That baseball game, last night's family visit and today's head hurting firing makes me want to go home and return to a normal life. I hope this is the final day. Today's firing has eased my gradual re-birth to our society.

With Two-Ply also being shipped out there is no one to even carry-on those systems put in place for the operational functioning of the unit. At least my original observation of that Lieutenant weeks ago was accurate. He causes problems due to his inability to think or act like an officer.

Showing him a hole in his security system is just like showing the SEC that naked short selling existed. They both prefer to deny the facts and kill the messenger. But the truth remains.

I was awakened to be told I had been rehired! As I got dressed, I didn't believe that it would happen without a meeting. I was right. I was cuffed and not rehired. The guards made a mistake. Keep thinking about what they do to the uneducated and the confused during these pages.

The CO's now with fright in their eyes came to my cell to tell me that all of the sheets and towels were in the dirty wash and they didn't have enough clean clothes to give to the inmates and the tier was not ready for inspection. One guard was honest enough to say, "You did tell us this would happen". Showers were cancelled unless the inmates didn't want a change of clothes or a towel.

They gave me a shower like the old days, and I spoke with a few of the guards who cannot understand the decision by the Lieutenant. Letting go of anyone in a corporation for cause or not for cause normally involves some sort of plan to continue operating uninterrupted. Not here.

This Lieutenant may have proudly exercised his authority and fired this orderly; however it raises some other prison quality control questions. I will just read the Bible until my legal visit or eventual release. I could see the neglected messy Day Room as I looked out of my shower, and I could hear the inmates calling my various names. I wonder what the guards will tell them. Will they say "he was too nice"? Will they say, "He followed what an officer ordered him to do"? Who knows? It certainly rounds out my stay in this governmental "think tank" of filth and disorder.

If tonight is my final night, it is a perfect way to remember the entire prison experience.

Chapter 103 – Black Plague in New York

Today, let me first set the stage because if I had tried to make up a dramatic ending (if today is to be that final day); I would never have even imagined what did actually happen.

Let's start at the morning.  I had a legal visit and upon my return I began the washing and preparation for what I had hoped was to be a perfect final shower presentation in which nothing could go wrong.  In case you are confused, of course, they rehired me without a word said.  Insanity and confusion exist here like filth, mice and contempt for sanity.

There was nothing left to wash as I prepared the big laundry shower cart, which I have made into a comet smelling white glove type presentation wagon.  I carefully took out 8 gray bins which were carefully marked with the sizes of every accessory.  It would be impossible for these guards to not know exactly where everything was.  On top of this rolling laundry cart I placed and neatly folded and marked seventy or more jumpsuits ranging in sizes from large to 7XL.  I must confess that it was quite thorough and professionally ready for the morning shift.

In addition, the evening crew wanted me to clean another thirty cells tonight.  Although I said it would not be necessary, that had to do something because they thought a "suit" was planning to visit.  So I carefully prepared the various brooms, brushes, mops, supplies and rags needed for the process.  To review, a comet can is not permitted to be given to the inmates because it has a metal top and if forgotten could be made into a knife.  So the comet is sprinkled into an envelope and handed to the inmate through the food slot.   I was coordinating the three officers who were doing ten cells each while I was cleaning stairs, providing supplies and getting whatever the inmates may have needed and the guards didn't want to get for them.  I was running to get items like a book, a pencil, toilet paper, a sock, or a form to request a phone call.  So while this very, very hectic unnecessary exercise which will now create sixty used blankets and thirty more used sheets, was going on, another Lieutenant began preaching to one of our inmates who has been upset of late due to the BOP's failure to move him to another prison, as they had promised.  This is a physically intimidating inmate who has been convicted of murder in a prison claiming self-defense. Whatever the background, he started a water flow by blocking his toilet. I rushed to stop the water when I heard of it because the last water mess clean-up just finished days ago. As I ran down with the dirty blankets I saw that the incompetent Lieutenant had already taken fifteen of my newly washed jumpsuits and thrown them on the ground to absorb and re-direct the water. I went ballistic because I do not have extra jumpsuits and any idiot would not upset such a pristine display like the one they were on. I threw down about twenty used blankets which was all that was ever needed. I was sent to the laundry during the count, and I then heard a fire alarm. That alarm went on for about five minutes before it stopped. Three other Lt.'s came in with a camera and about forty-five minutes went by until I saw three cadre tan suited workers being brought in to help me! As I walked out of the secluded laundry room, I could not intellectually process what I saw!

The inmate had broken the fire sprinkler in his cell and it activated all of the water sprinklers on that tier, Black water stored with chemicals for twenty years completely covered the entire tier and all of the cells. The black ink like water was everywhere except that all of my clean clothes had been thrown on the floor. Yes, all of the clothes! Not only wet but now blackened! In addition the soap, shaving cream and toothpaste boxes had all been dumped out! There were over a thousand small items spread and mixed all over the Day Room. I was numb when now one of the cadre pulled out a rubber devise that they have which avoids using linens to re-direct or absorb water. They didn't even need to use the clothes! I was unable to process this mess. So much of my work was wasted by their actions. Three hours later the four of us were trying to minimize the water damage and black soot which is still hardening as I write. I watched the Lieutenant giving the one inmate responsible for this mess new clothes and the Lieutenant couldn't believe I didn't have any of the clothing sizes he asked for! Now the other CO's who watched this happen wanted me to go to bed and to shower. "There's nothing we can do, it's not your fault", they said. "Let the daytime crew deal with it. If you stay past twelve o'clock, you won't get a shower and that black stuff should be washed off of you. If you don't shower now, you'll have to go to bed filthy covered with this black chemical."

Everything I had cleaned was covered with black water. The entire white floor was covered with black footprints. There is nothing for showers tomorrow! Nothing! Everything is lying all over the floor covered with black water. Trying to clean them will take days. The CO's who watched were both hysterical laughing towards the Lieutenant's actions and truly were sympathetic because of how hard I try to give them a dose of sanity in this insane world.

Even after writing this I wish it were a dream. Everything I did for the past few days was ignorantly undone and with no purpose. The clothes thrown on the ground did nothing to minimize the thousands of gallons of black water damage.

Since this may be my final prison entry, I wanted to relate a few stories which may have fallen through the cracks in the past few days.

1 -- One of the inmates left to go to population. When I cleaned his cell, I found 14 milk cartons with curdled milk and urine which were lined up in case he wanted to throw or stomp them against a CO, or hopefully not me.

2 -- "Evil" lost it tonight! Yes, he returned today. He actually assumed a different voice and appearance. He is now multi-personality and quite frightening. He threw 10 eggs and various things at the guards after his food slot was opened. He refused to let them close it. He is more lost than I originally thought. It pains me to feel this talented young man's confusion and desperation.

3 -- Prisoners have little except a desire to be "cool". I have a pair of sneakers which someone marked 12R on one and I2L on the other. No matter how often I gave them out, no inmate would take them. Since we don't have that many size 12 sneakers, I wear them. It has been a disarming and continued source of laughter when inmates comment on my shoes. I could have any new ones, but I have taken the least cool ones.

4 -- Because of my new gang status, I was given and put on a bandanna. Like the other gang members, I wear it only in my cell. It was a source of good fun when these inmates saw me wearing it while I was mopping tonight before the black plaque occurred!

5 -- I want you to research Unicore, the prison private business. They pay these inmates pennies an hour. How are these inmates to start their lives over when they get out of prison with no money? How come minimum wage is enforced on small businesses but not on our government?

6 -- Remember it costs between $175 and $200 daily to house a prisoner. Do the math. Reform is necessary. Two million prisoners. Many are incarcerated unnecessarily.

7 -- During the black flood removal tonight the cadre brought in two new water vacuums. They also didn't work! Added to our two previously non-functioning ones, who's buying them? What are the purchase requirements demanded for this equipment to perform?

8 -- Food quality and small portions are simply something that adds to the breakdown of these inmates. Weight loss and depression must be also considered.

As I go to bed tonight still hopeful it's my final "wakeup", my back hurts from lifting and mopping all of that water. (1000 gallons at least was estimated) The realization of what mess tomorrow brings, further depresses me. If I knew that I was being released, I would quit tonight. But if something else goes wrong with my release, I would have missed even having this horrific story to share with you.

By the way, during the Black Plague the guards covered the windows so the inmates couldn't see the damage or the work being done. All one could hear was their yelling to be let out of their wet, black cells. It was eerie and even frightening.

I have to be able to see these things first hand so I can report them to you accurately. That's why I stay out of my cell, working, so I can see and report on what's going on. In summary … For your sake, mine and our society, we need prison reform.

Chapter 104 – Heat on the Plantation

Today was the day of the five o'clock conference with the Judge, and I still know nothing. Knowing that my sad and frightened Wife is only blocks away either celebrating or feeling devastated is making it more difficult daily to hold my tongue.

Frankly I am tired or maybe bored is a better word of working with men of this emotional caliber. The inmates break my heart whenever I go on a tier to clean. Wanting to help them but not being able to, along with the extra non-productive work caused by inconsistent leadership makes the job tedious and repetitive. We never get better. We make the same mistakes over and over again, and they rationalize and justify the insanity that causes me to pray that each night is my last night. In fact, they create new mistakes daily.

My Wife's last visit was our worse. She is financially under massive pressure and my release is the only way I can try to help the backslide. I often wonder how a Judge is permitted to bankrupt citizens because he is either jealous or angry at them. My Wife holds no hope in any of our appeals and has lost all confidence in our legal system. I understand, but I don't agree with her conclusions yet.

It will be a stressful night. With no air conditioning and the cell temperature in the high nineties, with high humidity, as well - it won't be a comfortable night anyway. Despite the black water moisture hardening throughout, most of the day was spent with me planning my departure and every time the phone rang I thought it was my release. I must admit some concern now over our financial situation.

Let me try to recap the day. Upon coming out of the cell I had that massive black sludge clean-up and work to do. Although the Lieutenant told me not to help with showers, the CO's wanted me to do it! There goes another conflicting signal. The CO's don't improve their prisoner movements, food serving, and task completion any better from day to day. The apparent ease of simplifying and organizing these activities is not in their thought processes.

The psychopath who caused the flood last night was treated like a celebrity by the CO's and the other inmates. There was no mention of any consequence because I always "save the day" and clean up after them.

Despite my lists of supply requests we have run out of everything including now toilet paper. Tomorrow should be the day the inmates are told they can't have toilet paper. I clean without the soaps I need. We have zero socks for the sixty or so inmates. Not one pair. We have no towels so inmates reuse and reuse without washing their towels. Eight new inmates reported tonight. Four left. The four who left shook my hand and two hugged me with sincere appreciation. All this is an accomplishment, but home is where my heart is now.

There are so many things to correct. I have so many lawsuits to file. So many new businesses I must also create. Damn that judicial demagogue, but I remain confident of the eventual full circle of this travesty.

My poor 90 year old parents are sick with worry. How do we as Americans permit this type of unconstitutional behavior? Whenever I leave, I will legally and morally retaliate.

I do not know when my attorney will visit, but I am afraid of more bad news.

I am seeing too many return inmate performers here. Five more former inmates returned today.

Now that I am a gang member, I am included in prison "shower passing". Items are left in the shower vent for others to get and to pass other items on and on to the intended recipient. It is a fascinating system. I got an inmate in trouble today. I was asked to pass a "hood novel" to a particular murderer. I thought I did, but I accidentally gave it to another murderer. When I told murderer one, he threatened murderer two. Fortunately, I was able to avoid their anger from escalating by getting a second book.

By watching this prison chain of command, I can conclude that it is designed to frustrate inmates not rehabilitate them. This many people cannot be this non-functioning. Today alone I watched at least five inmates getting "tickets" or extended time. "Time is money here". Are the guards rewarded for additional time given to the inmates?

As I fear opening my eyes hoping that I am no longer here, the early morning sounds of chains, keys, doors and guards trying to organize breakfast and recreational visits remind me that my nightmare is still going on. It appears for the present that my entire future (if I still have one) is determined by a vindictive and vengeful Judge who has been given the power to destroy innocent lives with immunity.

Despite the slow moving morning and excessive heat in the cell, I wait for some outside communication and a definitive time for an end to this inappropriate incarceration.

My children, my grandchildren, friends, business associates. What do they think? Do they realize America is now under a different form of government?

The sounds of loud flushing toilets, slow prisoner movement and now my anxious silent waiting haunt this morning.

As I get dressed, I realize it is still too hot to sit dressed. How does one eradicate himself from the prison cycle? Should I stop-up the toilet? Should I break the fire sensors?

For what they have done to me, I scoff at their fearful vindictiveness. For what they have done to my Wife's life, I collapse in numbing pain. When will sanity and justice finally surface?

The 95 plus degree cell tonight coupled with my delayed release conference adds to my irritability. Before I speak of the day, I should tell you of my snacks which I eat every night. By eating the exact boring snacks for fifty or more days adds to the tastes of prison. I have attached to this diary a list of products they claim to sell. Not all are available, but the ones I get are granola bars, ice tea, matzo, cheese and peanut butter. After a while they become as boring as prison life. So while I am writing this diary, I am normally supplementing these inadequate meals with these regular commissary snacks permitted in my solitary cell.

Chapter 105 – Rat, I mean Rat

Today my day started with a legal visit which informed me of a further delay and then a two hour wait before I could go back to the unit. Why two hours? Because the guard sent to get me was flirting with a female guard. It made me think about the complete control these lesser developed BOP employees have over the prisoners. They are like flawed Gods with no one to answer to. In the case of a guard's poor judgment, the prisoner has no rights despite what their BOP paperwork claims they have. The UCMJ hangs like a sharp ax over their helpless heads.

A guard today got into a yelling argument with an inmate. When the inmate was verbally winning, the guard started calling him a "RAT". When the other prisoners heard this term, the "rat" prisoner was in trouble. The other guards took the inmate away to settle down the guard. If the inmate told anyone in authority about being called a rat in public by a CO, he puts his life in danger because the CO that called him a rat would simply deny it, and for going over the first CO's head … he would lose any guard protection he might have had. The words of one of the CO's rings clear. He said to the guard, "You don't have to argue with him, spit in his food or let him think you did! It's us against "them". How frightening a dialogue! What a corporate culture.

When I arrived back from my legal visit, they finally had brought in a pressure cleaner. What a disaster! Nothing has changed except the high pressure cleaner has blown away the rust and broken more tiles. Inmates can now break off the tiles as weapons and I have been cleaning up after yet another wasted and meaningless activity. The filth it created was extraordinary and unnecessary. It was like stripping the floors without polish available.

I decided to wax all of the tiers and the Day Room plus our entrance way tonight. I didn't ask permission because they thought I was only mopping, but I was laying down polish. When they found out, it was too late for them to stop me. Slipping and sliding on the waxed floors allowed the COs to stop letting corporate "suit" visitors come in, and gave them an idea. Since no one was bothering them, they thought we should polish every couple of days to keep the "suit" visitors away at night, as well. I prepared for my shower and retired early so I can prepare to leave if tomorrow is the day of departure.

The inmates were excited seeing the polish go down because they liked the smell and they believed me when I told them that the polish would keep the mice away. I made it up, but let's see tomorrow when they inform me if their nightly visitors were unable to run on the polish without slipping.

Morale seems good tonight. Guards and inmates are "hanging-out". They sound and look almost like men on an urban street comer. The guards spent time with the inmate "leaders" and seem to ignore the other faceless prisoners. I listen to many of these conversations and it's apparent that the "bonds" of prisoners and guards are created on evenings like this.

Tonight poor "Evil" is obsessed with the "rats" in his wall. His cell is the cell I had when I was tightly tucking in my covers. He's yelling at the rats and the guards. "Evil" has such potential, but he is reduced to yelling at rats in the walls.

I've got some extra mayonnaise for "Evil", coffee for the neighbor to my right and a stamp for the one across the hall. Hey, I don't get anything! I guess that's because there is nothing they have I need, and everything I have these poor lost souls need.

If tonight is the final wake-up, everything is polished and quiet. Whenever that phone in the Day Room rings, I hope it's my release.

I hope I don't have to order from the Commissary again. I'll know tomorrow. I hope that there are no floods, no yelling and "a roll of toilet paper in every cell" on this, my maybe final night.

Back to the pressure cleaning, even the guards know it was a disaster, but now they can tell the Warden that they pressure cleaned these twenty year old rusted and broken tile showers and get away with dirty showers. Their institutionalized behavior and thought process would disgust you.

The laundry room I work in is only six months old. I spoke with one of the prison cadre who built it. It was welded and taken down three times because of different opinions of "suits" and supervisors. One cadre refused to work until the "suits" stopped visiting and making changes. They had no thought out plans, only opinions and change orders. Some things never change.

Watching the different ego's strutting around here reminded me of the black flood of a few days ago. One of the vacuums burned up because of the Lieutenant's interference. Instead of letting us vacuum up the water, the Lieutenant asked us to stop and work on a small dry area that interested him. There was no water there to cool down the machine, as he was warned, and the machine burned immediately. I said nothing. I only tell you. If I ever told some of them what I think of them, I'd be looking at ten to twenty years extra by now. Say a prayer that tonight this insanity ends for me.

Chapter 106 – I'm Resigned to It

My final day came not with a "bang" but with a "whimper" (with apologies to William Blake). While I was in the laundry room at about 4:00PM washing clothes and beginning to prepare for Thursday's inspection, four COs came in to tell me, "the Judge wants to talk to you". "Does that mean I am leaving?", I asked, "because I have to pack my belongings and letters and say good-bye to my friends and also give away food and things that others may need." "No, you'll come back and do that, if you are leaving, but first you have to hurry down to Court to speak to him", they said.

Before I left, I handed my letter of resignation in case the day shift was gone before I returned. That resignation letter said the following:

To: 9 South COs From: IIC Altomare (Inmate In Charge)

Re: Departure Letter

In "To Sir With Love", there is a line that says "how do you thank someone who has taken you from crayons to perfume?" Well, how do I thank the men and women who have taken me from being handcuffed to being strip searched?

At the time of your receipt of this letter of appreciation and resignation from SHU 9 South, I will no longer have been a resident of yours.

Initially I want to thank you for many things:

1. Thank you for letting me help these inmates

2. Thank you for letting me meet some unforgettable characters

3. Thank you for allowing me to work as an orderly

4. Thank you for letting me clean up the place

5. Thank you for letting me out of my cell to work

6. Thank you for the laughs

7. Thank you for the friendships

8. Thank you for the material for my book

9. Thank you for trying to help me get books for these inmates

10. Thank you for opening cages and locks for me.


This indeed was a summer vacation I can never compare to another (except maybe Parris Island in 1969 in the Marine Corps.)

As crazy as the following phrases sound, I will miss you all. From the constant confusion to the completion of tasks and assignments, I will hold some fond memories of working with some new friends.

You have a job which is under appreciated and easy to criticize. I know many of you try your best in a difficult corporate maze.

Maybe our paths will cross again. I hope on my home field. I am glad to be going back to "my world". "Your world" touched my heart and made me feel young again.

Feel free to use my cell. It will not be necessary to "retire" it due to my orderly efforts. (They retired it for 30 days).

Although I will miss those inmates that I have met and served, please find and assign orderlies that will try to care for them and their replacements with the effort and love I tried to give.

Should I win my legal cases and I get an opportunity to run for political office and effectuate change which my book will address, I hope I can be invited to return to SHU 9 South for either an inspection, a Thursday walk through, or the opening of my paperback library.

In conclusion, I will always remember the courtesy extended and I hope "I didn't disappoint you, Mr. Rutgers for the work done and the respectful mood I tried to enhance.

Thank you,

Richard A. Altomare

Chapter 107 – Sent Me Off, Like it Never Happened

As I got off the elevator, I realized I wasn't going to Court!   I was going to Receiving and Departure!   "Hey, what about my stuff?" "We'll mail it to you", the officer said.   "Do you want to leave now or do you want to go back upstairs until next week?"   The answer requires no verbalization. "By the way CO Rutgers will retire your cell for 30 days.   It's been an honor to have watched you work."

They handed me clothes that looked like the ones I wore eighty-three days ago, but they couldn't be mine.   I had to actually hold up the pants and the shirt and sweater were hanging on my frame.   I had lost about 40 pounds during this show of power by a Judge who in my opinion has lost his own way.   I was then placed in a series of filthy holding rooms, and I imagined I would be greeted by my attorney or Wife to escort me out of prison.

That wasn't to be my exit plan.   I was greeted by two Marshals who tightly cuffed me as they rudely yelled at me as if I was a vicious incoming prisoner, not one finally being let free.   We then began walking down some dirty hallways.   At the end of the last filthy elevator and doorway, the handcuffs were gruffly removed, I was searched again, and I was actually pushed outside.   I had no money, no wallet, no identification and no one was there to meet me.   Just a rainy, crowded New York City rush hour with non-orange dressed people moving about awaited me while I stared in disbelief.   I attempted to make collect phone calls, but cell phones don't take collect calls.   Three strangers were frightened away by this disheveled unknown man, holding his pants up, with no shoe laces, as his sneakers flopped more than his uncombed hair (and don't forget fifty days of nail growth).   I was asking them to help me call someone.   This was rehabilitation?   This was how these other prisoners are also to be released?

I went back into the prison (yes, I had to).   Believe it or not, they laughingly asked me if I had any governmental identification.   They had just released me without a wallet or money, and now they refused to help me call to be picked up.   I walked around the neighborhood for almost two hours and surprisingly found one of the CO's and the Warden heading to work.   The Warden walked by me silently with fear in his eyes.   The

CO refused to help me, "because he wasn't allowed to help any former prisoner". How painful and disappointing. After all I tried to do for that CO, he failed his final exam with me. My thoughts of regret were filled with not getting to say goodbye to all of my friends, murderers and lost souls. Surprisingly, that human emotion of loss separation continually obsessed my departure mindset.

My Attorney came running up the street, and we jumped into a cab. Like two bank robbers, we sped to the airport. I finally called my Wife, got my wallet back from my Attorney, scheduled a flight to go home, combed my hair (with my nails in the cab rearview mirror) and put the shoe laces my Attorney gave me into my sneakers. I still had no belt.

A dark rainstorm had ominously delayed all flights out of New York, but I could get pizza, ice and candy. The colors and pace of the airport were unsettling to me. I still was observing this strange place called reality with multiple colors and non-orange people. I was in a daze when my name was called for my flight home, and I was one of the final two to board. The colors, human activity and airline TV were recognizable, but I was functioning on prison automatic pilot time, as I overly thanked the flight attendant for the snacks.

It was after 11:00PM and I was wide awake as the plane landed in Florida. I had watched my first baseball game of the 2008 season on July 23, 2008 - on the plane.

When I saw my Wife, her tears were unstoppable, I had no tears left. After over seven million seconds and eighty-three days away, I was afraid to drive home, as the rain continued to follow me this night. She gave me a belt. I noted that it was the wrong color. I must be re-entering society because my social consciousness of an incorrect belt color was reasserting itself.

Surprisingly I wasn't hungry when we got home, and I was shocked to see my emaciated post shower body in my first full length mirror in eighty-three days. This was the first time I realized what the horrific BOP diet did to my body shape. Previously without a mirror, I never imagined such a transformation.

Within days, my wife and I were on the road to visit family, friends and shareholder supporters. My almost 90 year old parents were hurt even more than I had been. This was not the America that they intended to leave me. Nor is it the judicial system I intend to leave to my grandchildren!

Included in the events of my first days out of jail, are countless e-mails and supportive messages received. I had promised to donate library books, but the Judge has frozen all of my possessions. He has demanded that videos are to be taken of my home belongings. Apparently his venom and injustice knows no bounds. America the Beautiful.

After I win an Appeal or Supreme Court hearing, future books or movies will tell about these challenges and our legal victories yet to come.

Since I've been out of prison, the SEC has admitted to naked short selling and they are now arrogantly banning it worldwide, as if it had just been uncovered as something illegal. That's a far cry from claiming that it didn't exist, destroying my company and illegally incarcerating me for a fictitious fine that will be proven unwarranted.

I guess it's not illegal if a hand-picked Judge says so. Now it is my job to prove that the Court's actions which ironically have caused my stay at MCC and this expose' into the BOP, can be turned into the most positive events of the rest of my life. You're invited to follow the journey. This story has only just begun!

USXP's story isn't the only one that has just begun and that you should follow. As we now prepare for our Federal Court of Claims case to correct these injustices, our judge has actually been promoted and the same disgraced agency responsible for the mistruths told to our country still continues to oversee our capital markets. They still operate, motivated by commissions, and through fear, inconsistent enforcement, and judicially protected closed financial books.

I guess, like Deliverance the guard, government job security and lifetime appointments can still operate with impunity. Making politically correct decisions still results in long time job retention and even promotions within our regulatory and justice agencies.

If a citizen is accused of lying to a government official, the punishment is swift. However, if a government employee lies about or lies to an American citizen, that punishment is non-existent.

When will our citizens who support these fiefdoms finally become outraged, recapture, and demand back the America we remember and we love?

Our America cannot continue to be governed by bullying agencies, fleecing our pockets, and unchecked judges, filling our prisons.

From "Mutiny on the Bounty" comes the quote, "decency and justice are in the heart of the Captain or they are not on-board at all."


Word of My Mother (remember, that means it's the truth),


R. A. Altomare
CEO USXP – Retired without consent
RT60981-054 – Happily retired
United States Marine Corps – Proudly retired

Court of Claims Case Profile

At the behest of the vindictive and conflicted SEC administration, this viable and growing American small public company that was Universal Express having a market capitalization during its fiscal year 2006 of $111 Million Dollars was fraudulently defamed in the business marketplace and improperly liquidated within a few days for $35,000 by a receiver of questionable credentials.

It is also estimated that since naked shorters never need to deliver or "cover" their positions with actual shares of companies thus forced into bankruptcy, their gains from these illegal activities have never been reported to the IRS. The Wall Street Journal stated in July 2007 that the naked shorting losses to American taxpayers were valued at $2.5 billion daily! Accordingly, the lost tax revenues from this illegal counterfeiting permitted by the previous SEC administrations over the relevant period was conservatively more than $7 trillion - sufficient to pay off the bulk of the national debt.

It is clear that the culture of previous SEC administrations was to defer to and not to regulate powerful Wall Street elites, and to target and eliminate less powerful companies at their direction. Despite the fact that the SEC's Charter mandates protection for ordinary investors, not just brokers and hedge funds; this now documented fact remains painfully true.

The revolving door of the SEC leading to huge accounting, legal and consulting salaries with these same Wall Street elites also fostered the SEC's culture of non-regulation.

Presidential Candidate Senator John McCain on September 18, 2008 called for the firing of former SEC Chairman Cox for failing to regulate the naked shorting scandal.

On December 18, 2008, President-Elect Obama, in nominating the new SEC Chairman, stated that the SEC, as the regulator assigned to oversee Wall Street had failed to regulate and had "dropped the ball" over the years, substantially causing the present financial crisis.

On January 27, 2009, the Senate Banking Committee at hearings accused the previous SEC administrations of a total failure to regulate Wall Street.

On February 4, 2009, the House Financial Services subcommittee determined at hearings that the previous SEC administrations had totally failed to regulate Wall Street and that the SEC had operated only to protect Wall Street institutions and not ordinary Main Street investors as charged by Congress in its charter.

On March 18, 2009, the Office of the Inspector General of the SEC issued a report finding that previous SEC administrations had failed to regulate the naked shorting scandal, that naked shorting was a significant factor in the present financial collapse and that the SEC had ignored many thousands of complaints on naked shorting from small public companies and investors.

On June 2, 2009, the Chief Executive of the NASDAQ told the U.S. Chamber of Commerce that naked shorting was the real problem underlying the present financial crisis.

On March 3, 2009, April 1, 2009, June 24, 2009 and July 22, 2009, numerous United States Senators sent joint letters to the new SEC Chairperson, Mary Shapiro, urging that the SEC ban naked shorting as a huge problem and a principal cause of the present financial crisis resulting in great damage to and destruction of public companies, especially smaller public companies like the now destroyed Universal Express.

On June 25, 2009, United States Senator Edward E. Kaufman in a floor speech to the Senate stressed in great detail the "fierce urgency" for the SEC to ban naked shorting as a huge problem and a principal cause of the present financial crisis and the cause of great damage to and destruction of public companies, especially smaller public companies.

On July 27, 2009, the present SEC, after more than ten years of denial, admitted that the naked shorting of the shares of all public companies including smaller public companies like Universal Express was a huge national problem.

On August 5, 2009, the present SEC finally, after more than ten years of actually denying that this illegal process existed, announced it had brought its first enforcement action against only small house brokers who naked shorted from 2005 to 2007.

These long overdue but still ineffective tentative actions were taken after more than a decade of previous SEC administrations denying that naked shorting existed or was even a problem. It ignored naked shorting. It actively covered-up and failed to regulate the naked shorting scandal. Its' inactions bordered on criminality and, at the very least, constituted gross fraud. Its' inactions were in the long-term and perpetual interests of Wall Street banks and firms who were illegally committing the naked shorting while at the same time the SEC illegally and vindictively incarcerated and sought to silence the most prominent and heroic whistleblower CEO, Mr. Richard A. Altomare.

On October 21, 2009, Senator Edward E. Kaufman in a floor speech to the Senate urged the SEC to finally and effectively ban naked shorting which has been a huge national problem for all public companies, now finally including small public companies.

In that same speech, Senator Kaufman referred to Senate Bill No. 605, to force the SEC to ban naked short selling, which he and a number of other Senators have introduced and cosponsored. He concluded, "We need to send a strong message to the SEC that the United States Congress will not tolerate (its' continued) inaction on this critical issue."

On February 3, 2010, Senator Kaufman in a video interview with Steve Forbes of Forbes Magazine indicated that naked short selling is not only a major factor in the financial meltdown but is a systemic financial fraud, criminal enterprise and a very dangerous situation which the SEC has failed to stop.

On February 24, 2010, Senators Isakson and Kaufman issued a bipartisan press release on the national scandal of naked short selling and again castigated the SEC for its long-term failure to protect the public from this scandal of naked-short selling.

Significantly, after more than ten years of the SEC's fraudulent cover-up of naked shorting, the Senators stated that "the real problem is that the SEC does not have an enforceable rule to punish those who undertake market manipulation through abusive naked short selling ...[SIC]"

On March 1, 2010, the whistleblower of Madoff's $65 Billion Ponzi scheme, Mr. Harry Markopolos was interviewed on numerous news networks concerning his book "No One Would Listen." He stated that for nine years he tried to convince the SEC that a massive financial fraud was being perpetrated by Madoff, but that the SEC turned a blind eye to Markopolos' detailed information on the scam which he said he had easily discovered in only a few minutes of analysis.

As previously indicated Madoff wrote, with the SEC's blessing, the short selling rules for the financial industry and was one of the biggest unregulated naked short sellers for decades.

When Madoff was arrested in December 2008, Mr. Markopolos said he was afraid that the SEC would come after him and that a friend high up in the SEC called him that day to warn him of the SEC's position that "we don't know you" and you had "better watch your back." Does this seem to be the actions of a legitimate governmental agency of our United States of America?

On March 15, 2010, Senator Kaufman in a speech to the Senate issued a manifesto against Wall Street corruption in the financial crisis and against the SEC's failure for years to regulate as well as take enforcement action against the perpetrators, including the Wall Street firms committing the naked shorting scandal.

On March 16, 2010, an article in the Huffington Post entitled "Senator Kaufman: Fraud Still at the Heart of Wall Street", described his speech as "devastating" including the very decisive statement that "fraud and potential criminal conduct were at the heart of the financial crisis."

On March 19, 2010, Arianna Huffington of the Huffington Post published an article on her interview with Senator Kaufman on his term as a Senator. Ms. Huffington commenced her article with the following statement: "At a time when our political and financial landscapes are littered with villains and those unwilling to take them on, it's refreshing to find someone in the halls of power that we can unabashedly celebrate."

Most importantly, she then quoted Senator Kaufman as follows: "In the beginning," he told me, "though I was very upset about what had happened on Wall Street, it wasn't one of my key objectives…. But then I started reading more and more about the way the SEC was failing to curb abusive practices when it came to short selling. So I started speaking out on that…."

On March 26, 2010, in a speech to the Senate on financial reform, Senator Kaufman stated as follows: "Meanwhile, as the consolidated supervisor of major investment banks, the SEC had similar powers to those of the Federal Reserve. And it goes without saying that its track record of regulatory enforcement was littered with colossal failures."

On April 13, 2010, the former CEO of Washington Mutual testified before the Senate's Permanent Subcommittee on Investigations that the principle reason for the biggest bank failure in US history was that Washington Mutual was the victim of naked short selling.

On May 14, 2010, the New York Times in a front page article on bank bailouts stated that the SEC is to blame for the financial meltdown. "The SEC., for one, is now eager to prove that it is on its game after failing to spot the global Ponzi scheme orchestrated by Bernard L. Madoff, or head off the Wall Street excesses that nearly sank the entire economy." (Emphasis added.)

On May 18, 2010, Germany banned naked short selling of the securities of financial institutions in connection with Europe's financial crisis.

During Senate debate on Wall Street Reform in May 2010, Senators condemned the SEC for failing to regulate trillions of dollars of mortgage backed securities, 90% of which failed setting the stage for the housing crisis and the financial meltdown.

On May 27, 2010, Senator Kaufman in an address to the Senate entitled "Redressing the Imbalance of Regulatory Capture" discussed the SEC's failures on the naked shorting scandal. He stated that "Since coming to office last year, I have highlighted this serious problem…along with seven other senators….""

He further stated in his speech, "The regulators are surrounded - indeed they consciously choose to surround themselves - with an echo chamber of industry players who are making literally billions of dollars under the current system. Who speaks to the regulators on behalf of the average investor?"

On June 2, 2010, Germany expanded its ban on naked short selling to the shares of all public companies.

On June 9, 2010, France and Germany jointly urged the European Union to ban naked short selling of securities.

On July 27, 2010, Japan announced a further extension of its October 2008 ban on naked short selling.

On September 28, 2010, the European Union announced that the EU plans to ban naked short selling.

In conclusion, Universal Express had corporately developed and had become globally recognized despite the rogue SEC harassment supporting the unrelenting attack since 1998 by naked short sellers, unscrupulous Wall Street financial interests, fraudulent brokers, hedge funds and market makers who sold into the market billions of USXP unregistered and counterfeit shares. This caused the collapse of the Company's stock price from $2.00 to $.02 (2 cents) per share and, thereafter, kept the Company's stock price well below fractions of a cent, despite the strong growth of the Company's businesses, including a tripling of revenues each quarter for more than five years.

In more than 100 press releases, letters and visits to government officials and in worldwide speeches and webcasts as well as a full page New York Times announcement, Universal Express, its' President and its General Counsel proved that naked short selling existed. These whistleblowers even showed by statistics that the volume of the Company's shares traded was 11 times the Company's outstanding shares and more than 68 times its average daily volume.

As stated, State court juries in Florida in 2001 and 2003 awarded the Company verdicts exceeding a total of $700,000,000 against naked short sellers. In a press release issued on September 23, 2003, entitled "Universal Express...Declares War on 'Naked Short Selling'," the Company stated "If normal everyday people acting as juries can understand this naked shorting scheme, why can't the SEC"?

Within a month after the Company's second jury verdict against the naked shorters and the extensive publicity attending the Company's verdicts, an embarrassed SEC, through its Denver office, commenced a fraudulent program of harassment against the Company with more than 13 subpoenas for thousands of documents demanded to be produced in only a few days. Not one attempt to aid the Company was offered by the SEC.

The Company volunteered to provide information on contracts for current proposed acquisitions and its' funding sources for those acquisitions.

Yet, before these documents were even received by the attorneys at the Denver office of the SEC, agents were actually calling and visiting those acquisition candidates' and funders' senior officers, threatening them with reprisals or tax audits so that they would move away from the Company and its imminent success.

This horrific and illegal SEC pattern of intimidation, attempting to prevent Universal Express' continued success was in full swing and successful since several large proposed acquisitions were inexplicably terminated.

The SEC's fraudulent harassment of the Company and its officers, as whistleblowers on naked shorting and the harassment of its business partners and potential business partners and funders continued unabated thereafter.

The Company, its President and General Counsel, who value free speech under our Constitution, were determined not to be bullied by a conflicted regulatory agency, which had failed the investing public on this national naked shorting scandal in favor of Wall Street interests in clear violation of its Congressional mandate.

This scandal, clearly ignored by previous SEC administrations, had destroyed the ongoing American dream of taking small private companies public and growing those businesses through the growth of their stock base has substantially contributed to today's high unemployment numbers.

Due to these SEC failures thousands of lost developmental products beneficial to the public and including Universal Express' innovative logistic businesses have never had a chance for the national market and have moved to other countries.

Trillions of dollars have been siphoned from the capitalizations of public companies by the naked shorters with the intent and result of bankrupting those companies so that the naked shorts would never have to be repurchased or "covered" by delivery of actual shares.

The present SEC's recent admissions that naked short selling has been a huge problem for all public companies, including small public companies like Universal Express and its recent announcement of its very first enforcement action after all these years, does not bring back Universal Express.

The above facts constitute the complete vindication of Universal Express and its officers in their over ten year battle against naked shorting.

These facts incriminate former SEC perjurers and sadly crystallize the history of the previous SEC administrations' fraudulent conduct against these courageous and long suffering whistleblowers.

It is time for the guilty to be exposed and punished, and the innocent to be vindicated and rewarded.

Further historical information is also available on the following website:

www.richardaltomare.com

# Universal Express on the Fast Track to Leadership in the Luggage Logistics Industry

## 10 Divisions Focus on Logistics, Transportation, and Finance Sectors

The rapid implementation of an innovative business vision with the clear potential of creating an huge conglomerate of consumer and business services with a worldwide reach – from delivery of packages and luggage, broad-based financial services, development of a private postal system, to transportation and equipment leasing – has established Universal Express, Inc. (OTC BB: USXP; Frankfurt: UEX) as a company to watch. The fact that Universal Express is operating in multiple multi-billion dollar industries adds even more interest for shareholders in this growing company.

A significant key to the success of Universal Express is the "synergy" of services within its multiple divisions. Perhaps one of the best examples of that synergy is dynamic between its flagship Luggage Express division and the newly created Luggage Express Found division. Luggage Express focuses on assisting travelers to avoid checking luggage at airports. Luggage Express Found specializes in delivering luggage, lost by airlines, back to the traveler.

Strategic partnerships are another important factor in the growth of Universal Express. For example, the Virtual Bellhop division partners with Windstar Cruises to provide premiere luggage logistics to the cruise line's customers. Universal Express' leasing division has close relationships with major manufacturers of limousine,

livery, small fleet, vehicle rental, delivery truck and van, bus and aircraft industries. In mid-2006, Universal Express announced a strategic partnership between its PostalNation affiliate and Enterprise Rent-A-Car.

### Active Acquisition Program Fuels New Divisions at Universal Express

"Acquisitions are part of our overall plan to become the leading expert when moving luggage for consumers or for airlines, and thereby creating a full service luggage transportation industry," says Universal Express President and CEO Richard Altomare.

Acquisitions to build many of the company's 10 divisions and affiliated subsidiaries highlighted much of the company's activities in 2006. In the fall, Universal Express completed

Universal Express' corporate vision aims to unify the worldwide delivery of packages and luggage for consumers and business, as well as developing synergistic services such as individual and corporate financing, business equipment leasing and transportation.

Reprinted from The Bull & Bear Financial Report, P.O. Box 917179, Longwood, FL 32791 • www.TheBullandBear.com • First Quarter 2007

413

# Universal Express Divisions

**UniversalPost Network –** Private postal store products and programs, offering growth opportunities

**Universal Express Capital –** Corporate and individual financing for transportation and equipment.

**Universal Cash Express** – Stored value cards for everyone... whether bad credit, no credit, or good credit.

**Universal Express Courier Assn.** – Discounted shipping rates & programs for the independent courier.

**Luggage Express Associate Program** – Opportunity to entrepreneurs to have their own Luggage Express territory.

**Luggage Express** – Domestic and international luggage transportation and delivery service.

**Virtual Bellhop** – Door-to-door premium luggage delivery service for individual, family and business travelers.

**UniversalPost International Delivery** – Express international delivery of documents and expedited air cargo.

**MadPackers** – Shipping and moving service solution for students, parents and schools and colleges worldwide.

**Luggage Express Found** – Delivery of lost or misplaced luggage from airports nationwide

---

designed specifically for the millions of people who send money overseas to their families. The customized debit card payment system allows people, including those who do not have checking accounts, to send money instantly worldwide.

Then there is Universal Express Realty Trust, Inc. which has begun contracting to own and manage commercial office properties and plans to market and resell real estate. USXP Capital specializes in providing capital acquisition funding or lease financing to the business community. The company's new MadPackers division focuses on a unique logistics niche – students who live at often far-away schools and colleges and need a reliable and cost-effective way to transport their belongings between school and home. The division is now expanding its "door to dorm" services to cater to diverse needs of students.

## Innovative Management Results in Rapid Growth

As President and CEO of Universal Express, Richard Altomare brings an infectious enthusiasm and utter belief in a vision that has put his company on the development fast track. Altomare's extensive background in investment banking and turning failing businesses around has proved to be a vital asset for Universal Express in the 1990s when the then-named Packaging Plus Services was $48 million in debt and facing bankruptcy. First as a bankruptcy trustee and then as president, Altomare's vision turned the company 180 degrees to become today's actively traded enterprise with operations that touch almost every aspect of the logistics, transportation and finance industries.

Altomare also brings to Universal Express an almost prescient ability to recognize under-exploited business opportunities and an aggressive and innovative marketing attitude.

"Our vision never changes, it is always to increase revenue, profits and shareholder equity by increasing our exposure to markets through new and innovative solutions," says Altomare. "The more we do, the better we do it, and the better the result for our loyal shareholders."

Altomare's innovative marketing vision led directly to the company's acquisition, with some entertainment partners, of Jackson Family mementos for $5.8 million. The collection of more

---

its purchase of a trucking company and announced the acquisition of a baggage delivery company, both key to the launch of another new company – Luggage Express Found. Universal Express also completed funding for Universal Jet Aviation, as part of a planned move into general aviation.

In 1988, Universal Express' initial big idea was to unite private postal stores and independent courier products and programs in a national partnership accessing unique logistics services to consumers and businesses.

The Universal Post Network quickly led to the creation of a series of affiliated businesses. Luggage

Express specialized in delivering luggage to and from airports, enabling passengers to bypass time-consuming luggage check-in. Virtual Bellhop took that idea a step further, delivering the luggage directly to a travelers' end destination. In effect, both companies have succeeded in separating travelers from their often burdensome suitcase to create a safer and more pleasurable travel experience.

Many of Universal Express' divisions and subsidiary companies are closely related to the original postal, courier and delivery logistics services. Others focus on niche financial services, such as the Universal Express Platinum Card

---

Reprinted from The Bull & Bear Financial Report, P.O. Box 917179, Longwood, FL 32791 • www.TheBullandBear.com • First Quarter 2007

415

than 10,000 items includes all Thriller costumes, platinum and gold records, costumes and master tape recordings. The items will be auctioned – and then delivered by Luggage Express.

Similarly, a Luggage Express suitcase "delivers' the opening puck to the center ice at every Florida Panther home game. Similar marketing agreements were recently signed with other major sports teams, including the New York Rangers (NHL), New York Islanders (NHL), the New York Knicks (NBA) and the New Jersey Nets (NBA.)

## Investment Considerations

"We are very pleased with the development and growth of all our businesses," says Altomare. "Revenues from out logistics and international shipping business almost doubled in 2006 compared to 2005 and we anticipate an exponential increase this year and in future years."

At the close of its 2006 fiscal year, Universal Express reported assets increased 180% to more than $6 million while revenues increased 100% over the previous year. The company's market capitalization soared to $89 million from $4.6 million in 2005.

The pace of that performance has continued into the 2007 fiscal year, with the company reporting a positive cash flow and assets increasing to $7.5 million.

The company's 2007 headline may well be a pending joint venture centering around the planned purchase of a New Jersey-based gasoline and oil operator. That purchase is intended to become the foundation of a nationwide chain of retail gasoline and diesel oil stations. The company recently announced the receipt of its first substantial installment from some of its initial Dubai and Saudi Arabian partners, with more fundings expected to follow.

"Virtually every facet of our business

"Universal Express has positioned itself to be a contender in the global economy for the next decade with the development of its complementary subsidiaries"...

Richard A. Altomare, Universal Express President & CEO

relies on the price, availability and delivery of fuel, whether it is our luggage division, our trucking component, our aviation company, or our courier network," says Altomare.

Meanwhile, Universal Express continues to attract a growing customer base, including U.S. Chamber of Commerce members, including CEOs of some of the country's largest companies attending an Association of 100 meeting in Las Vegas.

"Our company believes that an affordable outsourced distribution system is needed to suit consumers' needs," says Universal Express President and CEO Richard Altomare. "Universal Express has positioned itself to be a contender in the global economy for the next decade with the development of its complementary subsidiaries."

## UNIVERSAL EXPRESS INC.

**OTC BB: USXP • Frankfurt: UEX**

*Contact:*
Richard Altomare, President & CEO

**Corporate Offices:**
5295 Town Center Road
Boca Raton, Florida 33486
Phone: 561-367-6177 • Fax: 561-367-6124

**Manhattan Office:**
1230 Avenue of the Americas, Suite 771
7th Floor, Rockefeller Center
New York, NY 10020
Phone: 917-639-4154

E-Mail: info@usxp.com • Web Site: www.usxp.com

Shares Outstanding: 13.9 Billion

52 Week Trading Range:
Hi: $0.408 • Low: $0.0001

Reprinted from The Bull & Bear Financial Report, P.O. Box 917179, Longwood, FL 32791 • www.TheBullandBear.com • First Quarter 2007

417

# *An Overview for Offenders*

## *GENERAL INTRODUCTION*

As you were received at this facility, you were given a Federal Register Number which will identify you as long as you are in federal custody. That number is commonly known as your «number" or "reg. number." It is imperative for you to provide your family and friends with your number so you may receive correspondence from them while you are in our care. All mail and monies must be identified with committed name and your register number when received at this facility.

**Your committed name and register number**
**Metropolitan Correctional Center 150 Park Row**
**New York, New York 10007**

You will be screened by a Unit Team member, and given a quarters assignment based on your personal profile and security needs. While in Receiving and Discharging (R&D) you were given a cell assignment. Cadre inmates (inmates designated to serve a sentence at MCC New York) will participate in an Admission and Orientation Program as required by polity. During that program they will receive additional guidance and unit rules that will apply during their stay in the Cadre Unit.

Other inmates, (Holdover, Pre-trial inmates, Material Witnesses and Immigration Detainees) will receive an abbreviated familiarization and welcome to the facility. Rules and Regulations are posted in English and Spanish in all housing units and it is your responsibility to read and follow these rules.

## INMATE RIGHTS AND RESPONSIBILITIES

The following list of Rights (thing you can expect to enjoy) and Responsibilities (what the institution expects from you) will provide guidance in developing self-discipline within the Institution and establish the foundation for identification of disciplinary infractions and sanction.

Right: You have the right to expect that, as human being, you will be treated respectfully, impartially, and fairly by all personnel.

Responsibility: You have the responsibility to treat other, both employees and inmates, in the same manner.

Right: You have the right to be informed of the rules, procedures and schedules concerning the operation of the Institution.

Responsibility: You have the responsibility to know and abide by the rules.

Right: You have the right to freedom of religion affiliation and voluntary religious worship.

Responsibility: You have the responsibility to recognize and respect the rights of others in regard.

Right: You have the right to health care which includes nutrition meals, proper bedding and clothing, a laundry schedule for cleanliness of the same, an opportunity to shower regularly, proper ventilation for warmth and fresh air, a regular exercise period, toilet articles and medical and dental treatment.

Responsibility: It is your responsibility not to waste food, to follow the laundry and shower schedule, to maintain neat and clean-living quarters, to keep your area free of contraband, and to seek medical and dental care as you may need it.

Right: You have the right to visit and correspond with family members and friends, and correspond with members of the news media in keeping with Bureau rules and Institution guidelines.

Responsibility: It is your responsibility to conduct yourself properly during visits, not to accept or pass contraband, and not to violate the law, Bureau rules, or Institution guidelines through your correspondence

Right: You have the right to unrestricted and confidential access to the courts by correspondence on matters such as the legality of your conviction, civil matters, pending criminal cases, and conditions of your imprisonment.

Responsibility: You have the responsibility to present honestly and fairly your petition, questions, and problems to the court.

Right: You have the right to legal counsel from an attorney of your choice by interviews and correspondence.

Responsibility: It is your responsibility to use the services of an attorney honestly and fairly.

Right: You have the right to participate in the use of the law library reference materials to assist you in resolving legal problems. You also have the right to receive help when it is available through a legal assistance program

Responsibility: It is your responsibility to use these resources in keeping with the procedures and schedule prescribed and to respect the rights of other inmates in the use of materials and peer assistance.

Right: You have the right to a wide range of reading materials for educational purposes and for your own enjoyment These materials may include magazines and newspapers sent from the community, with certain restrictions.

Responsibility: It is your responsibility to seek and utilized such materials for your personal benefit, without depriving other of their equal rights to the use of this material

Right: You have the right to participate in education, vocational training, and employment as far as resources are available and in keeping with your interest, needs and abilities.

Responsibility: It is your responsibility to take advantage of activities which may help you live a successful and law-abiding life within the Institution and in the community. You will expect to abide by the regulations governing the use of such activities.

## *SECURITY PROCEDURES*

**Counts:** When a count is announced, each inmate must return to his/her assigned cell, and remain there quietly until it is announced that the count is clear. The staff will take disciplinary action if an inmate is not in his/her assigned area or leaves before the count is cleared. Official counts will be taken at about 12:00A.M., 3:00A.M., 5:00A.M., 4:00P.M. stand up count and 9:00P.M. Additionally, a 10:00A.M. count will occur on weekends and holidays. Other counts occur during the day and evening. The inmate must actually be seen at all counts, even if the inmate must be awakened.

**Special Counts:** A special count can be called at any time. Inmates should report to their housing unit or work detail, until the count is cleared.

**Unit Census:** After the work call in the morning and after noon meal, the unit officer is required to perform a census count of his assigned unit This officer must be presented with inmates' and number during this census. Inmates are to make their presence known to the staff member taking the census to assure proper accountability. If you do not belong in the unit and are discovered during the census, you can receive an incident report.

**Institution Lock Down Census:** At any time a lock down census may occur and will be announced by staff on the public address system In such instances, inmates will cease all movement and report to the closest staff member. You will give your name and number to this individual. There will be no movement to or from the area and any call-outs will be rescheduled. When the census is cleared, normal movement resumes.

**Emergency Counts / Lock Down:** Emergency Counts may be necessary for a number of reasons. When informed of an emergency count, inmates are to follow instructions given by staff immediately and without question.

**Out Counts:** You may be assigned to a detail where you will be counted outside of your assigned unit. Food Service is an example of a work assignment where (if authorized) you can be out counted. You cannot leave your assigned work area at any time without your work supervisor's authorization.

**Lock Down:** Weekday lock down in pretrial holdover housing units is at 10:45P.M. and 11:30P.M. for the Cadre Unit On weekends, the Cadre unit will lock down at 2:00A.M. Extended television viewing hours will be approved only by both the Captain and Unit Manager or by the Warden.

## VISITING

Inmates are encouraged to have visits in order to maintain family and community ties. Visitors may be limited on an hourly basis, or other allocation basis to ensure equitable access to visiting facilities.

Holdovers and Pre-Trial inmates may be limited to immediate family on their visiting list.

All visits will begin and end in the visiting room. Kissing, embracing, and handshaking are allowed only on arrival and departure.

Each institution has limits on the number and type of articles that can be taken into the Visiting Room. Typical items that may be taken into the Visiting Room by an inmate are limited to a wedding band, prescription eyeglasses, and religious medal. Items purchased in the Visiting Room may not be brought back into the institution by the inmate.

Visitors must be properly dressed. Short shorts, halter tops, and other clothing of a suggestive or revealing nature will not be permitted in the Visiting Room. Footwear must be worn by all visitors.

## CALL-OUTS AND CHANGE  SHEET

It is your responsibility to check the call-out sheet daily for appointments or job changes. Call-outs are a scheduling system for appointments (which include Health Services, Dental, Educational, team meetings and other activities) which are posted each day on the unit bulletin boards. Be especially attentive to call-outs since you are a new arrival at the institution. Your job assignment, medical appointments and educational appointments will be appearing on the call-outs as early as tomorrow. If you are listed on the call-out, notify your supervisor. Only the HOSPITAL or the AFW PROGRAMS can excuse you from your work assignment.

## *SMOKING POLICY*

The MCC New York is a non-smoking institution. All matches and smoking materials will be considered to be contraband; disciplinary action will be taken if you are found to possess items mentioned.

## *CONSULATE TELEPHONE CALLS OR VISIT*

### Telephone Calls

Submit an Inmate Request to Staff Member to your Unit Team requesting a telephone call to your consulate. Please provide the telephone number for the consulate and the address of the Embassy for verification. The Unit Manager will review your request and advise you if your request is approved. Ordinarily, the calls will be collect calls.

### Consulate Visits

Consulates wishing to visit inmates at this institution should make their requests through the Executive Assistant. The Executive Assistant will coordinate the visit with the Unit Team and other appropriate departments.

## *UNMONITORED LEGAL TELEPHONE CALLS*

Requests for unmonitored legal telephone calls should be made by submitting an Inmate Request to Staff Member to your Unit Team. Please provide the telephone number and address of the legal party. Also you must put on the request the reasons why the legal concerns cannot be addressed by the use of legal mail and show an imminent court deadline. Your unit team will review your request and coordinate a "collect call" to your attorney if approved.

## *POSTAGE STAMP FOR INDIGENT INMATES*

An inmate who has neither funds nor sufficient postage and who wishes to mail legal mail (includes courts and attorneys) or Administrative Remedy forms will be provided the postage stamps for such mailing. To prevent abuses of this provision, the Warden may impose restrictions on the legal and administrative remedy mailings. See Program Statement 5265.09, dated: July 9, 1999.

## *FOOD STORAGE*

Food items that are left open create a health hazard. These items must be properly sealed at all times. Empty containers will be disposed of and are not to be used for other storage. The food provided at each institution meal must be consumed or disposed of within 2 hours of being served. If not, it will be confiscated and disciplinary action may result

## *SUICDE PREVENTION*

It is not uncommon for people to experience depression and hopelessness while in jail or prison, particularly if they are newly incarcerated, are serving a long sentence, arc experiencing family problems or problems getting along with other inmates, or receive bad news. Sometimes, inmates consider committing suicide due to all of the pressure they are under. Staff is trained to monitor inmates for signs of suicide, and is trained to refer all concerns to the Psychology Department. However, staff do not always see what inmates see. If you are personally experiencing any of the problems noted above, or you or another inmate are showing signs of depression (sadness, tearfulness, lack of enjoyment in usual activities), withdrawal (staying away from others, reducing phone calls and/or visits), or hopelessness (giving away possessions, stating that "there is nothing to live for"), PLEASE alert a staff member right away. Your input can save a life.

## *PROBLEM RESOLUTIONS*

### Inmate Requests to Staff Member

The Bureau Form BP-Admin-70, commonly called a "cop-out", is used to make a written request to a staff member. Any type of request can be made with this form. "Cop-outs" may be obtained in the housing units from the Correctional Officer on duty. Staff members who receive a "Cop-Out" will answer the request in a "reasonable" period of time.

### Administrative Remedy Process

"The Bureau emphasizes and encourages the resolution of complaints on an informal basis. Hopefully, an inmate can resolve a problem informally by contact with staff members or "Cop-outs". When informal resolution is not successful, a formal complaint can be filed as an Administrative Remedy. Complaints regarding Tort Claims, Inmate Accident Compensation, Freedom of Information or Privacy Act Requests, and complaints on behalf of other inmates are not accepted under the Administrative Remedy Procedure.

Except for DHO Appeals, which are submitted directly to the Regional Director via a BP-l0 form, you must first present an issue of concern informally, via a "cop-out," to a staff member before filing a Request for Administrative Remedy, or Bp·8. You must attempt informal resolution and submit a formal written Request for Administrative Remedy ("BP-9") within 20 calendar days of the occurrence which gave rise to your complaint. If you demonstrate a valid reason for delay, requests for an extension in filing time may be granted. Sensitive issues, that is, where your safety or well-being would be placed in danger if the Request became known at the institution, may be marked "sensitive" and submitted directly to the Regional Director. All Administrative Remedy forms may be obtained from your Unit Counselor. Your complaint must be written in the space provided. Only one issue, or a reasonable number of closely related issues, may be placed on a single BP-9 form. Multiple, unrelated issues must be placed on separate forms. If more space is needed than is provided on a single form, you may attach a single 8 1/2" x 11" continuation sheet. Proof of your informal resolution attempt (generally a copy of the cop-out response) must be attached to your BP-9. The Warden has 20 calendar days from the date of receipt to respond to your Request.

If you are not satisfied with the Warden's response, you may file an appeal to the Northeast Regional Director, Federal Bureau of Prisons, U.S. Custom House, 2nd and Chestnut Streets, Philadelphia, P A 19106, within 20 days, on a form BP-l0. The Regional Director has 30 calendar days from the date of receipt to respond to your appeal. If you are not satisfied with this reply, you may file a final appeal to the General Counsel, Federal Bureau of Prisons, 320 First Street, N.W., Washington, DC 20534, within 30 calendar days of receipt of the Regional Director's response, on a form BP-11. The General Counsel has 40 calendar days form the date of receipt to respond to your appeal. Forms BP-10 and BP-11 may be obtained from your Unit Counselor.

Detailed information regarding the Bureau of Prisons' Administrative Remedy Program may be found in Title 28, Part 542 of the Code of Federal Regulations (28 C.F.R. 542JO et seq.), and Bureau of Prisons Program Statement 1330.13, Administrative Remedy Program. They are available in the Inmate Law Library.

## *PROHIBITED ACTS AND SANCTIONS* (PS 5270.07)

### *GREATEST CATEGORY*

The UDC shall refer all Greatest Severity Prohibited Acts to the 0110 with recommendations as to an appropriate disposition.

<u>CODE PROHIBITED ACTS</u>

100   Killing

101   Assaulting any person (includes sexual assault) or an armed assault on the institution's secure perimeter (a charge for assaulting any person at this level is to be used only when serious physical injury has been attempted or carried out by an inmate)

102   Escape from escort; escape from a secure institution (low, medium, and high security level and administrative institutions); or escape from a minimum institution with violence.

103   Setting a fire (charged with this act in this category only when found to pose a threat to life or a threat of serious bodily harm or in furtherance of a prohibited act of Greatest Severity, e.g. in furtherance of a riot or escape; otherwise the charge is properly classified Code 2) 8, or 329)

104   Possession, manufacture, or introduction of a gun, firearm, weapon, sharpened instrument, knife, dangerous chemical, explosive or any ammunition

105   Rioting

106   Encouraging others to riot

107   Taking hostage(s)

108   Possession, manufacture, or introduction of a hazardous tool (Tools most likely to be used in an escape or escape attempt or to serve as weapons capable of doing serious bodily harm to others; or those

hazardous to institutional security or personal safety; e.g., hack-saw blade)

109    (Not to be used)

110    Refusing to provide a urine sample or to take part in other drug-abuse testing.

111    Introduction of any narcotics, marijuana, drugs, or related paraphernalia not prescribed for the individual by the medical staff

112    Use of any narcotics, marijuana, drugs, or related paraphernalia not prescribed for the individual by the medical staff

113    Possession of any narcotics, marijuana, drugs, or related paraphernalia not prescribed for the individual by the medical staff

197    Use of the telephone to further criminal activity.

198    Interfering with a staff member in the performance of duties. (Conduct must be of the Greatest Severity nature.) This charge is to be used only when another charge of greatest severity is not applicable.

199    Conduct which disrupts or interferes with the security or orderly running of the institution or the Bureau of Prisons. (Conduct must be of the Greatest Severity nature.) This charge is to be used only when another charge of greatest severity is not applicable

*Sanctions A-G*

## SANCTIONS

A. Recommend parole date rescission or retardation.

B. Forfeit earned statutory good time or non-vested good conduct time (up to *100"10)* and/or terminate or disallow extra good time (an extra good time or good conduct time sanction may not be suspended).

B. Disallow ordinarily between 50 and 75% (27-41 days) of good conduct time credit available for year (a good conduct time sanction may not be suspended).

C. Disciplinary Transfer (recommend).

D. Disciplinary segregation (up to 60 days).

E. Make monetary restitution.

F. Withhold statutory good time (Note -can be in addition to A through E. (cannot be the only sanction executed).

G. Loss of privileges (Note-can be in addition to A through E (cannot be the only sanction executed).

## *HIGH CATEGORY*

CODE PROHJBITED ACTS

200   Escape from unescorted Community Programs and activities and Open Institutions (minimum) and from outside secure institutions--without violence.

201   Fighting with another person

202   (Not to be used)

203    Threatening another with bodily harm or any other offense

204    Extortion, blackmail, protection: Demanding or receiving money or anything of value in return for protection against others, to avoid bodily harm, or under threat of informing

205    Engaging in sexual acts

206    Making sexual proposals or threats to another

207    Wearing a disguise or a mask

208    Possession of any unauthorized locking device, or lock pick, or tampering with or blocking any lock device (includes keys), or destroying, altering, interfering with, improperly using, or damaging any security device, mechanism, or procedure

209    Adulteration of any food or drink

210    (Not to be used)

211    Possessing any officer's OJ staff clothing

212    Engaging in, or encouraging a group demonstration

213    Encouraging other to refuse to work, or to participate in a work stoppage

215    Introduction of alcohol into BOP facility

216    Giving or offering and official or staff member a bribe, or anything of value Giving money to, or receiving money from, any person for purposes of introducing contraband or for any other illegal or prohibited purposes

218    Destroying, altering, or damaging government property, or the property of another person, having a value in excess of $10.00 or destroying, altering, damaging life-safety devices (e.g., fire alarm) regardless of financial value

219 Stealing (theft; this includes data obtained through the unauthorized use of a communications facility, or through the unauthorized access to disks, tapes, or computer printouts or other automated equipment on which data is stored.)

220 Demonstrating, practicing, or using martial arts, boxing (except for use of a punching bag), wrestling, or other forms of physical encounter, or military exercises or drill (except for drill authorized and conducted by staff)

221 Being in an unauthorized area with a person of the opposite sex without staff permission

222 Making, possessing, or using intoxicants

223 Refusing to breathe into a breathalyzer or take part in other testing for use of alcohol

224 Assaulting any person (charged with this act only when less serious physical injury or contact has been attempted or carried out by an inmate)

297 Use of the telephone for abuses other than criminal activity (e.g., circumventing telephone monitoring procedures, possession and/or use of another inmate's PIN number; third party calling; third-party billing; using credit card numbers to place telephone calls; conference calling; talking in code).

298 Interfering with a staff member in the performance of duties. (Conduct must be of the High Severity nature.) This charge is to be used only when another charge of the high severity is not applicable.

299 Conduct which disrupts or interferes with the security or orderly running of the institution or the Bureau of Prisons. (Conduct must be of the High Severity nature.) This charge is to be used only when another charge of high severity is not applicable

## SANCTIONS:  A - M

A.     Recommend parole date rescission or retardation.

B.     Forfeit earned statutory good time or non-vested good conduct time up to 50% or up to 60 days, whichever is less, and/or terminate or disallow extra good time (an extra good time or good conduct time sanction may not be suspended).

B.     Disallow ordinarily between 25 and 50% (14-27 days) of good conduct time credit available for year (a good conduct time sanction may not be suspended).

C.     Disciplinary Transfer (recommend).

D.     Disciplinary segregation (up to 30 days).

E.     Make monetary restitution.

F.     Withhold statutory good time.

G.     Loss of privileges: commissary, movies, recreation, etc.

H.     Change housing (quarters)

I.     Remove from program and/or group activity

J.     Loss of job

K.     Impound inmate's personal property

L.     Confiscate contraband

M.     Restrict to quarters

N.     Extra duty

## LOW/MODERATE CATEGORY

### CODE PROHIBITED ACTS

400 Possession of property belonging to another person

401 Possessing unauthorized amount of otherwise authorized clothing

402 Malingering, feigning illness

404 Using abusive or obscene language

Tattooing or self-mutilation

406 Unauthorized use of mail (Restriction, or lose for a specific period of time, of these privileges and charges may often be an appropriate sanction (G) (May be categorized and charge in terms of grater severity, according to the nature of the unauthorized use; e.g., the mail is use for planning, facilitating, committing an armed assault on the institution's secure perimeter, would be charged as code 101, Assault)

407 Conduct with a visitor in violation of Bureau regulations (Restriction, or loss for a specific period of time, of these privileges may often be an appropriate sanction G)

Conducting a business

409 Unauthorized physical contact (e. G., kissing, embracing)

Use of the telephone for abuses other than criminal activities (c. G, exceeding the 15-minute time limit for telephone calls; using the telephone in an unauthorized area; placing of an unauthorized individual on the telephone list)

Interfering with a staff member in the performance of duties. Conduct must be of the Low Mode-rate Severity nature.) This charge is to be used only when another charge of low moderate severity if not applicable.

499     Conduct which disrupts or interferes with the security or orderly running of the institution or the Bureau of Prisons. (Conduct must be of the Low Moderate severity nature.) This charge is to be used only when another charge of low moderate severity is not applicable.

## SANCTIONS

B.1     Disallow ordinarily up to 12.5% (1-7 days) of good conduct time credit available for year (to be used only where inmate found to have committed a second violation of the same prohibited act within 6 months); Disallow ordinarily up to 25% (1-14 days) of good conduct time credit available for year (to be used only where inmate found to have committed a third violation of the same prohibited act within 6 months) (a good conduct time sanction may not be suspended).

E.     Make monetary restitution.

F.     Withhold statutory good time.

G.     Loss of privileges: commissary, movies, recreation, etc.

H.     Change housing (quarters).

I      Remove from program and/or group activity

J.     Loss of job

K.     Impound inmate's personal property.

L.     Confiscate contraband.

M.     Restrict to quartets.

N.     Extra duty

O.     Reprimand

P.       Warning.


NOTE: <u>Aiding</u> another person to commit any of these offenses, <u>attempting</u> to commit any of these offenses, and <u>making plans</u> to commit any of these offenses, in all categories of severity, shall be considered the same as a commission of the offenses itself.


## *MODERATE CATEGORY*


## CODE PROHIBITED ACTS

300     Indecent Exposure

301     (Not to be used)

302     Misuse of authorized medication

303     Possession of money or currency, unless specifically authorized, or in excess of the amount authorized.

304     Loaning of property or anything of valve for profit or increased return

305     Possession of anything not authorized for retention or receipt by the inmate, and not issued to him through regular channels

306     Refusing to work, or to accept a program assignment

307     Refusing to obey an order of any staff member (May be categorized and charged in terms of greater severity, according to the nature of the order being disobeyed; e.g., failure to obey an order which furthers a riot would be charged as 105, Rioting; refusing to obey an order which furthers a fight would be charged

as 201, Fighting; refusing to provide a urine sample when ordered would be charged as Code 110)

308    Violating a condition of a furlough

309    Violating a condition of a community program

310    Unexcused absence from work or any assignment

311    Failing to perform work as instructed by the supervisor

312    Insolence towards a staff member

       Lying or providing a false statement to a staff member

314    Counterfeiting or forging any documentation, article of identification, money or official paper

315    Participating in an unauthorized meeting or gathering

316    Being in an unauthorized area

317    Failure to follow safety or sanitation regulations

318    Using any equipment which is not specifically authorized

319    Using any equipment contrary to instructions, or posted safety standard

320    Failing to stand count

321    Interfering with the taking of count

324    Gambling

325    Preparing or conducting a gambling pool

326    Possession of gambling paraphernalia

327    Unauthorized contacts with the public

328    Giving money or anything of value to, or accepting money or anything of value from: another inmate, or any other person without staff authorization

329    Destroying, altering or damaging government property, or the property of another person, having a value of $100.00 or less.

330    Being unsanitary or untidy; failing to keep one's person and one's quarters in accordance with posted standards

331    Possession, manufacture, or introduction of a non-hazardous tool or other non-hazardous contraband (tool not likely to be used in an escape or escape attempt, or to serve as a weapon capable of doing serious bodily harm to others, or not hazardous to institutional security or personal safety; Other non-hazardous contraband includes such items as food or cosmetics

332    Smoking where prohibited

397    Use of the telephone for abuses other than criminal activity (e.g., conference calling, possession and/or use of another inmate's PIN number, three-way calling, providing false information for preparation of a telephone list).

398    Interfering with a staff member in the performance of duties (Conduct must be of the Moderate Severity nature.) This charge is to be used only when another charge of moderate severity is not applicable.

399    Conduct which disrupts or interferes with the security or orderly running of the institution or the Bureau of Prisons. (Conduct must be of the Moderate Severity nature) 'This charge is to be used only when another charge of moderate severity is not applicable.

## SANCTIONS

A.      Recommend parole date rescission or retardation.

B.      Forfeit earned statutory good time or non-vested good conduct time up to 25% or up to 30 days, whichever is less, and/or terminate or disallow extra good time (an extra good time or good conduct time sanction may not be suspended).

B.      Disallow ordinarily up to 25% (1-14 days) of good conduct time credit available for year (a good conduct time sanction may not be suspended).

C.      Disciplinary Transfer (recommend).

D.      Disciplinary Segregation (up to 15 days).

E.      Make monetary restitution

F.      Withhold statutory good time

G.      Loss of privileges: commissary, movies, recreation, etc.

H.      Change housing (quarters):

Remove from program and/or group activity

J.      Loss of job.

K.      Impound inmate's personal property.

L.      Confiscate contraband.

M.      Restrict to quartets.

N.      Extra duty

## Special Housing Unit Rules and Procedures - Inmate Copy

The attached information provides a clear and concise view of Special Housing procedures along with rules and regulations. This document is intended to inform Inmates of what to expect during their stay in the Special Housing Unit.

A.   Telephone Calls:   Inmates in Administrative Detention will be allowed use of the Unit telephone once every 30 days.   Telephone calls will not exceed the maximum amount of time allowed which is 10 minutes.   This will be accomplished by the inmates submitting an Inmate Request to Staff Member (Cop-Out).

Inmates in Disciplinary Segregation will receive one (1) telephone call every 30 days.   Legal Telephone calls will be handled by the members of your respective Unit Team.   This will be accomplished by the inmates submitting an Inmate Request to Staff Member (Cop-Out).   If an inmate is on telephone restriction, he/she will not be allowed to make social calls

B.   Law Library:   The Special Housing Unit has a law library for inmate use.   Inmates will submit an Inmate Request to Staff Member (Cop-Out) to the SHU OIC and will be placed on the waiting list for usage. Ordinarily, inmates will be allowed to use the Law Library for one hour.

C.   Barber Shop:   Inmates will submit an Inmate Request to a staff member to the Special Housing Unit OIC to be placed on the waiting list.

D.   Recreation:   Each inmate will be offered recreation at least five days a week.   The recreation period will last for one hour. Recreation will be held in the outdoor recreation cage.

E.   Mail:   Incoming inmate mail will be picked up by the Evening Watch Officer.   Mail will be distributed during the Evening Shift. All outgoing mail will be delivered to the mail room for mailing. This mail will be removed from the unit after the 2:00AM count.

Legal correspondence will be handled by the inmates Unit Team. Outgoing mail other than legal is not to be sealed.

F.     Commissary:   Commissary slips will be handed out and picked up on Thursdays. The specified items offered will be issued on Fridays.   Only those items on the commissary list for Administrative Detention or Disciplinary Segregation will be issued.

G.     Sanitation:  Inmates will be given an opportunity to clean their cells 3 times per week (SUN., TUE. and THUR.). Supplies such as mops, cleaning materials and sponges will be provided.   Inmates will have an opportunity to discard trash after the conclusion of each meal.

H.     Cell Inspection:   Upon an inmate arrival in the Special Housing Unit a cell will be assigned. The Officer will note any problems with the cell and upon agreement; the inmate will sign the inspection form. If any destruction or graffiti is present upon release the inmate(s) are subject to disciplinary action. Each inmate in a cell is responsible for sanitation.

I.     Personal Property:   Ordinarily, within 72 hours of an inmate arrival in the Special Housing Unit the inmate's personal property will Inventoried in the presence of the affected inmate.   At this time items allowed in the Special Housing Unit may be maintained by the inmates. - Legal Materials: A reasonable amount may be retained. Unit teams will determine how much space is needed on a case by case basis.

J.     Linen Exchange: This will be accomplished on Thursday. All linen will be turned in, and clean linen will be issued.

K.     Clothing Exchange: This will be accomplished on Monday, Wednesday, and Friday.

L.     Medical Treatment: Health Services Personnel will conduct rounds at least once daily.

M.    Visitation, Inmates housed in the Special Housing Unit will be allowed to visit in the Special Housing Unit Visiting Rooms. No children will be allowed to visit inmates in SHU.

N.    Attorney Visits: During legal visits the inmate and their Attorney will be allowed privacy in the visiting room in on the 3$^{rd}$ Floor.

O.    While in Special Housing Unit all inmates will receive three meals a day. The meals will be prepared in the Service Department and issued by the unit officers. The meals will be representative of what is served to the general population. NO fresh fruit can be purchased In Disciplinary Segregation. No metal or glass containers will be allowed in the Special Housing Unit.

P.    Unit Orderlies:    Inmates wanting to work as orderlies will submit an inmate Request to a Staff Member (Cop· Out) to the Special Housing Unit Lieutenant

Q.    Cell Condition:    Beds will be made and lights will be turned on by 7:30am. Beds are to remain made until 4:00pm. Inmates may lay on top of their bunks during the daytime hours. On weekends and holidays beds will be made and lights will be turned on by 10:00am. Any refusal to follow this policy will result in disciplinary actions.

R.    Razors will be issued on Sunday, Tuesday and Thursday. When the inmate is completed shaving staff will retrieve the razor for disposal. Any inmate who attempts to maintain any part of the razor will receive an incident report pending disciplinary action.

S.    Writing paper, envelopes, Inmate Request to a Staff Member (Cop-Out), and pens not more than three Inches long will be issued on an as needed basis

T.    Internal Movements: All inmates will be handcuffed behind the back during internal movements. The Special Housing Unit Lieutenant will approve any exceptions to this rule. A martin chain will be worn if cuffed in the front.

**NOTE: THESE RULES ARE SUBJECT TO CHANGE WITHOUT NOTICE.**